Contemporary Caribbean Women's Poetry

This book represents the very first sustained account of Caribbean women's poetry and provides detailed readings of an exciting range of innovative texts. The discussion is situated in relation to the predominantly male tradition of Caribbean poetry, and explores the factors which have resulted in the relative marginality of women poets within nationalistic poetic discourses. Denise deCaires Narain employs a range of cutting-edge feminist and postcolonial approaches to focus on a diverse range of themes, such as orality, sexuality, the body, performance and poetic identity.

The book begins with a discussion of two early Caribbean women poets, Una Marson and Phyllis Shand Allfrey, and suggests that their very different poetic identities and concerns highlight the hybridity of a nascent Caribbean women's tradition of poetry. Louise Bennett's work, with its emphasis on Creole and orality, has been widely acknowledged as inaugurating an authentically Caribbean voice – and the paradoxes and possibilities which her Creole voice represents are then explored in the work of Valerie Bloom, Jean 'Binta' Breeze, Merle Collins and Amryl Johnson. The work of Lorna Goodison, Mahadai Das, Grace Nichols and Marlene Nourbese Philip reveals the gendered implications of poetic voice and identity, particularly in relation to the representation of the Caribbean woman's body. Finally, Denise deCaires Narain appraises the ways in which Caribbean women's writing has come to constitute a discrete field of writing and the exclusions involved in such a constituency.

Contemporary Caribbean Women's Poetry provides detailed readings of individual poems by women poets whose work has not yet received the sustained critical attention it deserves. These readings are contextualized both within Caribbean cultural debates and postcolonial and feminist critical discourses in a lively and engaged way; re-visiting nationalist debates as well as topical issues about the performance of gendered and raced identities within poetic discourse. It will be ground-breaking reading for all those interested in postcolonialism, Gender Studies, Caribbean Studies and contemporary poetry.

Denise deCaires Narain is a Lecturer in English in the School of African and Asian Studies at the University of Sussex. Born and brought up in Guyana, she has also taught at the University of the West Indies.

Postcolonial Literatures

In collaboration with the Centre for Colonial and Postcolonial Studies at University of Kent at Canterbury

This series aims to present a wide range of scholarly and innovative research into postcolonial literatures by specialists in the field. Volumes will concentrate on writers and writing originating in previously (or presently) colonized areas, and will include material from non-anglophone as well as anglophone colonies and literatures. The series will also include collections of important essays from older journals, and re-issues of classic texts on postcolonial subjects.

The series comprises two strands:

Routledge Research in Postcolonial Literatures is a forum for innovative new research intended for a high-level specialist readership, and the titles will be available in hardback only. Titles include

1 **Magical Realism in West African Fiction**
   Brenda Cooper

2 **Austen in the World**
   Postcolonial Mappings
   edited by You-me Park and Rajeswari Sunder Rajan

3 **Contemporary Caribbean Women's Poetry**
   Making Style
   Denise deCaires Narain

4 **Animism and Politics in African Literature**
   Caroline Rooney

5 **Caribbean–English Passages**
   Intertextuality in a Postcolonial Tradition
   Tobias Doring

Readings in Postcolonial Literatures aims to address the needs of students and teachers, and the titles will be published in hardback and paperback. Titles include

1 **Selected Essays of Wilson Harris**
   edited by Andrew Bundy

Contemporary Caribbean Women's Poetry

Making style

Denise deCaires Narain

Routledge
Taylor & Francis Group

LONDON AND NEW YORK

**In memory of my Mum, Eileen Gertrude deCaires,
and for Atticus and Benjamin
and for Rzk**

First published 2002
by Routledge
11 New Fetter Lane, London EC4P 4EE

Simultaneously published in the USA and Canada
by Routledge
29 West 35th Street, New York, NY 10001

Transferred to Digital Printing 2003

Routledge is an imprint of the Taylor & Francis Group

© 2002 Denise deCaires Narain

Typeset in Baskerville by
RefineCatch Limited, Bungay, Suffolk
Printed and bound in Great Britain by
Biddles Short Run Books, King's Lynn

British Library Cataloguing in Publication Data
A catalogue record for this book is available
from the British Library

Library of Congress Cataloging in Publication Data
DeCaires Narain, Denise, 1953–
    Contemporary Caribbean women's poetry : making style/Denise
    deCaires Narain.
       p.   cm.—(Routledge research in postcolonial literatures)
    Includes bibliographical references and index.
       1. Caribbean poetry (English)—Women authors—History and
criticism.   2. Women and literature—Caribbean Area—History—20th
century.   3. Postcolonialism—Caribbean Area.   4. Caribbean Area—In
literature.   I. Title.   II. Series.
PR9205.2.D43   2001
811′.5099287′09729—dc21   2001048306

ISBN 0-415-21812-8

Contents

Preface

This book offers an account of Caribbean women's poetry which seeks both to introduce the uninitiated reader to this work as well as to offer an argument about the location of these texts within the broader context of Caribbean writing. It is motivated, in the first place, then, by an apparently straightforward agenda: that of making Caribbean women poets more visible in the literary discourse of the region. It is widely acknowledged that, historically, male writers have dominated the Caribbean literary landscape, and writers such as C.L.R. James, George Lamming, Sam Selvon, Wilson Harris, Derek Walcott, E.K. Brathwaite and V.S. Naipaul (among others) are generally recognized as the founding fathers of a West Indian literary tradition. The substantial increase in publications by women in the last two decades, however, has significantly altered the shape – and 'gender' – of this literary landscape. Since starting the research for this project some years ago, as part of a doctoral thesis, Caribbean women's writing has become a well-established field of literature, sustaining conferences on a regular basis and generating a steady stream of publications. Within this newly defined field of writing, it is fair to say that, while a handful of Caribbean women poets (such as Lorna Goodison, Grace Nichols, Dionne Brand and Marlene Nourbese Philip) have now established international reputations, it is women's *fiction* (by writers such as Jamaica Kincaid, Olive Senior, Erna Brodber, Pauline Melville and many others) which has made a much bigger impact in establishing Caribbean women's writing as a recognizable category of literature.

In focusing on Caribbean women's poetry and exploring the impact of gender on this genre, the aim here is also to contribute to a critical discourse which might help redress the rather exclusive focus on women's fiction. Nonetheless, in both prose and poetry, the *belatedness* of Caribbean women's 'arrival' on the literary scene raises concerns which provide another motivation for this book. I interrogate this belatedness by situating my discussion of Caribbean women's poetry alongside debates about definitions of a 'properly West Indian' poetics to ask questions about the 'origins' and gendering of this discourse. In doing so, I am motivated by a desire to explore the varied ways in which women poets have responded to the dominant tradition, rather than by a desire to construct a discrete 'tradition' of women's poetry. So, while the work of women poets is the main focus of my attention, male poets and critics are central to the arguments throughout this book.

Discussions of Caribbean poetry have often centred on the issue of language, notoriously summarized in the 1960s and 1970s in the polarized identification of the region's poetic giants, Derek Walcott, associated with a more European poetic discourse, and Edward Kamau Brathwaite, associated with a 'folk-centred' poetics. It is perhaps because discussions of poetry have been so intensely focused on the roles of Walcott and Brathwaite in the formation of an appropriately authentic and muscular 'indigenous' poetic identity, that it has been particularly difficult for both poetry *and* the figure of the poet to be perceived as not normatively male. I begin my discussion of Caribbean women's poetry with Una Marson and Phyllis Shand Allfrey because their work, though not very widely known, provides the opportunity to explore anxieties about authorship and about the 'Caribbeanness' of voice as well as to question the criteria conventionally invoked in defining Caribbean poetry. Louise Bennett, a poet whose sustained use of Creole in her poetry has established her reputation as a foundational figure, might appear to be a more obvious choice with which to begin this project. However, it is part of my argument to suggest that the privileging of the Creole voice in Caribbean poetry rests upon gendered assumptions about this voice which need to be interrogated. Chapter 1 argues, therefore, that the unevenness of poetic voice and accomplishment in Marson's oeuvre as well as the problematically 'raced' elements in Allfrey's output should be embraced in the spirit of recognizing fully the hybrid 'origins' of Caribbean literary culture. Chapter 2 extends this argument by focusing on the work of Louise Bennett and interrogating the attractions and ambiguities of continuing to identify the Creole voice and its associated values as the exclusive repository and source of a nativist poetics. Chapter 3 offers readings of the work of a selection of poets who make extensive use of Creole, Valerie Bloom, Jean 'Binta' Breeze, Merle Collins and Amryl Johnson, to gauge the continuing influence of Louise Bennett, to explore the meanings of Creole-use in diasporic locations and to pursue the proliferation of gendered meanings under the sign of 'orality'.

If, as I argue, the more performative mode associated with the Creole poetic voice has some troubling implications for the woman poet and the staging of poetic identity, then Chapter 4 explores the possibilities for more page-bound representations of the woman's body. Focusing on the work of Lorna Goodison, Mahadai Das, Grace Nichols and Marlene Nourbese Philip, this chapter discusses the significance of 'the body' in Caribbean discourse, and explores the diverse ways in which the female body has been *written about* and *written into* poetic discourse. Chapter 5 shifts away from detailed readings of individual poems to offer an overview of a selection of anthologies which have been instrumental in consolidating Caribbean women's poetry as a discrete literary entity, and explores the reception, via conferences and publications, of Caribbean women's writing more generally. I conclude, perhaps perversely given my own investment in such a category in this book, by suggesting that, although a specific focus on Caribbean women's poetry has usefully exposed some of the gendered implications in the region's poetic tradition, this grouping of women writers should remain *provisional* so that other versions of this 'tradition' can come into play, allowing for a continual mutation in definitions of Caribbean poetic identity, both male *and* female – and perhaps facilitating a shift *beyond* the category of gender altogether.

The arguments in this book have been shaped by the intersecting (and sometimes conflicting) critical interventions of feminist, Caribbeanist and postcolonial critics. While postcolonial and feminist perspectives have been extremely useful in destabilizing the limitations and prescriptions of a regionalist/nationalist approach, and, while it is true that most of the poets discussed in this book have written out of various diasporic locations as well as from within the region, the themes and issues treated in their work and the engagement with a shared corpus of literary texts remain strong enough for their work to be considered productively within a regional category, however porous that category. Nonetheless, the ongoing interrogation of bounded identities, whether of race, culture, geography or gender (while it occasionally generated a nostalgia, on my part, for the 'good old days' when defining a 'Caribbean woman writer' was relatively simple), provided the critical questions which both energized this research and complicated it. So, while this research initially set out to offer a comprehensive overview of Caribbean women's poetry, it quickly became apparent that there were too many 'fault lines' for such a narrative to be delivered. Further, as I became more interested in questioning some of the claims being made in the name of orality and Creole, and in pursuing the implications for representations of the female body attendant on these claims, the comprehensiveness of the project was eroded.

I regret that I have not been able to include more discussion of poets who have not been published widely, for there are many, many poems by little-known poets which offer innovative and insightful perspectives on Caribbean women's identities. But an even greater omission is that restrictions of space made it difficult to extend my arguments further to include sustained discussion of several well-known poets. In particular, I regret not being able to encompass the lyrical use of Creole made by Olive Senior and the nuanced exploration of Caribbean culture in her two collections of poetry. The extensive and powerfully complex poetic repertoire of Dionne Brand is also, regretfully, not discussed in this book. The work of many others, such as Claire Harris, Velma Pollard, Honor Ford-Smith, Ramabai Espinet, Pamela Mordecai, Christine Craig, Jane King and Joan Anim-Ado (among many others) has also not been discussed, though I have listed many of their publications in the bibliography. In the final analysis, I wanted to include detailed discussions of a range of poems by individual poets both to convey a sense of the distinctive poetic output of these poets, but also to situate these discussions in relation to broader concerns within Caribbean poetic discourse. As a result, I have, inevitably, also repeated some of the gaps and emphases which characterize Caribbean discourse, most notably, the emphasis on African Caribbean, and heterosexual, culture. On the other hand, to have discussed Dionne Brand's work, for example, 'simply' as an example of a 'representatively lesbian' poetics would have been reductive; indeed, perhaps impossible, for her work is so densely layered and metaphoric that reading the body in her texts was difficult to harness to my particular focus on Creole-use and the body. My decision to pursue a specific line of argument, combined with the tyranny of the word-limit, also meant that I was unable to offer as many detailed readings of individual poems by as representative a range of poets as I would have liked (but see, for example, J.E. Chamberlin's impressively nuanced *Come Back to Me My Language*).[1] Many fascinating trajectories have had to be deferred for another time and place.

The subtitle of this book, *Making style*, perhaps also requires explanation. The phrase is used popularly in the Caribbean to refer to someone who is showing off, or bragging – pretending to be 'bigger' than they 'really' are. I am attracted to the ambiguous ways in which this phrase can be used: admiringly – in 'watch how she making style!'; or censoriously – prefaced by a sucking of the teeth, in 'she only making style'. The phrase resonated both with the ambivalences and anxieties articulated in these women's texts about 'making style' in poetry and with the flourish with which such concerns about authorship were, paradoxically, explored – and challenged. That it is '*making* style', rather than 'having style' (or 'being stylish') seemed in keeping with an emphasis throughout this book on the constructedness of identities. The upbeat flamboyance of the phrase also captures something of the wonderful rhetorical swagger which many of these poems display.

It remains only for me to thank the many people who, given the time I have spent completing this research, may well have thought that I too was 'making style': Professor Lyn Innes, who supervised my doctoral research and kept me at it; Kadie Kanneh, with whom I shared many hours of vital 'thesisbabble'; François Lack, who helped on the keyboard at a critical moment when I was completing my thesis; colleagues, Jane Bryce and Evelyn O'Callaghan, at the Cave Hill Campus of the University of the West Indies where I taught for a year and whose comments on this material were extremely helpful; supportive colleagues at the University of Sussex, Laura Chrisman and Alan Sinfield; friends, Norma Kitson, Hilary Truscott and Ulele Burnham, for managing to appear interested always; my family, and especially my Dad, for continuing to enquire about the project; my sons, Atticus and Benjamin, for always being noisily around; and, finally, Abdulrazak, for listening and encouraging, and watching quietly as many of his books disappeared into my study.

Sadly, while in the final stages of completing this book, Amryl Johnson, a gifted poet and my good friend, died at her home in Coventry.

---

1   J.E. Chamberlin, *Come Back to Me My Language: Poetry and the West Indies*, Toronto, McClelland, 1993.

Acknowledgements

For permission to reproduce extracts from the poems discussed in this book, grateful acknowledgement is made to those listed below. Page references, given in parentheses, indicate where poems are located.

Lennox Honychurch for Phyllis Shand Allfrey's 'The Gipsy to her Baby' (p. 3), 'Decayed Gentlewoman' (p. 7), 'These People are Too Stolid' (p. 18), 'Salute' (p. 20), from *In Circles*, London, Raven Press, 1940; 'Nocturne' (p. 1) from *Contrasts*, Bridgetown, Barbados, Advocate Press, 1955; 'While the Young Sleep' (p. 5), from *Palm and Oak*, London, the author, 1950; 'Love for an Island' (p. 2), 'The Child's Return' (p. 7), 'The White Lady' (pp. 4–5), 'Resistance' (p. 14), 'Fugitive Hummingbird' (p. 11) from *Palm and Oak II*, Roseau, Dominica, 1973; 'Dominica: last haunt of the Caribs' from Allfrey's unpublished papers. McClelland & Stewart and Dionne Brand for 'Land to Light On' (p. 47), from *Land to Light On*, Toronto, McClelland & Stewart, 1997. Merle Collins for her poem, 'Because the Dawn Breaks' (pp. 88–90), from *Because the Dawn Breaks!* London, Karia Press, 1985. Peepal Tree Press for Mahadai Das's 'Flute' (p. 46) from *Bones*, Leeds, Peepal Tree Press, 1988. New Beacon Books for Lorna Goodison's 'I Am Becoming my Mother' (p. 38), 'On Becoming a Mermaid' (p. 30) from *I Am Becoming my Mother*, London, New Beacon, 1986; 'Farewell Wild Woman (1)' (p. 49) from *Heartease*, London, New Beacon, 1988. Marlene Nourbese Philip for her poems, 'Poisson' (p. 3) from *Thorns*, Toronto, Williams-Wallace, 1980; 'She' (p. 5) and 'Planned Obsolescence' (p. 36) from *Salmon Courage*, Toronto, Williams-Wallace, 1983; 'Discourse on the Logic of Language' (pp. 56–9) and 'Meditations' (p. 53) from *She Tries Her Tongue: Her Silence Softly Breaks*, Charlottetown, Prince Edward Island, Ragweed, 1989. Grace Nichols for 'epigraph' (p. 4), 'These Islands' (p. 31), 'Skin-teeth' (p. 50), 'Like a Flame' (p. 37), 'epilogue' (p. 80) from *i is a long memoried woman*, London, Karnak House, 1983; Grace Nichols and Virago Press for 'Beauty' (p. 7) from *The Fat Black Woman's Poems*, London, Virago, 1984; 'Configurations' (p. 31), 'On Poems and Crotches' (p. 16), 'Who Was It?' (p. 6), 'Ode to My Bleed' (p. 24) from *Lazy Thoughts of a Lazy Woman*, London, Virago, 1989.

Although I have made every effort to locate copyright holders, I have failed to establish contact in a few cases, and offer my apologies.

1 Literary mothers?

Una Marson and
Phyllis Shand Allfrey

The purple hills are calling and the orange is in bloom,
The dew is on the Myrtle and the violets fade so soon.
[. . .]
Oh, I'll arise and go again to my fair Tropic Isle
For I hear voices calling and I'm so sad meanwhile.[1]

Living in sunless reaches under rain,
how do exiles from enchanted isles
tend and sustain their rich nostalgic blaze?[2]

Beginning this account of contemporary Caribbean women poets with a discussion of the work of Una Marson (1905–65) and Phyllis Shand Allfrey (1908–86) inevitably accords them foundational status as literary 'mother-figures'. Mindful of some of the exclusions and limitations which have resulted from feminist and Caribbeanist reconstructions of literary traditions, however, I am motivated by a desire both to trace some kind of 'literary ancestry' as well as to question the grounds upon which such a notion of 'ancestry' might be constructed. In placing Allfrey alongside Marson and exploring the possibility that they might share a similarly pioneering poetic status, the imperative is both to extend the notion of who qualifies as a literary precursor and to interrogate the grounds upon which such categories are constructed. I would suggest that considering Marson and Allfrey *provisionally* as foundational literary figures is a productive way to begin a discussion of contemporary Caribbean women poets, for it allows sustained attention to be given to work which has, historically, been considered marginal to 'mainstream' literary activity, but it does not foreclose on the possibility of other 'foundational-figures' being substituted in further readings of Caribbean poetry. In other words, foundations *can* shift. I will argue, in the chapters that follow, that many of the issues raised here continue to inform both the writing and the reception of Caribbean women's poetry.

Both Una Marson and Phyllis Shand Allfrey were writing at roughly the same time and were among the few women of their time to have more than one collection of poetry published. Both women had extended periods of cultural/political activity in England, and elsewhere, and were involved in supportive roles for a variety of West Indians in London during the Second World War and with feminist organizations in Britain. Both Marson and Allfrey regarded the West Indies as 'home' and were actively involved in pre-independence developments there. Marson, a black Jamaican, died and was buried in Jamaica, while Allfrey, a white Dominican, lived most of her life, and was buried, in Dominica. Marson has recently gained recognition, in a variety of contexts, as a pioneering figure in Caribbean literary history, while Allfrey's reputation remains primarily associated with her political roles and, though her novel, *The Orchid House*, has accrued a steady readership,[3] her poetry is virtually unknown. Marson's four collections of poetry were published in 1930, 1931, 1937 and 1945, while Allfrey's first collection was published in 1940. Though Allfrey's last collection was published in 1973, most of these poems are taken from the earlier collections published in 1940, 1950 and 1955.[4] Despite this disjuncture in publication history, both women were writing at a turbulent time in West Indian history when both nationalism and feminism were incipient and contested ideologies. Part of the sociopolitical fall-out of both World Wars had been an intense challenging of received notions of woman's place in society *and* of the relationship of the colonized subject to 'the mother country'. Una Marson and Phyllis Allfrey were caught up, in different ways, in the dynamism of this profoundly transitionary moment.

Una Marson was the youngest of the six children of a Baptist minister, Soloman Marson, and his wife Maude, whose household also included three adopted children. Marson's father died when she was 10 and the family were forced to move from the parish in Santa Cruz to Kingston. With the help of a Free Foundationers Scholarship, Marson was able to continue her education at Hampton High School in Malvern, a fee-paying boarding school whose pupils were generally, unlike Marson, 'from moneyed white and creole families'.[5] After leaving school in 1922, Marson worked with the Salvation Army and YMCA in Kingston, before taking up a job as assistant editor of the sociopolitical monthly journal *Jamaica Critic*. There, she developed her writing skills and started the magazine *The Cosmopolitan*, becoming the first Jamaican woman to edit her own publication. Thereafter, Marson consolidated her interest in Jamaican culture and her commitment to promoting women's rights in various articles published in the newspapers. In June 1932, her play, *At What a Price*, was staged in Jamaica and, with the profits generated from it, she travelled to England in July 1932 where she became involved with the League of Coloured Peoples. In November 1933, *At What a Price* was performed by an all-League cast and was hailed as the first play by 'coloured colonials' to be staged in London. In 1935 she was the first, and only, black representative to take part in the first international women's conference to be held in Turkey. In 1935 Marson took up a post at the League of Nations headquarters in Geneva where, in 1936, she acted as Haile Selassie's secretary in his negotiations with the League of Nations. On her return to Jamaica in 1936, she founded the Readers and Writers Club and the Kingston Dramatic Club and two of her plays, *London Calling* and *Pocomania*, were performed; the latter was extremely successful and was hailed as indicating the future trajectory of a truly

Jamaican theatre. In March 1941, appointed as full-time programme assistant on the BBC's Empire Service, Marson compèred and co-ordinated a series of programmes, 'Calling the West Indies', which were to continue until her return to Jamaica in 1945. In her later years, Marson married briefly and it appears that she also suffered a 'breakdown'. Her varied literary activities in several locations resulted in acquaintances and friendships (and feuds) with diverse cultural figures, ranging from T.S. Eliot and George Orwell to Paul Robeson, James Weldon Johnson, Nancy Cunard, Winifred Holtby and Sir Nana Ofori Atta Omanhene of Ghana.[6] Despite these experiences and personal connections, there is a strong sense, in Marson's poetry and in Jarrett-Macauley's biography, that Marson remained something of an isolated and marginal figure.

Phyllis Shand Allfrey, as Lizabeth Paravisini-Gebert's biography makes clear, took great pride in being able to trace her ancestry on her father's side to an English lord, purportedly one of King Arthur's knights of the Round Table and, via the marriage of Major William Byam (a Royalist exiled to Barbados in 1645) to Dorothy Knollys (great-great-great-granddaughter of Mary Boleyn, Anne's sister), to the royal family in England. William's grandson married into the Warner family, establishing a family connection to another powerful West Indian family. On her mother's side, via French émigrés to Martinique, Allfrey claimed a family connection to the Empress Josephine.[7] Allfrey's father, Francis Shand, was the Crown Attorney in Dominica. He married Elfreda Nicholls in 1905 and they had four daughters; Allfrey was the second-born. The girls were educated at home by tutors because the only school on the island was Catholic and the Byam Shands were Anglican. In 1927, after working briefly for her father, Allfrey left Dominica to seek employment as a governess in New York. She later moved to England where she met and married Robert Allfrey in 1930, and together they resettled in America where their two children, Josephine and Philip, were born. Following the post-war depression, the Allfreys returned to England, where Allfrey took a position as secretary to the feminist writer Naomi Mitchison. There, Allfrey became actively involved in the Fabian Society and the Labour Party. In 1953, *In Circles* and, later in the year, *The Orchid House* were published. Phyllis then returned to Dominica, where Robert now worked, and there she became actively involved in cofounding the Dominica Labour Party. In 1958, she won the portfolio of Minister of Labour and Social Affairs in the West Indies Federation government (the only woman appointed at this level), and she moved to Trinidad until 1961 when the Federation collapsed. On returning to Dominica, she and Robert ran the *Dominica Herald* until 1965 when they established the weekly newspaper the *Star*, which they ran until the early 1980s. Following her expulsion from the Dominica Labour Party, Allfrey's involvement in politics continued in the regular satiric commentaries she wrote for the newspaper. The Allfreys had a daughter, Josephine (killed in a car crash in Botswana in 1977) and a son, Philip (diagnosed as schizophenic and institutionalized in England in 1953) and they also adopted two Carib boys, David and Robbie, and an African Dominican girl, Sonia. Ironically perhaps, given Allfrey's 'proud ancestry', she spent her latter years in poverty, often relying on donations from friends. She frequently voiced her disappointment at the way in which her political commitments impeded her development as a writer.

Clearly, both Una Marson and Phyllis Shand Allfrey were remarkable women whose place in the cultural history of the Caribbean is assured. Aside from the undeniable *archival* importance of retrieving these women's 'life stories' and texts, is it possible to make a case for their continuing relevance and importance to Caribbean writing? This chapter continues with an exploration of their work in an attempt to answer this question.

Most accounts of Caribbean literature locate its genesis in the late 1950s and early 1960s when several West Indian writers (Naipaul, Selvon, Lamming, Salkey, Harris), who had travelled to Britain in the 1950s, started to get their work published and publicly acknowledged. There *was* a considerable body of writing generated within the West Indies prior to this, but this writing was generally dismissed as *not truly West Indian*, partly because many of these writers were English, but also because of the unquestioning mimicry of colonial forms and the inscription of colonial ideology which characterized this writing.

God gives us a chance to be men!

Lloyd Brown's *West Indian Poetry*, first published in 1978,[8] and one of the first sustained accounts of West Indian poetry, suggests that 'modern' West Indian poetry begins in the 1940s and, while he makes reference to several earlier poets whose work helped shape this modern trajectory, his attitude to the early poetry is asserted forthrightly in the first sentence of the first chapter, 'The beginnings: 1760–1940': 'The first one hundred and eighty years of West Indian poetry are uneven at best, and in some respects are downright unpromising.' He acknowledges the importance of James Grainger's *Sugar Cane* (1764) as 'the first poem written in the West Indies to win any noticeable response from the outside world', despite its 'limited moral vision' (Grainger suggests that slavery is wrong but argues for 'upgrading' conditions, so that slaves might become 'servants' and work the cane fields by 'choice') and describes Francis Williams's poem 'Ode to George Haldane',[9] as 'the first poem on record which voices, albeit covertly, the duality of the West Indian as the despised and uprooted African ("Aethiop") and the dispossessed heir of the West'. Brown discusses these two as representative colonialist/ expatriate and postcolonial Caliban figures respectively, a dichotomy which is indicative of the binary at the heart of definitions of a West Indian literary tradition.

Once Brown moves away from these rather historically distant figures, his tone becomes less accommodating: 'the nineteenth century is the heyday of a Caribbean pastoral in which hackneyed nature verse in the Romantic mode alternates with the colonial's embarrassingly sycophantic verses in praise of the British Empire' (1978: 23). When discussing the work of the Jamaica Poetry League, he recognizes the importance of their attempts to name the Jamaican landscape but argues that, at best, this work introduces 'local colour', and, at worst, the incongruity of 'local content' indiscriminately inserted into 'imported form' results in poems which are 'nondescript' and 'insipidly escapist'. The gist of the argument here is that the work is embarrassingly derivative – 'the influence of Wordsworth is suffocating', 'it is merely a mechanical imitation of Swinburne' – with West Indian poets doing little more than display a more-or-less competent ability to mimic the poetic models provided by the mother culture.

Brown, clearly, is not the first to bemoan the overly derivative nature of West Indian letters, as the following quote from a 1933 Trinidad newspaper makes clear:

> One has only to glance through the various periodicals published in this and other islands to see what slaves we still are to English culture and tradition. There are some who lay great store by this conscious aping of another man's culture, but to us it seems merely a sign of the immaturity of our spirit.[10]

V.S. Naipaul's bleak description of the West Indian as a 'mimic man' has become a familiar formulation, recently given more mileage in Homi Bhabha's more ambivalently nuanced account, to which I will return later in this chapter. On occasion, however, if the anti-colonial content is strong enough, Brown is willing to forgive the mimicry of imported forms and inflated rhetoric, as in the example he cites from Walter M. Lawrence's 'Guiana':

> But Hope, high up the tenebrious sky, o'ershines the
> inglorious Night
> And a cry goes up (and the voice is the voice that
> speaketh of impotent might)
> From Gods, not men – what a people are here! Guiana,
> they're hoping again,
> For the cry goes up from the deepest despair; God gives us
> a chance to be men!
> (Brown 1978, p. 27)

The humanist rationale for accommodating this declamatory style, in the pursuit of a brotherhood of man – the normative subject is, of course, *male* – is made explicit in Brown's discussion of the poem:

> The colonial ambition to be free and to be achievers is a microcosm of the human spirit's need to fulfill its potential. It is this kind of potential that allows the poet to perceive human beings as 'Gods' in that they participate in the creation and growth of their own humanity. Their cry against the deadening impact of colonialism is therefore both a specifically Guyanese self-affirmation and a part of humanity's general quest for self-realization at all costs.
> (Brown 1978, p. 27)

The 'muscular morality' of Lawrence's declamatory appeal is consolidated in

Brown's discussion. It finds an echo later in a poem such as Claude McKay's 'If We Must Die', in which a strong and passionate plea for bravery, in the wake of the violent racism of the Southern states of America when lynching was rife, is made:

> What though before us lies the open grave?
> Like men we'll face the murderous, cowardly pack,
> Pressed to the wall, dying, but fighting back![11]

This poem is included in many anthologies and was famously referred to in a speech by Winston Churchill as a rallying cry for the troops in the Second World War. While noting its power and fine crafting, I want also to draw attention to the stridency and vigour of its poetics, and to foreground the way in which the *maleness* of heroic poetic discourse is presented here as the paradigmatic voice of resistance. Clearly, the colonial contexts of both Lawrence's and McKay's poems are ones in which the imperative to articulate black subjectivity and agency is absolutely crucial, but the gendering of this discourse so that it is exclusively black *manhood* that is at stake results in an elision of black womanhood.

Brown goes on to argue that this dramatic and declamatory speaking voice is a style which is overtaken, in slightly later work, by experiments to incorporate the 'ordinary' West Indian voice. Further, he suggests that the shift away from mimicry of imported poetic models and voices is one which allows a more authentically West Indian poetry to emerge; one in which 'the folk'[12] are evoked:

> The hackneyed nature verses and the songs of Empire hark back to, and celebrate, the black colonial's ingrained loyalties to the mother culture. But at the same time, the poems about the black, the Indian, and the poor represent a major breakthrough in nineteeth century West Indian poetry.
>
> (Brown 1978, p. 24)

This point about West Indian letters only becoming 'truly' West Indian when 'the folk' have been inscribed is made repeatedly in accounts of the region's literature and I will return to it in the following chapter. However, it is pertinent to note here some of the problems in distinguishing between 'authentic' representations of that folk voice and 'fake' versions of it. When Brown discusses Thomas MacDermot's 'A Basket in the Car', for example, he argues that, apart from 'hearing and attempting to reproduce folk language', it is a 'patronizing attempt to use folk dialect in poetry' and the poet – a white Jamaican – is considered to be 'severely handicapped not only by his individual shortcomings as a poet but by his social distance from his subject' (1978, p. 31). Earlier, when discussing MacDermot's 'The Mothers of the City', Brown pronounces it 'a very bad poem because the flaccid language reinforces the impression that the feeling is contrived and that the poet's imagination cannot bridge the enormous gap between his world and the lives of the Jamaican poor'.

Brown quotes a stanza from the poem to exemplify this point:

> Oh, who are the weary pilgrims
> >That caravan now on the way?
> 'Tis the women with market burdens
> >And their hampered donkeys gray.

I will argue later that there are many examples in Marson's poems of a similar awkwardness in her attempts to represent folk language, and that often, when remarking on the harsh realities of folk life, her poems echo the embarrassingly sentimental tone of MacDermot above. Clearly the ethnic and social markers which exclude MacDermot's poem are ones which allow Marson's to 'pass' in the terms invoked in Brown's discussion; in other words, the identities (race, class, gender) of the author act, problematically, to validate – or invalidate – particular interpretations.

'Race', gender and authorizing the text

Brown suggests that MacDermot's raced identity, and the particular 'lived' experience of the Caribbean which that would imply, preclude him from being able to represent the folk convincingly. If this emphasis on the author's identity, rather than on their facility with the representational codes of a particular genre, means that the white West Indian poet's work is often suspect, it also has consequences for the black West Indian poet. The dismissal of much early West Indian poetry as derivative hinges on the belief that poetic authority in these texts is being sought from an inappropriate cultural source, that of the former 'mother country'. Clearly, the stern tone of this nascent nationalism is a response to commonly held prejudices about who was *qualified* to write and the assumption that poetry – and the poet – belonged *elsewhere*. A.J. Seymour, the Guyanese poet, writing at the same time as Marson and Allfrey, commented on the sheer audacity required by the aspiring colonial poet to authorize his voice:

> When I was younger, I sometimes got the feeling from the educated and well placed individuals around me that it was positively indecent that a young Guyanese should want to write poetry. *That sort of thing was for a person in another country.* You should read about it happening in America but in a colony it meant that you were young and conceited and should be taken down a peg or two. [My emphasis][13]

N.E. Cameron, whose pioneering anthology, *Guianese Poetry*, was published in 1931, relates a telling anecdote in which he describes his embarrassment when, asked by his friends in Cambridge about the literature of Guiana:

> I replied, not without some embarrassment, that I did not think the people were much addicted to literature. [. . .] I subsequently made a list of all names of persons who had written anything – from a newspaper letter to a law book – classified them under political writers, moral philosophers, poets,

etc., and on subsequent occasions I was able to uphold the honour of good old British Guiana in the literary realm.[14]

The embarrassment and embattlement which characterize Cameron's defensive response resonate with the issues taken up, several decades later, by Henry Louis Gates, in his influential essay ' "Race", writing and difference':

> Hegel, echoing Hume and Kant, claimed that Africans had no history, because they had developed no systems of writing and had not mastered the art of writing in European languages. [. . .] *Ironically, Anglo-African writing arose as a response to allegations of its absence.* Black people responded to these profoundly serious allegations about their 'nature' as directly as they could: they wrote books, poetry, autobiographical narratives. [My emphasis][15]

Where Lloyd Brown's desire to construct an 'independent' tradition of West Indian poetry makes him rather briskly dismissive of some of the early West Indian poets – of the poets included in Cameron's *Guianese Poetry*, for example, he concludes, 'But it is doubtful that most of Cameron's nineteenth-century writers are of any importance to anyone except the literary antiquarian' – [16] Gates's approach is more permissive. Less interested in a literary 'ranking' of black writers, he foregrounds the ways in which the identity of the writer may make certain kinds of masks and voicings a strategic textual *necessity.*

Turning now to Una Marson's poetry, Lloyd Brown's comments on her work provide a useful preamble. He is generous in his acknowledgement of Marson's contribution:

> Marson's work as a whole represents a movement from one era to the next. She moves from the clichés and stasis of the pastoral tradition to the innovative exploration of her experience; and she undertakes that exploration in terms that are sophisticated enough to integrate political protest into a fairly complex and committed art.
>
> (Brown 1978, p. 38)

Brown's praise of Marson's work focuses on those poems which include an element of 'political protest' or where what he calls 'ethnosexual' themes are handled. Because his approach is organized so solidly around a notion of what might constitute a nationalist tradition of poetry, women poets and women's concerns in poetry are simply not part of the agenda.[17] Nonetheless, Brown's willingness to treat Marson's oeuvre seriously, whatever the omissions and emphasis of his approach, provides a platform from which to launch other interpretations.

A moth or a star?

There are several striking aspects about Una Marson's poetic output: the anxiety about the process of writing; the diverse range of poetic voices she makes use of;

the unevenness of the ambition and quality of her work; the frequent moving between locations out of which she wrote; and the sense of restlessness and lack of fulfilment which pervade much of her work. Given the emphasis on locating an authentically West Indian poetic voice and the embarrassment surrounding those works deemed to be overly derivative, it may be instructive to begin with those poems of Marson's which might generate such uneasy responses. From her earliest collection through to her last, Marson often wrote about the process of making poetry and about the role of the poet and, in these poems, her indebtedness to the Romantic poets and to the Georgians is most evident.

Her third volume, *The Moth and the Star*, opens with a poem, 'Invocation', which earnestly makes her lofty view of the poet's role explicit:

> God of the Daisied Meadows
> Who has opened my eyes
> To see the beauty in a blade of grass,
> The tenderness of little wayside flowers,
> The sweetness of the dew upon the rose,
> [. . .]
> God of the mighty Ocean
> Fill me full of courage,
> Of power to do the right
> When the wrong is so easy,
> Fill me full of the purpose of life,
> Let me not live and die
> Without having done some work
> That might bring thy heaven
> Nearer earth.
> (*The Moth*, pp. 3–4)

And in 'To Be a Poet', she begins:

> If I were a poet with gifts divine
> And all the blessings of earth were mine
> I'd sit all day 'neath a shady tree
> And keep the Daisies company;
> [. . .]
> If I were a poet I'd stir the world's heart
> From beauty and love she would never depart,
> But I'm just a fledgling too weak to alight,
> God of the Poets hasten my flight!
> (*The Moth*, p. 9)

The harnessing of a generalized religious ardour to the declamations of poetic ambitions, evident in the extracts above, is a recurring device in many of Marson's poems. Another poem, 'Pilgrimage', also constructs poetry as a kind of religious calling and, again, the poet agonizes about her ability to 'join the band of poets':

> Hearts of poets past and present
> I your anguish feel too well,
> Fortify my ailing spirit
> Let me in your greatness dwell.
> [. . .]
> Humbly now I seek to join you
> Here is love that overflows,
> May your spirits hear my pleading
> Set to music my dull prose.
> (*The Moth*, p. 67)

The anxiety here about the right to write is obvious, and one might read the construction of herself as a 'fledgling poet' (in 'To Be a Poet') as indicative of her embattled position within the patriarchal tradition she seeks to join. One might also argue that Marson deftly and strategically assumes the mask of decorous humility which befits the woman poet, and invokes a notion of 'the spiritual' to give herself access to an 'acceptable' kind of rhetorical power. (In other poems, such as 'Gettin de Spirit', she makes much more distinctive use of a spiritual voice.) This kind of dissemblingly humble voice might also be seen as a postcolonial masking of literary ambitions 'above one's station'. The gendered expectations of 'the poetess' would also compound the sense of a colonially designated inferiority.

The devotion to something afar

This kind of reading, while it has a recuperative appeal, from both a feminist and postcolonial stance, avoiding some of the narrow prescriptions of a nationalist approach, does also engender some uneasiness. The sheer number of poems in which Marson adopts the transcendental, all-seeing 'I' of the Romantic poet and the lack of irony within poems which use this viewpoint invites further questions about the nature of her indebtedness to the English poetic tradition and, in particular, to Shelley, Wordsworth and Byron. When Marson uses the following lines from Shelley as an epigraph to *The Moth and the Star*, for example, is it to camouflage her own poetic ambitions or is it 'simple' admiration? Are the ironies intentional or something the postcolonial reader inserts to 'explain' an uncomfortable cultural misfit?

> I can give not what men call love,
>   But wilt thou accept not
> The worship the heart lifts above
>   And the heavens reject not,
> The desire of the moth for the star
>   of the night for the morrow,

> The devotion to something afar
> From the sphere of our sorrow?
> (*The Moth*, p. 1)

Does the difference in social and literary power of Shelley's and Marson's cultural location and status make the meanings engendered by these lines irreconcilable? In asserting Marson's literary status as a pioneer, what should the reader do with those poems in which her devotion to 'something afar' is perhaps too unquestioning? The degree of slack in interpreting those poems which display the influence of English poetic traditions so overtly depends, of course, on the degree to which mimicry is viewed as disabling or not. If accounts of West Indian poetry have been hostile to such mimicry, dismissing it as evidence of cultural sycophancy, then some postcolonial reading strategies have offered more permissive readings of such texts. Homi Bhabha's notion of mimicry has been powerfully suggestive in recognizing the complicated ambivalences of colonial and postcolonial cultural transactions. Bhabha argues that the postcolonial 'mimic man', in the various rehearsals and repetitions of colonial cultural forms, displays a version of that colonial culture which unsettles and destabilizes the colonizer's authority:

> The *menace* of mimicry is its *double* vision which in disclosing the ambivalence of colonial discourse also disrupts its authority. [. . .] The ambivalence of colonial authority repeatedly turns from *mimicry* – a difference which is almost nothing but not quite – to *menace* – a difference that is almost total but not quite. And in that other scene of colonial power, where history turns to farce and presence to a 'part' can be seen the twin figures of narcissism and paranoia that repeat furiously, uncontrollably.[18]

The seductiveness of Bhabha's model is that it recognizes the power and *play* of colonial cultural meanings and, in its emphasis on the dynamic nature of colonial relations, allows a way out of the scenario articulated by V.S. Naipaul in which he characterizes the West Indies as forever doomed to mimicry, unable to create anything 'original':

> [I]n a society like ours, fragmented, inorganic, no link between man and the landscape, a society not held together by common interests, there was no true internal source of power, and that no power was real which did not come from the outside. Such was the controlled chaos we had, with such enthusiasm, brought upon ourselves.[19]

While Bhabha's argument refuses Naipaul's determinism and pessimism, it is not without its problems. His emphasis, in the essay 'Of Mimicry and Man', is largely focused on what the unfixing of colonial cultural authority means *to the colonizer*; his phrase, 'not quite, not white', may generate unsettling ambivalences in the metropolis for metropolitan subjects but, for the colonized subject, the gap between 'the original' and 'the copy' has perhaps been too rigidly ingrained by colonial prescriptions and *force* for so promiscuous a reading. Further qualifications may also be needed if Bhabha's argument is to make sense as 'Of Mimicry and *Woman*', for the male subject is taken as the normative colonizing – and colonized – subject, partly, of course, because the ideology, and practice, of empire-building *was* 'officially' male. The cultural models through which colonial values were promoted, and later challenged, assumed a dialogue, however unequal, *between men*. Hence, despite the anxieties expressed above by Seymour and Cameron about the right to write, Caribbean men were better placed to adopt *and* adapt canonical forms. They would have had wider access to education, but also cultural assumptions about the consumption and production of public culture took its 'maleness' as given and assumed women's participation to be peripheral – or decorative. Despite these reservations, however, Bhabha's model is an attractive alternative to the fixity of many nationalist or feminist models. It also suggests possibilities for recuperating *some* sense of agency – and voice – (however circuitous) from colonial cultural exchanges. So, to return to Marson's 'devotion to something afar', I want to explore the ways in which this devotion manifests itself, and to see what kinds of conclusions can be made about such usage.

To be a (woman) poet

The influence of the Romantics is sometimes evident 'straightforwardly' in the way Marson uses quotes from their texts to preface her own words, as in the example from Shelley above. But, in a more generalized and profound way, it is at the heart of the very conception of the role of the poet which is explicitly asserted in many of the poems. This professed poetic identity is qualified and challenged by the *implicit* poetic identity available in other poems, which I will discuss further on, but here I want to cite from 'Vagabond Creed', in which Marson idealizes the figure of the poet as a roaming vagabond, floating free from all material considerations:

> For the body is merely a cloak,
> It's the spirit and soul that live on,
> *And I am a real happy bloke*
> *For the whole world to me doth belong.*
>   (*The Moth*; my emphasis, p. 8)

The disjunction between the poet's black female identity and that of the speaker in the poem is awkward to negotiate; of course, the poet could 'simply' be using the male persona, 'vagabond', to flirt with an idea of freedom not generally recognized as 'belonging' to women. But poems written by poets *about* poetry invite connections to be made between poet and persona and, in this poem, any possibility of there being a tension in this relationship is elided. Instead, the jaunty rhythm and relentless rhyme, in tandem with the repetition of the main theme of the poem, results in a false sense of consolidation, culminating in the final two lines, 'And I am a real happy bloke/For the whole world to me doth belong'. The self-consciousness or irony which might have retrieved this poem simply doesn't surface, resulting in a kind of disjuncture between persona and poet which *does* jar with this reader; perhaps because it dramatizes the more traumatic, internalized dislocations and traumas which characterize the colonial subject – and which Bhabha's notion of mimicry tends to sidestep? Marson appears, here, to be too naively the ventriloquist of Wordsworth's notion of the poet as 'a man speaking to all men'. A comparison with Sylvia Plath's, 'Ode to Ted', a poem explicity affirming her happiness to play 'Eve' to his Adamic poetic role, may help to clarify:

> From under crunch of my man's boot
> Green oat sprouts spring
> [. . .]
> How but most glad
> Could be this Adam's Eve

The comparison may be contrived and the weight of Plath's iconic status as a feminist poet may make any other kind of reading impossible, but the poem is too taut and self-consciously convoluted grammatically for the tension between 'form' and 'content' here to be inadvertent.

Remembering daffodils

Another way in which Marson's devotion to her poetic masters manifests itself is in her reworkings of their words within her own poems. 'Spring in England', for example, includes a stanza in which, having noted the beauty of various budding trees in London, the poet asks:

> 'And what are daffodils, daffodils,
> Daffodils that Wordsworth praised?'
> I asked. 'Wait for Spring,
> Wait for the Spring,' the birds replied.
> I waited for Spring, and lo they came,
> 'A host of shining daffodils
> Beside the lake beneath the trees'
> They stood. What gift of Spring
> Could equal this? Daffodils everywhere!
> What season boasts such loveliness?
> > (*The Moth*, p. 6)

The echo of the first line of Keats's 'Ode to Autumn' in the final line of the stanza above is also, clearly, not accidental. In 'Darlingford', later on in the collection, Wordsworth's daffodils have become, 'Waves, sparkling waves/Dancing merrily in the breeze' in a Jamaican seascape. Wordsworth's, 'I Wandered Lonely as a Cloud', is probably now the most often cited poem when symbols of the alienating effect of colonial education are invoked. For example, Lucy (in Jamaica Kincaid's eponymous novel), has the following response when her joyous employee shows her the spring daffodils:

> I did not know what these flowers were and so it was a mystery to me why I wanted to kill them. Just like that. I wanted to kill them. I wished that I had an enormous scythe: I would just walk down the path, dragging it alongside me, and I would cut these flowers down.[20]

Initially, when Lucy tries to articulate this rage to Mariah, she stammers and bites her tongue, foregrounding the muting effect of master texts on the postcolonial woman. When Lucy does get her voice back, she says, 'Mariah, do you realize that at ten years of age, I had to *learn by heart* a poem about some flowers that I would not see *in real life* until I was nineteen?' (p. 30; my emphasis).

'Learning by heart' and 'real life' are phrases which resonate powerfully with ambivalences and contradictions that may illuminate some of the difficulties in interpreting Marson's poetic voice. Kincaid, writing in the 1990s, has her protagonist express, in absolutely unequivocal terms, her outrage at the cultural distortions which resulted from colonial educational structures. Marson, by contrast, writing in the 1930s, does not signal any cultural unease about inhabiting the land/wordscape of her beloved Wordsworth; rather, the excitement generated by his account of the daffodils is presented as *anticipating*, and, indeed, *shaping*, her own response. In other words, the expression of excitement in Marson's poem appears to me to be *sincerely* felt. Rather than interpreting this as evidence of her false consciousness, I would interpret my own unease with Marson's euphoric response to the daffodils (and that of Wordsworth, for that matter) as an index of the preference in contemporary culture for less epiphanic modes of discourse.

Another contemporary Caribbean novelist, Erna Brodber, in her novel *Myal*,[21] describes a scene in which the young Jamaican protagonist, Ella O'Grady, recites perfectly two poems by Rudyard Kipling that she has learned 'by heart', including 'Take up the White Man's Burden'. Brodber's novel then explores the processes by which Ella must first recognize the foreignness of the culture she has imbibed and then learn how to expel what she cannot adapt from the imposed culture. Marson does write poems which express the kind of outrage apparent in the quote from Kincaid; and she does explore the possibilities for other kinds of poetic voices which might appear to be more culturally appropriate, in Brodber's terms. But there is perhaps another resonance to 'learning by heart' which isn't quite accounted for in these accounts. To 'learn by heart' is to commit to memory, to internalize a piece of text so that it is a part of the many memories, experiences and texts which constitute our subjectivity. However much these memorized pieces may be revisited and revised in the light of new knowledge and experience, as part of the memory bank, they are always free to resonate in not always predictable ways. Reinscribing the memorized text in one's own poem, then, need not automatically signal a naive or 'false' consciousness but can also be read as an intimate act of remembrance, an act of love. This, it seems to me, is the spirit in which Marson delivers a poem, such as 'Spring in England', and recognition of this is important in an evaluation of her contribution. The poem 'To Hampton', dedicated to the girls' school Marson attended in Jamaica, and included in her first collection, *Tropic Reveries*, is nostalgic for the values and culture of her schooling, all of which bear the hallmark of a solid colonial education:

> Ah me, the cares of Latin and French,
> And of the long hours spent upon the bench,
> The toils of writing prose and conning rhymes
> To us no doubt, did seem large ones at times.
> [. . .]
> How oft in dreams I live those days again,
> Chasing a hockey ball with might and main,
> Or sit and list without a thought of fear
> To dearest Mona reading great Shakespeare.
> (*Tropic Reveries*, p. 70)

Olive Senior, a fellow Jamaican writing several decades later, constructs a very different picture, and response, to her colonial education in 'Colonial Girl's School':

> Borrowed images
> willed our skins pale
> muffled our laughter
> lowered our voices
> let out our hems
> dekinked our hair
> denied our sex in gym tunics and bloomers
> harnessed our voices to madrigals
> and genteel airs
> yoked our minds to declensions in Latin
> and the language of Shakespeare
> > Told us nothing about ourselves
> > There was nothing about us at all[22]

It could be argued that the self-reflexivity in Senior's catalogue of the detailed ways in which colonial education attempted to erase the West Indian girl-child's selfhood exposes the political naivety of Marson's nostalgia for her schooldays. But such an argument would involve refusing the middle-class aspirations which characterize Marson's life (as Jarrett-Macauley's biography makes clear) and the contradictory nature of her embrace of English culture, as well as ignoring the more complex and confident nationalist and feminist discourses available to Senior. Further, the nostalgia for her colonial education which Marson expresses in this poem needs to be read alongside her public statements about colonial education. So, for example, Jarrett-Macauley cites a newspaper report of

Marson's address to the British Commonwealth League Conference in May 1935, in which she argued that the colonies had all had 'far too much of the old Imperialist propaganda and British training. [. . .] The aim of colonial education should be to produce useful citizens of their countries and not flag-waving Britishers.'[23] Here, Marson's take on colonial education, when expressed publicly in her role as a black spokeswoman, is sharply anti-imperialist. The perspective expressed in 'To Hampton', by contrast, invokes a much more intimate, affectionate and ambivalent relationship between colonial subject and colonial education.

The intimacy involved in 'learning by heart' is also characteristic of another kind of 'devotional' activity, that of rewriting poems by the 'master', for in such rewrites, the 'original' is often shadowed line by line by the imitator. Marson published several of these in *Tropic Reveries* and, though they are carefully listed as parodies in the table of contents and each poem includes an apology to the particular 'master poet', these poems are, with varying degrees of playfulness, counter-canonical in dramatizing the kinds of *difference* (with regard to race and/ or gender) which the originals elide. So, in 'To Wed or Not to Wed', Marson matches the phrasing and metre of that most canonical of soliloquies, Shakespeare's Hamlet agonizing about the miseries of his life, using the soliloquy to reflect on the supposed advantages of marriage for women:

> To wed, or not to wed: that is the question:
> Whether 'tis nobler in the mind to suffer
> The fret and loneliness of spinsterhood
> Or to take arms against the single state
> And by marrying, end it?
>
> (*Tropic Reveries*, pp. 81–2)

The poem concludes that the risks of a 'mismatch' are great enough to justify remaining inactive – and single. Grace Nichols, a Guyanese poet, has also published a (partial) rewrite of this soliloquy in her poem, 'With Apologies to Hamlet'.[24] The poem, which opens, 'To pee or not to pee/That is the question', explores the 'dilemma' facing the woman poet suffering the 'discomforting slings/ Of a full and pressing bladder'. Although Marson's feminist rewrite refuses the supposed fulfilment afforded by marriage, it does appear pretty tame alongside Nichols' more irreverent version; Shakespeare doesn't get a mention in the latter (Nichols' apology is to 'Hamlet') and she is much more cavalier than Marson in her use of the original. Clearly too, in refusing to parallel exactly the phrasing and weight of Shakespeare's lines, and, in replacing Hamlet's existential angst with the figure of the woman poet 'dying for a pee', Nichols challenges the idea of the thinker-poet as a transcendental 'I'. Instead, the writing of poetry is placed firmly within the realms of the ordinary and the embodied. Nonetheless, Marson's rewrite, given that she was writing when anti-patriarchal discourses were much less established, anticipates something of Nichols' witty challenge. It demonstrates, too, that, Marson is as capable of critiquing patriarchal bards as she is of mimicking them. In another poem, 'Politeness', Marson's challenge to the bards is absolutely unequivocal; here she responds to William Blake's poem, 'Little Black Boy'. The first stanza of Blake's poem reads:[25]

> My mother bore me in the southern wild,
> And I am black, but O! my soul is white;
> White as an angel is the English child:
> But I am black as if bereaved of light.

And here is Marson's poem, 'Politeness', in its entirety:

> They tell us
> That our skin is black
> But our hearts are white.
>
> We tell them
> That their skin is white
> But their hearts are black.
> (*Tropic Reveries*, p. 44)

In these poems, then, Marson's indebtedness to her 'European poetic masters' is displayed in such various forms that dismissing them as 'fakery' or 'not authentically West Indian' is to refuse the ambivalent and contradictory nature of Marson's poetic oeuvre and some of the more nuanced strands of colonial cultural exchanges between England and the West Indies. The uncertainty about voice which characterizes Marson's work is an indicator of the degree of her sense of cultural unbelonging and of a desire to both belong to, *and* challenge, the poetic status quo.

Picnicking among the wreckage

John Clare McFarlane, who founded the Jamaica Poetry League in 1923 and published *A Literature in the Making* in 1956, notes the restlessness in Marson's work, foregrounded above, but comes to quite different conclusions:

> And Miss Marson's *Confession* is the confession of all youth of today. It has inherited a spiritual domain that is more or less in ruins, with good things and evil things lying in a confused and confusing mass, and with no one to sort out the wreckage. [. . .] But for the present youth has decided to have a picnic among the wreckage and to pretend to itself that it does not care; that at all events it is living its life. [. . .] It *knows* it is not secure, and that any building it erects, with all that ruin lying about, is but a temporary makeshift.[26]

'Confession' opens with the bold assertion:

I regret nothing –
I have lived
I have loved
I have known laughter
And dance and song,
I have sighed
I have prayed,
I have soared
On fleecy clouds
To the gates
Of heaven,
I have sunk
Deep down
In the pit
Of hell.
                (*The Moth*, p. 63)

And it concludes, 'Why should I/Sorrowing go?/Have I not lived?' McFarlane objects to the easy acceptance of the unpredictable and the transient in Marson's work, and to the modernist sensibility he associates with such an outlook. By contrast, the other women poets discussed in *A Literature in the Making*, all of whom, apart from Marson, were white, represent a more conservative and 'traditional' poetics. So, for example, McFarlane singles out a poem by Albinia Catherine Hutton, 'The Empire's Flag', for special praise because 'The admirable restraint with which the poem is written lends to it just that touch of power in tranquility which a contemplation of the Union Jack brings' (1956, p. 27). While not wishing to labour the point, I offer the stanza McFarlane quotes from this poem to emphasize the degree to which Marson's concerns, however much she mimicked colonial cultural forms, were out of kilter with the prevalent attitude of her peers in the Jamaica Poetry League:

I fly where'er the birds fly, where'er the sun doth shine
I've sons of every colour, in every land and clime,
I 'witch them all with beauty and make them forever mine.
Set on the crests of mountains, Queen of the boundless sea,
Proudly they walk beneath me, they who are truly free:
I am the Flag of Freedom, where'er my children be.
                            (McFarlane 1956, p. 28)

   By contrast, Marson's poem 'He Called Us Brethren' exposes the hypocrisy beneath this myth of freedom and equality; Marson travelled to 'the heart of the Empire' in 1932 and had cause to question seriously the values of the mother country:

The preacher called them brethren
And who were they but coloured folk!
And who was the preacher but English!
He called us brethren and the Press
Was pleased to publish this strange news.
[. . .]
O England, England, heart of an Empire
That reaches to the remotest parts of earth,
Beneath thy flag are men in every clime;
How slow thou art to comprehend the truth,
The universal truth that all must learn –
And thou the foremost for thou hast set
Great claim upon the holy words of God.
For greater than all battles
That are fought in freedom's name,
[. . .]
. . . stronger than the bonds
That bind the peoples of one Race
Is that same blood that flows –
That flows alike through black and white
Making us one in Christ.

(The Moth, p. 15)

The poem consolidates its message adroitly with a fairly conventional appeal to 'true' Christianity which facilitates the poem's closure; this 'predictable' closure, however, seems here to be deployed strategically to contain the fury generating the poem in the first place. In a poem which Marson published in *Keys*, the publication of the League of Coloured People, this challenge is made even more forcefully:

They called me 'Nigger'
Those little white urchins
[. . .]
What made me keep my fingers
From choking the words in their
    throats?[27]

Marson's travels and, in particular, her stay in England, sharpened her perspective on many issues and several of the poems in *The Moth and the Star*, published after her arrival in England, exploit these insights in innovative ways.

The poem 'Little Brown Girl' (*The Moth*, pp. 11–13),[28] for example, does not make use of the self-consciously poetic 'I' of poems such as 'Spring in England' (published in the same volume); instead, the poem dramatizes a dialogue of sorts between a white Londoner and a West Indian girl. The Londoner, whose gender is left ambiguous, is intrigued by the strangeness of this 'little brown girl' in the city and asks a series of questions of the young woman:

Why do you start and wince
When white folk stare at you?
Don't you think they wonder
Why a little brown girl
Should roam about their city
Their white, white city?

Little brown girl
Why did you leave
Your little sunlit land
Where we sometimes go
To rest and get brown
So we may look healthy?

The bulk of the poem is spoken by the white speaker, and Marson uses this device both to dramatize the sense of strangeness and difference which the brown girl represents to the white gaze and to tease out some of the assumptions made by the speaker as she/he attempts to understand the desires of the young brown girl. In the process, the discontent and desire of the white speaker are also revealed. The poem concludes:

Little brown girl
You are exotic
And you make me wonder
All sorts of things
When you stroll about London
Seeking, seeking, seeking.
What are you seeking
To discover in this dismal
City of ours?

When the brown girl herself speaks, it is to comment on the lack of laughter and vitality in the streets of London:

Nothing but people clad
In Coats, Coats, Coats,
Coats in autumn, winter and spring,
And often in the Summer –
A city of coated people
But little to charm the eye.

And the foks are all white –
White, white, white,
And they all seem the same
As they say that Negroes seem.

Here Marson neatly reverses the stereotype of blacks all 'seem[ing] the same' to the white gaze and then goes on to catalogue the copper, black, brown and bronze which are homogenized by the label 'black'. The poem then contrasts the friendliness and vibrancy of 'back home' in ways which at times risk re-introducing, and endorsing, stereotypical images of blacks, 'country folk/Parading the city/With bare feet,/Bright attractive bandanas,/Black faces, pearly teeth/And flashing eyes'. Nonetheless, the poem conveys a haunting sense of the strangeness and isolation of the brown girl's existence in the city; an isolation which the structure of the poem emphasizes for, although there are two speakers, their voices speak *at*, rather than *to* each other. The white speaker presents a series of staccato questions which he/she answers her/himself, while the brown girl's response does not directly address any of the questions and is positioned in the middle of the poem, 'framed' on either side by the white speaker's desire to know and *consume* the other. The sense of 'double-take' and the subtle shifting of perspectives which results from this use of two speakers indicates Marson's modernist concerns but can perhaps also be regarded as the beginnings of a diasporic poetics.

The limer and the *flâneuse*

If Sam Selvon's *The Lonely Londoners*, published in 1956, has become a text which is read as providing early examples of diasporic black figures, then Marson's 'little black girl' provides a useful reminder that some of these migrants were *women*. In Selvon's text, 'de boys dem' roam endlessly and aimlessly through the city, their 'liming' punctuated by the repeated question, 'Wha' happenin'?' These 'limers',[29] constrained by London's racism, exercise their limited agency within the arena of their sexual relationships with white, mostly working-class, women where they (the West Indian men) act out the required myth of their sexual potency in 'jungle games'.[30] Marson represents the encounter between the black woman and the city in more whimsical and ambivalent ways to conjure the experience more elusively. Where Selvon's 'lonely Londoners' lime in a group, Marson's speakers are alone *and* lonely. The experimentation with form and with voice, which is characteristic of both Selvon's and Marson's work, clearly relates to a broader modernist project in which representations of a unified self are questioned. Unlike 'mainstream' modernists and the emphasis on the internal/psychological dimensions of subjectivity, however, both Selvon and Marson are more emphatic on the degree to which 'race' – and the effects of racism – require sharp attention to the 'external' factors which shape identity. Placed alongside Rachel Bowlby's discussion of the modernist woman as a *flâneuse*,[31] walking the streets of the city (with Virginia Woolf as exemplar), Marson's figure of the brown girl is a reminder of the particular kind of audacity such 'street walking' would require of the *black* woman. As well as poetic evocations of the woman-as-walker in Marson's poetry, Delia Jarrett-Macauley's biography refers many times to Marson's penchant for strolling around the city on her own. What emerges from these accounts, and even more powerfully from the poems, is a figure imbued neither with the noisy flamboyance of the limer, nor the confident panache of the *flâneuse*; rather, the figure of the black/brown woman in the city is one acutely aware of her otherness and isolation.

'The Stranger', also published in *The Moth and the Star*, repeats some of the insights found in 'Little Brown Girl', in its self-reflexive awareness of the different ways in which 'strangeness' is activated. The 'I' of the poem recognizes that she is constructed as exotic or strange:

> So you like talking to people like me
> Friend with the wistful smile,
> To foreign girls who are brown of skin
> And have black kinky hair
> And strange black eyes.
>   (*The Moth*, p. 16)

In the heightened stories she tells of her 'tropic paradise', there is a sense that the speaker is manipulating the expectations of the 'friend' about her 'strangeness'. The concluding lines, by reversing the estranging gaze and describing the English friend as strange, suggests the relativity of the concept of 'strangeness' itself:

> I like to listen to you,
> Friend with the wistful smile,
> It's not to hear of your great country
> And tales of your marvellous land,
> But to watch the wistful smile
> That plays around your mouth,
> The strange look in your eyes
> And hear the calm sweet tone of your voice.
>   (*The Moth*, p. 16)

In other poems, such as 'Black Burden', the 'double-take' strategy is less playfully utilized and the weight of the 'burden' of blackness is asserted in heavy, resigned tones:

> I am black
> And so I must be
> More clever than white folk,
> More wise than white folk,
> More discreet than white folk.
>   (*The Moth*, p. 16)

Caught in the perverse logic of racist stereotypes, the speaker acknowledges that restraint is also required:

> I must not laugh too much,
> They say black folk can only laugh,
> I must not weep too much,

They say black folk weep always
I must not pray too much
They say black folk can only pray.
(*The Moth*, p. 93)

In the final stanza of the poem, the speaking voice shifts from the first person to the third person in a manoeuvre which suggests that the 'I' is speaking to itself. Here, Marson seems to rehearse Fanon's insights in *Black Skin, White Masks* about the splitting of 'self' under the colonial gaze:

Black girl – what a burden –
But your shoulders
Are broad
Black girl – what a burden –
But your courage is strong –
Black girl your burden
Will fall from your shoulders
For there is love
In your soul
And a song
In your heart.
(*The Moth*, p. 93)

The shift in tone effects a kind of up-beat closure which sits rather uneasily with the mournful and resigned tone of the rest of the poem. But perhaps, rather than reading the last lines as escapist or trite, this internal tension should be read as a defiant insistence on consciousness-raising, as the most appropriate response to the relentlessness of the racist gaze. 'Cinema Eyes', a poem in which a black mother addresses her 18-year-old daughter, makes its consciousness-raising agenda explicit:

Come, I will let you go
When black beauties
Are chosen for the screen;
That you may know
Your own sweet beauty
And not the white loveliness
Of others for envy.
(*The Moth*, p. 88)

The narrative line in this poem verges on the melodramatic – the mother's 'fair' husband ends up killing himself and the 'black god' (who had been the mother's first suitor, rejected because he was too dark). The moral of the story is clumsily executed but, in its awareness of the importance of popularly disseminated images, it makes a daring point. Another poem in which Marson explores con-structions – and reconstructions – of black female identity is 'Black is Fancy'. In this poem a black servant speaks, in a dramatic monologue, to her image in a mirror, contrasting it with the picture of 'a beautiful white lady' and deciding, in the end, to replace the picture of the white woman with the mirror so that she can affirm her own sense of beauty. The poem perhaps strains to make the point, particularly in the concluding stanza:

> My John told me I was sweet,
> I did not believe him,
> Thought he would go mooning around
> Some whitewash girl,
> But maybe he means it,
> For I am not so dull,
> Yes, I am sure he loves me
> His black ivory girl,
> And I love him
> For he is young, and strong and black.
> (*The Moth*, p. 76)

But there are some lines that are irresistibly assertive:

> There is something about me
> That has a dash in it
> Especially when I put on
> My bandana.
> (*The Moth*, p. 75)

There is something of Zora Neale Hurston's rhetorical swagger in these lines: 'I love myself when I am laughing. And then again when I am looking mean and impressive.'[32] Unlike many of the poems discussed earlier, the poems in which black female identities are explored make use of more fragmented forms, uneven line lengths, less rigid rhyme schemes and slippery-voiced speakers. Marson's poetic identity in these poems is less directly asserted and, in its tentativeness and contradictions, more convincingly engaging. The fact that it is in those poems which, in some way, interrogate black (female) identity that Marson experiments most actively with different voices suggests that masquerading as 'a real happy bloke' might be understood as providing 'poetic relief' from the business of representing her own troubled subjectivity.

'Kinky Hair Blues'

In other poems, in what I read as an indication of her restless quest for a more effective poetic voice, Marson experiments with the African American speech rhythms and musical influences characteristic of the work of Langston Hughes and others involved in the Harlem Renaissance.[33] This is evident in poems such as 'Kinky Hair Blues', 'Canefield Blues', 'Lonesome Blues' and 'Brown Baby Blues'.

In these, Marson uses the melancholy tenor of 'the blues' to document aspects of black experiences. In 'Canefield Blues', a male speaker mourns the sudden death of his 'sweet Mandy' while they are together in the cane field. While the political significance of this location is not exploited overtly in the way that more recent poets have done,[34] the poem operates here as the voicing of a folk testimony to the grief caused on the cane plantations. 'Brown Baby Blues' is a dirge sung by a black mother to her 'high brown' baby, following the (white) father's disappearance; the poem sets up intertextual echoes with the lines of a popular calypso, 'brown-skin gal stay home and mind baby',[35] but concludes with an ironic affirmation of the baby's 'high' (light) colour:

> My sweet brown baby
> Don't you cry
> My sweet brown baby
> Don't you cry.
> Your mamma does love you
> And your colour is high.
> > (*The Moth*, p. 97)

'Kinky Hair Blues' is one of Marson's best-known poems, and is included in *The Penguin Book of Caribbean Verse in English*[36] and discussed by both Lloyd Brown and, later, Rhonda Cobham (see below). The poem bemoans the oppressive 'beauty regime' which the young black woman must submit to and, after repeating that 'I like me black face/And me kinky hair', the poem concludes with a reluctant and resigned capitulation:

> Now I's gwine press me hair
> And bleach me skin.
> I's gwine press me hair
> And bleach me skin.
> What won't a gal do
> Some kind of man to win.
> > (*The Moth*, p. 91)

The poem is an early and important representation of the oppressive cultural prescriptions which curtail black women's selfhood, and of the pressures which force complicity with such oppression. The use of the demotic in these poems is sometimes an uneasy mix of African American and Jamaican and this, when combined with the dictates of rhythm and rhyme, can make for rather stilted readings. Sometimes, as in the poem. 'Banjo Boy', Marson represents African American culture in ways which, though perhaps intended as celebratory, verge on minstrelsy:

> Black boy,
> How you play that banjo!

Gee – it goes right to my toes,
[. . .]
Where did you get that rhythm?
That swing and that motion
[. . .] I have it too,
I can feel it going through me,
But I can't express like you do.
                              (*The Moth*, p. 68)

Marson read this poem on the BBC programme 'Voice' in November 1942 with an introduction by the editor of the programme, George Orwell (then Eric Blair), 'Before we go on to the nineteenth-century writers we must have something to represent the Negro writers'. As Delia Jarrett-Macauley astutely puts it: 'For those with more than a cursory knowledge of African-American poetry, this scripted exchange was a pathetic window on that field and the impact of Una's reading "Banjo Boy" might have been to suggest that minstrelsy and coyness characterized Black poetry.'[37]

Marson also experimented with incorporating Jamaican speech rhythms into her poetry. There was little published poetry which made sustained use of Creole; Claude McKay had written several 'dialect poems' but had shifted away from this after his migration to America. Marson's experiments with Creole were, undoubtedly, pioneering. Nonetheless, her success with using Creole in her poetry, I would argue, is fairly limited. In 'Quashie Comes to Town' (*The Moth*, pp. 17–21), the speaker is a Jamaican 'quashie', a 'man from the country'[38] who, in a letter home, extols the many pleasures of London – its theatres, music halls, cinemas and restaurants, and the general hustle and bustle of the city. The speaker also proclaims his preference for black women, ('black pearls'), black music ('An' if you hear Paul Robeson sing/You feel you wan' fe bawl'), and for Jamaican food ('Me good ole rice an' peas'), before concluding:

It not gwine be anoder year
Before you see me face,
Dere's plenty dat is really nice
But I sick fe see white face.

The poem is an uneasy mixture of the assertion of black pride – most stridently in the final line of the poem, 'But I sick fe see white face' – and a demonstration of Quashie's ability to consume the culture of the city discriminatingly. The speaker's use of Creole is uneven, driven more by the demands of the iambic pentameter and the abcb rhyme scheme in which it is written, than by verisimilitude in replicating spoken Creole on the page. The jaunty tone, combined with the adherence to a tight rhythm and rhyme which does not easily accommodate the Jamaican Creole of the speaker, results in some rather unwieldy images, such as, 'An' talkin 'bout de Bobbie dem,/Dem is nice as nice can be,/An' some o' dem is tall me boy/'Mos' like a coconut tree'. These lines make for uneasy reading; not simply because of the post-Lawrence suspicion surrounding the Metropolitan Police Force in Britain in the 'new' millennium but because social history of the 1940s would suggest a decidedly less 'jolly' relationship between the police and black male 'arrivants' than Marson suggests. In the final analysis, Quashie's monologue is so readily accommodated to the familiar role of Creole-speaker as entertainer that the subversive racial politics embedded in the poem resonates in rather circumscribed ways. Caught between shifting loyalties to cultures 'over here' and 'over there', the poem dramatizes the double bind of the migrant-person – and poet.

Marson also made more 'serious' use of Creole in her poems, as in 'The Stone Breakers', in which two women, breaking stones by the roadside for a living, register, fatalistically, the hardships they suffer in this employment. Marson presents the dialogue between 'Cousin Mary' and 'Liza' with economy and without the jaunty closure characteristic of so many of her poems:

'But whey fe do, Cousin Mary,
Me haf fe buy frack fe de pickney dem,
Ebry day dem hab fe feed.
Dem wotless pupa tan roun' de bar
A trow dice all de day –
De groun' is dat dry,
Not a ting will grow –
Massy Lard, dis life is hard.'
                                    (*The Moth*, p. 70)

The less rigid rhythm and rhyme scheme and the tight thematic focus give this poem a more authoritative tone. It is also worth noting, in passing, the links between Marson's poem and that of the much anthologized poem 'History Makers' by George Campbell. If Marson attempts to convey the realities of these working-class women's lives through the simulation of their speech, creating the illusion that they present their experiences *in their own words*, Campbell's (very fine) poem mythicizes the women into silent but statuesque monuments of strength and endurance:

Women stone breakers
Hammers and rocks
[. . .]
Strong thigh
Rigid head
[. . .]
No smiles
No sigh
No moan.[39]

In pointing to the differences between the two poems, I do not wish to offer a simplified response which explains these differences entirely in terms of innate empathy: because Marson was a woman she is better able to empathize with her women subjects than is Campbell, though this may well have *some* valency. Rather, I would argue that the gendered differences be read as an indication of the powerful symbolic currency of 'the strong (but silent) black woman' in early nationalist writing, a symbolic value which, because of its mythic proportions, the black woman writer was perhaps less disposed towards using in her own work. Black Caribbean women poets have since constructed different myths of their own strengths and Una Marson's life and work have been mobilized to this end (see below).

With this issue of 'women' as a collective identity in mind, Marson's poem, 'Gettin' de Spirit' may be read as an early attempt to 'break the silence' and to mobilize and empower a sisterly solidarity. The poem presents the unmediated voice of a woman, in a series of exuberant calls to the 'sisters' to 'shout':

> Join de chorus,
> We feel it flowing o'er us –
> You is no chile of satan
> So get de spirit
> And shout – sister – shout –
> Hellelujah – Amen –
> Shout – Sister – shout!
> (*The Moth*, p. 76)

Unlike the decorously coy voice of some of the poems discussed earlier, where the tropes of Christian spirituality are used to legitimize the poetic voice, here an 'indigenized Christianity' is dramatized and its energetic power is presented as an avenue to collective vocal empowerment. In the final analysis, the dynamic poetic voice of 'Gettin' de Spirit' is not the one which dominates Marson's work when taken as a whole. Instead, it is perhaps the tension *between* poetic identities which leaves the most lasting impression and, coupled with this, a sense of a poet who perceived herself as writing very much in isolation. To consolidate this point and by way of conclusion, here are the last two stanzas of 'Lonesome Blues':

> Nobody cares
> If I don't come home,
> Nobody cares
> If I don't come home,
> What's de good o' dis life
> Jes as well I roam.
>
> It's kinda hard
> Being a lonesome gal
> It's kinda hard
> Being a lonesome gal

But I bet it's worse
Wid a no good pal.
(*The Moth*, p. 96)

Here, Marson is able to forge the influence of African American women blues singers, such as Bessie Smith and Billie Holliday, to her own experiences and identities as a migrant, black woman poet. In its reluctant promotion of 'roaming alone', the poem, as in 'Little Brown Girl' and other poems discussed above, evokes a poignantly nuanced image of Una Marson as a black woman and as a poet. Read alongside the poem discussed earlier, 'Vagabond Creed' and Marson's troublesome declamation, 'And I am a real happy bloke/For the whole world to me doth belong', it foregrounds the many 'masters', and cultural centres, Marson looked towards for inspiration, and emphasizes the diverse, diasporic aesthetics of her poetic output. The unevenness of the poems and the very partiality of their 'success' as poems, is as much an index of the transitional moment at which Marson was writing and of her dissatisfaction with inherited poetic forms, as it is a marker of her accomplishment as poet.

Between the palm and the oak

While Phyllis Shand Allfrey's poetry shares little of Marson's concerns or stylistic innovation, biographical information suggests that both women were unhappy (for different reasons) with their literary output. In addition to her novel, *The Orchid House*, and several short stories published in various newspapers, journals and anthologies, Phyllis Shand Allfrey published four collections of poetry: *In Circles* (1940), *Palm and Oak I* (1950), *Contrasts* (1955) and *Palm and Oak II* (1973).[40] These volumes of poetry are not widely available; the Public Library in Dominica, for example, while it had multiple copies of the Virago edition of *The Orchid House*, had only one copy of one volume of Allfrey's poetry.[41] Aside from this practical, but significant, example of inaccessibility, and combined with the distinctive isolations of her 'small island' location, Allfrey's poetic voice and style are often both secretive and self-enclosed, contributing further to the sense of obscurity surrounding her poetry. She frequently allegorizes her poetic material, drawing on the details of her own family history as well as the broader sweep of colonial history. 'Clues' for interpreting these allegories are not always inscribed within the poems and this, coupled with the penchant for archaic diction, can sometimes result in frustratingly obfuscatory texts. It is certainly likely that *part* of the reason for the cryptic nature of Allfrey's poetry is connected to the difficulties of maintaining privacy when living in 'a small place',[42] but it is also related to her own perception of the role of the poet as somehow out-of-the-ordinary or 'enchanted'. The fact that Allfrey is a white West Indian would also mean that her credentials as an 'authentic' West Indian would not have been readily assumed. Further, Allfrey seldom inscribes 'West Indianness' in obviously recognizable ways in her poetry; neither does she express dissatisfaction with colonially inherited traditions of poetry by experimenting with a range of forms, as did Una Marson.

Allfrey's appeals to 'universal' alliances between women and amongst 'comrades' may also have distracted attention from her 'West Indianness'. Marson's work, on the other hand, in putting black identity on the poetic agenda and in, however unevenly, challenging inherited poetic forms, is more immediately and *recognizably* West Indian.

The title of Lizabeth Paravisini-Gebert's excellent biography of Phyllis Shand Allfrey, *Phyllis Shand Allfrey: A Caribbean Life*, suggests what the book itself argues through in convincing detail, that Allfrey lived most of her life in Dominica and that her contributions to Dominica, both in the realms of politics and culture, have been significant and lasting. But the subtle distinction implied in the title between a Caribbean *life* and a Caribbean *woman* is an interesting one, suggesting something of the ambivalence surrounding Allfrey's Caribbean 'birthright'. Certainly, Allfrey claimed and articulated her Dominican identity in her poetry, proclaiming her love for the island itself and seeking to come to terms with the historical legacy of colonialism. She also, however, claims the 'Nordic' strain of her ancestry pretty unequivocally; Paravisini-Gebert quotes Allfrey as saying, 'After all, I have been here for 356 years (since Thomas Warner came).'[43] The title chosen for two volumes of her poetry, *Palm and Oak*, makes explicit this sense of a dual cultural heritage and her insistence on claiming *both*. The degree of comfort with which Allfrey claimed her 'Nordic strain', is evident in an early poem, such as 'Transfiguration', in which the speaker confidently and unselfconsciously describes Buffalo city in America, transformed by heavy snowfall. In the poem, there is nothing exotic or spectacular in 'snow':

> Carrying precious weight,
>   The noble trees
> Proud of their snowy freight
>   Solemnly freeze.[44]

Instead, it is exploited for its potential to transform the grubby materialism which usually defines the city. Allfrey's poetic claims to a West Indian landscape, by contrast, is made in a much more self-conscious and declamatory manner. In the poem 'Love for an Island' (probably the most frequently anthologized of Allfrey's poems), the speaker voices her love for Dominica most unequivocally and passionately:

> Love for an island is the sternest passion:
> pulsing beyond the blood through roots and loam
> it overflows the boundary of bedrooms
> and courses past the fragile walls of home.
>   (*Palm and Oak I*, p. 2)

What is interesting here is the way in which the soil of the homeland/island, '*pulsing beyond the blood* through roots and loam', is presented as overriding 'blood ties' and connections with people. The poem continues, shifting to colonial tropes of rapacious possession:

Theirs is no mild attachment, but rapacious
craving for a possession rude and whole;
lovers of islands drive their stake, prospecting
to run the flag of ego up the pole.

The poem concludes by commenting on the futility of such efforts to erect
monuments which might secure claims to the island:

Salesmen and termites occupy their dwellings,
their legendary politics decay.
Yet they achieve an ultimate memorial:
they blend their flesh with the beloved clay.

The poem balances between a nostalgia for the past and for monuments to testify
to that past and an acknowledgement of the futility and hubris of such a 'monumental' view of history. This tension is 'resolved' in the final two lines when the
body *becomes* the land, albeit in a kind of 'death-rite/right'. This notion of
laying claim to the island in a death-rite/right is repeated in the poem 'The
Child's Return', dedicated to Jean Rhys and inspired by a line in one of Rhys's
letters to Allfrey about coming back to 'lay her bones in Dominica'.[15] The poem's
concluding stanza reads:

The timbers will creak and my heart will break
and the sailors will lay my bones
on the stiff rich grass, as sharp as spikes,
by the volcanic stones.

(*Palm and Oak I*, p. 7)

By way of contrast, in Una Marson's poem, 'Home Thoughts', the red blooms
of the poinciana tree are presented as 'calling, calling me home', but 'blood' in
this poem is associated much more firmly with the living and with the future (there
is no reference to the past) and, in its appeal to a notion of black diaspora, suggests
a much more mobile notion of 'belonging' than appears in Allfrey's poem. Here is
an extract from Marson's 'Home Thoughts':

O pride and glory of our tropic Isle,
As thy red and golden petals
Drip blood drops on the sod
That thou mayst bring forth
Mighty pods of fertile seed,
So children of your tropic land
With broken hearts that bleed
In foreign lands afar
Strain every nerve to bring forth
Fruit that may enrich the race

And are anew inspired
With hope and loyal longing.
(*The Moth*, p. 23)

There are numerous images of the luxuriant, exotic beauty of the landscape of Dominica in both Rhys and Allfrey, testifying to its 'terrible beauty' and the 'hothouse' intensity of the vegetation. It is tempting (space does not permit me to make a more consolidated argument) to suggest that there is a greater self-consciousness about laying claim to the land in the writing of white West Indians than there is in their black counterparts, and that the passionate claim to the land is both a symptom of the alienation felt by whites and a substitute for affiliations with the black populace. If the 'peoplescape' provides little sense of belonging, then the landscape is often represented as a refuge. Jean Rhys suggests such a scenario in the extract below from *Wide Sargasso Sea*:

> I took another road, past the old sugar works and the water wheel that had not turned for years. I went to parts of Coulibri that I had not seen, where there was no road, no path, no track. And if the razor grass cut my legs and arms I would think 'It's better than people.' Black ants or red ones, tall nests swarming with white ants, rain that soaked me to the skin – once I saw a snake. All better than people.
> Better. Better, than people.[46]

In other poems, like 'Nocturne', Allfrey presents the island as an enchanted place full of sensual pleasures which dwarf human life; the moon 'hovers like some perfume-laden kite/or drips and sways, a carnival balloon.' Later on in the poem, the moon 'drips/intoxicating silver on an isle/of dark seduction'. The lines which follow make use of a highly suggestive dark/light imagery:

> . . . Round her sable hips
> the sea, a pleated sparkling petticoat,
> unfurls to girdle closer. In a white
> delirium we humans drift afloat
> within the pallor of a tropic night,
> our mortal shadows gliding brown as bark
> spangled with nutmeg, cinnamon and lime.
> (*Contrasts*, p. 1)

It is difficult not to read the contrasts set up in the poem – between the darkly seductive island and the pale floating humans – as being racially inflected, particularly when the 'brown', 'mortal shadows' of the pale folk are aligned with the fruit and spices of the land. Allfrey may intend the 'we' to refer to a universal humanity, but 'accidentally' the poem's symbolism evokes images which associate blacks with rootedness in the land and whites with the peripheral and ethereal. This interpretation is supported by the recurrence in Allfrey's work of imagery which associates whites/whiteness with the ethereal or decaying. The precarious position of all the white characters in *The Orchid House*, for example, indicates their peripheral location in a new postcolonial order and Allfrey compounds this, at least with regard to the male characters, by associating them with disease as well as decay. Certainly, other poems endorse the sense of a decaying white order which is so prevalent in the novel. The concluding stanza of 'Decayed Gentlewoman', for example, reads:

> Oh sad winter, drain the clot
> Of sap from the decaying tree,
> Fell it straight and let it rot
> For other lives' fertility.
> > (*In Circles*, p. 7)

Allfrey specifically genders the poem and, given her own high profile in Dominica as a 'character', invites an autobiographical reading. This insistence on the necessity of the old making way for the new is also part of a romantic belief in an 'island philosophy', as in 'The True-born Villager', where West Indian migrants in Britain (to whom the poem is dedicated) are presented as having an innate ability to understand and domesticate their metropolitan context, 'The true-born villager will thatch a village/deep in the metropolis' and 'has alchemy to turn/flats into cottages!' The poem concludes with a summary of this philosophy:

> . . . What's love to him?
> A long and stoical mating. And what's death?
> The hewing of a tree that's served its term:
> > logs for the living.
> > (*Palm and Oak I*, p. 6)

The calm, intuitive wisdom of the migrant is asserted: 'He gleans the primrose faces of the young,/paled by unnatural lighting, reading them/simply as other men absorb the news.' Allfrey's image of the migrant figure here makes an interesting contrast to that of 'Quashie' in Marson's poem, 'Quashie Comes to London', discussed above.[47] Where Marson, in a narrative poem of some forty-two four-line stanzas, *demonstrates* Quashie's ability to appreciate and critique metropolitan culture, Allfrey simply, in an eighteen-line poem, *asserts* the migrant's knowledge. Clearly, this difference can partly be explained in terms of their respective poetic styles, but, read together, this difference suggests that Marson's own experience of migration, charted in the poems, may have given her a much more intensely nuanced sense of the 'strangeness' of the migrant and, consequently, a greater impetus to *prove* Quashie's cultural credentials than Allfrey's experiences might have generated.

Allfrey draws upon the experiences of exile in many poems, but she does so explicitly in two poems which will allow me to elaborate on some of the differences between Allfrey's and Marson's representations of migration. In an untitled poem included in her first collection, *In Circles*, Allfrey sets up a contrast between the 'stolid spirits' and the 'frail spirits' in which the former 'feed on wood and iron,/they grow stolid/on a diet of plumbing,/books, chairs, lamb cutlets/houses and hard facts'; while the latter 'are fed on hurricanes,/songs by moonlight, pomalaks,/coconut milk, yams and the/mysterious grenadilla'. The speaker of the poem declares her/himself as one of the frail spirits at the outset:

> These people are too stolid
> for my frail self.
> Insubstantially I watch them,
> like a waiter at the Ritz,
> like a skeleton waiter
> padded with the defence
> of a different way of life –
> a birth between the palms
> of a Caribbean mound.
>
> (*In Circles*, p. 18)

The poem's concluding lines read:

> there is always a war on
> between the stolid spirits and the frail,
> and the stolid spirits always win:
> but the frail spirits have a final strategy
> – they vanish.
>
> (*In Circles*, p. 18)

In this poem, 'difference' is not made specific with reference to the details of context which characterized a poem such as Marson's 'Little Brown Girl'; instead, Allfrey *allegorizes* difference so that the basis upon which the distinction is made between the stolid and the frail spirits is not made explicit. Here, Allfrey constructs a romanticized distinction between the imaginative, exotic islander and the stolid realism of 'these people' who, given the reference to 'lamb cutlets', 'plumbing' and so on, appear to be English. What is interesting in this poem is the way in which the speaker cherishes the *invisibility* of her difference – 'Insubstantially I watch them [. . .] padded with the defence/of a different way of life' – an 'invisibility' of difference which alludes to the way Allfrey might herself have been perceived in London as not *visibly* different. Marson's representations of the experience of exile are also often couched in terms of opposites ('grey-coated women', 'glad darkies', etc.) but difference, in her poems, is always something *visible* to the gaze of the white city-dweller. For Marson, the apparently immutable physicality of racial difference makes invisiblity, as a strategy *or* a trope, an impossible one.

In 'Exiles', *Palm and Oak I* (later republished in *Palm and Oak II* as 'Expatriates', with the subtitle 'West Indians in Britain'), Allfrey asks:

> Living in sunless reaches under rain,
> how do the exiles from enchanted isles
> tend and sustain their rich nostalgic blaze?
>
> (*Palm and Oak I*, p. 1)

The answers to this question are listed: some 'ignite in pain', others 'grow charred to ash on memories' and so on, with the lines, 'one estranged beats poems thin as leaves/out of stored tropic heat on brumal nights/of fearful mist and chill', suggesting an image of the poet herself as the 'one estranged'.

Happy we are to be brown and strong and lissome

If the speakers in many of Allfrey's poems present themselves as 'insubstantial' or 'frail', 'afloat/within the pallor of a tropic night', the poem 'The White Lady', subtitled 'Martinique', offers a different perspective as the speakers here are black women. The speaking voice of the poem slips from 'We are the trees, we are the silent spies', to 'happy we are to be brown and strong and lissome'. These black women are presented as observing 'the untarnished ones, the wives of officials' promenading in 'precious gowns, imported from Paris', between the royal palms which surround the famous statue of 'Napoleon's Josephine', situated in 'La Savane' in Fort de France in Martinique. The use of the first person *plural* is unusual; most of Allfrey's poems make use of first-person or omniscient speakers – ironically perhaps, given her socialist convictions. The poem continues:

> we know that they conceive their children in rooms
> with the jalousie blinds drawn, the mosquito net tucked in.
> We are not jealous of that love-making:
> happy we are to dig our roots firm into the earth,
> happy we are to be brown and strong and lissome.
> Our children are multiple, and all have beauty:
> we fear not dirt, nor age. There was but one we feared,
> and she was a queen.
>
> (*In Circles*, p. 4)

The poem then describes the mesmerizing beauty of Napoleon's Creole wife, Josephine, whose beauty eclipses that of the black/brown women: 'and the poets turned their eyes away from us,/to write poems about her: sweet lewd poems'. Here, the black woman is constructed as being deeply and comfortably rooted in the fecundity of the soil while the white ladies are presented as 'uptight', conceiving their children in sanitized privacy. The association of black women with fecundity and warmth and the parallel association of white women with sterile frigidity is a familiar one in the literature of the region. Jean Rhys, most obviously, invokes this dichotomy in *Voyage in the Dark*: 'I wanted to be black. I always wanted to be black. [. . .] Being black is warm and gay, being white is cold and sad',[18] while Grace Nichols dramatizes this opposition in 'Love Act'.[19] The poem conveys the harsh realities of the plantation system in which the black woman's body is 'the fuel/that keep them all going', including the Master who, in forcing himself upon the black servant, releases his 'mistresswife' from the 'love act':

> And his mistresswife
> spending her days in rings
> of vacant smiling
> is glad to be rid of the
> love act
>> (*i is a long memorial*
>> *woman*, p. 49)

The insistence in the Nichols poem on detailing the sociopolitical realities which inform relationships between black and white women offers a sobering corrective to the romantic essentialism of both Rhys's and Allfrey's constructions. Allfrey's poem concludes with a series of images in which romantic associations of Josephine proliferate:

> now we have no rival:
> she stands among the palms,
> among the royal palms,
> whiter than the wives of officials
> and whiter than Caribbean surf,
> as white as marble, with her face lifted to the wind,
> listening for the word Phina
> in the deep of the night,
> and the tourists say
> her gown is Empire.
>
>> (*In Circles*, p. 5)

There are contradictory and troubling resonances in this poem with regard to Allfrey's choice of *voice*: While the black women *do* assert a sense of their own identity and agency, it is articulated in terms which are almost entirely nature-bound; and, while the preciousness of the white wives of the officials is parodied, the poem concludes with the black woman's admiring gaze turned upon and held by the statuesque image of Josephine. Finally, it is the tourists, and not the speaker, who make the connection with Empire: 'the tourists say/her gown is Empire.' However, while the poem opens by setting up a familiarly 'raced' binary in the image of the silent black women observing the white women, the fact that Josephine, like Allfrey, was a white Creole while the wives of the officials would have been 'French whites' (that is, 'proper' whites, *not* 'white cockroach', Creoles) complicates the neat binary. The title of the poem, nonetheless, in its use of the singular ' "The" White Lady', implies that Josephine, despite being Creole, is 'the' white lady – by virtue of her real power and beauty (unlike the superficial power of the officials) and, more playfully, because of the marble out of which the statue is made. Allfrey appears in this poem to be using the black women speakers to consolidate a wished-for affiliation between blacks and white Creoles. In the absence of a *recognizably* white-Creole speaking voice, Allfrey mediates this Creole subject position *through* that of the black women who *do* have a recognized voice as the disenfranchised. It could be argued that Allfrey's use of a black narrator is generated by a desire to signal clearly an ideological affiliation with the black masses. For this 'signal' to be recognized as radical, she cannot trust a white Creole-speaker. On the other hand, it might also be argued that Allfrey uses black women speakers provocatively in 'The White Lady' (and with the servant-narrator, Lally, in *The Orchid House*) as a way of displaying the conservative cultural and political values of the black masses.

These readings are further complicated by Allfrey's well-documented investment in her 'ancestry'. Paravisini-Gebert suggests that:

> The sheer romance of her family's connection to the empress delighted Phyllis. It gratified her romantic nature and deep sense of 'family' and nurtured a conviction that her ancestry marked her as someone deeply linked to *history*, someone whose family chronicle could be traced in books.[50]

Allfrey, then, makes a personal claim to Josephine, and to the statue which the poem celebrates. The fact that she named her daughter Josephine confirms the intensity of Allfrey's romance with her past. That the poem does not question what the statue might mean to black Martiniquans has to be read as an indication of the limitation of Allfrey's imaginative connection with 'the people', whatever the extent of her political involvement and popularity. Aimé Césaire in *Notebook of a Return to My Native Land*, for example, emphasizes the distance separating Martiniquans from the Empress:

> In this inert town, this strange crowd that does not cram up together, does not mingle [. . .] This crowd which doesn't know how to be a crowd, this crowd, one realises, so perfectly alone under the sun like a woman who, seemingly engrossed in her lyrical beat, suddenly summons a hypothetical rain and commands it not to fall; or like a quick apparently unmotivated sign of the cross; or like a peasant urinating on her feet, her stiff legs parted.
>
> In this inert town, this sorry crowd under the sun, taking part in nothing which expresses, asserts, frees itself in the broad daylight of its own land. Nor in Empress Josephine of the French dreaming high, high above negridom.[51]

The fact that the statue has recently been decapitated suggests that Césaire's perception has some popular appeal. The postcard image of the statue, promoted as a tourist attraction, shows a Martiniquan woman, black, colourfully dressed and wearing a straw hat, looking into the distance, alongside the statue, suggesting an easy parallel between the two images which denies any historically generated tension.[52] Césaire's juxtaposition of the image of the peasant woman urinating, followed by the image of Josephine dreaming on high, deliberately disturbs this touristic (and Creole) fantasy; it does so, of course, by invoking the peasant *woman* as symbolic shorthand for everything the statue does *not* represent. The gendered implications of negritude will be revisited later; here it is perhaps sufficient to note the way in which both Allfrey and Césaire, with their Creole and negritude agendas, elide the subjectivity of the black woman herself.

The great and gracious days

Allfrey's pride in her 'noble' ancestry sometimes combined uneasily with her passionate commitment to socialism and to a more egalitarian Dominican society. Her involvement with the Federation led her to believe that 'the West Indies could be the best small nation of *mixed* people in the world. After all, I have been here for 356 years (since Thomas Warner came). *Then* I strolled to the Trinidad Library and found my one novel on a shelf for "white people's fiction".'[53] The poetry, too, reflects these contradictory impulses. In the poem 'The Great Days', for example:

> Those were the great days, and the gracious days!
> But did you say, my dear antagonist,
> the past is all our treasure – that we live
> now in the second-rate and the half-best?
>
> Dear enemy, the times are always great
> for the large-hearted. History is now,
> [. . .]
> The light is strong because it pours from him:
> the times are great when humans make them so.
> (*Contrasts*, p. 11)

The ambivalent way in which the speaker both affirms and rejects traditional accounts of History suggests that the poem is a kind of internal dialogue, in which 'the enemy' being addressed is the 'other self' of the speaker. While in 'Ghosts in a Plantation House' the presence of a violent colonial past haunts the present, it is 'Small wonder the slave girl moans and the French priest talks' as the absentee landlord puts off the moment of occupation until his 'youngling son inherits'. The image with which the poem concludes, of predators, ghosts and lawyers suspended in perpetual struggle for possession of the land, suggests a critique of such struggles but one which, in its description of the past as an 'enchanted enclave', resonates ambivalently:

> But land is land and the predators are busy.
> From an enchanted enclave of long days past
> Nobody wants to move. Both ghosts and lawyers are waiting
> Deep in the shadows: the struggle not yet abating.
> (*Palm and Oak II*, p. 20)

In 'Salute', however, Allfrey's socialist politics is presented as a universal buffer against colonial histories:

Meeting me in the road, he greets me: comrade.
Rough music in that word, rude magic
In grip of clenching fist on willing hand.
This is our barricade against the tragic
Creeping decomposition of our land.

(*In Circles*, p. 20)

And in 'Colonial Committee' (which Allfrey notes was first published in Aneurin Bevan's newspaper, *Tribune*), Allfrey's political take is unequivocally anti-colonial:

the olive and mahogany and white
of the assembled faces, but no frown

hints at the terminating trusteeship,
or at the adolescence too prolonged;
for in this civil jungle scarce a snarl
or yap of pain attests the deeply wronged.

(*Palm and Oak I*, p. 8)

The leaves of the book blow wild for its reader

Allfrey's extensive political involvements clearly impinged on her writing career: 'Politics became more important than writing. I regret that now. I shouldn't have given up writing for politics. [. . .] O yes, Politics ruined me as a writer.'[54] Some of the poems dramatize the struggle between her various roles as politician, feminist, mother and writer, and it is this struggle which dominates her work, rather than, as was the case with Marson, a struggle with literary precursors. In 'Resistance', the speaker notes 'how sad we lay our book, our sleeping child,/our need for symphony and safety by' when political action is required:

Against our cheeks the tendrils of reproach
whip in the storm; the leaves of the book blow wild
for their lost reader; the infant screams, abandoned;
the symphony fades, the safe walls hug no tenant.
Reproach without reward – that is our choice;
for in a world well stacked with organized armies
we, spurning armchair trenches, join the guerrillas,
and plunge in the dark to seek that pilgrim band
whose faces we shall always recognize.

(*Palm and Oak I*, p. 14)

The figure of the political radical is presented confidently here, without any irony to offset the romantic focus. In her prize-winning poem 'While the Young Sleep', the figure of the radical is again a woman but here the domestic context is presented in more detail and the romanticism slightly more muted. After clearing up the 'tangled debris' of her sleeping 'striplings', the mother has a moment of calm:

> Marvellous freedom of a lonely room,
> Treasures at handsreach dormant, all the past
> In the slow downsweep of a silver brush
> Through burnished hair . . . banished the lively fume
> Of growth and challenge, now at this languid last
> Comes self-remembrance in delicious hush.
>
> Sleep, younglings, sleep. She dreams; you lie quite still,
> but she is quick with liberated thought
> and over all the night broods like a dove.
>
> (*Palm and Oak I*, p. 5)

The appeal to a feminist reader in the construction of the mother as 'quick with liberated thought' is obvious and helps explain its choice as the prize-winning poem in 1950 in the international poetry competition organized by the Society of Women Writers and Journalists based in London. It is perhaps worth noting, too, that a context of some degree of privilege is implied in the line, 'all the past/in the slow downsweep of a silver brush/through burnished hair'. While, in 'The Gipsy to Her Baby' (dedicated to her daughter), the feminist thrust of the poem, that her baby daughter should inhabit the world boldly, is presented in terms which evoke, apparently unselfconsciously, a history of buccaneering and adventure:

> Out of my body's darkness rudely torn
> To navigate the ocean of the world
> [. . .]
> How will you roam, and whither, who can guess?
> All that I give you is a heritage
> Of bold adventuring and loveliness
> Of merriment, and wisdom amply sage;
>
> (*In Circles*, p. 3)

Allfrey also wrote a poem dedicated to one of her adopted sons, David, a Carib from the designated 'Carib Territory' in Dominica. Allfrey had considerable interest in, and some support from the Caribs[55] and felt (somewhat naively) that the fact that their ancestries were 'connected' (via her distant relative, Thomas Warner, who had 'married' a Carib woman), gave her a special empathy with the them. 'Trio by Lamplight' recalls nostalgically, in its dedication, 'For David once upon a time', childhood and happier times. The poem opens:

> Hiawatha
> Huckleberry
> Fauntleroy . . .

Look long, for this may be the last year when within
   one taut skin
three story-book boys are tangled into one
                (*Palm and Oak II*, p. 1)

It then continues to interpret the swift changes in mood of the boy in line with his three literary counterparts; so he attacks the arithmetic column, 'just like an Indian warrior stern and solemn', after declaring in a 'precise, patrician voice (Lord Fauntleroy's)' that 'Arithmetic's not fair!' When the homework is complete he is Huckleberry, 'Gosh darn it, nine times eight are seventy-two!/jumps to his feet, crows cockadoodledo'. The poem continues making such parallels until 'the three/inseparable boys eat sleepily/at last; well-loved well-fed/tumbling in one brown body up to bed'. What is interesting here is the way in which American and English literary models are used as a vehicle for representing the boy's identities, including his Carib-ness. The conflictual relationship between identities is staged, in this poem, entirely in terms of literary models with the 'facts' of the boy's 'real' identity reduced to skin colour ('within one taut brown skin', 'in one brown body', 'slanting eyes', 'raven fringe'). The speaker's sustained use of an 'imported' literary map for 'reading' the boy suggests an inability to imagine the boy's difference in any other terms. Perhaps, too, the poem, in constructing the child's boyhood nostalgically ('this may be the last year when within/one taut brown skin/three story-book boys are tangled into one') implies a repressed anxiety about his raced identity in manhood – when the literary parallels may no longer be sustainable?

An unpublished poem, 'Dominica, Last Haunt of the Caribs', also appears reticent, if not anxious, about representing 'the' Carib. In this poem descriptions of nature abound but, in the last three lines, the Caribs finally appear:

Green palms stand out with leaves like ancient lace,
Tall trees begemmed with raindrops take new grace,
As Nature beautifies the beautiful. And then
In sheltered nooks appear the huts of men,
Then men themselves, last vestige of the race
That Dominica's mountains still embrace.[56]

The Caribs here are conflated with nature and Dominica, presented as being caught in a pre-lapsarian space and time. Representing Carib subjects does not appear to prompt Allfrey to move beyond the designated remit of the familiarly 'literary'. Instead, the speaker presents the Caribs through a familiar ethnographic lens as 'the noble savage'.

That Allfrey appears untroubled by her collusion in 'othering' the Caribs should perhaps be placed in relation to the way in which poetry is frequently conceptualized in her work as separate from the mundane realities of the everyday, as an enchanted discourse. Paravisini-Gebert quotes Allfrey as saying that she refused, like her sisters, to learn to sew but 'used to climb into trees and write poems instead'.[57] The poem 'Changeling' opens: 'The child was not bewitched,

but was translated/into a strange and unfamilial grove', and proceeds to dramatize the tension between the world of books/fantasy and the demands of the real.
It concludes:

> Then the rush basket lost its twinkling freight,
> The infant, torn from her enchanted tree,
> Landed behind a closed suburban gate
> Leaving as trace a scrap of poetry.
>
> (*Palm and Oak I*, p. 9)

Allfrey constructs the poet as a highly romanticized, 'otherworldly', figure; the
reference to an infant in a 'rush basket' inviting a parallel with Moses which
inflates the metaphor further.

Throughout her four volumes of poetry Allfrey's style remains fairly consistent,
and there is little by way of the experimentation with voices, so characteristic of
Marson, which might suggest an uneasiness about the largely European poetic
forms she inherited and imbibed. Her attitude to, and use of Creole – or patois[58] –
is also interesting in relation to her literary choices. Allfrey's father was a member
of the League for the Suppression of French-patois, and Phyllis and her sisters
were forbidden to use patois (or to involve themselves in Carnival). Paravisini-
Gebert quotes Allfrey recounting how angry their music teacher was when she
caught the young Phyllis 'translating a Beethoven sonata into calypso rhythm at
the piano'.[59] Nonetheless, the Shand sisters learned patois from their cook, Julia,
and her daughters, and Allfrey was later to tell Polly Patullo that it was very useful
in her political career: 'I would never have won the elections without it.'[60] Allfrey
made extensive, if strategic, use of patois, then, in her political career but did not
incorporate it into her literary work except for some of the dialogue in *The Orchid
House* and for some of the pieces she published under the pseudonym 'Rose O', a
pun on 'Roseau', in *The Star*. These items usually offered sharp commentary on
the news of the day and Allfrey occasionally combined her satiric approach with
the use of patois. Allfrey's patois in these pieces is, for the most part, less interested
in accurately inscribing patois speech than in indicating that it is an 'ordinary'
Dominican challenging 'big' political figures. So, in 'Courtesy Awards Dialogue',
for example, Miss Rosie and Miss Hetty conclude that they are not being awarded
any prizes because their attitudes to the 'Guvment' is less than courteous:

> Goodbye den Miss Hetty
> I shoh disappointed;
> We ack so politely
> When de Minstah passin!
> Mus be all de naybohs
> Tell dem how we cussin
> Puttin hell on Guvment
> Foh de way *dey* actin.
> Good marnin Miss Hetty.[61]

The emphasis in this and many of the patois pieces published in *The Star* is on the political implications of the patois-speaker as representative of 'the people' and not on the aesthetic possibilities which patois might signal. That 'Rose O' often 'speaks' using Standard English suggests that Allfrey does not share the commitment to Creole-speakers or Creole cultural values, in the broader sense, that is so clearly evident in the work of Louise Bennett, whose work is the focus of the next chapter. In the final analysis, Allfrey's own assessment, that she was *for* the people, not *of* the people, may provide the most insightful gloss on her use of the demotic.

Literary reputations

There is no evidence that Allfrey or Marson were aware of each other or that they had read each other's work. What their work does share is a pervasive sense of isolation and of writing at a time, and from locations, in which their particular poetic concerns, and voices, were not recognized. Una Marson has often been heralded as a pioneering figure in accounts which seek to construct a literary history of women's writing in the Caribbean. Phyllis Shand Allfrey's literary reputation remains, to date, a much more precarious one.

It is perhaps worth noting here that, unlike Allfrey, Marson did have some sense of being connected to a literary community, however fraught the connection. Her work was discussed in J.E.C. McFarlane's *A Literature in the Making*,[62] alongside that of other (white) women who were active members of the Jamaica Poetry League, which McFarlane, a black Jamaican, had founded in 1923. McFarlane is full of praise for Marson's fellow women poets. Praising Albinia Hutton's nature poetry he says, 'Poetry such as this carries a special message in these hectic days when in the pursuit of wealth and its material concomitants men have divorced themselves from nature'; or of Lena Kent he says, 'In Lena Kent we have simplicity and soft music'; while of Constance Hollar he writes, 'Her character was itself a poem'. Arabel Moulton-Barrett is described as having a 'full-throated lyricism' and the 'dainty' Tropica's poetry is 'delicate, like a scent drifting from afar'. McFarlane is clearly less comfortable with Marson's oeuvre, 'a new spiritual tone, an element of unrest and discontent, of uncertainty and questioning' (p. 92), though he recognizes 'the modern' in her work. While he acknowledges Marson's contribution to Jamaican poetry as 'her revival of interest in the thought and sentiment of the common people' (p. 86), McFarlane is more powerfully persuaded by the cultural certainties represented by Hutton, Hollar, Tropica and others, commenting that, by contrast, with Marson's work 'Something of great value has been lost to the modern Jamaican' (p. 93).

It is precisely the forward-looking restlessness of Marson's work which has made her such a magnet for contemporary women critics. Erika Smilowitz, one of the earliest commentators on Marson's work, while defensive about the uneven quality of her work, concludes: 'However, her poetry, it must be noted and emphasized, is of uneven quality; [. . .] Viewed from a literary-historical perspective, however, Marson's poetry, in general, is worth studying, for Marson leaves her contemporaries behind, set in their pastoral clichés, while she explores issues of womanhood, race and identity.'[63]

Delia Jarrett-Macauley makes more extensive claims for Marson:

> As *the first black British feminist* to speak out against racism and sexism in Britain, Una Marson emerges as a significant forerunner to contemporary black feminists operating within Euro-American contexts as well as to those who are concerned with debates on 'Third World' feminism. [My emphasis][64]

The emphasis on Marson as a black feminist is repeated in *Watchers and Seekers*, a collection of black women's writing, edited by Rhonda Cobham and Merle Collins.[65] Cobham gives Marson this symbolic power partly, simply, because she wrote at all but also because of her defiant assertion of black female identity at an historical moment, and in a literary genre, in which black women had had very little representation.

> This is why Una Marson's significance for the writers in this volume goes further than the coincidence of race, gender and social situation. Marson was a pioneer for her time in the search for an authentic literary style: a style that could reflect and utilise the heritage of those half-forgotten voices, skills and gestures.[66]

Here, Marson's oeuvre is seen as embodying, and preserving, a distinctly black female presence and poetics. Despite reservations about the essentialism this implies, Cobham's recuperation of Marson also has to be understood as a feminist re-reading of West Indian literary history which seeks to challenge the dominant notion of the male writer as the *normative* writerly subject.

Phyllis Shand Allfrey's contribution to Caribbean women's literary/cultural history has not, until very recently, received significant recognition. Prior to the publication in 1996 of Lizabeth Paravisini-Gebert's biography, very little sustained critical attention was given to Allfrey's poetic output. It was the London-based Virago Press which reprinted *The Orchid House* in 1982, and another Virago publication, *Writing Lives*, edited by Mary Chamberlain and published in 1988, included Polly Pattullo's interview with Allfrey. Yet another Virago publication, *Chaos of the Night: Women's Poetry and Verse of the Second World War*, edited by Catherine W. Reilly and published in 1985, included two of Allfrey's 'war poems'; 'Cunard Liner 1940' and 'Young Lady Dancing with Soldier'. Allfrey's poetry had gained recognition much earlier on from 'the centre' when, in 1950, she was awarded the second prize in an international poetry competition sponsored by the London-based Society of Women Writers and Journalists, Vita Sackville-West being one of the judges. The prize-winning poem was entitled 'While the Young Sleep', and it was the prize money from this award which made the writing of *The Orchid House* possible. The prize-winning poem makes reference only to an unspecific domestic context and the 'war poems' mentioned above invoke images of wartime London. There is, then, nothing distinctively 'West Indian' in the three poems which gained attention at the time of publication and this perhaps explains their success in England and parallel *lack* of success in the West Indies.

The fact, too, that Allfrey came from Dominica and was, therefore, a 'small islander' is also worth noting. Jamaica, by contrast, afforded Una Marson a much larger literary culture and the opportunity to start and sustain exchanges with other Jamaican poets in the form of various local publications and poetry societies, such as the Jamaica Poetry League. This was not the case in Dominica, where Allfrey's minority status as 'white' would have been compounded by her minority status, and isolation, as 'writer'. The Guyanese writer A.J. Seymour visited Dominica in 1978 when he spent time with Allfrey and urged her to take up her writing again. On his return to Guyana, he wrote:

> You were a name on a page. You were the most mature creative example of the White West Indian that I knew. I had read of your novel in the pages of Ken Ramchand's book, but I had never seen the book itself. [. . .] The world of which you spoke is a world that is being lost completely and unless you recount it, however succinctly, it will be no more.[67]

Here, Seymour urges Allfrey to record the decline in fortunes of the white population in Dominica and to testify to their life experiences before it disappears. Interestingly, where Allfrey's *political* associations were, however ambivalently, with 'the people', her *literary* associations are represented as being with 'a dying order' – the 'lost' world of white Dominicans. Marson, by contrast, is associated unequivocally with the black masses – and with a *new* postcolonial order.

Kenneth Ramchand, in the book referred to by Seymour, *The West Indian Novel and Its Background*, published in 1970, suggests that the work of white West Indian writers is characterized by a sense of embattlement:

> Adapting from Fanon we might use the phrase 'terrified consciousness' to suggest the White minority's sensations of shock and disorientation as a massive and smouldering Black population is released into an awareness of its power. [. . .] To consider them at all is to bring forward some imaginative works that tend to be neglected in the demanding contexts of black nationalism.[68]

Ramchand's argument, despite the apocalyptic tone and heightened language, was a timely one. However, assessing its applicability to Allfrey's poetry is not straightforward for, while *The Orchid House* does convey a powerful sense of the impossibility (and undesirability) of the continuation of the white plantocracy's power, the poetry presents this dynamic in much more ambivalent terms. Evelyn O'Callaghan suggests that it is precisely the ambivalent location of the white woman writer which is useful: 'It is precisely because of this paradoxical place in West Indian socio-history – distanced from, yet bound up in the cultural emergence of the "broadly ex-African base" – that the white creole woman writer can make a valuable literary contribution to the developing tradition.'[69]

Early white West Indian women's writing offers insights precisely because they are simultaneously located inside *and* outside of West Indian sociocultural histories. One might argue, in relation to Allfrey's poetry, that the aesthetic choices she made generally aligned her work much more securely *outside* the region, with the 'Nordic' strand of her ancestry. I would also argue that some of Una Marson's aesthetic choices suggest a desire for alignment outside the region too, despite the fact that her confidence in claiming these 'external' cultural influences could not be made with recourse to a 'legitimate' personal history, in the same way that Allfrey's could – and did. In other words, the ambivalence with regard to location inside and outside the region is one which marks the poetic output of *both* Marson and Allfrey, problematizing the categories of 'native' and 'outsider'. Despite the obvious differences between the two poets, then, I would suggest that both Marson and Allfrey share a sense of 'in-betweenness', of being situated *between the palm and the oak*, though this liminality may have generated different kinds of anxieties for the two poets about their sense of belonging to either or both cultural worlds.

I concur with those who have already made a case for Una Marson as a pioneering literary figure, though I would argue that her reputation need not rest so exclusively on those poems in which she handles themes that are explicitly concerned with black women's realities. Reading Marson's more 'derivative' poems offers valuable insights into the intimacy of the relationship between the Caribbean subject and the 'mother country', and her 'devotion to something afar' may be read more permissively for the ambivalences which continue to mark cultural production in the Caribbean. Reading Phyllis Shand Allfrey alongside Una Marson may confirm the importance of 'race' in the writing of the region but it also further nuances our understanding of its contradictory impact.

I will close this chapter by referring to two poems which capture something of the dilemma concerning the poetic ambitions and reputations of Una Marson and Phyllis Shand Allfrey. The speaker in Marson's 'Winged Ants' inadvertently removes the wings of a flying ant as it crawls on the blank sheet of paper in front of her:

> You will fly no more
> And now I feel your woe;
> Has not life's hard caress
> Forced from me glad wings
> That bore me to the stars
> When first I saw the wonder
> And beauty of the world?
> (*The Moth*, p. 36)

The poem invites a reading which draws parallels with Marson's perception of her own poetic identity and ambition and her anxious aspiration and 'devotion to something afar'. While the following lines from Allfrey's 'Fugitive Humming-bird' convey something of Allfrey's perception of her own 'mistaken identity' – and lack of recognition – as a white West Indian writer:

> Now only the enchanted songless lark,
>   the small one, the feerique
>   flesh finer than beak,
> hummer and fusser, darting untrapped spark,
>   will rise at dawn
>   as bird from lawn:
> mistaken for a moth in citrus dark.
>   (*Palm and Oak II*, p. 11)

In these images of flight, both Marson and Allfrey signal, in different ways and for different reasons, their desire to transcend the parameters of 'the real'. In the following chapter, I will focus attention on a poet, Louise Bennett, who has consistently grounded her poetics in 'the real' and whose reputation as 'the mother' of Caribbean poetry is widely acknowledged. Neither Marson nor Allfrey has been sufficiently widely read for a case to be made about their influence on contemporary poets, though clearly Marson is the better known of the two. Nonetheless, considering Una Marson and Phyllis Shand Allfrey alongside each other has allowed me to foreground several issues which continue to be important in reading contemporary Caribbean women's poetry, however unstable their status as literary mothers.

Notes

1 Una Marson, 'Nostalgia', *The Moth and the Star*, Kingston, Jamaica, published by the author, 1937, p. 24.
2 Phyllis Shand Allfrey, 'Exiles', *Palm and Oak I*, London, n.p., 1950, p. 1.
3 I shall make passing reference to *The Orchid House*, London, Virago, 1982 [1953], but my interest here is in Allfrey's poetry.
4 Una Marson's publications include: *Tropic Reveries*, Kingston, Jamaica, published by the author, 1930; *Heights and Depths*, Kingston, Jamaica, published by the author, 1931; *The Moth and the Star*, Kingston, Jamaica, published by the author, 1937; *Towards the Stars*, London, University of London Press, 1945. Phyllis Shand Allfrey's publications include: *In Circles: Poems*, Harrow Weald, Middlesex. UK, Raven Press, 1940; *Palm and Oak: Poems*, London, n.p., 1950; *Contrasts*, Bridgetown, Barbados, Advocate Press, 1955; *Palm and Oak II*, Roseau, Dominica, Star Printery, 1973.
5 Delia Jarrett-Macauley, *The Life of Una Marson: 1905–1965*, Manchester, Manchester University Press, 1998, p. 16.
6 These friendships and acquaintances are fascinatingly documented in Jarrett-Macauley's account.
7 Lizabeth Paravisini-Gebert, *Phyllis Shand Allfrey: A Caribbean Life*, New Brunswick, NJ, Rutgers University Press, 1996. See especially pp. 6–18 for a full account of Allfrey's ancestry.
8 All references here are to the second edition: Lloyd Brown, *West Indian Poetry*, London, Heinemann, 1984 [1978].

9   Francis Williams (b1770) was a freed black Jamaican who, under the patronage of the Duke of Montague, was educated at grammar school and Cambridge University as part of an 'experiment' to prove that the black man was as educable into civilized culture as a white man.

10 *The Beacon II* (June 1933) in *From Trinidad*, ed. R. Sander, London, Hodder & Stoughton, 1978, p. 31.

11 Claude McKay, 'If We Must Die', in Paula Burnett (ed.), *The Penguin Book of Caribbean Verse in English*, London, Penguin, 1986, p. 144.

12 'The folk' is a clumsy term but, given its pervasive use by various commentators, I shall continue to use it throughout this book without flagging its imprecision.

13 A.J. Seymour quoted in E. Baugh, *West Indian Poetry 1900–1970: A Study in Cultural Decolonization*, Kingston, Savacou,1970. Interestingly, in this quote, America's not-so-distant colonial status is elided.

14 N.E. Cameron (ed.), *Guianese Poetry: 1831–1931*, Georgetown, Guyana, Argosy, 1931.

15 Henry Louis Gates, Jr (ed.), *'Race', Writing and Difference*, Chicago, University of Chicago Press, 1985, p. 11.

16 Lloyd Brown, *West Indian Poetry*, p. 23.

17 See Alison Donnell, 'Sentimental Subversion: the Poetry and Politics of Devotion in the Work of Una Marson', V. Bertram, *Kicking Daffodils: Twentieth-century Women Poets*, Edinburgh, Edinburgh University Press, 1997, pp. 113–24, for a sustained argument about the 'misreading' of Marson's love sonnets.

18 Homi K. Bhabha, *The Location of Culture*, London, Routledge, 1994, pp. 85–92.

19 V.S. Naipaul, *The Mimic Men*, London, Penguin, 1980, [1967], p. 206.

20 Jamaica Kincaid, *Lucy*, New York, Plume, 1991, pp. 29–30.

21 Erna Brodber, *Myal*, London, New Beacon, 1988, pp. 5–6.

22 Olive Senior, *Talking of Trees*, Kingston, Jamaica, Calabash, 1985, p. 26.

23 Una Marson cited in Jarrett-Macauley, *Life of Una Marson*, p. 73.

24 Grace Nichols, *Lazy Thoughts of a Lazy Woman*, London, Virago, 1989, p. 6.

25 William Blake, *William Blake*, J. Bronowski (ed.), London, Penguin, 1982 [1958], pp. 28–9.

26 Clare McFarlane, *A Literature in the Making*, Kingston, Jamaica, Pioneer Press, 1956, p. 95.

27 Quoted by Erika Smilowitz in 'Una Marson: Woman before her Time', in *Jamaica Journal*, 16, 2 May 1983.

28 There is an ironic 'coincidence' in Winifred Holtby's reference to Una Marson as 'a brown girl from Jamaica' in a letter to a friend, cited in Jarrett-Macauley, *Life of Una Marson*, p. 77.

29 Richard Allsopp, *Dictionary of Caribbean English Usage*, Oxford, Oxford University Press, 1996, defines a limer thus, 'An idler; a time-waster; one (usu a man) who stands around with others on the sidewalk or in some public place watching people go by, and sometimes being mischievous,' p. 349.

30 Samuel Selvon, *The Lonely Londoners*, London, Longman, 1981 [1956], pp. 92–3.

31 Bowlby explores the relationship of women writers, like Woolf and Rhys, to the model of the male writer as *flâneur*, 'The figure of the *flâneur* epitomizes a distinctive nineteenth-century conception of the writer as walker, a sort of man about town with ample leisure and money to roam the city and look about him.' Space does not allow me to explore the fascinating possibilities of if, and how, Selvon's 'boys' might – or might not – be accommodated in Bowlby's model. Rachel Bowlby, *Still Crazy After All These Years: Women, Writing and Psychoanalysis*, London, Routledge, 1992, p. 5.

32 Zora Neale Hurston, cited as the epigraph to Alice Walker, (ed.), *I Love Myself When I Am Laughing . . . A Zora Neale Hurston Reader*, New York, The Feminist Press, 1979.

33 D. Jarrett-Macauley's biography, *Life of Una Marson*, includes detailed references to the African American writers who influenced Marson.

34 See, for example, Grace Nichols' poem: 'Sugar Cane', in *i is a long memoried woman*, London, Karnak House, 1984, pp. 32–5.
35 I have relied on memory for the following: 'Brown skin gal stay home and mind baby/ Brown skin gal stay home and mind baby/I am going away on a sailing ship/And if I don't come back/trow way de damn baby.'
36 Paula Burnett (ed.), *Penguin Caribbean Verse*, pp. 158–9.
37 Jarrett-Macauley, *Life of Una Marson*, pp. 157–8.
38 The definition of 'Quashie' offered by Richard Allsopp. op. cit., p. 459, is worth quoting: 'A black man who is considered gullible or stupid, esp such a person who is not familiar with city-life; [by extension] any Black person who is considered to be of no importance.'
39 George Campbell, 'History Makers', in Paula Burnett (ed.), *Penguin Caribbean Verse*, p. 177.
40 Phyllis Shand Allfrey, *In Circles: Poems*, Harrow Weald, Middlesex, Raven Press, 1940; *Palm and Oak: Poems*, London, n.p., 1950; *Contrasts*, Bridgetown, Barbados, Advocate Press, 1955; *Palm and Oak II*, Roseau, Dominica, Star Printery, 1973.
41 This information is based on a visit I made to the Public Library in Dominica in 1988.
42 See Jamaica Kincaid's polemical essay, *A Small Place*, London: Virago, 1988, and her novel, *Annie John*, London, Picador, 1985, p. 127, where the protagonist longs 'to be in a place where nobody knew a thing about me'.
43 Paravisini-Gebert, *Phyllis Shand Allfrey*, p. 255.
44 Paravisini-Gebert includes 'Transfiguration' in her forthcoming *Collected Poems of Phyllis Shand Allfrey*, suggesting that the poem may be one of the earliest surviving poems by Allfrey. I am indebted to Juliette Meyers for allowing me access to the draft copy of the manuscript, generously given to her by Paravisini-Gebert. The poem 'Maine' displays a similar confidence in its evocation of a winter landscape in Maine, in *In Circles*, p. 15.
45 Cited in Paravisini-Gebert, *Phyllis Shand Allfrey*, p. 245.
46 Jean Rhys, *Wide Sargasso Sea*, London, Penguin, 1966, p. 24. This passsage is preceded by the scene in which the speaker, Antoinette, is humiliated by her black companion, Tia.
47 Space does not permit me to pursue the obvious intertextual links with Jonathan Swift's satirical poem 'The True-born Englishman'.
48 Jean Rhys, *Voyage in the Dark*, London, Penguin, 1988 [1934] p. 27; one might also read Robert Antoni's novel, *Blessed Is the Fruit*, London, Faber, 1998, as an extended exploration of this dynamic.
49 Grace Nichols, *i is a long memoried woman*, p. 49.
50 Ibid., p. 11.
51 Aimé Césaire, *Notebook of a Return to My Native Land*, trans. M. Rosello and A. Pritchard, London, Bloodaxe, 1995, p. 75.
52 I am indebted to my colleague at the University of Sussex, Professor Richard Burton, for alerting me to the images discussed here.
53 Cited in Paravisini-Gebert, *Phyllis Shand Allfrey*, p. 255.
54 Cited in Polly Patullo, 'Phyllis Shand Allfrey', in Mary Chamberlain (ed.), *Writing Lives*, London, Virago, 1988, p. 230.
55 Paravisini-Gebert, *Phyllis Shand Allfrey*, pp. 114–15.
56 I am indebteded again to J. Meyers for access to Paravisini-Gebert's manuscript, *The Collected Poems of Phyllis Shand Allfrey*.
57 Ibid., p. 27.
58 Generally speaking, where there is a strong French influence on the Creole spoken in the West Indies, as in Dominica, Grenada and St Lucia, 'patois' tends to be the preferred term, rather than 'Creole'.
59 Paravisini-Gebert, *Phyllis Shand Allfrey*, p. 26.
60 P. Patullo,'Phyllis Shand Allfrey', p. 231. See also Paravisini-Gebert, *Phyllis Shand Allfrey*, p. 117, where Allfrey is described as justifying 'her rather French-laden patois to her Dominican audience by describing it as *patois parisien!*'

61 Again, I am indebted for access to this poem to Paravisini-Gebert's manuscript, *The Collected Poems of Phyllis Shand Allfrey*.
62 J.E.C. McFarlane, *A Literature in the Making*, Kingston, Pioneer Press, 1956.
63 Erika Sollish Smilowitz, ' "Weary of Life and All My Heart's Dull Pain": The Poetry of Una Marson', R. Knowles and E. Smilowitz (eds), *Critical Issues in West Indian Literature*, Iowa, Caribbean Books, 1984, pp. 19–32.
64 Jarrett-Macauley, *Life of Una Marson*, p. vii.
65 Rhonda Cobham and Merle Collins (eds) *Watchers and Seekers: Creative Writing by Black Women in Britain*, London, The Women's Press, 1987.
66 Ibid., pp. 6–7.
67 Paravisini-Gibert, *Phyllis Shand Allfrey*, p. 253.
68 Kenneth Ramchand, *The West Indian Novel and Its Background*, London, Faber, 1970, p. 225.
69 Evelyn O'Callaghan, ' "The Outsider's Voice": White Creole Women Novelists in the Caribbean Literary Tradition', *Journal of West Indian Literature*, 1, 1, October 1986, pp. 74–88.

2 The lure of the folk

Louise Bennett and the politics of Creole

More than any other single writer, Louise Bennett brought local language into the foreground of West Indian cultural life.[1]

Dem dont want dis concert end
dem want carry home dis legend
like beads of boonoonoonoos words/
dis pride in *mudder language giver*
dis lady who could sing in C
but prefer to sing in river[2]

. . . all of us, I think, have been influenced by Louise Bennett, who was a pioneer in writing Creole and speaking it – because it was something revolutionary.[3]

It is largely thanks to one woman's warmth that the prejudice against dialect has gradually melted away, and that a climate has been established in which a whole new generation of creative users of the vernacular could flourish.[4]

By fortuitous circumstances in 1943, a 24-year-old Jamaican lady, Louise Bennett, was allowed to read a few of her dialect poems on Jamaica's first radio station. *That event launched a people's voice.*[5]

[My emphasis]

In the previous chapter, I outlined some of the concerns which militate against Una Marson being celebrated, unreservedly, as a literary mother-figure; I also discussed the kinds of issues which may have 'disqualified' Phyllis Shand Allfrey from sharing that platform with her. Louise Bennett's reputation as a literary mother-figure, by comparison, is broadly recognized and her work is celebrated as being unequivocally West Indian. In contrast to some of the complications and ambiguities surrounding the work of Marson and Allfrey, Louise Bennett's poetry, as the epigraphs above demonstrate, is often cited as marking the birth of an 'authentic' West Indian poetry, the moment when the region *finds its voice*. Where Marson's oeuvre is constrained by an over-reliance on European poetic models and where Allfrey's West Indianness is contested (at least as it is manifested in her poetry), Louise Bennett's work has been consistently received as being grounded firmly in a Jamaican context and, in her exclusive use of Creole, her work is seen as redefining, and *indigenizing*, the contours of 'the poetic'. This chapter will interrogate some of the criteria involved in the consolidation of Louise Bennett as 'the mother of Creole'. Bennett's *literary* reputation was relatively late in coming, and, to date, discussion of her work has largely been dominated by the focus on the importance of her innovative use of Creole, rather than on detailed readings of her poetry. My discussion, as a result, will include a brief outline of the literary debates which may account for this time-lag and focus, in the literary reception of her work, as well as offering detailed readings of specific poems.

Louise Bennett was born in 1919 in Kingston, Jamaica, where she grew up and was educated. Her father, a baker, died when she was 7, and her mother, Kerene, supported the family by working as a seamstress. Bennett was encouraged by her mother when she expressed a desire, as a teenager, to make a living by writing: 'If you can write as well as I can make a frock, I'll be satisfied.'[6] Mervyn Morris, in the introductory essay to *Selected Poems*, quotes a very early unpublished poem by Bennett which recalls, in many ways, the declamations of unworthiness for the poetic calling which punctuate Marson's work. In the extract below the poet wishes for:

> . . . power to express my thought
> And whims in dulcet poetry.
> 'I wish' I wished, 'that I could be
> A poet great and with my pen
> Trace paths of peace and harmony
> For the uncertain minds of men.
> Inspire me O tiny cloud
> O messenger of god
> Strengthen any ability
> I have already had.'
> 		(*Selected Poems*, p. iv)

But, unlike Marson, who continued in her fourth collection of poetry to agonize about her right to write, Bennett did not spend years grappling with the weight of an inherited tradition, deciding instead to abandon 'dulcet poetry' in favour of writing that would draw upon the speech and rhythms of her own Jamaican context. Morris recounts the genesis of Bennett's first 'dialect poem':

> One day she set out, a young teenager all dressed up, for a matinee film show in Cross Roads. On the electric tramcars which were then the basis of public transport in Kingston, people with baskets were required to sit at the back, and they were sometimes resentful of other people who, when the tram was full, tried to join them there. As Louise was boarding the tram she heard a country woman say: 'Pread out yuhself, one dress-oman a come.' That vivid

remark made a great impression on her, and on returning home she wrote her first dialect poem, 'On a Tramcar'.

(Selected Poems, p. iv)

This 'originary' moment is telling for several reasons. The incident above is one in which Bennett's social distance, as a 'dress-oman', from the women on the tram is cause for action – they spread themselves out so there is no room for *her*. Following this 'epiphany', Bennett will make frequent use of women speakers modelled on women like those in the tram so that, paradoxically, their recognition of *her* – as a well-dressed, middle-class young woman – results in her recognition of *them*: as powerful manipulators of the word. The social distance between the poet and the people she chooses to represent does not appear to have generated similarly troubling questions to those generated by early, white, colonial writers (as discussed in Chapter 1). Carolyn Cooper, for example, also comments on the same account of the genesis of Bennett's first dialect poem:

> The literal spreading out of self is an evocative metaphor for the irrepressible survival instincts of Jamaica's dispossessed who refuse to be squeezed out of existence. The amplitude of the body becomes a figure for the verbal expansiveness that is often the only weapon of the politically powerless; tracings and other forms of verbal abuse are essential armaments in class warfare. The well-dressed young woman who is not allowed to sit with the market women – at her convenience – must know her place; she cannot violate the social space that the ostracised market-women have come to claim as their own.[7]

I will return to Cooper's larger argument about the innate 'slackness' and amplitude of Jamaican culture. Here I will simply draw attention to the way in which her argument does not ask questions about Bennett's appropriation of voice – the *linguistic* space occupied by these market women – or what's at stake in the 'translation' of their voices into the printed text and the commodification which might result from such a process. In other words, the well-dressed young woman may be forced to *know her place* on the bus but can restore some of that power by commentating on the event.

In an interview with the Jamaican poet Dennis Scott, Bennett presents the choice of dialect as deliberate and one which self-consciously, and simultaneously, rejects inherited poetic models:

> I began to wonder why more of our poets and writers were not taking more of an interest in the kind of language usage and the kind of experiences of living which were all around us, and writing in the medium of dialect instead of writing *in the same old English way about Autumn and things like that*. [My emphasis].[8]

Here, the pastoral, as the definitive mode of English poetry, is presented as irreconcilable with the realities and culture of Jamaica. In the same interview, Bennett also comments on the way in which the vernacular, and the irreverence of the culture in which it is embedded, intruded upon and disrupted her attempts to write 'serious nature poetry'. Recalling the embarrassment generated by early West Indian attempts at the pastoral, it is tempting, though not altogether satisfactory, to argue that Bennett's explicit choice of subject matter and voice allow her to avoid metropolitan cultural models altogether and to circumnavigate the troubled waters of derivativeness and mimicry. Certainly, the forthright way in which Jamaican culture is spoken and performed in Bennett's work is perceived as a welcome release from the constraints and sense of cultural 'misfit' which characterized earlier poetry. The authority and confidence of Bennett's voice are reassuringly definite and, indeed, many of her poems explicitly take as their theme the superiority of Jamaican culture over imported 'high' cultural norms. So, for example, the poem 'Sammy Intres' stages 'a contest' between the inherited poetic models of Europe, represented by Henry Wadsworth Longfellow's 'Excelsior', and the storytelling of 'Miss Della'. The speaker, Sammy's mother, encouraged by the teacher to take more of an interest in her son's education, has written down the poem 'Excelsior', which her son has 'learned by heart', and which *she* now plans to study. Miss Della's arrival interrupts this process and the poem proceeds to alternate deftly between the lines of the poem and the chatty, colloquial comments of the speaker to her visitor. The Longfellow poem is parodied by these unlikely juxtapositions and, at the same time, Bennett gets considerable political mileage by foregrounding the deeper ironies of which the speaker seems to be unaware, as in the seventh stanza:

> Den ow is fi-yuh lickle gal?
> Me hear har – clarion rung –
> Me hear har singing wid – *de accent*
> *Of dat unknown tongue.*
>   (*Selected Poems*, p. 7; my emphasis)[9]

The poem concludes with an assertion of the much greater appeal of 'talk-story', or gossip, over the stiff, unnaturalness of the poem (and its *unknown tongue*), a conclusion which the preceding stanzas have already prepared the reader for:

> Pop tory gimme, Della – all
> De labrish from yuh yard.
> Me cyaan study pickney intres
> Ef a so it a go hard.
>   (*Selected Poems*, p. 7)

In 'Independence Dignity', a poem documenting the dignified celebration of independence in Jamaica, a similar intertextual strategy is used. Here, Bennett parallels closely the phrasing and metre of Charles Wolfe's 'The Burial of Sir John Moore at Corunna', which begins:

Not a drum was heard, not a funeral note,
   As his corse [*sic*] to the rampart we hurried;
Not a soldier discharged his farewell shot,
   O'er the grave where our hero we buried.[10]

The 'matching' stanza in the Bennett poem reads:

Not a stone was fling, not a samfie sting,
Not a soul gwan bad an lowrated;
Not a fight bruk out, not a bad-wud shout
As Independence was celebrated.
   (*Selected Poems*, p. 116; 'samfie': trickster)

The insertion of 'ordinary' Creole words works immediately, and obviously, to parody the pomp and ceremony of the Wolfe poem with its archaic words and funereal iambics. Bennett's strategy might also be described, using Henry Gates's formulation, as 'signifying':

This rhetorical naming by indirection is, of course, central to our notions of figuration, troping, and of the parody of forms, or pastiche, in evidence when one writer repeats another's structure by one of several means, including a fairly exact repetition of a given narrative or rhetorical structure, filled incongruously with a ludicrous or incongruent content. [. . .] Another example of formal parody is to suggest a given structure precisely by failing to coincide with it – that is, to suggest it by dissemblance.[11]

Given that the speaker in 'Independence Dignity' is female and that the Wolfe poem is redolent of the trappings of patriarchy (in both thematic and aesthetic terms), the strategy, advocated in French feminist discourse, of mimicking patriarchal discourse in order to *undo* it is also relevant.[12] In addition, the poem also gently mocks the precariousness of the 'good behaviour' being exhibited by Jamaicans especially for the Independence celebrations. Bennett's use of a speaking voice which is signalled as that of an 'ordinary' woman (writing to her cousin abroad) allows these several layers of mockery to function unobtrusively in the poem, 'disguised' by the speaker's dramatic presentation and enthusiasm. Finally, the relish with which the canonical poem is parodied – Morris suggests that 'it is as if the colonizer is being buried while a new nation is born'[13] – may also disguise the degree to which this parody serves, simultaneously, to reinscribe canonical notions of form even as the content of such poems is ridiculed. The regularity of the rhyme scheme and rhythm in Wolfe's poem facilitates 'learning by heart', partly because of its obvious mnemonic qualities but also because poems such as these were important vehicles, in colonial education, in the dissemination of colonial cultural values. Routinely and efficiently drilled into the minds – and 'hearts' – of Caribbean schoolchildren (like Bennett herself), these poems become, in effect, paradigms for the 'memorable', long after their colonial 'content' has been refused.

Ironically, in Bennett's version of the Wolfe poem, it is possible for 'the local' to be memorized, and *memorialized*, via the instrumental use of the 'imported' poetic container. The ironies proliferate when one considers the fact that Bennett's poems themselves are now regularly memorized for performances of various kinds, presumably by schoolchildren who, in post-Independence Jamaica, will no longer have memorized a repertoire of poems such as those by Longfellow and Wolfe. The traces of these canonical texts, then, will resonate in the rhymes and iambic rhythm of Bennett's poems, as a submerged cultural residue (offering a neat reversal of Brathwaite's suggestion that Creole is the submerged language of the Caribbean).[14] Such intertextual intimacies suggest that Bennett's work is deeply indebted to the canon in ways which are self-consciously combative, challenging and utilitarian *as well as* derivative. Further, the formal poetic conventions which Bennett adheres to in all of her poems serve as a reminder that this is a *stylized*, rather than *naturalistic*, delivery of voice: Jamaicans clearly do not, in everyday parlance, speak in rhyming couplets or iambic pentameter. I would suggest that rather than 'launching a people's voice', as James Berry suggests above, Louise Bennett's poems and performances of those poems might be better described as *staging* the *performance* of a people's voice. The implications of this distinction will punctuate the discussion in the remainder of this chapter.

The young Louise Bennett entertained her school friends with performances of her own poems, and, encouraged by their enjoyment, she gradually started performing at local concerts, reaching a wider and wider audience until, at Christmas 1938 she gave her first paid performance (earning 2 guineas) at the popular Christmas morning concerts arranged by Eric Coverley, whom she later married. In 1942, she published her first collection of poems *(Jamaica) Dialect Verses*, and the following year she performed at a dinner party attended by the Chief Editor of the *Gleaner*, who was impressed enough by Bennett's work to pay her to write a weekly column in his newspaper on Sundays. During this period, Bennett had also completed a correspondence course in journalism and embarked (in 1943) on a course at Friends' College, Highgate, where she also began her serious study of Jamaican folklore. By 1945, having acquired considerable experience of performance, Bennett won a scholarship to study drama at the Royal Academy of Dramatic Art in London. She was highly successful on this course and also ran a BBC radio programme of her own, shortly after arriving in England.

Bennett returned to Jamaica in 1947 where she taught for a while and was involved in setting up the Little Theatre Movement pantomime, but financial difficulties forced her to return to England where she worked for BBC radio in charge of 'West Indian Guest Night' and performed with a range of repertory companies. In 1953, she moved to New York where she eventually collaborated with Eric Coverley again to co-direct a musical, *Day in Jamaica*, which toured New Jersey, New York and Connecticut. In 1954, Bennett and Coverley were married and they both returned to Jamaica where she worked for four years for the Jamaica Social Welfare Commission; this involved extensive travel throughout Jamaica and she was able to continue collating Jamaican folklore and oral history. Bennett also lectured on drama and Jamaican folklore for the Extra Mural

Department of the University of the West Indies and worked for the Jamaica Broadcasting Corporation in their first year of operation.

Through these varied activities, Louise Bennett has become a household name in Jamaica, appearing regularly on stage, radio and television and has been central in developing Jamaican pantomime. In 1949 she collaborated with Noel Vaz to write *Busha Bluebeard*, which Mervyn Morris describes as one of the first distinctively Jamaican pantomimes.[15] Louise Bennett has received numerous awards for her contributions to Jamaican culture, including an MBE, a Silver Musgrave Medal from the Institute of Jamaica, the Norman Manley Award for Excellence in the Arts (1972), the Order of Jamaica (1974) and the Musgrave Gold Medal of the Institute of Jamaica (1978). In January 1983 she was awarded an honorary doctorate from the University of the West Indies. The publication of *Jamaica Labrish* in 1966 and *Selected Poems* in 1982 helped to establish Bennett's literary reputation.[16] She is well known in the wider Caribbean and, in various metropolitan contexts, amongst the Caribbean diaspora.

Indeed, within Jamaica, Louise Bennett has become something of a national icon or heritage figure; certainly, the kinds of awards referred to above suggest that official recognition has been very substantive. Few individual artists in the region have received this level of institutional recognition, though many governments have sponsored cultural endeavour in various ways. Jamaica Kincaid's comments in relation to Antigua are a useful reminder of some of the potential dangers of a self-conscious promotion of 'national culture': 'In countries that have no culture or are afraid they have no culture, there is a Minister of Culture.'[17] One does not have to share the degree of Kincaid's scepticism to recognize that official sponsorship of culture invariably involves politically partisan agendas of some kind or other. With regard to Louise Bennett's poetic output, her emphasis on 'folk culture' results in performances of national identity which may appear more unthreateningly recuperable to nationalist agendas than other forms of literary protest, such as Jamaica Kincaid's *A Small Place*, to take an obvious example. Kincaid's sharp critique of Antiguan politics resulted in her being declared *persona non grata* in Antigua.

Having noted that reservation, it is pertinent to mention here that Louise Bennett, in recording, disseminating and celebrating indigenous cultural forms, shares the platform of 'cultural archivist/activist' with many other Caribbean women writers (Merle Hodge, Olive Senior, Dionne Brand and Erna Brodber, to name a few) – writers who have documented or commented on Caribbean culture in discourses other than the literary. There is evidence to suggest that Una Marson and Phyllis Shand Allfrey were similarly involved in cultural activities where they played a supportive role, rather than pursuing their writing careers more single-mindedly. One can only speculate about the degree to which this pattern reflects a lack of confidence in their respective writing abilities, the harsh financial circumstances facing the writer, or a consensual pull to the traditional association of women as 'keepers of culture'.

Bennett has, more so than any of the women listed above, been most visible as a recorder of culture; indeed, her collections of poems are cited so often that they appear to have become a kind of *source book* of Jamaican culture. The interpenetration of the worlds of script and orality which this suggests, so frequently elided in celebrations of Bennett's rootedness in the oral, is important. In an introductory essay to the 1966 edition of *Jamaica Song and Story*, Bennett says:

> [W]hen I was collecting Jamaican folklore for use on the stage and trying desperately to remember some of the stories I knew as a child, a friend gave me a copy of Walter Jekyll's book of Jamaican stories and songs. I was overjoyed to find accurate retellings of many of the stories which I had forgotten. [. . .] *Now there they all were in black and white.* [My emphasis][18]

Bennett is clear here about the importance of having these stories available in print – *there they were in black and white* – as permanent reminders of what she had experienced, *in live, living colour*, as it were. That Bennett's work is also available in print, and that its literariness would only be *recognized* in print also testifies to the mutually constitutive nature of the relationship between the spoken and the written. Walter Jekyll's preface to the 1906 edition of *Jamaica Song and Story* concludes with the following: 'The book as a whole is a tribute to my love for Jamaica and its dusky inhabitants, with their winning ways and their many good qualities, among which is to be reckoned that supreme virtue, *Cheerfulness*.'[19]

That Bennett (as well as Philip Sherlock and Rex Nettleford) should endorse the text so unequivocally, despite the patronizing tenor of the above, attests to her (and their) belief in the multiple possibilities for interpretations, rehearsals and re-presentations of the stories within the book. It is part of Bennett's achievement that the cumulative power of her performances have recuperated Jamaican folk culture from its colonialist moorings in anthropological texts.

Certainly the performativity of Bennett's work has had a powerful impact on increasing the size of her readership/audience in ways completely unparalleled by Marson or Allfrey. The introspective privacy of Allfrey's poetry does not suggest public performance at all. And, while Marson's plays were performed, and she read her poem 'Banjo Boy' on the BBC radio programme 'Voice', the unsettled and uneven register of many of her more performative pieces makes for a much more ambiguously performative oeuvre, and Jamaican speech rhythms are seldom incorporated fluidly into the adopted poetic models. Delia Jarrett-Macauley cites a telling comment by the English critic Esther Chapman, in her review of an elocution contest in which Marson participated:

> Miss Marson has a pleasant manner and a nice clear voice; her intonation is good. [. . .] She displays great promise *and properly trained*, should do well. Her principal fault is the pronunciation of certain words, especially the vowel sound in words like 'there' and 'stairs' which she pronounces 'theere' and 'steers'. [My emphasis][20]

It is easy to appreciate the release from constraint which the performance of

Bennett's Creole signifies, given the contortions of voice required of Marson in the 'correct' elocution of English. While the performance of Bennett's poems clearly involves regulatory practices to professionalize the delivery, her re-centring of indigenous culture shifted cultural authority 'back home' and effected a radical transformation of the popular perception of the role of the poet.

Many critics and writers have commented on the difference between the performative modes used in the telling of stories in Creole and in the formal recital of poems from the canon; the former associated with an expansive expressiveness in which a variety of bodily gestures are essential, while the latter requires the performer to stand erect with hands clasped and head held high to keep bodily movement to a minimum. The version of performativity associated with national identity, with its more 'natural' body language, provided a dramatic demonstration of freedom from the embarrassing ironies of 'the good native' mimicking her 'master's voice'.

Olive Senior, a writer often commended for the effective use of Creole in her short stories, comments on Louise Bennett's influence:

> Louise Bennett was a high school graduate, and yet she dared to get up and talk in Creole. Now, when I was a child we all learned Louise Bennett poems, but we did them, like, at school concerts so that people would laugh. It still was not accepted – in other words, it was something you laughed at.[21]

Like Senior, I remember attending concerts (some as recently as the 1980s, though in a different West Indian location) and registering the way in which an audience immediately relaxes into amusement and laughter as soon as a Creole performance begins. I am not sure that the laughter stems *entirely* from the fact that an unacceptable, 'inferior' language is being used, though, undoubtedly, that *is* part of the transgressive impact – and pleasure – of the moment. Some of the laughter may also be produced by the unfamiliar transplanting of Creole-use from its familiar context of the home/yard or street, where it had its own theatricality, to the more formal theatrics of the stage. The fact that the performer, in the case of Louise Bennett, was an educated woman – *a high school graduate*, and *a dress-oman* – may further heighten the sense of uneasiness in the performance. In addition, the very stylized use of Creole may also have generated uneasy laughter. Depending on whether the audience was largely middle class or working class, the laughter might be nuanced accordingly. So, for example, in the former, it might be a distancing laughter, 'we *can* "talk dat talk" too when we choose', while in the latter, it might be a righteously outraged laughter, 'A dat yuh mudder sen yuh a school fa?'[22] Gordon Rohlehr points to a similar disjunction between audiences in an article published in *Bim*, in which he argues:

> The community for which this poem is meant would accept these aphorisms as meaningful bits of advice, wisdom which they can test by experience. The average reader of *Savacou*, however, comes from a world in which proverbs and aphorisms are meaningless.[23]

In other words, I want to suggest that there may well be a dimension of embarrassment in the audience's response and that this embarrassment may not be *entirely* dissimilar to that generated by Caribbean poets attempting to ventriloquize in the mode of canonical English poets. 'Cultural unease', then, comes in many guises and the performance of poetry in the demotic does not completely short-circuit some of the tensions explored in the previous chapter with regard to poetic identity and voice.

Tek bad tings mek good

These qualifications, offered in the spirit of nuancing the debate, do not detract from the skilful way in which Bennett has made humour, as it is manifested in everyday, 'ordinary' situations, essential to her work. Bennett argues that comedy and dialect are inextricably, and profoundly, linked:

> I have found a medium through which I can pretend to be laughing. Most of the time when we laugh it is so that we may not weep. Isn't that so? We can laugh at ourselves. . . . The nature of the Jamaican dialect is the nature of comedy, I feel. As it is used by the people to express their feelings, the dialect is very adaptable.[24]

Bennett's poems invariably make use of 'ordinary' Creole speakers, often women, whose linguistic dexterity and inventiveness are emphasized and whose feisty resilience in the face of hardship is often 'the point'. Many of Bennett's poems were originally written for publication in her weekly newspaper column, and she exploited the potential for irreverence which Creole afforded her in commenting on the issues and concerns of the day. These concerns included the West Indian Federation, the hardships facing Jamaicans between the two World Wars, the Women's Movement, the cost of living, racial politics, local politics and the move towards independence. In the breadth and range of issues tackled, Bennett's poems provide a fascinating catalogue of current events over an extended period (roughly the 1940s to the early 1970s); read alongside more conventional, historical accounts of the period, her poems offer distinctive and insightful comments from the 'marginal' perspectives of 'ordinary Jamaicans'.

The majority of Bennett's poems are set in an urban context and the speaker's class status is signalled not just by the Creole register of the language used but often with reference to the speakers' employment – most frequently, higglering, paid work as domestics as well as everyday domestic duties. The frequent declamations of the kind found in 'War-time Grocery' (*Jamaica Labrish*, p. 83) of 'Wha poor people dah-go do?' consolidates the overwhelming sense of the speakers' marginal status. The poem 'Hard Time', for example, dramatizes the way in which Miss Matty attempts to solve the problem of shortages and high prices in the inter-war years. Advised by her friend to 'try fe mek it stretch', Miss Matty stretches the note *literally* until it tears. In re-telling the tale of Miss Matty's foolishness, the friend concludes:

Lawd ah pity po' Miss Matty,
But she is a real ole goat,
She tink me hooda feel hard time
Ef me coulda stretch poun note?
(*Jamaica Labrish*, p. 119)

The poem conveys the difficulties of the time, while the stoicism of the speaker's
advice also hints at the ways in which women maintain the labour force while
remaining 'invisible' in national economic categories. The 'common-sense' aspect
of this advice is characteristic of many of Bennett's poems and there is always the
risk, in such approaches, of common sense resulting in a pressure to conform to
the status quo. 'Hard Time' opens with Miss Matty being advised *not* to make a
commotion about the inflationary economy but to get on with *coping*. Neverthe-
less, the poem itself, in highlighting the comic potential of the situation, presents
humour as a way of making that coping bearable.

If, in 'Hard Time', Miss Matty is the butt of the joke because she does not see
the metaphoric use being made of language, in many poems it is precisely the
inventiveness and dexterity of the Creole speaker's use of language which is
celebrated. So, in 'South Parade Peddler' and 'Candy Seller', Bennett dramatizes
the verbal enticements which the higglers use to attract custom and the verbal
abuse which immediately follows if they decide not to buy. In the process, she
celebrates the higgler's dexterity in switching deftly from flattery to abuse. The
first stanza of 'South Parade Peddler' reads:

Hairnet, scissors, fine teeth comb!
Wey de nice lady dey?
Buy a scissors from me noh lady?
Hair pin? toot' pase? Goh wey!
Me say go-wey aready, ef
Yuh doan like it see me.
Yuh dah-swell like bombin' plane fun'
Yuh soon bus up like Graff Spe.
(*Jamaica Labrish*, p. 27)

While in 'Candy Seller' a customer's white skin does not, as might be expected,
signal privilege but is the occasion for the higgler to fine-tune her abuse:

Cho goh way – Come here nice white man
Don't pass me by soh sah!
See me beggin by de roadside
Come buy a nice wangla.
Wen w'ite people go fe ugly
Massa dem ugly sah.
Koo 'ow dat deh man face heng dung
Lacka wen jackass feel bad.
(*Jamaica Labrish*, p. 29)

If the higgler is often perceived as existing on the margins of power, Bennett dramatizes the ways in which this figure exercises considerable *linguistic* power, particularly in the inventive use of invective. In documenting this *women's* tradition of 'tracing', Bennett offers an important corrective to the trend in many anthropological and sociological accounts for the public trade in invective to be represented as an exclusively *male* domain.

Louise Bennett's poems often demonstrate the various ways in which Jamaican Creole can be used to 'cuss' effectively but, invariably, while the location of such 'cussing' is public in the sense that the speakers are located in 'the yard' and the market, and therefore a communal space, it is not the same kind of politicized public arena as those occupied by men in their ritualized verbal battles on the street. In the poem, 'Cuss-Cuss', Bennett stages a 'cussing-match' between two women. The nine stanzas alternate between the two women's voices with each speaker establishing a distinctive platform from which to abuse the other. The poem culminates with an exchange in which both speakers (wo)man-handle 'big words':

> Is grudge yuh grudgeful, me kean cook
> But me ben goh dah good school,
> Me got intelligency yuh
> Illiterated fool!
>
> Me sorry fe de man yuh get
> De po' ting hooden nyam
> When you ackebus him salt-fish
> An bwilivous him yam.
>   (*Jamaica Labrish*, p. 189)

The circumstances which caused the quarrel are not given, endorsing the sense that it is the inventiveness of the cursing itself which is the point of the poem. In other poems, Bennett exploits the humour generated when speakers attempt to rise (verbally) to the occasion. In 'Speechify', the bestman trips over his verbs in his attempts at a formal speech –

> Let I takes in hand wine glasses,
> Let I full it to de tip,
> While Miss Clemmy share de cakeses
> Let I rise an let I sip.
>   (*Selected Poems*, p. 68)

– while in 'Love Letter', the speaker gets into a similar rhetorical tangle as he attempts to convey his love for his lady:

> As ah puts me pen to paper
> An me pen-nib start fi fly

Me rememberance remember
De fus day yuh ketch me yeye!
(*Selected Poems*, p. 67)

The speaker then makes use of a series of cumbersome and unlikely similes
before, stretched beyond his linguistic capacity, he draws images of his love which
he then interprets, 'de plate wid yam an saltfish mean/Dat we can never part'.
This poem demonstrates some of the risks involved in Bennett's use of Creole
speakers for, although the imaginative use of the local is being acknowledged, the
poem also veers uneasily in the direction of presenting the speaker as something
of a buffoon. Bennett is on more secure ground in 'Big Wuds', where it is the
'speaky-spokey' language of newspaper coverage of the short-lived West Indian
Federation which is made fun of:

History makin delegation, an
De growin population,
Most outstandin' observations
Dem all rhyme wid Federation!

Me like sey de big wuds dem, gwan like
Me learnin is fus rate;
But me hope dat me jawbone noh bus
Before we federate.
(*Jamaica Labrish*, p. 165)

Here the language of political power is gently ridiculed by the speaker, who
recognizes that, despite all the seductive rhetoric, the promise of Federation is just
'big-talk'. Bennett also uses the 'common-sense' commentary of women speakers
to undercut any easy assumption of a celebratory stance in relation to the
Independence movement in Jamaica, as in 'Independence':

Independence wid a vengeance!
Independence raisin Cain!
Jamaica start grow beard, ah hope
We chin can stan de strain!
(*Jamaica Labrish*, p. 169)

In 'Is Me', Bennett ridicules the ostentatious display of power of many recently
elected political figures in the new nation, who feel it beneath their dignity to have
to identify themselves to any member of the ordinary public. The poem begins:

Is who dat a-sey 'who dat'?
Wat a piece o' libaty,
Gal yuh know is who yuh talkin to?
Teck a good look, is Me!
(*Jamaica Labrish*, p. 140)

It is interesting to note the difference in tone when Michael Smith takes up the question 'Ah who dat?', in what I take to be a deliberately intertextual reference, in his poem, 'Me Cyaan Believe It',[25] though in his poem the repetition of the question functions to emphasize the paranoia, madness and hardship of life in Jamaica:

> Sittin on de corner wid me frien
> talkin bout tings an time
> me hear one voice seh
> 'Who dat?'
> 'Me seh 'A who dat?'
> 'A who a seh who dat
> when me a seh who dat?
>
> When yuh teck a stock
> dem lick we dung flat
> teet start fly
> an big man start cry
> me seh me cyaan believe it
> me seh me cyaan believe it

Where Bennett's construction of the power-hungry politician shows him up as a deluded figure of fun, there is a sense in which the energetic humour works to diffuse some of the political bite of her point. In Smith's poem, the staccato repetition of this question (in a poem which is deliberately and structurally much more disjointed and unsettling than Bennett's seamlessly rhythmic one) evokes a much more sinister and disquieting effect. Nonetheless, Bennett's poem conveys well the inflated sense of power of the local politician and a sense of the paranoia surrounding such figures in the newly independent Jamaica:

> I is de rulin powah, gal!
> I is Authority!
> I mek dis country jump wid joy,
> Or rock wid misery!
>   (*Jamaica Labrish*, p. 140)

In several poems, Jamaican Creole is the explicit focus of the poem itself, as in the first three poems in Bennett's *Selected Poems*. In 'Dry-Foot Bwoy', it is the affectation of an English accent which the boy insists on using after a stay in 'foreign' that is ridiculed:

> For me notice dat him answer
> To nearly all me seh
> Was 'Actually', 'What, 'Oh deah!'
> An all dem sinting deh.
>   (*Selected Poems*, p. 1)

In 'No Lickle Twang', by contrast, it is the boy who returns from a six-month stay in America *without* any evidence, by way of an accent or clothes or jewellery, that is cause for consternation:

> Bwoy, yuh no shame? Is so yuh come?
> After yuh tan so long!
> Not even lickle language, bwoy?
> Not even lickle twang?
>
> (*Selected Poems*, p. 3)

And in 'Bans a Killin', faced with Mas Charlie's plans to 'kill dialec', the speaker offers a cogent argument about the embeddedness of all languages, including English, in dialect roots:

> Yuh wi haffi kill de Lancashire,
> De Yorkshire, de Cockney,
> De broad Scotch and de Irish brogue
> Before yuh start kill me!
>
> (*Selected Poems*, p. 5)

As the discussion above indicates, Bennett's appeal lies both in the way she makes 'ordinary Jamaicans' the *subject* of her poetry and in her assertion of a poetic voice which claims its authority in the indigenous language and its associated values. This is a highly seductive strategy, particularly in light of the stiltedness associated with earlier West Indian poetic voices. This chapter will now proceed to explore the cultural debates which resulted in Bennett's work being recognized as *poetry* and, eventually as an *authentically* West Indian poetic voice – as *the real thing*. In the process of revisiting the discussions surrounding the literary use of Creole, the *gendered* implications of the debates will also be foregrounded.

Mudder-language and the politics of Creole-use in literature

The Creole spoken by the majority of the population in the anglophone Caribbean, as is well documented, is a hybrid language created under the impact of a divisive colonial regime in which Africans brought to the West Indies as slave-labour for the plantations were forced to communicate using the master's tongue – English – and were punished if they were found communicating in their native tongues.

In his essay 'History of the Voice', Edward Kamau Brathwaite describes the process thus:

> What these languages had to do, however, was to submerge themselves, because officially the conquering peoples – the Spaniards, the English, the

French, and the Dutch – did not wish to hear people speaking Ashanti or any of the Congolese languages. *So there was a submergence of this imported language. Its status became one of inferiority.*[26] [My emphasis]

It is easy to see, given this history, why Creole language, *per se*, should function as such a powerful signifier of a spirit of resistance and survivalism, as well as being celebrated as encapsulating the generally syncretic and hybrid nature of Caribbean culture and society. This recognition of Creole involved considerable debate and I will consider these debates in some detail below. The denigration of Creole was clearly the result of colonialism and the relentless promotion of European cultural values which was an intrinsic part of its strategy for control. There are many cases of colonial administrators (Walter Jekyll's encouragement of the dialect poetry of his protégé, Claude McKay, is a well-known example) actively encouraging the documentation of 'local culture', but this was invariably more in line with the colonial obsession with information retrieval, of an archival kind, about 'the native', than with any serious desire to authorize indigenous culture in the colonies. The impetus for a break with colonial culture and the development of an 'indigenous' culture and language came later, as pressure mounted for self-government in the 1930s and 1940s.

   The impetus towards Creole-use was also clearly prompted by a desire for Caribbean writing to speak of, and to, a more representative notion of 'the people' than the small coterie of the intelligentsia. The imperative to appeal to 'the folk' was evidenced in several novels written in the 1950s where there was a strong focus on representing life in the yard, as in, say, C.L.R. James's *Minty Alley*, 1952, George Lamming's *In the Castle of My Skin*, 1953, and Roger Mais's *Brother Man*, 1954. Simultaneously, attempts were being made to capture the speech rhythms and language of the folk on the page. Lamming, in the following quote, argues that the work of some West Indian novelists was crucial in humanizing and validating the West Indian peasant:

> For the first time the West Indian peasant became other than a cheap source of labour. He became, through the novelist's eye, a living existence, living in silence and joy and fear, involved in riot and carnival. It is the West Indian novel that has restored the peasant to his true and original status of personality.[27]

Lamming goes on to praise writers like V.S. Reid and Sam Selvon for capturing the rhythms of 'the peasant tongue' on the page:

> The peasant tongue has its own rhythms which are Selvon's and Reid's rhythms; and no artifice of technique, no sophisticated gimmicks leading to the mutilation of form, can achieve the specific taste and sound of Selvon's prose. *For this prose is, really, the people's speech, the organic music of the earth* [. . .]. *For soil is a large part of what the West Indian novel has brought back to reading; lumps of earth: unrefined, perhaps, but good, warm, fertile earth.*[28] [My emphasis]

The Guyanese critic Gordon Rohlehr rightly takes Lamming to task for the hyperbolic role that he ascribes to the novelist:

> Long before the advent of the West Indian novelist, the peasant was visibly working against tremendous odds towards an essential independence. [. . .] It was not therefore the isolated efforts of the novelists which, in Lamming's words, 'restored the West Indian peasant to his true and original status of personality'. It was the efforts of the West Indian peoples as a whole which provided a dynamic powerful enough to charge the writers of the fifties. These writers *reflected* an awareness which had been there for some time; they could neither *create* nor *restore* what was already present in the creative struggle, rebellion and movement of the West Indian people.[29]

Lamming's association of the people's language with fertility and the land is, of course, an association which genders literary discourse in familiar ways by mobilizing metaphors of maternal fecundity. Moreover, Lamming's emphasis on the *lack of artifice* involved in transposing the people's tongue onto the page evokes notions of *the natural* which have also, historically, been routinely associated with women. Further, he appears to be *willing* a kind of transformative agency – and relevance – on 'writing the folk' within the context of a region where a large portion of the population are illiterate and where the writer is not valued. Olive Senior suggests that 'in a society whose base is so intensely materialistic, where the majority of the people spend their lives confronting the issues of sheer *survival*, it [writing] is also regarded as something irrelevant, eccentric, foolhardy, quixotic.'[30]

Lamming privileges the status of the literary text, while Rohlehr emphasizes the political sphere, which writing *reflects*. However, both Lamming and Rohlehr suggest a mimetic view of art, indicating that the relationship between the text and 'reality' is one where the latter reflects the former. Rohlehr states this, while Lamming implies it in his stress on the lack of conventions or artifice in Reid's and Selvon's rendering of Creole on the page.

This emphasis on the ability of the writer to mimic the folk tongue resulted in a stress, in fiction in particular, on Creole as a *spoken* language, signalled to the reader via various textual devices, most obviously with the use of speech marks. Sam Selvon's 1956 novel, *The Lonely Londoners*, marked a broadening of the possibilities for Creole-use in its use of a creolized authorial voice throughout and in its attempts to render contemplative, unspoken, moments in the text in a stylized Creole. The use of Creole *in poetry* has involved far more heated contestation because of this emphasis on *the speaking voice*. Clearly one of the reasons for the greater ease with which Creole could be incorporated into fiction is that Creole in fiction was, as indicated above, often quite easily contained within the speech marks which signalled its status as dialogue. Making use of Creole in poetry, and the particular kind of spoken voice associated with Creole, would involve a radical revamping of the dominant conventions of the genre itself. Gerald Moore elaborates on this as follows:

By contrast it seems to have taken rather longer for West Indian poetry to develop a full consciousness of the living language situation which surrounds it. Although we might wish the Creole ballads of Louise Bennett and the best of the Calypso lyrics as poetry – indeed I believe we should – they were not perhaps fully apprehended as such by the audiences which first heard them, in the forties, fifties and even the sixties. Poetry was something else, something which appeared in little magazines, on BBC programmes, in rare anthologies and even rarer slim volumes.[31]

Poetry, as a genre, has long been considered the most sacrosanct of literary discourses, the one for which a 'classical education' is required, and is, therefore, perhaps the hardest of genres for the aspiring colonial writer to participate in. Feminist critics have similarly emphasized the exclusivity and prestige of poetry as a genre, with regard to women's participation in the production of poetry. It seems reasonable to assume, therefore, that these dif-ficulties would be compounded for the postcolonial woman-who-would-be-poet. The decorum associated with received notions of what constituted 'the poetic' increased the perception of cultural distance between the Caribbean and the metropolis, where poetry was actually *produced*. Poetry, more so than prose, was both something else and *somewhere* else. If, as Gerald Moore suggests, poetry was perceived as rare and prestigious, then the Creole used by Louise Bennett, and by calypsonians, lacked the necessary refinement to qualify as poetry.

As argued in the previous chapter, early attempts in the 1940s at an 'authen-tic' Caribbean poetry had tended to focus on incorporating descriptions of the Caribbean landscape into the inherited poetic forms available. This poetry was dominated by male writers and by attempts to name – and claim – the Carib-bean landscape. Later on, when a more radical version of nationalism had developed, naming was not enough; poetic voice and language had also to be transformed and harnessed to nationalist agendas for self-definition. As early as 1912, Claude McKay had published a collection of poems which included a large number written in Jamaican Creole. Una Marson had also experimented tentatively with Jamaican Creole in the 1930s. It is interesting to note too that McKay's poetic output after leaving Jamaica in 1912 did not include any Creole usage, in keeping with his desire to write 'serious' poetry. McKay's passionate sonnets protesting against the violent racism he witnessed in America employed a powerful and formal English, as in 'The White House':

Oh, I must keep my heart inviolate
Against the potent poison of your hate.[32]

The literary Creole available in McKay's historical moment made the conception or 'translation' of sentiments such as those above, or of another of his famous sonnets, 'If We Must Die', into the demotic impossible to imagine.

McKay's difficulty in incorporating Creole into 'serious poetry' also explains the general tendency in much of this pre-independence poetry for the Creole-speaking voice to be restricted to easily recognizable Creole characters. The persona often used for articulating Creole speech was the 'Quashie' figure (a gullible country person), in *either* its male or female representations. Julie Pearn describes a well-known Jamaican actor, Ernest Cupidon, as being 'famous for his impersonations of women. He brought Jamaican dialect into "respectable" theatre for the first time.'[33] Cupidon, incidentally, was part of the cast when Una Marson's play, *At What a Price*, was staged in Jamaica in 1932. That Cupidon should bring dialect to the stage via female personae is clearly not accidental. Women have often been associated with 'chattering tongues' and the black woman has often functioned as the most vocal user of Creole speech. That women in the Caribbean (and, no doubt, elsewhere) are often characterized as loquacious grumblers is summed up in the proverb cited in an article by Carole Boyce Davies, 'Woman Is a Nation Grumble Too Much.'[34] This association of women with the demotic is partly also a reflection of their relative absence from more public discourses. Space does not allow me to pursue in detail the interesting implications of the kind of cross-dressing involved in a male *performance* of a female gender role (is Cupidon, here, a literary drag queen?) and the way in which his performance *translates* the woman's words from the domestic space into the public arena. Nonetheless, Cupidon's use of female personae is a recognition of an association of women's talk with domestic space, the space where Creole is the norm.

In the context of print, several male writers have adopted female Creole speakers in their work, particularly when intimate, domestic matters are being related or when some notion of a Creole/woman's wisdom is being invoked. Four brief examples will have to suffice here. The first is a stanza from James Berry's 'Lucy's Letter' in which Lucy (around whom the collection *Lucy's Letters and Loving* is focused) writes home to Leela:

> Things harness me here. I long
> for we labrish bad. Doors
> not fixed open here.
> No Leela either. No Cousin
> Lil, Miss Lottie or Bro'-Uncle.[35]

The nostalgia of this stanza is tempered later on when Lucy describes the advantages offered by life in London.

Edward Kamau Brathwaite's 'The Dust' revolves around the speaking voices of several women who have congregated in the corner shop. It concludes with them puzzling over the strange volcanic dust which has settled on the land around them:

> An' then suddenly so
> widdout rhyme
> widdout reason

you crops start to die
you can't even see the sun in the sky;
an' suddenly so, without rhyme,
without reason, all you hope gone
ev'rything look like it comin' out wrong.
Why is that? What it mean?[36]

Brathwaite's ear for the spoken rhythms of Bajan Creole is remarkably evocative of 'real' speech, and the poem has been regularly, and rightly, praised as one of the finest renderings of Creole. With regard to the gendered use of Creole, it is worth noting that this is one of the few places in Brathwaite's trilogy where women are the direct focus of attention, and so it is interesting that the women's voices are far more tentative and puzzled than those of, say, the 'fuckin' negro man' in 'Folkways' or 'Brother Man the Rasta' in 'Wings of a Dove'.[37] Fred D'Aguiar, in his 'Mama Dot' poems, seldom speaks *as* Mama Dot (though her warning, 'doan fly no kite is good-friday' punctuates the poem, 'Mama Dot Warns against an Easter Rising').[38] Rather, his 'Mama Dot' functions as poetic shorthand for 'woman's wisdom' encapsulated in the grandmother figure:

Her rocking chair counselling:
Forwards, backwards, unflinching
To our worst imaginable tales;
Her words rocking us backwards
And forwards into a calm light.[39]

In a less reverential vein, Paul Keens Douglas, a Trinidadian poet who writes and performs exclusively in Creole, offers yet another version of the Creole woman in his poem 'Tantie Merle at the Oval'. His representation offers an excellent example of the particular kind of power and presence associated with the 'Tantie' figure. In this poem, the speaker who has gone with his aunt to watch an important cricket match at the Oval in Trinidad is constantly disrupted by Tantie's 'largesse'; she doles out huge amounts of food, puts up her umbrella, makes inappropriate, gossipy comments and generally transgresses all the ritual boundaries associated with cricket by her larger-than-life female presence. She spreads herself out from the moment she gets in the taxi to the cricket ground:

Ah never hear ah taxi-man cuss so yet
But Tanti Merle eh take he on,
She just freeze him with one bad eye
Haul open de back door,
An' take over de whole backseat
As if she is de Queen of Sheba.[40]

In the realms of fiction, the Caribbean literary landscape is littered with various versions of 'Tantie' (Aunt/Auntie) figures or maternal substitutes: large, strong, black women whose facility with Creole makes them formidable agents and whose presence in the text is often to act as repositories of Creole culture. In Selvon's *The Lonely Londoners*,[41] for example, apart from the various (undifferentiated) 'white girls' with whom 'the boys' have sexual encounters, Tantie is the only woman given any kind of presence in the text and it is her ability to negotiate her own way with the English shopkeepers – and so stake a claim to her piece of the metropolis – by manipulating (Creole) language, which marks her out as more convincingly empowered than the assorted men who roam restlessly through the text.

One might also read Christophine in Rhys's *Wide Sargasso Sea* as another Tantie or mother-substitute figure whose powerfully succinct use of Creole language, and its associated cultural values, signals the parameters of her power within a white, patriarchal world.[42] But it is perhaps Merle Hodge in her novel *Crick, Crack Monkey* who most obviously exploits the aunt/mother-substitute figure as repository of a cluster of Creole values.[43] Hodge positions the young protagonist, Tee, as caught between the opposing value systems of her aunt in the country, 'Tantie', and her Aunt Beatrice in town. The former is associated with a rich, expressive Creole verbosity, a frankness about bodily functions and sexuality, and an appreciation of community connections – all of which Tee's Aunt Beatrice dismisses persistently throughout the text as 'niggeryness'. Instead, Aunt Beatrice cultivates, and represents, a mincing mimicry of European middle-class values and culture. Beatrice's inability to fit into this Eurocentric paradigm is most effectively foregrounded by Hodge in the way Beatrice frequently trips up when trying to 'speak properly' (that is, to use Standard English), so that she says 'arktully' for 'actually' or 'dorncing' for 'dancing' and so on. Tee's alienation from her 'niggery' roots in the country is dramatized at the end of the novel in her revulsion at the spectacle of Tantie – complete with oozing bags of 'coolie' food and speaking 'bad English' – invading the pristine sterility of Aunt Beatrice's living room:

> The worst moment of all was when they drew forth a series of greasy paper bags, announcing that they contained the polorie, anchar, roti from Neighb' Ramlaal-Wife, and accra and fry-bake and zaboca from Tantie, with a few other things I had almost forgotten existed, in short, all manner of ordinary nastiness.[44]

I use this fictional example because it succinctly captures a dichotomy which is at the heart of debates about language in the Caribbean literary context; a binarism which might, formularized, look something like this:

Eurocentric	Afrocentric
Standard English	Creole
sterile/asexual/uptight	physical/sexual/laid-back
individual	community
culture of books	oral culture/carnival/calypso
artifice	natural
male aesthetic	female aesthetic

This is a binarism which had, by the late 1960s, become cemented (in rather reductive fashion) around the two giants of Caribbean poetry, Derek Walcott and Kamau Brathwaite, and I will return to this in the next chapter. My argument here is that women speakers of Creole, in the Tantie figure, feature prominently, as 'cultural shorthand', when Creole value systems are invoked. This Tantie figure exudes a kind of power associated with the largeness of her physical presence and with the expressiveness – and excesses – of Creole speech. If, as I have argued in my discussion of Bennett's poems, she utilizes the largesse and linguistic excess of the market women and, using Creole, 'spreads herself' out in her poems, it is notable that *the poet herself* is seldom identifiable in the poems. Instead, Bennett shifts from speaker to speaker, acting as a ventriloquizer *par excellence*, so that, paradoxically, while her performances are often regarded as hugely successful because of the energy and ebullience of her physical *presence*, the lack of authorial commentary reminds us, simultaneously, of the author's *absence*. This absence is even more marked in the printed text when the poet's performative embellishments might help make some of the more conservative viewpoints being expressed more acceptable.

Mudder language

Louise Bennett's chosen focus on women Creole speakers and their 'labrish' is obviously signalled in the title of her first collection of poems, *Jamaican Labrish*, and it is a mode of discourse which many of the poems embody. Rex Nettleford defines the word as meaning 'gossip, chatter',[45] while Mervyn Morris's definition reads, 'gossip, chatter, bear tales; idle talk, stories, gossip, news; gossipy, talkative'.[46] Bennett self-consciously signals her role as a 'gossip', and, in performances, uses body language and intonation of voice to create an atmosphere of intimacy with the audience, inviting the audience to 'collude', as listeners, in the spreading of gossip. In the printed text, this positioning of the reader as salacious listener is signalled by the frequent declamations and rhetorical questions which assume a reader who is both familiar with, and interested in, the various personalities being described. The fact that the personality being focused on in many of the poems is often carefully located via an intimate web of connections helps to convey the illusion of recognition in the reader, as in the example below:

> Is a good ting say de policeman
> Was somebody me know,
> Leah husban outside darta son
> Wha dem call knock-knee Joe.
> (*Jamaica Labrish*, p. 88)

Gossip, as a discourse, has long been associated (pejoratively) with women and the domestic sphere. Feminists have begun the process of re-evaluating this discourse; Deborah Jones, for example, describes gossip as a 'language of intimacy' and as a 'basic element of female subculture', and she quotes Kate Millett: 'Like the members of any repressed group, [women] are verbal persons, talking because they are permitted no other form of expression [. . .] *those out of power must settle for talk*. [My emphasis][47]

Many of Louise Bennett's poems, as indicated in the earlier discussion of her work above, do suggest speakers whose facility with language affords them some recognition despite their marginal social status. In addition, many commentators have made the point that the black *male* West Indian's hyperbolic use of language is often performed as a public display to counteract, or compensate for, his relative lack of power in socioeconomic terms – verbal style, here, masking marginal status. There are significant differences, however, between the 'verbal disguises' available to the male performer as opposed to the female performer.

A brief discussion of one of Louise Bennett's most frequently anthologized poems, 'Colonization in Reverse', is pertinent at this point. Here, Bennett makes use of an intimate context, one woman speaking informally to another, to address the issue of Jamaican migration to the 'mother country'. She effectively exploits gossip, as a 'low-status' discourse, to make some sharply astute observations about the implications of migration, arguing that the flux of migrants from Jamaica to England is so sizeable that it turns 'History upside dung', effecting a 'colonization in reverse':

An week by week dem shippin off
Dem countryman like fire
Fi immigrate an populate
De seat a de Empire.
(*Selected Poems*, p. 106)

The poem outlines the pull of the metropolis:

Dem a pour out a Jamaica;
Everybody future plan
Is fi get a big-time job
An settle in de motherlan.
(*Selected Poems*, p. 106)

The speaker makes fun of the way in which Jamaicans throw themselves into the process even if they themselves don't intend to travel, 'Dem all a open up cheap-fare-/To-Englan agency', and then details the ways in which the Jamaican migrants make their presence felt in England, by competing with the English for jobs and by making use of the state welfare system:

Oonoo se how life is funny,
Oonoo see de turnabout?
Jamaica live fi box bread
Out a English people mout.
(*Selected Poems*, p. 106)

The joyful humour with which the speaker describes the arrival of the migrants and the insistence on their continued presence in 'De seat a de Empire' works to disguise the subversively political agenda of the poem in turning 'History upside dung'. The poem also charts the ways in which 'the margins' impact upon and hybridize 'the centre'. Carolyn Cooper argues that 'Colonization in Reverse' is a poem which 'gleefully celebrates the transforming power of Jamaican culture as it implants itself on British soil in a parodic gesture of "colonization". History is turned upside down as the "margins" move to the "centre" and irreparably dislocate that centre.'[48]

While such celebrations of the hybridizing impact of diasporic communities tend towards an exaggeration of the agency of the migrant in hostile metropolitan contexts, the gist of Cooper's argument is appealing. Rex Nettleford, by contrast, has this to say about 'Colonization in Reverse': '[it] is a classic of her brand of satire and the biting irony of the situation is brought out even more forcibly when Miss Bennett recites this with *her peculiar relish and clean fun!*[49] (My emphasis)

Nettleford appears here, while recognizing its sharp irony, to want to *understate* the subversive potential of the poem and to emphasize its wholesomeness, its 'clean fun'. Carolyn Cooper's argument, made some twenty-six years later than Nettleford's, is part of a larger argument about the excesses, irreverence and slackness of Jamaican popular cultural forms, particularly as embodied in Creole language. The difference in emphasis between the two interpretations of the poem offered by these two notable Jamaican critics provides a useful platform from which to discuss the gendered implications of Creole-use. Nettleford's emphasis on the effect of Louise Bennett's literal *presence* – and her 'real' personality – in consolidating the sense of 'good clean fun' in the poem can be read in terms of his own gendered expectations of a woman's poem, but it would also be true to say that Louise Bennett consistently makes use of speakers who, however much they may parody the pretensions of their social 'betters', always remain within the parameters of suitable linguistic decorum themselves. They may be cheeky and forthright but they are never indecent or 'slack'; indeed, while Bennett makes almost exclusive use of female speakers, there is very little overt reference made to the sexual. Carolyn Cooper's argument concerning the irreverent slackness of Creole, with its sexual punning and carnivalesque subversions, does not apply straightforwardly to the work of Louise Bennett.[50] The linguistic power associated with the female Creole-speaker in Bennett's work, as consolidated in the 'Tantie'/labrisher figure, may refuse conventional definitions of 'ladyhood' but it does so within carefully inscribed parameters of propriety of its own.

The man-of-words in the West Indies[51]

Lloyd Brown, in *West Indian Poetry*,[52] includes a discussion of Louise Bennett and the calypsonian the Mighty Sparrow, in a chapter entitled, 'The Oral Tradition: Sparrow and Louise Bennett'. The general thrust of Brown's argument is that their work utilizes oral forms, derived from African culture, whose characteristics include the dramatization of the power of the spoken/performed word: 'In effect language becomes a substsitute for physical violence [. . .] because it carries with it a violence of its own, and because its flow and energy display an awesome imaginative power.'[53] That culture also uses what Brown calls 'the grinning mask': 'The grinning mask of the oral tradition therefore represents a deeply ingrained irony that goes back to the original rebellion of the African slave through the Westerner's language.'[54]

While I agree with the overall thrust of this argument, Brown's neat coupling of Bennett and Sparrow as 'the oral tradition' elides the difference which gender makes to their use of oral forms, producing very different kinds of poetic/performative identities or 'masks'. Bennett's poetic/performative iden-tity, as argued above, is very much that of the jovial, gossipy Tantie figure. Rex Nettleford's comment is indicative of this view: 'The charm of her winning personality is essential in all this and she uses it with unqualified success.'[55] By contrast, the identity of the calypsonian generally, and of Sparrow in particu-lar, is much more aggressively confrontational, even when it is drawing on similar 'yard-life' concerns. Historically, calypso, with its focus on politics as well as on sexually explicit material, has largely been the domain of male performers – for all the familiar reasons by which social mores ascribe women to the domestic space and men to the public. Social and cultural codes have, for the most part, allowed men a much greater freedom to manoeuvre in public life in the Caribbean. The kind of licence to be licentious, a hallmark of calypso, is not readily accorded to women, though there are contemporary exceptions and, historically, there has been active involvement in aspects of carnival by women. Space does not permit a detailed outline of the trajectories followed in the history of calypso, but many commentators have remarked on the way in which more overt expressions of misogyny have been routinely incorporated alongside the more politically inflected repertoire of the calypsonian. Gordon Rohlehr describes the shift in focus of the calypsonian's art as follows:

> What marks the differences between the 1900–1920 and the 1920–1940 periods is the fact that to the delight in a purely verbal self-inflation were added two elements: a growing concern for social and political issues and the calypsonian's self-celebration as a 'sweet man', a macho man in 'control' of several women or a man who lived in the barrack-yard and could therefore impart intimate knowledge of its 'comesse', scandal and 'bacchanal'.[56]

Implicit in the above remark is the idea that the disempowered 'yard-man' dis-guises his lack of power in the wider sociopolitical context by exercising his (very real) power over the women in the yard. By contrast, in Bennett's poem 'Jamaica Oman' the black woman is presented as having to *disguise* the considerable power she wields in relationship to men:

Neck an neck an foot an foot wid man
she buckle hole her own;
While man a call her 'so-so rib'
Oman a tun backbone!
                                    (*Selected Poems*, p. 22)

The theatrical display of sexual power by men, disguising their relative political impotence, has to be read here as *requiring* the disguise (or mask) of relative
powerlessness by women for the performance of gender roles to be recognized
and affirmed popularly. Clearly, wearing the mask of 'helplessness' can offer
only limited long-term effectiveness for women. Rohlehr suggests that the calypsonian, in taking and disseminating publicly the women's discourse of gossip,
transforms it into a more sexualized currency; 'comesse', 'scandal', 'bacchanal'
are words which mark a sharp contrast to the kind of 'good clean fun' associated with 'Miss Lou' (as she is fondly known). Any calypso described as providing 'good clean fun' might perhaps be considered a contradiction in terms –
though calypsonians like David Rudder in the 1980s and 1990s have struggled to
shift the macho ethos of the calypso and to refuse the routinely misogynous in
their lyrics.

A brief discussion of Sparrow's calypso 'Congo Man', which Lloyd Brown also
discusses, will help to consolidate this point. The calypso opens with drum beats
and the sound of exaggeratedly demented laughter, and then proceeds to
describe, with great relish, a 'cannibal headhunter', the 'Congo Man', who is
about to consume two white women:

Two white women travellin' through Africa
    Fin' themselves in the hands of a cannibal headhunter.
    He cook up one an' he eat one raw
    They tas'e so good he wanted more . . .
        I envy the Congo Man
        I wish I coulda go an' shake he han'
        He eat until he stomach upset,
        An' I . . . I never eat a white meat yet![57]

Brown rightly acknowledges the ambiguities generated by Sparrow's energetically
parodic treatment:

the black male's desire-hatred for the white woman, as object of sexual craving and racial revenge, is dramatized by the sadistic overtones of the cannibal
motif; and on her side, the white woman's loathing for, and fear of, the savage
cannibal actually reinforces a certain yearning for the forbidden.[58]

While, as Brown argues, the calypso dramatizes the 'atmosphere of paranoia, the
nightmarish sense of insecurity' which has resulted in ethnosexual stereotypes of
'the black stud' – and of the white woman as the epitome of desirability – the

parodic mask of the calypsonian might also be seen as a device which distances him (Sparrow, the West Indian) from the 'Congo Man' whose Africanness he (Sparrow) both recognizes *and* (uneasily) disavows. In the process, the distance signalled between one black man and another, between the West Indian and the African, reinscribes a familiar hierarchy of otherness. Clearly, the exaggerated treatment of both stereotypes – of the black man and of the white woman – is deliberately provocative and intended to be wickedly, *illicitly* funny. And it is. Nonetheless, the way in which physical violence is shadowed by sexual violence throughout in the repetition of 'I never eat a white meat', anticipates the white woman being *consumed* by the black man. The parody and inventiveness of Sparrow's wordplay disguise but do not erase the threat of violence which energizes the calypso, and there is a sense that one is positioned uneasily as voyeur in a process which dramatizes, but also reinscribes, the erotic potency of raced/sexed stereotypes. The black woman is significantly absent in the drama played out in Sparrow's 'jungle' and this is indicative, perhaps, of the very different ways in which black and white women are idealized, and/or demonized, in popular cultural forms, such as calypso. If Sparrow's 'Congo Man' inscribes Africa ambivalently, when Bennett does engage with 'Africa', in her poem, 'Back to Africa', she adopts a no-nonsense approach which might be read as suggesting the irrelevance of connections with Africa:

> Go a foreign seek yuh fortune,
> But no tell nobody she
> Yuh dah-go fe seek yuh homelan
> For a right deh so yuh deh!
> (*Jamaica Labrish*, p. 215)[59]

While violence in relation to the (often idealized) white woman is highly sexualized, violence in the context of 'real' relationships with (more socially accessible) black women is often represented as much more physically controlling. For example, Sparrow, reworking a calypso, 'Treat Em Rough', which Gordon Rohlehr attributes to Atilla, offers advice on how men should behave towards their women:

> Every now and then cuff dem down
> They'll love you long and they'll love you strong
> Black up their eye, bruise up their knee
> Then they'll love you eternally.

The earlier version by Atilla made the violence much less explicit:

> Every now and then turn dem down
> They'll love you long and they'll love you strong
> You must be robust, you must be tough
> Don't throw no punches but treat them rough.[60]

Where Atilla cautions, however disingenuously, 'Don't throw no punches but treat them rough', Sparrow provides detailed images of violence. Sparrow's 'linguistic violence' resonates with the threat of 'real' violence behind it. If physical and sexual prowess was to become increasingly important (as Rohlehr convincingly documents) in constructions of black West Indian masculinity, Sparrow harnesses the power of such symbols to his art. The masculinist terms in which these potently sexual signifiers were manipulated by the calypsonian would, for obvious reasons, prohibit a woman performer, like Louise Bennett, from actively participating in such a discourse.

This masculinist bias has, at times, been perpetuated implicitly in sociological and anthropological texts which have examined Caribbean culture from a revisionist viewpoint. Peter Wilson's paradigm in *Crab Antics*,[61] for example, suggests that the cultural spaces occupied by men and women in the Caribbean are fairly rigidly demarcated, with men occupying the outside/public space, associated with *reputation*, and women occupying the inside/domestic space, associated with *respectability*. Reputation and respectability represent different value systems: the indigenous and internally generated on the one hand, and the colonially inherited, externally driven, on the other. Apart from the overly neat dichotomizing of inside and outside (Caribbean concepts of 'the yard' may well complicate such boundaries), Wilson's model posits resistance as an inevitably male phenomenon, a point made succinctly by Jean Besson:

> In particular, I challenge Wilson's thesis that Afro-Caribbean women are passive imitators of Eurocentric cultural values of respectability; that the counter-culture of reputation is male-oriented; and that cultural resistance to colonial culture is therefore confined to Afro-Caribbean males.[62]

Another influential anthropological study, Roger Abrahams', *The Man-of-Words in the West Indies*, also, in its drive to re-read Caribbean culture and to recuperate some notion of agency for the West Indian male, pays scant attention to the *woman*-of-words in the West Indies, and, simultaneously, inflates the word-warrior of the West Indian man. Abrahams argues that the stylized, public displays of verbal skill which West Indian men engage in on the streets, in rum shops or, more formally, in tea meetings held in halls, are all part of a competitive but socializing process for the West Indian man:

> A man-of-words is worth nothing unless he can, on the one hand, stitch together a startling piece of oratorical rhetoric and, on the other, capture the attention, the allegiance, and the admiration of the audience through his fluency, his strength of voice, and his social maneuverability and psychological resilience.[63]

This competitive verbal dexterity is linked to 'an essentially oral, African attitude towards eloquence',[64] a connection which Lloyd Brown also makes. Abrahams acknowledges that certain kinds of oral performances are heavily indebted to a range of printed sources – of various degrees of canonicity – particularly when the performer wants to impress his audience with a certain kind of authority, but this does not unsettle the oral/scribal binary used. Nonetheless, the boundaries of page/printed word and stage/spoken word declare their porousness, at least in terms of cultural practices, despite the ideological imperative in much critical commentary to reinscribe this boundary.

Abrahams also documents the way in which the exhibition of sexual prowess is central to establishing the standing of a particular performer. This can take a variety of forms, from boasting about virility to verbally abusing the sexual part-ners of rivals or, of their mothers. For example, Abrahams includes a depressing litany of rhymes which 'focus on the maternal figure' engaged in by adolescent Tobagonians:

> 16. A little boy with a cocky suit
> Fuck your mother for a bowl of soup.
> [. . .]
> 18. I put your mother on a electric wire,
> And every wood I give she, porky send fire.
> (Abrahams 1983, pp. 62–3)

There are examples, too, of jokes and rhymes which Abrahams presents as straightforwardly complimentary to women:

> This fascination with incest and female genitalia is exhibited in any number of other ways during the bongo. One example that stands out in my memory is a fifteen-minute exercise in metaphor in which a woman's genitalia were compared to a water well, the major point being the pleasures attendant upon digging and finding water.
> (Abrahams 1983, p. 61)

This may reverse the emphasis of the rhymes in the previous examples but still draws its metaphors of woman/sexuality from a similar system of symbols, one in which women are defined *entirely* in terms of sexuality, a sexuality which exists only in relation to the sexual *agency* of men. *The Man-of-Words in the West Indies* gives serious, scholarly treatment to cultural practices normally relegated to the mar-gins and is an important intervention, given the distortions and erasures of colo-nial accounts of the West Indies. Nonetheless, the notion of the West Indian man as word-warrior, enshrined in the title of the book itself, ignores the gendered implications of such a focus and simultaneously romanticizes verbal resistance as an *exclusively male* phenomenon. It is perhaps also worth noting that a great deal of leisure/liming time is required for the kinds of lengthy verbal sparring which Abrahams describes; 'spare' time which may also partially account for the relative absence of Caribbean women from this discourse.

In foregrounding the emphasis on sexual and physical violence in many popu-lar cultural forms, it is not my intention to contribute to the consolidation of damaging stereotypes about the West Indian male, but to examine some of the tensions which arise when the work of women poets and performers are interpreted within such a cultural framework. Neither am I arguing here that the word equals the deed or that 'linguistic violence' and 'real violence' are bound in a neat causal relationship. However, it remains pertinent to acknowledge the widespread culture of sexual violence which permeates many Caribbean popular cultural forms, and which, in challenging the dominance of 'elite Western culture', we are in danger of celebrating too uncritically. Many Caribbean writers, particularly women writers, have stressed the damaging impact of such a culture of violence; Olive Senior, in an interview with Anna Rutherford, makes a connection between physical violence and 'linguistic violence':

> I think we do live in a violent society. It starts with domestic violence, it starts with violence against the child. [. . .] People are very aggressive in the language they employ and in the way they deal with one another. And of course then it goes out into the street. We all grew up with this sense of one group of people threatening another; there is a whole manipulation of the weaker people by the more powerful, and in our society a lot of the powerful people in the domestic situation are men.[65]

Louise Bennett's poems do make use of images which might be described as 'violent', but these are not presented as prescriptions on how to behave, and the use of inflated rhetorical threats invariably involves the speaker being ridiculed precisely for *not* being able to deliver the promised violence of her words. In the poem, 'Colonization in Reverse', for example, the concluding stanza reads:

> Oonoo see how life is funny?
> Oonoo see de turnabout?
> Jamaica live fi box bread
> Out a English people mout.
> (*Selected Poems*, p. 107)

The aggressiveness of the line 'Jamaica live fi box bread/Out a English people mout', is part of the ironic take on migration which Bennett offers throughout the poem. Bennett's use of an apparently naive speaker is not meant to fool the reader; the inflated rhetoric is a mischievous strategy but the detailing of the ways in which Jamaicans manoeuvre when they *do* get to the mother country (taking jobs which 'the natives' don't want and collecting the dole) makes clear that this is a very different kind of 'colonization'. In other words, the poem's 'punch' is generated by the gap between the inflated signifier of 'colonization' and the realities of Jamaican migration to the UK. Violent images here are clearly *masquerading* as 'the real thing'.

As the examples in this chapter demonstrate, it is *not* the case that Louise Bennett does not project confrontation and resistance in her work. Rather, given that the models of resistance and confrontation have been consolidated so unquestioningly around the man-of-words in the West Indies, it is perhaps not surprising that the *woman*-of-words has not always been *recognized* as contributing to this discourse. If Sparrow is able to capitalize on the notion of the man in the West Indies as a 'natural' word-warrior, then Bennett astutely capitalizes on the verbal prowess associated with the Tantie figure. It is not surprising, given the weight of colonially instituted cultural prejudices, that the recognition given to 'the oral' (as embodied in calypso and other public displays of verbal skill) was accorded retrospectively, and that this recognition might repeat the male bias of colonial culture. If, as a result, the *man*-of-words has come to dominate the discussion of the *performed* Creole word, the concluding section of this chapter will return to the more conventionally literary arena to examine the discussion surrounding the *printed* Creole word.

From stage to page

Louise Bennett's work, as argued above, frequently makes use of the archetypal 'Tantie' figure: a strong, resilient, cheerful, black woman. This persona may not have 'book-learning' or middle-class status, but she asserts her right to speech and to exercise some control over her difficult circumstances by naming them and choosing to be pragmatically philosophical about them. This choice of persona made it easy for Bennett's work to be excluded from consideration alongside the more conventionally 'literary' work of her contemporaries. In an interview with Dennis Scott, Bennett comments:

> I have been set apart by other creative writers a long time ago because of the language I speak and work in. From the beginning nobody ever recognized me as a writer. 'Well, she is "doing" dialect'; *it wasn't even writing you know.*' Up to now a lot of people don't even think I write. They say 'Oh you just stand up and say these things!' [My emphasis][66]

The above comment confirms a point made throughout this chapter, about the crucial function of 'the book' in the production and performance of 'the oral'. I place Bennett as following on from some of the earlier attempts to incorporate Creole into literary forms. With the early McKay and Cupidon, this use of Creole tended to be focused on celebrating the excesses, the exaggerated expressiveness, the physicality and lack of pretensions of the language itself. It seemed to be defining itself precisely in terms of its difference from conventional European poetry of the kind aspired to by members of the Jamaica Poetry League; Bennett comments that, 'You know I wasn't ever asked to a Jamaican Poetry League meeting?'[67] This performative Creole poetry did not really feature significantly in the debates about Caribbean poetry in the 1960s and 1970s, partly because, as Gerald Moore points out in the quote cited above, it was '*not* perhaps *fully apprehended as such* by the audiences which first heard them'. The willingness to discuss Bennett's and Sparrow's lyrics as poetry was not to become institutionalized until the 1980s, when cultural paradigms (in the Caribbean and broader 'postcolonial' context generally) were questioned at a more fundamental level and notions of 'the literary' were hotly contested. By this time, too, the more visible/audible presence of women writers was also to add to the challenge being made to notions of 'the literary'.

The discussion of the place of Creole or 'the folk tongue' in more conventional or 'serious' Caribbean poetry circles began in earnest in the 1960s and came to a head with the publication of a special joint issue of *Savacou* in 1971, entitled *New Writing 1970*. Gerald Moore summarizes the significance of this anthology in an article, titled 'Use Men Language': 'The distance travelled stylistically and intellectually over the thirty odd years of Bim's existence received impressive confirmation with the appearance of the *Savacou* special issue in March 1971.'[68]

This publication had included a range of work by newer writers, predominantly Jamaican, who often emphasized the need to liberate the poetic voice from the restrictive conventions of Standard English and other 'niceties' associated with European forms. One of the more arresting pieces in this anthology – and one which captures the strident aesthetic of protest which marks 'the resistance path' along which Creole-use diverged – is a well-known poem by Bongo Jerry, 'Mabrak', in which he urges a move away from colonially inherited poetic discourses to what he calls 'Men Language':

> BLACK ELECTRIC STORM
> IS HERE
> How long you feel 'fair to fine'
> (WHITE) would last?
>
> How long calm in darkness
> when out of BLACK
> come forth LIGHT? . . .
> MABRAK is righting the wrongs and brain-whitening –
> Not just by washing out the straightening and wearing
> dashiki t'ing:
> MOSTOFTHESTRAIGHTENINGISINTHETONGUE –
> so . . .
> Save the YOUNG
> from the language that MEN teach,
> the doctrine Pope preach
> skin bleach . . .
> MAN must use MEN language
> to carry dis message:
>
> SILENCE BABEL TONGUES; recall and
> recollect BLACK SPEECH.[69]

The extract above also points up a difference in the version of Creole being exploited; where Bennett uses what might be described as a more naturalistic, colloquial register of Jamaican Creole, Bongo Jerry makes selective use of a much more declamatory and 'ideologized' Creole and, alongside this, he incorporates Rasta idiom or 'dread talk'. This combination of Creole/Rasta usage, markedly different from Bennett's usage, is one which was to dominate much of the protest poetry of the region.

How to behave on paper

Laurence Breiner, in a paper entitled 'How to Behave on Paper: the *Savacou* Debate', gives a good summary of the issues upon which the responses to the poetry in *Savacou* focused:

> Above all, the *Savacou* debate was about what amounts to the decorum of poetry – a matter of values, standards, the rules of the game [. . .] the critical furore over the *Savacou* anthology was most particularly about what should be printed, and about how a poem should look on paper. No one was fighting about techniques of improvisation, or about what should happen in a poetry reading or on the radio. The discussion was about written texts, and so about the canon created by print: about what should be in an anthology.[70]

Breiner's phrasing neatly captures the focus of much of the discussion generated by the *Savacou* anthology and foregrounds the way in which aesthetic considerations (focused on language) were crucially informed by the medium of print.

Discussions about the interface between print and performance, 'secondary orality',[71] continue into the 1990s but the roots of these discussions are clearly identifiable in this nationalist phase of cultural production. Louis James, in an article printed in another edition of *Savacou*, in 1970, generated some controversy in his discussion of the problems for Caribbean poetry. Anne Walmsley offers a useful summary of this debate in her *History of the Caribbean Artists Movement*,[72] describing the challenge made by Rohlehr, Brathwaite and John La Rose, who argued that the vernacular spoken in the Caribbean was just as capable of complex and expressive richness as Standard English.

In his introduction to *The Islands in Between*, James had argued that the main problem for the Caribbean poet was in finding an authentically Caribbean poetic voice; the early pioneers of West Indian verse, he claimed, were 'writing consciously as West Indians' but, in the final analysis, 'their literary sensibility is too English'. When discussing Mervyn Morris's work, James says: 'One could claim that Morris's work shows a fusion of European verbal complexity with the shrewd commonsense of Caribbean popular culture which we see, for example, in the work of Louise Bennett.'[73]

The highly loaded binary of cultural value which James invokes here was strongly challenged, with many arguing that other definitions of 'literary sensibility' had to be forged. The basis for this new Caribbean literary sensibility was hotly debated. Breiner quotes Wayne Brown's criticism of 'the breakdown of literary standards in the islands, as evinced by a rash of publications of mostly worthless verse – publications which were nonetheless championed by certain academics as heralding a breakthrough of the oral tradition into scribal literature, and as socially relevant.'[74]

Eric Roach's reservations about the anthology were similar, stressing his belief in the need for crafted poetry rather than 'simple', rhetorical protest. He argued:

> Colour, trumpeted on so many pages, gives the impression that one is listening to 'Air on the nigger string', or to the monstrous thumping of a mad shango drummer on his drum 'in sibylline frenzy blind'. [. . .] Are we going to tie the drum of Africa to our tails and bay like mad dogs at the Nordic world to which our geography and history tie us?[75]

Rohlehr's response to this was to challenge Roach's implicit assumption that, to be a good poet, the West Indian must be schooled in the craft of 'the great English poets'. Rohlehr also usefully stresses the diversity of popular oral cultural forms which were influencing 'the new poetry' (kaiso and reggae, for example) and argued, convincingly, for a critical approach which would rise to the challenge posed by the younger poets rather than simply short-circuiting this process by dismissing them in the way that Roach and others had done.

What is at stake here is the kind of poetic identity and voice which might be constructed out of the recognition of the literary potential of the Creole register. Rohlehr, in the article cited above, urges a connection between the protesting and experimental West Indian voices of the *Savacou* anthology and those of young African American poets: 'For example, familiarity with the Wright–Baldwin–Howe–Ellison–Cleaver exchange on "protest" fiction would redeem a lot of West Indian fiction from its naivety.'[76]

He also stresses connections between the angry new poets of the West Indies and the harsh, turbulent sociopolitical realities in the region which produce such cultural forms. Rohlehr then focuses on a particular articulation of black identity, that of Rasta culture, arguably still one of the most potent symbols of a strong black identity. He argues that in the context of Caribbean culture in the late 1960s and the 1970s, it is Rasta culture that most powerfully impacts upon poetic forms and language use. And it is the naked energy and menacing power of 'the Dread', he suggests, which makes Roach uneasy. Here is Rohlehr's account of 'Dread':

> 'Dread' is indeed a frightening quality; the image of naked elemental survival and the mythical sense of Apocalypse with which the Rastafarian lives day after day, are indeed awe-inspiring. [. . .] For what really is 'Dreadness'? The Rastafarian locksman claims to possess the quality, his Dread locks symbolizing both his leonine fierceness and his inner strength. [. . .] Dread is that quality which defines the static fear-bound relationship between the 'have-gots' and the 'have-nots'.[77]

While the power and intensity of 'the Dread' offers a highly focused image of resistance, it generates a discourse which is emphatically male. A brief discussion of Louise Bennett's poem 'Pinnacle' may help foreground some of these issues. The poem refers to a community of Rastas who squatted near Spanish Town in the early 1940s. The poem, focused on 'Mass John's' return from Pinnacle, presents the Rasta figure in degraded and relentlessly unheroic terms, concluding with the following:

> De whole o' him face chamba up,
> Cow-itch bump up him han
> Nuff bur-bur an' dutty all ova him clothes
> Yuh waan see how him tan!
> (*Jamaica Labrish*, p. 123)

The speaker deliberately reverses the image of the Rasta as the roaring lion of Judah and presents him as a timid cat:

> Him dah-tell 'bout how one time
> Him meck nize wen him crawl,
> One police look an him haffe 'Meaw'!
> Mek dem tink is puss a-bawl.
> (*Jamaica Labrish*, p. 122)

The relentless denigration of the Rasta man here can clearly be read as an indication of the more conservative trend in Bennett's oeuvre, and as a reflection of the hostility to Rastafarianism in Jamaica in the 1940s. Certainly, there are many other poems by Bennett with which to sustain an argument about the conservatism of values being expressed. There is, for this reader, something rather too nastily vindictive in the poem's sustained erosion of the Rasta man's 'leonine' status. Having said that, the intensity of this emasculation might be read as a direct commentary on the inflated rhetoric of maleness which is claimed by Dreads. Bennett's speaker deflates such hyperbolic masculinity vigorously and undermines the platform from which it is launched by asserting a familiar 'common-sense' *woman's* logic. Without wishing to collude with Bennett's speaker in trivializing Rastafarianism, the poem suggests a refusal of the apocalyptic discourse of 'Dread poetics' which draws attention to its gendered status.

The point about the gender-blindness of discourses of black resistance has been made many times in relation to the black power struggle in America, coming to a head in the 1980s in the angry debates over the 'emasculating' image of black manhood in literary texts, in the wake of the phenomenal success of black women writers such as Alice Walker, Toni Morrison, Maya Angelou and others. As indicated earlier, these reservations continue to inflect discussions about the relevance of feminist critical perspectives on Caribbean writing and culture, with arguments being made that the historical emasculation of the black man by oppressive colonial structures makes questions of gender irrelevant. However, I would argue that recognition of the gendered implications of debates about Caribbean writing and culture is essential for the (re)construction of more productive and enabling 'femininities' *and* 'masculinities'.

To conclude, the 'protest' poetry of the 1960s and 1970s, which experimented with the use of oral forms, Creole speech and 'Dread talk', was one which was dominated by a stridently male aesthetic. Critical discussions of the *Savacou* anthology tended to emphasize the process as a battle: in Eric Roach's terms (quoted in Breiner, cited above) as a battle between the 'tribe boys' and the 'Afro-Saxons'. The tone of aggressive masculinity which marks the poetry of this period, and discussions of it, helps to explain the very sparse representation of women's voices in anthologies or individual collections and suggests reasons for the particular difference of the trajectory in Creole-use taken by Louise Bennett, and for the belatedness of the recognition for this trajectory. Further, a gendered reading of Caribbean poetry and its relationship to Creole-usage suggests that male protest poetry is associated with a declamatory public anger while the kind of Creole-use associated with Louise Bennett and women speakers generally is interpreted (and, indeed presents itself) as an intimate, humorous, private discourse, located in relatively circumscribed domestic spaces.

In the following chapter I explore the work of four contemporary Caribbean women poets who make extensive use of Creole, and 'the performative', in their work, and discuss the degree to which their work can be seen to follow a similar trajectory to that of Louise Bennett. The discussion will also engage with some of the issues raised in more recent critical discussions about Creole-use and 'the oral' to ask whether the gendered dichotomy identified above continues to structure responses to Caribbean poetry.

Notes

1   J. Edward Chamberlin, *Come Back to Me My Language*, Toronto, McClelland & Stewart Inc., 1993, p. 95.
2   John Agard, 'Miss Lou on Stage at the Commonwealth Institute, London 1983'; in *Mangoes and Bullets*, London, Pluto Press, 1985, p. 57.
3   Olive Senior, interview with Marlies Glaser in M. Glaser and M. Pausch (eds), *Caribbean Writers: Between Orality and Writing*, Amsterdam-Atlanta, Editions Rodopi, 1994, p. 82.
4   Paula Burnett, *The Penguin Book of Caribbean Verse in English*, London, Penguin, 1986, p. xxxix.
5   James Berry, *News for Babylon: The Chatto Book of Westindian-British Poetry*, London, Chatto & Windus, 1984, p. xvi.
6   Louise Bennett (ed.), *Selected Poems*, Mervyn Morris, Kingston, Jamaica, Sangster's, 1982, p. vi.
7   Carolyn Cooper, *Noises in the Blood: Orality, Gender and the 'Vulgar' Body of Jamaican Popular Culture*, London, Macmillan, 1993, p. 41.
8   Louise Bennett interviewed by Dennis Scott in E.A. Markham (ed.) *Hinterland: Caribbean Poetry from the West Indies and Britain*, Newcastle upon Tyne, Bloodaxe, 1989, p. 47.
9   Mervyn Morris very helpfully includes the relevant stanzas of the Longfellow poem in the notes which accompany this collection; Bennett, *Selected Poems*, p. 123:

> His brow was sad; his eye beneath
> Flashed like a falchion from its sheath;
> And like a silver clarion rung
> The accents of that unknown tongue –
> Excelsior!

10 I am again grateful to Mervyn Morris for helpfully including the relevant stanza of this poem.
11 Henry Louis Gates, *The Signifying Monkey*, New York, Oxford University Press, 1988.
12 See the arguments presented in Elaine Marks and Isabelle de Courtivron (eds), *The New French Feminisms*, Brighton, Harvester Press, 1981.
13 Bennett, *Selected Poems*, p. 162.
14 Edward Kamau Brathwaite, 'History of the Voice', *Roots*, Ann Arbor, University of Michigan Press, 1993, pp. 259–304.
15 Bennett, *Selected Poems*, p. viii.
16 Bennett, *Jamaica Labrish*, Kingston, Sangster's, 1966; Bennett, *Selected Poems*, 1982.
17 Jamaica Kincaid, *A Small Place*, London, Virago, 1988, p. 49.
18 Louise Bennett in Walter Jekyll, *Jamaican Song and Story*, New York, Dover Publications Inc., 1966 [1906], p. x.
19 Ibid., no page reference indicated in the text.
20 Delia Jarrett-Macauley, *The Life of Una Marson 1905–1965*, Manchester, Manchester University Press, 1998, pp. 27–8.
21 Olive Senior, *Caribbean Writers*, p. 82.
22 Bennett, *Selected Poems*, pp. xii–xiii.
23 Gordon Rohlehr, 'West Indian Poetry: Some Problems of Assessment' in *Bim*, 55, 1971, p. 135.
24 Bennett, quoted in Markham, *Hinterland*, p. 45.
25 Michael Smith, *It a Come*, London, Race Today Publications, 1988, p. 15.
26 Brathwaite, 'History', p. 262.
27 George Lamming, 'The Peasant Roots of the West Indian Novel' in E. Baugh (ed.), *Critics on Caribbean Literature*, London, George Allen & Unwin, 1978, p. 25.
28 Ibid., pp. 25–6.
29 Gordon Rohlehr, 'The Folk in Caribbean Literature', in Baugh, *Critics*, p. 29.
30 Olive Senior, in an interview with Charles H. Rowell, *Callaloo*, 36, 11, Summer 1998, pp. 477–546.
31 Gerald Moore, 'The Language of West Indian Poetry', in Baugh, *Critics*, p. 131.
32 Claude McKay, 'The White House', in Paula Burnett (ed.), *The Penguin Book of Caribbean Verse in English*, p. 144. Burnett notes that McKay's *Selected Poems*, from which 'The White House' is taken, were selected by McKay himself and did not include any poems in the vernacular.
33 Julie Pearn, *Poetry in the Caribbean*, London, Hodder & Stoughton, 1985, p. 17.
34 Carole Boyce Davies, 'Woman Is a Nation: Women in Caribbean Oral Literature' in Carole Boyce Davies and Elaine Savory Fido (eds), *Out of the Kumbla: Caribbean Women and Literature*, Trenton, NJ, Africa World Press, 1990, p. 165.
35 Berry, *News for Babylon*, p. 194.
36 Edward Brathwaite, *The Arrivants: A New World Trilogy*, Oxford, Oxford University Press, 1973, pp. 68–9.
37 Ibid., p. 30 and p. 42 respectively.
38 Fred D'Aguiar, reprinted in Berry, *News for Babylon*, p. 30.
39 Ibid., p. 28.
40 Paul Keens Douglas, 'Tantie Merle at the Oval', in *Tim Tim*, Port of Spain, Keesdee Publications, 1977, p. 28.
41 Samuel Selvon, *The Lonely Londoners*, London, Longman, 1956.
42 Jean Rhys, *Wide Sargasso Sea*, Harmondsworth, Penguin, 1968 [1966].
43 Merle Hodge, *Crick, Crack Monkey*, London, Heinemann, 1981 [1970].
44 Ibid., p. 106.
45 Rex Nettleford, glossary, in Bennett, *Jamaica Labrish*, p. 223.
46 Mervyn Morris, glossary, in Bennett, *Selected Poems*, p. 169.
47 D. Jones, in D. Cameron (ed.), *The Feminist Critique of Language*, London, Routledge, 1990, p. 244.

48 Cooper, *Noises in the Blood*, p. 175.
49 Rex Nettleford, in Bennett, *Jamaica Labrista*, 1983, p. 15.
50 Cooper, *Noises in the Blood*, pp. 1–18.
51 I take the title of this section from Roger D. Abrahams, *The Man-of-Words in the West Indies: Performance and the Emergence of Creole Culture*, Baltimore, Johns Hopkins University Press, 1983.
52 Lloyd Brown, *West Indian Poetry*, London, Heinemann, 1984.
53 Ibid., p. 111.
54 Ibid., p. 101.
55 Nettleford, Introduction to *Jamaica Labrish*, p. 16.
56 Gordon Rohlehr, 'Images of Men and Women in 1930s Calypsos', P. Mohammed and C. Shepherd (eds), *Gender in Caribbean Development*, St Augustine, Trinidad, University of the West Indies Women and Development Project, 1988, p. 233.
57 I have taken this quote in its entirety from Lloyd Brown's *West Indian Poetry*, p. 103.
58 Ibid., p. 104.
59 See Louise Bennett, 'Nayga Yard', in Bennett, *Selected Poems*, 1982, pp. 102–3, for a poem in which an unequivocally Jamaica-based black identity politics is asserted:

> So, nayga people, carry awn;
> Leggo yuh talents broad.
> Member de place a fi-yuh –
> Jamaica is nayga yard.

60 I am indebted for the quotes from both calypsos to Gordon Rohlehr in Mohammed and Shepherd, *Gender*, pp. 289–90.
61 Peter Wilson, *Crab Antics: The Social Anthropology of English-speaking Negro Societies in the Caribbean*, New Haven, Yale University Press, 1973.
62 Jean Besson, 'Reputation and Respectability Reconsidered: A New Perspective on Afro-Caribbean Women', in *Women and Change in the Caribbean*, Janet H. Momsen (ed.), London, James Curry, 1992, p. 30.
63 Abrahams, *Man-of-Words*, p. xxx.
64 Ibid., p. 33.
65 Olive Senior, interviewed by Anna Rutherford in *Kunapipi*, 8, 1986, p. 20.
66 Louise Bennett, interviewed by Dennis Scott in Markham, *Hinterland*, p. 46.
67 Ibid., p. 46.
68 Gerald Moore, 'Use Men Language', in *Bim*, 57, 1974, p. 69.
69 Bongo Jerry, 'Mabrak', reprinted in Burnett, *Penguin Caribbean Verse*, p. 70.
70 Laurence Breiner, 'How to Behave on Paper: The *Savacou* Debate', in *Journal of West Indian Literature*, 6, 1, 1993, pp. 1–10. I am indebted to Evelyn O'Callaghan for drawing my attention to this paper.
71 Walter J. Ong, *Orality and Literacy: The Technologizing of the Word*, London, Routledge, 1989 [1982]. Ong's insights have informed the discussion of 'the oral' throughout this chapter.
72 Anne Walmsley, *The Caribbean Artists Movement 1966–1972*, London, New Beacon Books, 1992, pp. 105–7.
73 Louis James, *The Islands in Between*, London, Oxford University Press, 1968, p. 25.
74 Ibid., p. 33.
75 Eric Roach, quoted in Gordon Rohlehr, 'West Indian Poetry; Some Problems of Assessment', *Bim*, 54, 1971, p. 83.
76 Gordon Rohlehr, 'West Indian Poetry: Some Problems of Assessment, Part 2', *Bim*, 55, 1971, p. 140.
77 Ibid., p. 139.

3 Speaking and performing the Creole word

The work of Valerie Bloom, Jean 'Binta' Breeze, Merle Collins and Amryl Johnson

One culture's 'knowledge' is another's 'noise'. The metonymy of blood and bone embodies the text, the marrow of literary tradition assuming a particularized cultural character. The artist as *griot* transmits a body of knowledge that is the accreted wisdom of generations. [...] Assumed by the in-group, this figure of speech denotes a genealogy of ideas, a blood-line of beliefs and practices that are transmitted in the body, in oral discourse.[1]

Paradoxically, Plato could formulate his phonocentrism, his preference for orality over writing, clearly and effectively only because he could write. Plato's phonocentrism is textually contrived and textually defended.[2]

Gender is not a fact, the various acts of gender create the idea of gender, and without these acts, there would be no gender at all. Gender is, thus, a construction that regularly conceals its genesis. [...] The abiding gendered self will then be shown to be structured by repeated acts that seek to approximate the ideal of a substantial ground of identity, but which, in their occasional *dis*continuity, reveal the temporal and contingent groundlessness of this 'ground'.[3]

Bodily presence and awareness in one sense or another is one of the features which is central to postcolonial rejections of the Eurocentric and logocentric emphasis on 'absence', a rejection which positions the Derridean dominance of the 'written' sign within a larger discursive economy of voice and movement. In its turn this alter/native discursive and inscriptive economy which stresses the oral and the performative is predicated upon an idea of an exchange in which those engaged are physically present to one another.[4]

This chapter continues the discussion of Creole-use, taking it into the 1980s and beyond to ask questions about the degree to which contemporary Caribbean women poets have followed the trajectory established by Louise Bennett, to explore the poetic uses to which Creole is put in the work of a selection of poets and to interrogate further the gendered implications of such use. The epigraphs above indicate the broad discursive parameters within which the discussion is framed as I forground some of the contradictions, ambivalences and complications which proliferate under the sign of 'orality'. Before discussing the work of the four poets in question, it is necessary to return to the literary history which informed my argument in the previous chapter in order to make explicit the gendered implications involved when women poets lay claim to 'the oral' and choose to engage actively with the performative dimensions of the Creole word. I argued in the previous chapter that Creole-use has often been seen as most succinctly embodied in the 'Tantie' figure, consolidated in Louise Bennett's performances in Creole. The kind of ebullience and excess involved in Bennett's Creole performativity generally signals *maternal* rather than *sexual* largesse, and it is part of this chapter's focus to explore the degree to which contemporary poets have followed this trajectory or not.

Creole is often characterized as a language of *excess*: excess in the sense that repetition and hyperbolic imagery are frequent features of the discourse but also in the sense of the expansive *body language* and *physical presence* which are a feature of performing Creole. This association of Creole with linguistic and bodily excess might be read as expressing a misogynistic view which stereotypes women's discourse as anarchic and chaotic. But it might also be read, more positively, in line with French feminist notions of excess, or plenitude, in which the 'chaos' associated with woman's voice and body signals transgressively multiple possibilities for 'textual empowerment'. Louise Bennett suggests that Creole appeals to her precisley because it refuses the dictates of patriarchal, grammatical rules, when she describes Creole as 'the free expression of the people [. . .] a manner of speaking unhampered by the rules of (Standard English) grammar, a free expression'.[5] This recalls Lamming's celebration of the 'folk tongue' as involving 'no artifice of technique, no sophisticated gimmicks [. . . just] the organic music of the earth'.[6] Rex Nettleford refers to Creole as a 'shapeless and unruly substance [. . .] a bastard tongue.'[7] And Mervyn Morris stresses the way in which Louise Bennett's texts cannot be easily categorized, anarchically transgressing the boundaries which divide texts into 'the oral' or 'the scribal'.[8] Edward Kamau Brathwaite is perhaps the figure whose arguments about Creole and 'nation language' make the most sustained use of woman as symbol.

In *The Arrivants*, Brathwaite stresses a symbolic connection between mother and mother *tongue*. The most dramatic way in which he indicates this connection is in his decision in a later edition of the trilogy to include an epigraph quoting Miss Queenie, one of the priestesses in the Kumina religion of Jamaica:

> Well, muh gran'parents, she teach me some of the African languages an' the rest I get it at the cotton-tree root. . . . I take twenty-one days to get all the balance . . .
> So I just travel up to hey, an' gradually come up, an' gradually come up, until I experience all about . . . the African set-up.[9]

This epigraph functions to locate Miss Queenie – because of her ability to speak in tongues – as the symbolic 'source' or originary moment both for his own voice and text, and for the creation of Creole. This gesture suggests the deliberate *(re)invention* of tradition and an insistence on women's central role in this (re)invention. Interestingly, in the body of the trilogy, Brathwaite's focus is on the black *man's* struggle in the face of a range of emasculating processes associated with colonial and postcolonial economic and cultural systems. As discussed in the previous chapter, when women are focused on in their own right, as they are in 'The Dust', they are representative of a kind of timeless 'folk wisdom', the signifi-cance of which they do not themselves appear to grasp. So, 'Francina', in the poem of that name, is also associated with a kind of 'submerged knowledge' when she insists on spending money purchasing an old turtle, 'when she can't keep/she body an' soul-seam together';[10] the turtle clearly represents some notion of an ancestral past but Francina does not articulate this meaning. I am not interested in making crude accusations of 'sexism' here; rather, I wish to point to a tension between the symbolic weighting given to woman/woman's voice in Brathwaite's poetics and the strange *lack* of voice accorded women in his poetry.

But it is Brathwaite's essay 'History of the Voice' which is most pertinent to my argument here, offering an extended account of Creole as a 'nation language'. Brathwaite distinguishes Creole English from 'nation language' as follows:

> We have also what is called *nation language*, which is the kind of English spoken by the people who were brought to the Caribbean, not the official English now, but the language of slaves and labourers, the servants who were brought in by the conquistadors.[11]

Later on in the essay he elaborates on this difference:

> Dialect is the language when you want to make fun of someone. Caricature speaks in dialect. Dialect has a long history coming from the plantation where people's dignity was distorted through their languages and the descriptions which the dialect gave to them. Nation language, on the other hand, is the *submerged* area of that dialect that is much more closely allied to the African aspect of experience in the Caribbean. It may be in English, but often it is in an English which is like a howl, or a shout, or a machine-gun, or the wind, or a wave.[12]

What Brathwaite is doing here is not really pinpointing a distinctive language-use but *renaming* dialect as a way of *reclaiming* it from its low-status categorization. 'History of the Voice' has become a seminal essay in both Caribbean and post-colonial critical contexts, foregrounding the two central Caribbean/postcolonial concerns of language and nationalism. Of course, in Brathwaite's account, 'nation' is very much an 'imagined community' in that notions of Caribbean Creole speakers constituting any kind of shared 'nationhood' are subject to being fractured linguistically (Creoles vary considerably between Caribbean nations) and politically (the failure of a West Indian Federal government, for example). Further, in privileging 'the African aspect of experience', it is a *Pan-African* identity which is invoked, rather than an ethnically inclusive one. But Brathwaite is mak-ing use of poetic licence here and his hyperbolic claims for 'nation language' have to be read in the light of his imperative to reclaim the *lost continent* of Africa itself as much as to his commitment to valorizing Creole. In this scenario, Africa functions as a version of the lost maternal body – the same maternal body of psychoanalytic discourse, but writ large – a kind of *collective imaginary*. One of the ways to reconnect with the lost body of 'Mother Africa', Brathwaite suggests, is to read the body of the New World African for traces of Africa inscripted upon that body. These 'traces' – reminiscent of Julia Kristeva's semiotic *chora* – Brathwaite argues, are embedded in the rhythm of Creole speech and in the body language associated with it. Nation language in this schema is defined in opposition to the cerebral, the scribal, the patriarchal – characteristics which feminists have also defined as those which women's writing must challenge. Thus Brathwaite argues:

> The poetry, the culture itself, exists not in the dictionary but in the tradition of the spoken word. It is based as much on sound as it is on song. That is to say, the noise that it makes is part of the meaning, and if you ignore the noise (or what you would *think* of as noise, shall I say) then you lose part of the meaning. When it is written, you lose the sound or the noise, and therefore you lose part of the meaning.[13]

What Brathwaite characterizes as the *noise* or sound of nation language is then associated with the rhythms of the Caribbean landscape:

> But basically the pentameter remained, and it carries with it a certain kind of experience, which is not the experience of a hurricane. The hurricane does not roar in pentameters. And that's the problem: how do you get a rhythm which approximates the *natural* experience, the environmental experience?
>
> (p. 265)

In a talk given at the University of Kent at Canterbury in 1988, Brathwaite, in foregrounding the question of rhythm, said with characteristic aplomb that 'the empire was won in iambic pentameter', and, when he wanted the most succinct example of the way in which this dominant iambic beat was being challenged, he described the groups of women (from various religious sects) who could be found 'breaking away' at the end of the various military-style parades in Barbados, *wining their waist* in such a way that their body language subtly undermined the formality of the procession. In *Poetry as Discourse*, Antony Easthope, coming at the issue of iambic pentameter from a different angle, also stresses the ideological weight 'behind' this poetic form:

> The metre can be seen not as a neutral form of poetic necessity but a specific historical form producing certain meanings and acting to exclude others. [. . .] Pentameter aims to preclude shouting and 'improper' excitement; it enhances the poise of a moderate yet uplifted tone of voice, an individual voice self-possessed, self-controlled, impersonally self-expressive.[14]

Brathwaite argues that it is precisely this 'improper excitement' which Creole speech rhythms, and the unruliness of its body language (especially as it is consolidated in the figure of 'the' Creole woman), represent and which should be recuperated into Caribbean poetry. Brathwaite's 'History of the Voice' posits women as the symbolic receptacles of a particular kind of body language and rhythm; one associated with the 'inherent' naturalness and spontaneity of Creole. He cites Louise Bennett and Miss Queenie as the two most important culture keepers. He describes Louise Bennett as a 'poet who has been writing *nation* all her life' and praises her persistence with Creole:

> Anancy, Auntie Roachie and *boonoonoonoos* an *parangles* an *ting*, when she could have opted for 'And how are you today': the teeth and lips tight and closed around the mailed fist of a smile. But her instincts were that she should use the language of her people.[15]

Brathwaite's choice of a word like 'boonoonoonoos' (a term of endearment) captures precisely the sense of *excess* associated with Creole, while the mincing uptightness of the 'how are you today' operates as shorthand for 'uptight' Standard English poetic forms. The frequent use which Bennett makes of iambic pentameter does not appear to disturb this construction. When he discusses Miss Queenie, he describes her language as '*fundamental nation*':

> (*seeing* her of course completes the experience because then you would know how she uses her eyes, her mouth, her whole face; how her arms encircle and reject; how her fingers can become water or spear); but without hearing her, you would miss the dynamics of the narrative: the blue notes of the voice; its whispers and pauses and repetitions and stutters and elisions; its high pitch emphases and its low fall trails; [. . .] *With Miss Queenie we are in the very ancient dawn of nation language* and to be able to come to terms with oral literature at all, our critics must be able to understand the complex forces that have led to this classical expression. [My emphasis][16]

The organic wholeness of Miss Queenie's performance – '*this total expression*' – is what makes her so suggestive to Brathwaite as the originary, foundational voice, and body, for nation language. He also points to figures such as the calypsonian, Sparrow, and the dub poets, Bongo Jerry, Linton Kwesi Johnson, Oku Onuora and Mikey Smith, but none of these is given the powerful symbolic weighting attributed to Louise Bennett or, more emphatically, to Miss Queenie. The latter are associated with a kind of unruly, natural bodily excess or fecundity, while the former are perceived as the revolutionary shaping consciousnesses positioned between oppressive white power structures on the one hand and the feminized raw material of black folk culture on the other.

Folkways and fakeways

By contrast to Brathwaite's folk-centred poetics, Derek Walcott's suspicion of the folk is articulated sharply in the long essay 'What the Twilight Says'.[17] In this essay, first published in 1970, Walcott challenges the (then) current orthodoxy amongst West Indian intellectuals of sentimentalizing so-called folk culture, much of which he felt was the deliberate invention of politicians, intellectuals and other 'culture vultures':

> The folk arts have become the symbol of a carefree, accommodating culture, an adjunct to tourism, since the state is impatient with anything which it cannot trade. [...] Today they are artificially resurrected by the anthropologist's tape recorder and in the folk archives of departments of culture.[18]

As with Brathwaite, the tenor of Walcott's critical essays is often strikingly hyperbolic, but here I want to draw attention to the way in which Walcott focuses on women's bodies when he wants to make his most scathing point about the *excesses* of fake folk, which in this example he characterizes as almost pornographic in its lurid detail:

> The women of the choir are dressed in the standard imitation frippery of Mexican or Venezuelan peasants: black skirts appliquéd with cushion-sized flowers, low-necked, lace-edged cotton bodices and prim shoes, the plainest of the women with, unless argument is dominating memory, a lurid bloody hibiscus in her greased hair.[19]

Earlier in the same essay Walcott again uses the image of a woman in order to evoke a sense of history as an ancient but living, *embodied* presence; he catalogues country-shop smells which are 'all folded round the fusty smell of the proprietor, some exact magical, frightening woman in tinted glasses, who emerged from the darkness like history' (p. 24). Finally, when he wants a symbol of promise with which to end this assault on fake folk, Walcott chooses the image of a young, windswept girl with flowing hair, clutching a shawl around her: 'She was white, and that no longer mattered. Her stillness annihilated years of anger. [...] She was a vessel caught at the moment of departure of their Muse' (p. 34). The pale stasis of this image is in marked contrast to the *physicality* of the black women in the choir. Women's bodies, then, provide Walcott with fertile ground for interrogating the limitations of folk culture. Further, his comments suggest a refusal to endorse the increasing tendency in Caribbean nationalist discourse for the black woman's body to operate as the most suitable symbolic repository of Creole values. Here, Walcott deliberately (and at times problematically) writes against the grain of many of his nationalist contemporaries.

It may be timely here to offer examples from more recent texts, from the wider Caribbean, in which the black woman functions as symbolic repository of Creole culture to emphasize the continued valency of such symbolism. The Cuban writer, Antonio Benitez-Rojo, in *The Repeating Island: The Caribbean and the Post-modern Perspective*, argues for the use of chaos theory as an effective model for interpreting Caribbean culture as a series of minutely patterned repetitions and rehearsals. Space does not permit me to do more than note the gendered implications of his arguments by drawing attention to the way in which the black woman functions powerfully in the epiphanic moment when Benitez-Rojo *recognizes* the pattern, the *certain kind of way*, which characterizes the postmodern-ness of his Caribbean:

> I can isolate with frightening exactitude – like the hero of Sartre's novel – the moment at which I reached the age of reason. It was a stunning October afternoon, years ago, when the atomization of the meta-archipelago under the dread umbrella of nuclear catastrophe seemed imminent. [. . .] While the state bureaucracy searched for news off the shortwave or hid behind official speeches and communiqués, two old black women passed 'in a certain kind of way' beneath my balcony. I cannot describe this 'certain kind of way'; I will say only that there was a kind of ancient and golden powder between their gnarled legs, a scent of basil and mint in their dress, a symbolic, ritual wisdom in their gesture and their gay chatter. I knew at once that there would be no apocalypse. The swords and the angels and the beasts and the trumpets and the breaking of the last seal were not going to come, for the simple reason that the Caribbean is not an apocalyptic world; it is not a phallic world in pursuit of the vertical desires of ejaculation and castration.[20]

In the Martiniquan Patrick Chamoiseau's *Childhood*, the powerful figure of Ma Ninotte exudes a similar physical presence and verbal power:

> Ma Ninotte then dropped her laundry, inspired as all get-out; hands on her hips, concentrating on the reach of her voice, she entered into a truly resounding serenade. [. . .] Nothing could stop her anymore, she forgot everything, preoccupied solely with defeating whoever'd had the nerve to challenge her by means of the unquestionable breadth of her repertory, the imperial resources of her voice, the cavernous echoes of her chest. Soon the adversary stopped. Silence.[21]

In 'Creolite Bites: A Conversation with Patrick Chamoiseau, Raphael Confiant and Jean Bernabé', the question, posed by Lucien Taylor, 'What about gender in all this? And the criticism that your novels don't give very empowering roles to women', elicits this sharp response from Chamoiseau:

> *But that's simply how Creole women are.* I refuse to budge before this criticism. Those who make it presume that literature is simply an intellectual discourse about a culture; they forget that it's also a way of bearing witness to that culture, a form of testimony. We can't plaster feminist principles over our

narratives just to look good in the eyes of the great feminist discourses still in fashion in the West. [My emphasis][22]

Derek Walcott, despite the high praise he accords to Chamoiseau's *Texaco*,[23] does not appear to be seduced by the all-consuming power of the Creole woman as articulated in Creolite. And, where the submerged mother-figure in Brathwaite's poetics provides access to the past and to multiple textual possibilities (for him, as writer), Walcott dismisses 'the maternal' as naively escapist nostalgia:

> The West Indian mind historically hungover, exhausted, prefers to take its revenge in nostalgia, to narrow its eyelids in a schizophrenic daydream of an Eden that existed before its exile. Its fixation is for the breasts of a nourishing mother, and this is true not only of the generation of slaves' children but of those brought here through indigence or necessity, in fact, through the threat of hunger.[24]

By way of comparison, this chapter will now shift its focus away from the possibilities, or limitations, represented by the mother-figure to explore a text which places the black *man* centre page – and stage. If, as argued in the previous chapter, the debate over Creole-use became centred on 'how to behave on paper', then the discussion, for the purpose of this chapter, might best be characterized as 'how to behave on stage'.

How to behave on stage: poetry with attitude?

Christian Habekost, in the introduction to *Dub Poetry*,[25] makes several statements about the kind of identity associated with dub poetry, and the dub poet, which merit quoting at length:

> One only has to look at the word 'poetry' to see how strongly we are dominated and formed by Western culture and values. Dub Poetry has nothing to do with the lyricists' poetry that fills traditional (classic) poetry anthologies. Neither has Dub Poetry anything to do with the 'iambic pentameter' which in school stifled many a person's interests in poetry. Nor has Dub Poetry anything to do with that form of 'Concrete Poetry' where one word, printed in different sizes, is elevated to a literary piece of art. The word 'poetry' is, therefore, nothing more than a loose, but nevertheless helpful definition which is used due to the lack of a more fitting expression.
>   'Dub', on the contrary, can't even be roughly clarified by looking into a dictionary. For 'dub' is not a word but a phenomenon, a movement, a musical hypnosis, bass & drum, *the heartbeat of a people*.[26]

Dub appears here to be bigger than – or beyond – definition. Later on in the introduction, the 'pulsating and continuously flowing' rhythm of dub is described as aiming, not 'at the head but at the belly, the underground area of the human body which is the breeding ground for the artistic expression of a singer, Dee-Jay ("toaster") or Dub Poet' (p. 14).

Contemporary poetry, on the other hand, is described as 'the expression of a decadent, saturated and computerised society' (p. 15). Dub poetry, then, is defined precisely in opposition to 'classic English poetry', and to avant-garde poetry; the naked, elemental black body is pitted against the contrived, excessively intellectual formalism of the book. This definition of 'dub', as everything which 'conventional poetry' is *not*, would seem to imply that it is an inherently reactionary phenomenon, and many of the texts included in the anthology point up the reactionary limitations of the form itself as much as they point up the limitations of Habekost's approach to dub. In Habekost's account, the question of 'aesthetic value' is made irrelevant and elitist. Nonetheless, I would argue that many of the pieces in the anthology fall into the category described by Carolyn Cooper (in relation to one of Benjamin Zephaniah's poems) as 'pure greeting-card doggerel'.[27] Stewart Brown's remarks on the commercialization of dub poetry – cited by Cooper – are also relevant here:

> As dub poetry becomes a commercial product, as its performers [. . .] become media Stars and strive to entertain a mass, multi-cultural audience, there seems to me to be a real danger that the protest, the anger, the fire, becomes an act, while the image, the dub/rant/chant/dance becomes the real substance of the performance.[28]

I think Brown is right: commercialized dub does run the risk of being celebrated as a solely theatrical *display* of anger/protest with the specificity of the *cause* of the rage – the content of the poem, if you like – being entirely ignored. I would add to Brown's comments that *all* dub is a *display*, an *acting out* of anger/protest. The test for dub, then, should perhaps be less focused on the authenticity of feeling of the poet/performer than on how much attention has been paid to the crafting of the act so that it gives an engaged *illusion* of conviction – and authenticity. What happens in facile dub is that the anger is, precisely, *not* acted out but asserted baldly. In emphasizing dub as angry, impolite and *raw*, by comparison to the effete contrivances of Western poetic forms, Habekost's argument is as suggestive of what he perceives as *missing* from Western culture as it is a portrayal of dub:

> And it is only at a live performance that the visual power of the Dub Poets can be experienced. [. . .] Their performance is perfect – the poems are almost always recited freely without manuscript or book, and the sound of the voice, together with the outward appearance, give the performance the true and forceful power, something hardly ever found at a poetry reading in Western society.
>
> (*Dub Poetry*, p. 36)

Habekost then makes several references to 'the glass of wine and the table,' which become bizarrely inflated signifiers of the elitist contrivance of Western poetry, and concludes: 'Wherever a performance takes place it remains, in essence, a [*sic*] unpretentious affair since neither chair, table nor glass of wine is needed, not even a book or a manuscript, *just the poet him/herself*' (*Dub Poetry*, p. 37; [my emphasis].

This emphasis on the poet *him/herself* romanticizes the figure – and body language – of the angry black man (there is little discussion of the difference gender might make to the characteristic voicing of poetic identity in dub) and results in an interpretive framework which hinges on the (angry black) presence of the dub poet to authorize the performance. Here is Habekost's account of what's missing if one does not *see* as well as hear the dub performance:

> [T]he poet on stage with flying dreadlocks, an angry expression on his black face, murderously kicking into the air with his motorbike-boots just as the police boots kicked him. [. . .] Mutabaruka comes on stage half naked, chains around his bare feet and when he lets the gunshot ring out, his face distorted by pain, in 'Ev'rytime Aear de Soun'' then it gets under the whitest of skins and is enough to 'blacken' the whitest soul.
>
> (*Dub Poetry*, p. 36)

Even Desmond Johnson, whose performative style is self-consciously understated, is described as having 'the force of a brick through a window' (ibid.). The hyperbolic thrust of Habekost's admiration strikes an uneasy note, invoking an almost reverential treatment of black male anger which does not allow any critical distance between performer and critic/audience, rendering the performance 'untouchable'.

Gordon Rohlehr's discussion of dub and music-related poetic forms in *Voiceprint*[29] offers a discussion of dub which usefully embeds it in the contexts – socio-economic as well as cultural – within which it was produced. This results in a much more engaged discussion and one which does not treat the dub poet as an unproblematically romantic hero: he admits, for instance, that dub poetry can be a 'kind of tedious jabber to a monotonous rhythm' (p. 18). What Rohlehr's introduction usefully emphasizes, and which Habekost elides, is the way in which music/performance-related poetic forms in the Caribbean are male dominated. This is partly because the role of political commentator associated with the calypsonian has been historically male but is also due to the fact that the control of the technology associated with reggae, dub, deejaying and, latterly, ragga, is invariably male dominated. Rohlehr argues:

> Technological change in the mixing of music, the advent of the 16-track tape and easy-overdubbing, the development of the synthesizer, intensified the DJ's role as manipulator of sound, juggler of gimmicks, controller of rhythm and pace, exhorter of the audience, who would be soldiered into jumping, prancing, raising their hands in the air, wining, grinding, and jamming, getting up or getting down to it. The DJ became high priest in the cathedral of

canned sound, fragmented discotheque image projections, broken lights, and youth seeking lost rituals amid the smoke of amnesia.[30]

Although Rohlehr is not explicitly concerned with the gendered implications of this context, his account makes apparent the structural ways in which women are peripheral to oral and performative modes in the Caribbean. He refers to the tendency of black men, African American as well as West Indian, to 'heroic self-identification' and many of the categories used to organize the material in *Voice-print* are largely male dominated (calypso, robber talk, rapso, dub, dreadtalk, tracing). As mentioned in the previous chapter, anthroplogical accounts, such as those of Roger Abrahams,[31] have similarly emphasized the way men dominate the domain of the publicly performed word. While this emphasis may, to some degree, reflect 'the reality', it remains important to pose questions about where and how these performative paradigms might be recuperated by women and to account for the nature of *female* youth culture. This provides a suitable cue for the Jamaican critic, Carolyn Cooper, to enter – centre stage – for she is the critic who has most explicitly focused on the gendered implications of Creole discourses. It is in the spirit of Cooper's own theatricality that I offer the following, punning heading.

Re-cooper-ating Jamaican popular culture

Carolyn Cooper, in *Noises in the Blood*, emphatically makes the connection between Creole and the 'vulgar body of Jamaican popular culture' in which she posits a feminization of Jamaican popular culture using the notion of the 'promiscuously dilated body of woman' as an image of the 'porous openings in the oral text'. Drawing heavily on Bakhtin's notion of 'the carnivalesque', Cooper reads examples of Jamaican orature (including Louise Bennett's texts) as disruptive subversions of patriarchal, scribal discourses. The rude 'noises' of Jamaican popular culture, she argues, challenge and subvert canonical notions of culture. The 'noise in the blood' of her title is taken from Vic Reid's *Nanny Town*, which Cooper quotes as one of her epigraphs to the introduction, 'when a knowledge comes to me like an echo in the bone or a noise in the blood', which, in turn, is echoed by Brathwaite's references to the noises of the oral tradition in his 'History of the Voice' (which Cooper also cites in an epigraph). Cooper extends the familiar configuration of the black body as a carrier of culture to offer a comprehensive argument about orature.

In her account, she sets the polyphonic, 'slack' oral text against the tightly sealed and closed scribal text: 'These vulgar products of illicit procreation may be conceived – in poor taste – as perverse invasions of the tightly-closed orifices of the Great Tradition' (p. 9). The connection is then established between woman and the oral: 'Transgressive Woman is Slackness personified, embodying the porous openings in the oral text' (p. 11); Slackness is defined as follows:

Slackness is not mere sexual looseness – though it is certainly that. Slackness is a metaphorical revolt against law and order; an undermining of consensual standards of decency. [. . .] Slackness as an (h)ideology of escape from the authority of omniscient Culture is negotiated in a coded language of evasive double-entendre.[32]

Despite the seductive slackness of Cooper's own discourse, the conflation of 'slack woman' with the 'promiscuous oral text' results in some problematic formulations. It hinges on a binary opposition between the oral and the scribal in which all oral texts are essentially subversive and all scribal texts are inherently conservative. In the process, the consolidation of conservative *values* in some forms of orature, however radical the *form*, is elided. So, while many of the texts Cooper discusses directly challenge the status quo with regard to respectable sexual mores, there are troubling implications, because this subversive battle is often enacted on the terrain of women's bodies. This approach also overstates the fixity of even the most canonical of scribal texts and ignores the 'dilatory' status of many printed texts – and the possibility of multiple interpretations of *any* text. Further, the reliance on biologistic tropes, 'bloodline', 'heritage' and so on, to describe the *embodiment* of Jamaican popular culture, does suggest an essentialist and exclusivist approach to 'national' culture which is worrying.[33] The kind of fancy footwork which Cooper has to engage in to keep the 'slack woman'/'slack oral text' parallel in play is under most pressure in the chapter on ragga culture, 'Slackness hiding from culture: erotic play in the dance hall' in which the infamously misogynistic and homophobic lyrics of ragga – and its accompanying body language – are interpreted as evidence of black working-class masculinity in crisis:

> Disempowered working-class men cannot be simply stigmatised and dismissed as unqualified 'oppressors' of women. Their own oppression by gender-blind classism and notions of matriarchy itself motivates their attempted oppression of women [. . .] a chain of disempowerment. The raw sexism of some DJs can thus be seen as an expression of a diminished masculinity seeking to assert itself at the most basic, and often the only level where it is allowed free play.
>
> (*Noises*, pp. 164–5)

Cooper does acknowledge that 'it is the sexuality of women, much more so than that of men, which is both celebrated and devalued in the culture of the dance hall', but she explains this double-take on female sexuality by arguing that the flamboyant way in which women display their bodies in the dance hall is indicative of their power: 'The dance hall is the social space in which the smell of female power is exuded in the extravagant display of flashy jewellery, expensive clothes, elaborate hairstyles and rigidly attendant men that altogether represent substantial wealth' (*Noises*, p. 5). The violent homophobia and misogyny of ragga culture cannot be satisfactorily explained away by invoking black working-class men's oppressed status. Neither can the display of women's bodies in dance hall culture be read as simply celebrating female sexuality. Cooper is right in saying that the spectacular and famously revealing clothing worn by dance hall women challenges colonially inherited, middle-class definitions of femininity, but this class is not necessarily the primary audience for such display. When this erotic display is read in the immediate arena of the dance hall itself, it is much more difficult to interpret this display of the female body as a display of female power. The documented reality suggests that it is ragga *men* who control what women are actually allowed to do with their bodies. The display by ragga queens of sexual power dramatized in the dance hall remains, precisely, *a display of power* for as long as men control the circumstances in which that power can be *acted out.*

Orature: the real thing?

> My people have been separated from themselves, White Hen, by several means, one of them being the printed word and the ideas it carries.[34]

If, as Brodber suggests, the printed word is associated with a kind of 'zombifying power',[35] then the spoken word, by contrast, is invested with a life-enhancing authenticity. The resulting binarism defines the oral text as everything which the printed text is *not*. In postcolonial discourse, with its oppositional agenda, there is often an ideological imperative to invoke oral texts as subversive 'alter/natives' to canonical, page-bound texts, as the fourth of my epigraphs at the beginning of this chapter suggests. But, as Karin Barber argues, citing the scant attention paid to indigenous languages in *The Empire Writes Back*, often 'The oral tradition is not interpreted, it is exemplified or *gestured to*'.[36] By comparison, Carolyn Cooper's detailed attention to the 'noisy texts' of Jamaican popular culture, despite the problematics of gender, at least starts the process of developing a critical vocabulary which would allow a shift away from simple celebration – or apology. The other pitfall of this fetishizing of the spoken word is that it brings the author back onto the centre stage – alive and kicking (*literally*, in Habekost's account!) – in ways which may reduce the impact of a particular performance to the embodied *presence* of the poet as the authenticating origin of a text.

In practice, performances of poems are as open to multiple interpretations as is the written word – despite the common-sense notion that the presence/voice of a speaker expresses the unmediated intention of the speaker. As Antony Easthope suggests, 'In every text, written or spoken, read silently or performed aloud, there will always be some "gap" between intention and reading.'[37] Rather than triggering alarm about a proliferation of interpretations, this 'gap' can be productively used to develop the skills for learning to *listen* critically. These skills will not be completely alien to those required for reading because, as Mervyn Morris argues in 'Printing the Performance', it is unrealistic to continue to separate 'the oral' and 'the literary' in the Caribbean context because of the constant interaction between the two modes: 'Most of our West Indian poets inhabit the differing contexts – and must wrestle with the differing requirements – of print and performance.'[38] Karin Barber similarly argues, 'The two domains are in fact mutually defining to such an extent that to overlook the former is gravely

to disfigure our perceptions of the latter.'[39] Caribbean poets constantly demonstrate, in their writing practice, the creative traffic between the oral and the
literary – in *both* directions. But the critical *reception* of this oral/scribal hybridity
has often not risen to this challenge and continues to inflate the difference – and
authenticity – of 'the oral', reinscribing the binary relationship of scribal/oral.
If creative practice straddles both page and stage, critical practice still struggles,
because of its embeddedness in institutions centred on the printed word, to
develop a vocabulary and critical criteria which can deal adequately with the
'oraliterary'. Perhaps it is *because* of its print-centred orbit that critical commentary still yearns nostalgically for the spontaneity and freedom associated with the
oral?

Caribbean women poets: on the page and on the stage

In the final section of this chapter, I explore the ways in which a selection of
contemporary women poets, who make extensive use of Creole in their work,
might be located in relation to the issues discussed above. What follows does not
aim to give a comprehensive overview of their output nor does it provide many
detailed readings of individual poems. Rather, the work of the poets chosen is
used to foreground the variety of poetic possibilitites for Creole-use and to further
the discussion about the gendered implications of such use. It is also not the case
that the poets discussed here are the only poets to make extensive use of Creole;
three of the poets discussed in Chapter 4, for example, all make some use of
Creole in their work but, given my interest in the (en)gendering of Creole
discourse, the poets focused on in this chapter provide the most interesting
symptomatic readings.

Valerie Bloom: Jamaica language sweet yuh know bwoy

Valerie Bloom is the poet who has most obviously followed in Louise Bennett's
footsteps, as Linton Kwesi Johnson suggests in his introduction to her first collection of poems, *Touch Mi; Tell Mi!* (1983): 'Valerie Bloom's poetry bears a remarkable similarity to that of Louise Bennett's in form, style and language.'[40] The
poems in this collection are written exclusively in Creole, often involve female
speakers and, as in Louise Bennett's poems, it is often the farcical possibilities of
Creole speech itself which provide the poem's thematic focus. So, in the poem
with which the collection opens, 'Mek Ah Ketch Har', Bloom presents a speaker
who is 'all mouth' but whose 'big' words are comically undermined by her actions.
The speaker asks her neighbours to hold her back from attacking 'Dat mawga gal
name Sue' who has accused her of thieving but, when Sue appears – with her
brother and sister – the speaker retreats, only to return with more threats and then
to retreat again:

> Ah gwine mek she kno' mi a big ooman,
> A no yesterday mi bawn,

Lawd ha' massey, dem a come back,
Oono gi mi pass, mi gawn!
(*Touch Mi; Tell Mi!*, p. 13)

This sense of enjoying the operatic, hyperbolic rhetorical possibilities of Creole language features in many of Bloom's poems, and is suggestive of a phrase used by Jamaica Kincaid in *A Small Place*, where she describes West Indians as 'people for whom making a spectacle of yourself through speech is everything'.[41] Part of this 'spectacle' also includes the use of violent imagery for effect, as in 'Mout' Ha' Massey', where a mother displays her concern for her injured child by threatening vengeance on whoever caused the injury, but in the eleventh stanza the target of her anger shifts to the child himself when he tells her that he is crying because he has lost two of his marbles:

– A dat yuh di deh cry fah, bwoy?
But fada tek de case,
Bwoy, move go feed de hag
Befo' a re-arrange yuh face!
(*Touch Mi; Tell Mi!*, p. 29)

In other poems it is the gossip figure who is centre stage, as in 'Carry-Go-Bring-Come', where the speaker who proclaims that 'Mi no carry news about', does precisely that and, when the person she addresses refuses to play the game and trade gossip for gossip, the speaker reads her silence as evidence that she endorses the gossip:

A gawn yuh gawn, yuh nah tell mi
Well silent mean consent.
Dat mean what mi sey mussa true
Mek a run go tell Miss Clement.
(*Touch Mi; Tell Mi!*, p. 33)

Gossip here functions as a kind of 'social glue' which, unlike its other, more benign manifestations, may function to *enforce* 'community values'. Other kinds of yard-life pressures are also exposed as in 'Tenement Yard' (pp. 43–4), where the many difficulties involved in sharing the bathroom, television, kitchen and bills must be stoically accepted: 'But a dat yuh might haffe put up wid/When yuh eena tenement yard.' While, in 'Insec' Lesson' (pp. 45–6), the speaker suggests that some of the constraints and difficulties of yard life might be overcome if, instead of fighting and cussing, 'uman been' (human beings) pulled together in the way exemplified by arrangements in the insect world. In other words, like Bennett, Bloom's Creole poems also contain a sharp critique of Creole culture.

Again, like Bennett, Bloom also uses various devices to convey the illusion that events are happening in the present tense with the reader/listener inscribed as

part of 'the scene'. In many of the poems, such as 'Mek a Ketch Har', the reader/
listener is given no scene-setting introduction but is immersed in the action of the
moment: 'Onoo hole mi yaw, onoo hole mi good,/No mek mi get wey do' (p. 12).
In others, such as 'Mashalaw' (p. 15), the speaker's excited appeal to 'Miss Amy' to
'Cum siddong lissen to dis' acts, simultaneously, as an invitation to the reader/
listener to do the same. The immediacy and intimacy of the tone emphasize that
no 'introduction' is deemed necessary.

There is also a sense in Bloom's work, as in Bennett's, that the use of a gallery
of Creole speakers works cumulatively to convey the illusion that the reader/
listener is as intimately acquainted with the various addressees of the poems as the
speakers are themselves.

In other poems Bloom creates a climate which suggests that performer and
audience form a community with shared political values, consolidating the poet's
own political platform. In the poem 'Yuh Hear Bout', Bloom astutely and economically uses the phrase 'yuh hear bout', with its promise that a juicy bit of
gossip is imminent, as a tellingly understated comment on racism in Britain. The
speaker poses a series of questions which anticipate *just* responses to racism before
cryptically commenting on the lack of such justice:

> Yuh hear bout di policeman dem lock up
> Fi beat up di black bwoy widout a cause?
> [. . .]
> Yuh no hear bout dem?
> Me neida.
> (*Touch Mi; Tell Mi!*, p. 78)

The sharp-edged political agenda is effectively harnessed to the poet's more familiar 'labrisher' voice, with Creole here signalling economy and understatement,
rather than its more usual association with excess and overstatement. On a similar
theme, but using a more gentle and 'teacherly' rhetorical strategy, the poem 'Show
Dem (dedicated to all black children in British schools)', urges black children, in
an explicitly 'consciousness-raising' style, to refuse racist assumptions about their
'failure' and make the most of their education:

> Show dem even doah yuh different,
> Yuh noh wussar off dan dem,
> For aldoah tree-leaf a ride high
> Him couldn ride without de stem.
> (*Touch Mi; Tell Mi!*, p. 60)

Poems such as these *assume* a reader/listener with similar values and beliefs, so that
the poem works to consolidate community and communally held views, rather
than attempting to convince those 'outside'. The poet, by implication, merges any
sense of her *individual* poetic voice with that of the community and, in the process,
attempts to *embody* that community, reflecting – and shaping – their concerns.[42]

Creole is a crucial medium for constituting this writer–performer/reader–listener relationship. As argued in the previous chapter, there is substantial agreement that Louise Bennett's exclusive use of Creole in her poetry has been invaluable in creating a climate in which Creole language (and culture) is perceived as creative and complex, rather than as an inferior side-kick to Standard English. Creole-use in literary production can no longer be read as an 'experiment'; indeed, it has almost become *de rigueur* for the Caribbean poet. What, then, are the continued attractions of Creole for a poet like Valerie Bloom, writing and performing, mostly in the UK, in the 1980s and 1990s?

Clearly, the answer to this question lies partly in the cultural context of Britain in the 1980s and the contestation over notions of *Englishness*, in which many black writers and critics were involved. Valerie Bloom came to England from Jamaica in 1979 when she was 23 and became involved in writing and performing very soon after her arrival. Although Louise Bennett often performed in Britain and in the USA, her primary affiliation was to Jamaica, and very few of her poems tackle black British social realities in the way that Bloom and others have felt it necessary to do. Bennett's poems were essentially an encapsulation of folk and yard life – in all its rich diversity – not an attempt to make a claim for the place of Creole culture and language *in Britain*. So, while the battle over the appropriateness of Creole-use in writing may have peaked in the Caribbean in the 1960s and 1970s, it resurfaces in Britain in the late 1970s and early 1980s and becomes inextricably linked to articulations of black Britishness and to contestatory discourses more generally.

Three of Bloom's poems were included in an anthology, *News for Babylon: The Chatto Book of Westindian-British Poetry*, published in 1984, which was one of the many publications to chart the emergence of 'black British' identities and concerns.[43] James Berry, who edited the collection, argued in his introduction that 'The poems in this book all shout a crucially unsettled relationship. Hurt not diffused either by retaliation or by sublimation in art becomes exposed.'[44] Many of the poems, as the combative title of the anthology implies, focused on black–white relationships in Britain, where Enoch Powell's 'rivers of blood' speech still reverberated. The 'street style' poetics of Linton Kwesi Johnson captured the gritty aesthetics which seemed most appropriate to the times. Jimi Rand's 'Talk, Talk: Nigger Talk Talk', also signalled clearly the emphasis on the need for a more challenging linguistic register, which many of the pieces in the anthology also argue for:

> Cause me no talk no London talk
> Me no talk no Europe talk
> Me talking black, nigger talk;
> Funky talk
> Nitty gritty grass-root talk.
> Das wha I da talk
> So if ahna don't like nigger talk
> Ga![45]

Valerie Bloom's work, by contrast, does not address the reader in the same confrontational manner. Bloom is one of only four women, out of a total of forty poets, to be included in the anthology, and this imbalance can be read as a clear indication of the ways in which the notion of 'black British' writing tended to cohere around male writers (particularly poets) and a more 'robust' and 'gritty' poetic voice. Bloom herself explicitly associates her use of Creole with the broader category of 'African orality', rather than the 'dub' or 'protest' forms which characterized black British poetry of the 1980s: 'I work within the oral tradition that goes back to Africa, rather than the newer one of reggae and dub poetry.'[46] This choice, evident both in the focus on largely 'domestic' subject matter and in the 'chatty' tone in which many of the poems are delivered, either on the page, on cassette or in live performances, suggests that Bloom is appealing by way of consensus, rather than confrontation. Alongside this, there is what might be described as the 'nostalgia factor' in Bloom's work, especially, as is often the case, when the audience includes a large representation of West Indian Brits. Bloom herself comments on this function of her performances:

> In England the situation is very different. The old oral tradition seems to have been neglected or lost. My poetry appears to remind people of it. Especially when I perform to a 'community audience' rather than a poetry-going audience. I often find that people, older people in particular, are astonishingly gratified. This is clearly not just a response to my work as such, but it is because something has been restored which they felt they had left behind.
>
> (*Let It Be Told*, pp. 86–7)

For a white British audience, perhaps, Creole poems may evoke nostalgia too – for a sense of community and belonging which they feel is lost in post-industrial, 'high-tech' Britain. The Grenadian novelist Jean Buffong argues further that Creole is, in effect, an *endangered* language:

> With the modern advent of technology, that age old tradition of storytelling is slowly being killed off. Oral storytelling with all its cultural 'semmi demmi' is being extinguished. That's where the role of Caribbean women writers comes into play in keeping tradition alive. [. . .] Caribbean women writers are preserving an existence in their writing which will otherwise be lost. They are cementing their cultural identity for future generations.[47]

In this account, orality is not perceived as a mutable cultural form which might be changed and enhanced by technology, for example,[48] or by the different diasporic contexts to which it is transported. Further, women, cemented into their traditional roles as 'keepers of culture', appear to be required to police the boundary of authentic Creole-use.

One crucial element of artifice in the performance of Creole poetry is, of course, the various mnemonic devices to ensure the poem *can* be 'learned by heart'. Indeed, when Bloom describes her indebtedness to Louise Bennett, whose work she memorized and performed while she was at school, she also foregrounds the security which Bennett's mnemonic devices afforded her: '"iambic quatrain with its ABCB rhyming scheme", which was the form I had taken from Louise Bennett and relied on in my early writing, carried with it a built-in sense of security born of long familiarity.'[49] What this suggests is that the very rigidity of iambics – which Brathwaite and others have commented on as inappropriate to Caribbean rhythms of speech and landscape – provides a useful way for this performance poet to harness the unruly 'noise' of Creole speech into a shape that can be memorized and performed. It also implies a belief that colonially inherited genres *can* be exploited to different poetic ends.

Bloom also talks of the page/stage dynamic in her work, arguing that, 'only fifty per cent of the poems are actually on the page, the other fifty per cent being in the performance'.[50] While this is problematic, for, as Mervyn Morris argues (when discussing Habekost's arguments on dub poetry), 'Why then bother with the book?',[51] perhaps it is also the case that, as with many of Louise Bennett's poems, their value on the page may be in documenting social realities which do not make their way into other, more official, kinds of records. This kind of 'topicality' may require the dynamics of a live audience to 'activate' a poem fully. However, a live audience may not always solve the problem of reception in relation to the performed poem: the *kind* of audience also makes a difference. I have been in several audiences, for example, in which Bloom (and other perform-ance poets) have attempted to get a largely non-Caribbean audience to participate in call-and-response poems. The tepidness of some responses has effectively killed off many a performance poem. Perhaps what this dramatizes is the way in which certain oral forms are so dependent on the context out of which they were produced as to be resistant to transplantation. In a sense, what Bloom and Bennett have done is to try to capture the 'operatic' quality of everyday Caribbean speech events – Kincaid's 'making a spectacle of yourself in language' – but when this spectacle is removed from its context, the dynamism and volatility become frozen, paradoxically, at the very moment of performance.

While Bennett's poetry has functioned as an important literary vehicle to valid-ate the possibilities for the literary use of Creole, it may be that this strategy is no longer a productive one. It is certainly the case that, of the large numbers of references to Louise Bennett's poetry, very few go beyond registering the sub-versive potential of Creole-use to analyse the individual poems in any detail. Valerie Bloom talks of experimenting with other poetic forms besides those she has inherited from Louise Bennett and it will be interesting to see the direction this work takes. However, as yet a second collection of poetry has not been published (though Bloom has published several volumes of verse for children). She recorded an audio cassette of her work in 1997, *Yuh Hear Bout: Selected Spoken Works*,[52] which includes many of the poems from *Touch Mi; Tell Mi!* as well as others, though a transcript of the poems is not included with the tape. The performances of poems on this recording demonstrate a desire to diversify the use of Creole speech beyond that of the dramatic monologue, Miss Lou style. She had already done this in *Touch Mi; Tell Mi!* with 'Yuh Hear Bout' (mentioned above) and 'A Soh Life Goh', both of which utilize a terser and more understated irony than the more straightforwardly 'comic' loquaciousness of her other Creole poems.

Bloom also experiments with making more nuanced use of Creole personae, so the tape includes 'Bitter Season', in which the death of a young boy (at the hands of bullying male neighbours) is told by the grieving grandmother. There are also poems performed in Standard English, such as 'Dusk', and others in which Bloom sings refrains, often in a hymnal mode. The taped performance certainly foregrounds the great tonal range of Bloom's voice in performance and of Creole speech itself though, by contrast to the theatricality of the poet's live performances, it represents a pared-down version of the 'performance'. The taped recording, clearly, in enunciating Creole speech and intonation, assists the non-Creole speaker. Some published Creole poems are presented with a glossary as a way of overcoming the question of unintelligibility (both of Louise Bennett's collections discussed in the previous chapters come with extensive glossaries).

Other poets, like Jean 'Binta' Breeze and Linton Kwesi Johnson, use a phonetic rendition of Creole both to indicate the pronunciation and to act as a defamiliarizing strategy to unsettle the reader's expectations of the printed word in 'English'. Another method (less commonly used)[53] has been to include 'translations' of the Creole into Standard English. Three of the four poems by Bloom included in *Let It Be Told* are accompanied by such translations – 'Mek Ah Ketch Har', 'Yuh Hear Bout' and 'Trench Town Shock (A Soh Dem Sey)', which become 'Let Me Get Hold of Her', 'Did You Hear About?' and 'That's What They Say', respectively. As even the translations of the titles indicate, this is not a satisfactory device, for the translations appear reductive by contrast to the original. A comparison of one of the stanzas from 'Mek Ah Ketch Har' with its translated version is set out below, as an example:

> Ah gwine mek she kno' mi a big ooman,
> Ah no yesterday mu bawn,
> Lawd ha' massey, dem a come back,
> Onoo gi mi pass, mi gawn!

> I'm going to let her know I'm a big woman,
> It's not yesterday I was born,
> Lord have mercy, they're coming back,
> Out of my way, I've gone.
>
> (*Let It Be Told*, pp. 89–90)

Not only does the very fact of the translation exaggerate the 'strangeness' of Creole (there are too few 'difficult' words to warrant a translation in the three poems), but the use of a 'correct' or 'neutral' Standard English simply ignores the class status of the speaker and the nature of this particular speech event, so that the enjoyment in the 'big-up' qualities of the language itself – which is, largely, what the poem is about – are completely missed. At the same time, this 'untranslatability' may also indicate why poems like 'Mek Ah Ketch Har' seem to fall flat on the page.

The fourth of Bloom's poems included in *Let It Be Told* (and, interestingly, *not* translated) is 'For Michael', written in memory of Michael Smith who was murdered in Jamaica in August 1983. The poem is a beautifully orchestrated tribute to Smith, in which Bloom's own text is comprised largely of lines from Smith's well-known poems. On the taped version of this poem, Bloom even mimics his famous voicing of an extended 'Laaaawwwwd' (this is not replicated in the print version of the poem), and this phrase has its counterpoint in the lines from a hymn which Bloom sings: 'It's a hard road to travel/and a mighty long way to go.' The intimacy of the intertextual relationship between Bloom's poem and Smith's poems and the deliberate mimicking of poetic voice, including the specific *voice-print*[54] associated with Smith's performance of the poem, together, in the explicitness of their use, invite a comparison with the mimicry associated with earlier writers such as Marson. 'Mimicry', in Bloom's poem, is clearly signalled as an act of remembrance and a tribute to Smith's poetic accomplishments; the confidence and self-consciousness with which she weaves direct 'quotes' from his poems alongside lines of her own suggest richer possibilities for 'devotional' poetry (in the looser definition of this term) than some of the more derivative, devotional poems of Marson's discussed earlier. Clearly, this is largely due to the much greater sociocultural proximity of Smith's work to Bloom's concerns than, say, Shelley's were to Marson. But it is perhaps also due to the greater accessibility of a wider range of poetic *voices* which Bloom is able to exploit than was the case for Marson. Smith's poems frequently utilized the possibilities of multiple voices, and his performances of the poems dramatized the effectiveness of this even further; his poem 'Mi Caan Believe It', with its deft shifts of tone and pitch, is a classic example. Bloom's poem 'For Mikey', released from the demands of representing a Creole-speaker in her more usual 'labrisher' mode, demonstrates both the lyrical and elegiac possibilities for Creole-use, and the effectiveness of combining a more public/political voice with a more contemplative/personal voice:

> Ten cent a bundle fi di callaloo dread, ten cent a bundle
> But wi cyan eat callaloo whey fertilize wid blood
> An wi cyan afford fi lose
> No more prophet no more scribe
> For ratta, ratta nuh bring back new life
> An di pickney still a bawl
> An di rent deh fi pay
> An when wi lose di prophet
> Only Jesus know di way.
>
> (*Let It Be Told*, pp. 93–4)

The fact that it is in tribute to a *male* poet that Bloom writes one of her finest poems is not incidental to the feminist perspective pursued in this book; women poets of the region have been influenced profoundly by male poets, 'local' and 'foreign', in ways which have produced interesting intertextual relationships of great diversity and creativity – they have not simply reproduced *in their master's voice*. Poetic 'masters' have provided many women poets with models, both to mimic and to challenge.

Jean 'Binta' Breeze: riding on de riddym

Jean 'Binta' Breeze is Jamaican, has lived in England for over a decade and now divides her time between England and Jamaica. She attended drama school in Jamaica and started performing there in 1983 before leaving for England, where she gave her first performance in 1985. She writes and performs extensively in Creole but, increasingly, also makes use of Standard English in her poetry. She has published two collections of poetry, *Riddym Ravings and Other Poems* (1988), and *Spring Cleaning* (1992), and a collection of poems and short stories, *On the Edge of an Island* (1997). Her work is also available on cassette and long playing record.[55]

Breeze has travelled widely to perform her work and is one of the few women poets to have made a name for herself as a 'dub poet'; she has toured extensively with other dub poets and with a reggae band. She is one of only three women to be included in Habekost's *Dub Poetry* and, as Breeze mentions in her essay 'Can a Dub Poet Be a Woman?',[56] she was acclaimed by one magazine as 'the first female dub poet in a male-dominated field'. Her poem, 'Riddym Ravings' is described by Mervyn Morris as 'one of the great performance poems of Caribbean literature' (cited on the backcover of *Spring Cleaning*), and Breeze herself as 'the best of performers',[57] while Carolyn Cooper refers to 'Breeze's repeatedly spectacular performance of her "Riddym Ravings" classic'.[58]

Recently, Breeze has chosen to distance herself from dub poetry despite her considerable reputation within this field. The reasons she gives for this 'withdrawal', partly to do with the form of dub itself with its heavily rhythm/rhyme-driven imperatives but also because of the specific limitations attendant upon the *woman* poet's performance identity, are pertinent to my argument about the gendered implications of poetic discourses. Christian Habekost quotes from an interview he conducted with Breeze in London in 1985, where she says:

> I had to get out of the confines of dub poetry . . . it was so restricting having to write poetry to a one drop reggae rhythm. That can't be good for any poet. . . .
>
> I'm not screeching and shouting my poetry anymore. . . . I've discovered that poetry is not synonymous with preaching. My poetry has become a lot more personal.[59]

Creole, then, when harnessed to the rhythms associated with dub, signals constriction rather than the 'free expression' it is more usually equated with. Further, because the backing music used in dub performances is invariably controlled by male performers (as is the music industry more generally), the woman dub poet may well find herself 'at the mercy of the beat' in a more literal sense as well.

Breeze, in a workshop she conducted as part of the 'Kicking Daffodils Conference' in Oxford,[60] described her experiences of travelling with a largely male band of musicians and performers, and recounted their tendency to use the paraphernalia of music technology as a kind of 'stage protection', while she preferred to move freely around the stage. And, in a short article, 'Can a Dub Poet Be a Woman?', she clarified the gendered implications of working within dub with a dramatic example:

> Mutabaruka offered to re-record some of my work in his voice and many people thought they were lyrics much more suited to a male voice and someone even suggested that they had been written by a man. This was with particular reference to 'Aid Travels With a Bomb', my anti-IMF poem, and seemed to suggest that it was more masculine to achieve such distance from the subjective or the personal.[61]

In this construction, dub is 'man's work'; a hard-hitting, strident voice is seen to require the famously *leonine* physical presence of Mutabaruka,[62] rather than Breeze's more *feminine* presence. The poem begins:

> (Four hundren years, from
> the plantation whip to the
> I.M.F. grip)

and ends:

> You don't know if they're on C.I.A. fee
> or even with the K.G.B.
> cause you think your country is O so free
> until you look at your economy
>
> Aid travels with a bomb
>
> WATCHOUT
> (*Dub Poetry*, pp. 44–5)

   Many of Breeze's poems are informed by a similarly acerbic perspective on the international economic order, so it is difficult to fathom what makes this particular poem so unsuitable for her to perform on stage. The poem 'Big Time Tief', included on the *Riddym Ravings* cassette recording (but not in the print collection, *Riddym Ravings*), for example, makes very similar accusations about exploitation of the 'smaller economies' by the West, and Breeze's performance, to a lively reggae backing, seems perfectly at ease with the lyrics.
   On the other hand, Breezes's more 'personal' poems were perceived as not properly part of a dub tradition:

   I had my first album turned down by the American company that had put on my previous work, on the grounds that my new work was becoming far too personal and that there were too many pieces dealing with love.

('Can a Dub Poet Be a Woman?', p. 48)

The contradictory demands and expectations for the woman dub poet are dramatically obvious in the two comments, a double-bind which appears to have propelled Breeze out of dub. The emphasis on performance in the dub context, and on a particular kind of performance – as in Habekost's account discussed in the earlier part of this chapter – appears to result in quite precise kinds of exclusions for women poets. Breeze elaborates on another, related dimension of her poetic identity which was not acceptable in dub performance:

I was told by many people that a radical dub poet should not be 'wining up her waist' on the stage as it presented a sexual image rather than a radical one. This led me into an era of wearing military khaki uniforms for performing, but I soon realised that even if I wore sackcloth it would not reduce the sexual energy I carry normally as an individual and which becomes the source of creative energy on stage.

('Can a Dub Poet Be a Woman?', p. 48)

This apparent taboo on the personal and the sexual in the performance of dub suggests that 'mainstream' dub, with its clear political thrust, is somehow *not* a sexual display; the power and anger which male poets project in their performances are simply part and parcel of being 'a man'. In other words, the expression of male sexuality has a taken-for-granted status which makes the expression, or performance, of female sexuality appear as a deviation from the norm. Habekost's discussion of dub poetry placed the angry dreadlocked figure of the dub poet centre stage and, while sexuality may not have been explicitly asserted, it is obviously a subliminal dimension of their anger and energy as he describes it. Carolyn Cooper's argument, that many Jamaican popular cultural forms make use of the explicitly sexual, of *slackness*, to challenge the constraints of the dominant social order, is difficult to reconcile with the double standard which operates with regard to the display of female sexuality, as described by Breeze above. Perhaps this double-take on sexuality needs to be located in the larger, contradictory picture of a Caribbean sexual landscape in which attitudes to sex and sexuality veer between *both* poles – of 'decency/decorum' and 'slackness/crudity'. In this fluctuating scenario, however, men, more easily and in far greater numbers than women, inhabit those genres of cultural production which are most associated with a confrontational energy and anti-establishment power.

In the case of ragga, an aggressive attitude to the establishment and an aggressive attitude to women and so-called 'sexual deviants' are inextricably bound together, making this an even more problematic genre for women to participate in. While reggae, which has so heavily influenced dub poetry, is nowhere near as violently anti-women in its lyrics as ragga (reggae's offshoot), it, too, often refuses women status as equal agents in the struggle against 'Babylon'. Breeze wryly comments on this in the poem, 'Going Home', where she represents a dialogue in which a Rasta advises his woman to 'go home to ya madda/she will help you wid de youth/go home to ya madda/I a tell you is de truth'; to which the woman replies, 'for when I lef I madda/a go to dis Afrikan/I never did expec no/more a dis Babylon'.[63]

Clearly, then, the performance of both 'national' and gendered identity, as exemplified in dub, is subject to a variety of limitations and prohibitions. Together, these constraints endorse Judith Butler's argument, summarized in the third of the epigraphs to this chapter, that 'gender' – and, I would argue, national identity – is produced via the repetition of a series of *acts* which seek to license certain versions (of gender, of nation) as 'natural'. The processes which supposedly *reflect* gendered and national identities operate, instead, in Butler's account, to demonstrate their *constructedness*. The policing of poetic identity, as outlined above, dramatically foregrounds the gendered restraints imposed in pursuit of the performance of an acceptably robust national poetic identity.

It is clear from even the most cursory reading of Breeze's poems that her frequent focus on 'the personal' and 'the sexual' are invariably embedded in the broader sociopolitical context in such a way as to make any neat separation of the personal, sexual and political very difficult. For example, in the poem 'Ordinary Mawning', a woman doing her regular round of housework contemplates the trials and tribulations of her life. Here, Breeze's skilful interweaving of a variety of problems (her children, neighbours, South Africa, the price of sugar) gives equal status to the personal and the political while also managing to maintain the credibility of the speaker. The poem concludes:

> so it did hard fi understand
> why de ordinary sight of
> mi own frock
> heng up pon line
> wid some clothespin
> should a stop mi from do nutten
> but jus
> bawl
> (*Riddym Ravings*, p. 49)

That Breeze should continue to personalize the political and politicize (and sexualize) the personal is testimony to her refusal to be 'dubbed out' by dub. One might also read Breeze's restlessness within the genre as pointing to the limitations of the genre itself, with its gender constraints and rhythm-driven imperatives. Mervyn Morris's suggestion that 'performance poetry' might be a better label than 'dub' because of its ability to include a wide range of performative styles – including the dramatic potential of stillness[64] – is a sensible one, despite the terse refusal of it by Jamaican dub poet, Lillian Allen: 'I think that's bullshit [...] I don't think it's performance poetry, what we do. It is dub poetry. What do we have to do – whip those guys over their head? It's something new in the world, guys; no, it is not "performance poetry".[65]

'Riddym Ravings', Breeze's 'classic', is a good example of a poem which fits more comfortably in the 'performance' rather than 'dub' category. For, although the poem makes a powerful claim for 'rhythm' and includes a refrain which (at least in some versions of the poem) is sung to a reggae beat, it is not *driven* by a reggae beat nor is the reader/listener addressed in the much more confrontation-ally political manner associated with dub, as indicated in Oku Onuora's definition:

> [T]hat is what dub poetry mean. It's dubbing out the little penta-metre and the little highfalutin business and dubbing in the rootsical, yard, basic rhythm that I-an-I know. Using the language, using the body. It also mean to dub out the isms and schisms and to dub consciousness into the people-dem head.[66]

A brief comparison of Breeze's 'Riddym Ravings' with another classic dub poem, Mikey Smith's 'Mi Cyaan Believe It', will help to sharpen the distinctive-ness I want to claim for Breeze's performative style. Both poems take (roughly) similar material as their focus: the 'madness' of surviving in the urban jungle of Kingston, Jamaica. One of the key differences between the two poems is that Breeze's is narrated by the 'mad' woman herself while Smith's is narrated by a visionary poetic persona who walks the city streets crying out in despair at what he sees. The poem's opening lines, 'Me seh me cyaan believe it/me seh me cyaan believe it'[67] punctuate the text as the poet-persona voices the pain of the sufferers, building up in momentum to the penultimate stanza in which the reader/audience is challenged directly:

Yuh believe it?
How yuh fi believe it
when yuh laugh
an yuh blind yuh eye to it?
          (*It A Come*, p. 15)

The apocalyptic tone throughout the poem and the emotive rendering of the final three lines, 'But me know yuh believe it/Lawwwwwwwwd/me know yuh believe it' (p. 15), are powerfully authoritative and, here, the poet *claims* the right to speak out and to confront the reader/audience. Breeze's construction of the 'madness' of Kingston is located intimately within the narrative of one woman who offers her story to the reader/listener with the minimum of analysis, so that conclusions have to be arrived at; they are not delivered. While this point is made on the slim basis of a brief discussion of two poems (about which all sorts of qualifications could be made), it seems to me that the strident delivery of Smith's poem, by contrast to the understated intimacy of the appeal for understanding in Breeze's poem, are suggestive indicators of a gendered difference between dub and performance. This is not to say, however, that Smith's performance of 'Me

Cyaan Believe It' is not compellingly evocative. I share the respect for Smith's visionary work which Breeze pays tribute to in a poem which takes its title, 'Tek a Trip from Kingston to Jamaica', from a line from 'Me Cyaan Believe It'. In the poem the speaker acknowledges, 'so often, uncle/yuh voice/come chanting true', in which the suggestion is made that, with Smith's demise, this 'true' dub voice is no longer around:

> seem like revolution come an gawn
> an revolutionary son
> full im house fram merica
> an talk like spida man.[68]

In addition to pointing up the slippery distinctions between dub and performance, a discussion of 'Riddym Ravings' is useful for foregrounding distinctions between page and stage. There are, one can argue, several versions of the poem: the one on the page, the one on the audio cassette, and the various 'live' performances which Breeze has done of this poem. There is, moreover, more than one version of the poem as it is printed – on page and on poster – and as it is performed on recordings. In the poem, the various hardships, trials and traumas which the 'mad woman' endures are narrated as if the mad woman were speaking directly to the reader/listener/audience. The poem is not framed by any direct commentary from the poet and we are immersed immediately in the narrative the woman offers of her life:

> de fus time dem kar me go a Bellevue
> was fit di dactar an de lanlord operate
> an tek de radio outa mi head.[69]

The repeated use of a refrain, in which the woman remembers 'her D.J.' and the music he plays, operates as a powerful reminder of the way in which she survives the harsh realities of her life:

> *Eh, Eh,*
> *no feel no way*
> *town is a place dat ah really kean stay*
> *dem kudda – ribbit mi han*
> *eh – ribbit mi toe*
> *mi waan go a country go look mango.*[70]

In a discussion of one of the performances Breeze made of this poem, at the Commonwealth Institute, Mervyn Morris argues:

Watching Jean Breeze on stage, one senses that she has prepared with similar thoroughness [as that of Mikey Smith]. I still remember details of a performance she did in London in October 1986, when, with disturbing authority, she created the world of a derelict psychotic, the persona of 'Riddym Ravings'. [. . .] I remember, for example, feeling shivers when, with a very sudden gesture, the woman pushes in the plug again, so she can 'hear the DJ . . . a play'.[71]

I was also at the performance Morris describes and share his sense of being spell-bound by the precise, understated, dramatic skill with which Breeze conveyed the poignancy of the 'mad' woman's situation. The detailed attention to small movements and the subtlety with which Breeze deployed body language were striking features of the performance. So, while the speaking voice throughout used a baselectal Jamaican Creole register, there was none of the confrontational energy, or angry presence, which Habekost claims as an essential ingredient of dub, nor any of the hand movements, or other body language associated with Creole performance à la Lou. Breeze, like many of the dub poets to come out of Jamaica, trained at the Jamaica School of Drama in Kingston, so it is very likely that her performances are carefully prepared for. Spontaneity, in this context, then, has to be read as a carefully crafted *illusion* of spontaneity and not the more naive sense of spontaneity often associated with oral forms, symbolized in Habekost's insistence that the dub poet comes on stage with no books as 'props'.

In the two taped versions of the poem, while Breeze's dramatic *physical* pres-ence is (obviously) missing, careful attention is paid to the modulation of voice to convey a similar, if not as comprehensive, sense of drama. But, precisely because Breeze's performance is so compelling, I think an argument can be made that there is an equally powerful, if qualitatively different, sense of disturbance evoked when one reads the poem, *without* the presence of the poet or the poet's voice, precisely because the poet *is missing*. Breeze's performance/voicing of the poem gives a definite shape and 'polish' to the woman's turmoil, where an individual reading may, at least initially, produce a more fractured and ragged version. The intimacy of address which the presence, or voice, of the poet facilitates and which helps the audience/listener to internalize the alienation of the woman, has to be worked at, more patiently, in a *reading* of the poem.

As is evident in the extracts from the poem above, the orthography preferred by Breeze is one which privileges phonetics, and therefore also facilitates 'correct' pronunciation. But, as Morris rightly points out,[72] this does not iron out all difficul-ties in translating the performance from the stage to the page. In most printed versions of the poem, the refrain is rendered in italics, and, while this does not indicate that the refrain might be sung, or to what kind of melody, it clearly signals its difference from the main narrative of the poem. Breeze's own recordings of the poem suggest very different ways of representing the refrain. In the version recorded for Ayeola Records, Breeze sings the refrain to a 'live' reggae backing and, in the final lines, '*Murther/Pull up Missa Operator!*' (*Riddym Ravings*, p. 61), various electronically produced sounds are used to emphasize parallels between the electric shock treatment which is being forced on the 'mad' woman and her own attempts to keep her sanity via the radio she plugs in 'eena mi belly' (p. 60). In the more recent recording of the poem, for 57 Productions, Breeze performs in a much more understated and soft-spoken voice than the previous recording; the refrain is sung, to the same melody as on the earlier version, but without live music, and the last phrase of the refrain, 'go look mango' is delivered in a faltering voice. The final lines of the poem, *'murther/Pull up Missa Operator!'* are subtly, electronically amplified.

One can speculate on the reasons for these changes: Breeze's declared shift away from dub? The very fame of the poem, 'Riddym Ravings', perhaps required a more understated performance from the poet? Or perhaps, more practical considerations, concerning the specific contract with the recording company, may have dictated a 'voice only' version. In addition, there are 'misfits' between the Ayeola recording and the print version of the text when, between lines 72 and 80, the sequence of lines does not match, as if Breeze is either extemporizing when memory (or script) fails her, or is responding to a live situation. This proliferation of versions of the poem, each of which works effectively, but differently, in their respective contexts, foregrounds the multiple possibilities for interpretation of the 'performed poem' and allows the presence of the poet in performance a function beyond simply an *authenticating* or *authorizing* one.

The multiplicity of readings/interpretations of Breeze's work, which the discussion of 'Riddym Ravings' foregrounds, has its parallel in the poem 'I Poet', in which Breeze offers an account of the way in which the speaker/poet has been shaped by both the written and oral cultures in which she grew up:

ah was readin
readin all de time
fram book
fram play
fram t.v.
fram life
in odder words
fram yuh all
[. . .]

ah read all yuh poems
ah read all yuh plays
ah read all tea leaf, palm,
anyting wid a good story
even if it didn't always have
a happy endin
(*Spring Cleaning*, pp. 88–9)

The speaker stresses that her idea of poetry is informed powerfully by the oral culture, in all its forms, of the community, *and* by the world of books. What is interesting here is the way in which 'reading' is used throughout the poem as synonymous with 'interpretation' and that it, therefore, applies to the understanding of a broad range of cultural forms – not just 'the book'. This, in turn, suggests a 'reading' of culture which refuses the boundary between the worlds of the 'scribal' and the 'oral'. There is a suggestion, too, in the lines, 'so doah I was well hurt inside/wen yuh all did sey/I wasn't no poet' (p. 89), that Breeze is aware of, and willing to comment on, the fact that her 'performance poems' were not considered 'proper poetry'. In the title poem, 'Riding on de Riddym', recorded on cassette (by 57 Productions) in 1996, Breeze proclaims her intentions to ground her poetics once again in 'the oral' – though not necessarily the orality associated with dub – when she says:

> de cap couldn't fit
> de muse pack har grip
> move outa egypt
> now she rovin like a gypsy
> cause accommodation – it not easy
> an too much craft was reachin har by telephone
> [. . .]
> the muse now say she comin live
> she didn't like how her influence get prioritze
> wid de five percent ah like demself and aestheticize
> an de majority doan even realize
> dat is dem retain de culture dat keep har alive
> [. . .]
> so she jump off ah de page
> jump up pon de stage
> mongst de dejay, dance hall,
> de jazz, de blues, de graze
> [. . .]
> an de muse sey to tell yuh
> she havin a rapsi-ragga-raving time[73]

This poem suggests an ongoing interest in the possibilities afforded by 'riddym'. Where the earlier 'Riddym Ravings' had described the sustaining power for the 'mad' woman of 'de Channel One riddym box', in 'Riding de Riddym', Breeze proclaims her ability to manipulate and *ride* the rhythms of her choice and to refuse to be limited to any one beat. Diverse rhythms have always been a key feature in Breeze's work, from the more obviously 'dub' rhythm of 'eena mi corner', 'me jus a/skengeh/skengeh/me jus a/skengeh/pon some cords/eena me corner' (*Riddym Ravings*, p. 27) to the more blues rhythm of 'Third World Blues (for Grenada)' (*Riddym Ravings*, p. 38); to the more nuanced rhythms in the title poem from *Spring Cleaning*, where it is the everyday rhythm of the woman's domestic chores which is interleaved with lines from the twenty-third psalm to create beautifully contrapuntal rhythms:

> de Lord is my shepherd
> I shall not want

an she scrapin
de las crumbs
aff de plate
knowing ants will feed

maketh me to lie down
in green pastures
leadeth me besides de still
waters

an she han washing clothes
spotless
lifting dem outa de water
    (*Spring Cleaning*, p. 12)

In her last collection, there is still an appeal to dub rhythms 'fi fling up wi distress', but it is a modulated and subtle appeal, rather than the use of dub to 'dub consciousness into the people-dem head'.[74] The poem, 'one last dub', opens:

dis is one time dat de
message laas
to de constant bubblin
   of de riddim below
   de waisline
fah people packet did lang time
   absalete
cep fi few crumbs
   (*On the Edge of an Island*, p. 78)

Given the diversity of the range of the poems included on this cassette, and the many trajectories taken in her work, one suspects that Jean 'Binta' Breeze will continue to hybridize poetic form and to ride whatever riddym takes her fancy:

> Now, I am told, my work has advanced beyond the confines of dub poetry, but that is not to say I am achieving as much as other women writers in conventional poetry, and to tell you the truth, I don't much care. I like this space, there are no rules here.[75]

Merle Collins: she sits on the train and sings inside

Unlike Jean 'Binta' Breeze and many other dub and performance poets who define their poetic voices in opposition to the government 'shitstim'[76] and 'polytricks', Merle Collins began her work as a poet during the years of the 'Grenada Revolution' under Maurice Bishop. As part of their commitment to socialism, the People's Revolutionary Government of Grenada (PRG) initiated a variety of programmes which sought to validate Caribbean culture generally, and Grenadian culture in particular. Many individuals in the region looked to Grenada as an inspirational model, even if other governments did not follow suit.[77] Merle Collins worked in Grenada as a teacher and as a Research Officer on Latin American Affairs from 1979 to 1983, when, following the American invasion of Grenada, she moved to Britain; more recently, she has moved to the USA, where she now lives and teaches.[78]

Collins describes the central role of the specific politcal context of Grenada in her development as a writer:

> The sociopolitical context within which my writing really emerged in a stronger more political way, was the revolutionary period, particularly for me between 1981 and 1983, in Grenada. The political situation gave me the urge to write. [. . .] Later on, the response of larger audiences to my ideas and expressions gave me the confidence to continue writing. I did not really think of writing with a view to publication until after 1983 [. . .] after the American invasion.[79]

Ngugi Wa Thiong'o, in his introduction to *Because the Dawn Breaks!* claims Collins's work for a *global* constituency because of its radical politics:

> Merle Collins speaks to more than Grenada. This collection of her poems belongs to Asia, to Africa, to Latin America, to all those in the world who are struggling to create a new world free from US imperialism and all the other forms of parasitism.
>
> (*Because the Dawn Breaks!*, p. xiv)

The publishers also emphatically locate Collins's work as 'committed poetry':

> There is a struggle between two forms of poetry. One is concerned with assisting in the process of liberation and the other seeks to divert our attention from those issues. [. . .] The poet in order to play a meaningful role in this process must, among other things, be an educator giving strength to the struggles we wage. Karia Press, by publishing this collection, celebrates the tradition of committed writing.
>
> (Publisher's Note)

Certainly, many of the poems in *Because the Dawn Breaks!* convey powerfully and energetically the dynamic of a poet whose identity is constructed out of a commitment to representing the concerns of 'the people'. In the title poem of the collection, the poet confidently declaims:

We speak
because
when the rain falls
in the mountains
the river slowly swells

Comes rushing down
over boulders
    (*Because the Dawn*
      Breaks!, p. 88)

Here, Collins harnesses the power and inevitability of 'nature' to evoke a sense of the righteousness of this struggle and a conviction that it will succeed:

We speak
because
your plan
is not our plan
our plan
we speak because we dream[80]
because
our dreams
are not of living in pig pens
in any other body's
backyard
[. . .]
We speak
not to agitate you
but in spite of your agitation
because
we are workers
peasants
leaders
you see
and were not born
to be your vassals
    (*Because the Dawn Breaks!*,
        pp. 89–90)

While the Marxist language which informs and shapes this poem may appear anachronistic in a post-Cold War context, the truthfulness of its use here is compelling. In a poem, 'Up the Hill', from her second collection, *Rotten Pomerack*, Collins comments on the disappointments, following the collapse of the Grenada Revolutionary Government, which now force her to be suspicious of such rhetoric:

and I think of you, too
when I think of words like
petit-bourgeois
like vacillation
like intellectuals

> I think of you
> when I scratch from a poem the word
> anti-imperialist
> and seek some more everyday
> poetic phrase
>> (*Rotten Pomerack*, pp. 44–5)[81]

In other poems, Collins eschews a self-consciously Marxist vocabulary in favour of Creole, as a way of voicing the concerns of her community, in a more 'everyday poetic phrase'. In 'Callaloo', the celebration of a 'truly' independent sense of nation is evoked using a domestic and indigenous image, that of a thick, 'mix-up' pot of callaloo soup:

> Dat is what it feel like
> to be part o' dis
> Revolution reality
> O' dis
> wakin up reality
> o' dis
> no more hidin' you passport
> reality
> no more
> hangin' you head
> [. . .]
> but out loud an' bole
> like you make de name
> GRENADA!
>> (*Because the Dawn Breaks!*,
>>> pp. 23–4)

The poem manages to weld several facets of 'Grenadian-ness' together by using an 'everyday', local dish as metaphor, as well as the 'everyday' language of Grenadians, to capture something of the euphoria many associated with Grenada's re-invention of itself under the revolutionary government.

Collins has spoken in several places about the importance of 'body language' in the expression and understanding of Creole language. In 'Themes and Trends in Caribbean Writing Today', she talks of the persistent 'devaluation of both the spoken language and the body language which included considerable movement of the hands' (p. 186). Moreover, in a talk given at Sussex University in March 1994, Collins elaborated on this by demonstrating the dramatic difference in posture and body language students in Grenada were required to adopt when reciting, for example, a Thomas Hardy poem – body rigid, head held high and hands clasped tightly together at waist height – and the kind of body language associated with Caribbean storytelling traditions – expansive gestures, frequent asides and, generally, a sense of continuous interaction with the listener. In 'Callaloo', the speaker's use of Creole is securely rooted in the demotic:

> No more
> Playin' you doh hear
> Or sayin' some shit like
> A . . . a . . a . . . island
> Near by Trinidad
> Or
> a . . . a few mile
> off Venezuela
> (*Because the Dawn Breaks!*,
>   p. 24)

And this, along with the confident tone of celebration, suggests a speaker who is, assuredly, *staging* or *performing* the nation. Collins describes the origins of the poem 'Callaloo': 'The first poem written within Grenada during this period, "Callaloo", was performed within a women's group. They decided when they heard it to work on it for presentation at a bigger event.'[82] This consolidates the sense that the poem, rather than being the exclusive and unique work of the individual poet, is reworked and re-presented in the interests of national cultural identity. One imagines that, in performance, in the context of Grenada during the revolution years, the body language implied in the declamatory tone – very evident in the written script – would combine with the nationalist rhetoric of the poem's theme to emblematize powerfully the spirit and sensibility of the 'new nation'.

Collins claims 'the oral' from twin trajectories: she was involved, in her early years in Britain, with an Africa-oriented group involved in mime, music and poetry in which she developed a broader sense of the oral, as one of the acknowledgements makes clear: 'In appreciation/to the members of African Dawn/whose work with the integration/of various art forms/has unravelled for me/new dimensions of creativity' (*Because the Dawn Breaks!*, acknowledgements). Another acknowledgement is 'In appreciation/to my mother/oral poetess and dramatist/whom old structures buried within/house and home.' In the talk given at the University of Sussex referred to above, Collins 'performed' the memories she had of her grandmother's gestures and body language when telling her (the grandmother's) 'stories' of European monarchs and distant geographical places. Her grandmother, she said, would use various gestures and ritualized movements, such as ticking off the line of kings on her fingers, to aid her in memorizing detailed bits of information. Collins then went on to perform her own (scripted) poem, 'The Lesson', in which she, in turn, memorializes her grandmother's ability to internalize, so intimately, such 'foreign' texts and distant realities:

> Great Grand-mammy
> Brain tired
> And wandering

Walkin' an' talkin'
[...]
Talked knowingly
Of William de conqueror
Who was de fourth son
Of de Duke of Normandy
He married Matilda
His children were
Robert
Richard
Henry
William and
Adella
[...]
Is not no Nancy-story
Nuh
Is a serious
joke
I used to
laugh at Grannie
Repeat after her
Till one day
Ah check de map
Fin' de spellin'
little different
to how
I did think
But de geography
Straight
like a arrow
Tip focusing
on de
Arctic ocean
    (*Because the Dawn Breaks!*,
        pp. 18–19)[83]

What Collins's preamble and the performance of the poem itself encapsulates is the incestuous intimacy of the relationship between 'the oral' and 'the scribal' (articulated clearly by Ong in the second of the epigraphs with which this chapter opened): the grandmother's internalizing and then performing of the printed word is, in turn, internalized and performed by Collins, the poet/granddaughter. History as text is inscripted in the memory/on the body of the grandmother and the language of the grandmother's body is inscripted in the memory/on the body of the granddaughter. Collins has developed a distinctive mode of delivery when performing her work, making use of an incantatory tone of voice which, in its rhythmic regularity, is almost like a chant. The recent recording of her *Butterfly: Selected Spoken Works*[84] makes use of no music or 'extra' audio props, just the poet reading the poems in her distinctively calm manner. The comparative under-statedness of her style is no less a professional performance than, say, the power-packed precision of Jean 'Binta' Breeze, and, in 'live' performative contexts, Collins shifts gear to project a powerfully dramatic voicing of her work.[85]

If, in 'The Lesson', the figure of the grandmother is an ambivalently rendered figure, representing wisdom and strength but also 'false consciousness', then *mother*-figures are often similarly ambivalent. In 'The Butterfly Born',

> Mother
> Teaching
> As she was taught
> Little girls
> Must learn
> To be seen and not heard
> Or is certain
> Destruction
> Is pillar of saltness
> Oh God!
> Look how Lot
> Smart
> An' he wife
> So fas'
> A pillar of salt!
> (*Because the Dawn Breaks!*,
>   p. 30)

The rise to power of the New Jewel Movement in 1979, however, provides the catalyst for entrenched attitudes to change and for the butterfly to emerge:

> From
> Zot fouten twop
> You too fas'
> To Woman step forward
> To Woman
> Equal in Defense
> Huh
> You tink it easy?
> [. . .]
> The caterpillar dead
> The butterfly born!
> (*Because the Dawn Breaks!*,
>   pp. 30–3)

The speaking voice in the poem slips in and out of patois Creole and standard English, tempering the embrace of progressive slogans, 'Woman step forward', with a sympathetic awareness of the realities which make ideas of 'progress' appear threatening. As with many of the poems in *Because the Dawn Breaks!*, translations of any patois used are offered within the poem or in footnotes. The seamless weaving of registers of language – Creole, patois, Standard English and the Marxist-inflected discourse of politics – are a striking feature in Collins's first collection of poetry. The easy movement between these registers and the accessible structuring of the poems suggest a poet responsive to the demands of a live audience. In talking of her own development as a poet during the years of Grenada's revolutionary government, Collins says: 'writing meant having a vocal and participatory audience, having people respond verbally to the work. *So it was really with the loss of that audience that I began to think of publication'.*[86] [My emphasis]

Increasingly, in Collins's published poetry, it is this sense of loss which punctuates her work. There are poems, in *Because the Dawn Breaks!*, which chart the disappointments following the fall of the Bishop government ('To Trample Dreams', for example) but these have a precision and energy which suggest a poet still in touch with a familiar constituency:

> so many Judases
> so many Simon-Peters
> I tell you again
> I know not him
>
> But ask
> dat man dere
> dis woman here
> Dat
> is one o' dem
>
> . . . a ten dollars please
> people must live
> (*Because the Dawn Breaks!*,
>   pp. 74–8)[87]

Disconnected from sustained involvement with her Grenadian audience, and without the clear focus of a politically exhilarating agenda, Collins *has* written poems which are informed by the political realities facing black British constituencies, but seldom are these in the up-beat voice of, say, 'Callaloo'. In 'No Dialects Please', published in *Watchers and Seekers*, Collins offers a scathing critique of the hypocrisy of a poetry competition which 'was lookin for poetry of worth' but warned entrants, 'Send them to us/but NO DIALECTS PLEASE'.[88] The second stanza begins:

> Ay!
> Well ah laugh till me boushet near drop

Is not only dat ah tink
of de dialect of de Normans and de Saxons
dat combine and reformulate
to create a language-elect
         (*Watchers and Seekers*, p. 118)

This is reminiscent of Louise Bennett's 'Bans a Killin', which argues that, if
Jamaican 'dialect' is banned, then the 'dialect' of Chaucer, Burns, Lady Grizelle
and Shakespeare will have to be banned too. The poem concludes:

And mine how yuh dah read dem English
Book deh pon yuh shelf,
For ef yuh drop a 'h' yuh mighta
Haffi kill yuhself![89]

Collins acknowledges the importance of Louise Bennett, who, she claims, 'broke
new ground by her use of the Jamaican language to explore the sociopolitical
reality'.[90] But Collins's harnessing of Creole and patois to a progressively political
agenda marks her own use of the vernacular as significantly different, in its
explicitly radical politics, from that of Louise Bennett. While, in 'Bans a Killin',
Bennett sharply exposes the skewed logic of denying Jamaican dialects while
retaining those dialects of 'high culture', the poem's drive towards the very witty
final stanza (cited above) allows the political bite of the piece to be diffused to
some extent. Collins, in 'No Dialects Please', is more insistent on the detail of
specific historical moments in which 'Britishness' is strategically denied or
extended to the postcolonial migrant. The poem uses 'dialect' throughout to
underscore the thrust of the argument being presented and the many exclamation
marks and capital letters help to convey the manner in which the anger propelling
the poem should be performed.

In another poem in *Watchers and Seekers* – 'Images' – Collins addresses the specifically black feminist agenda around which the anthology is organized, in a poem
which powerfully dramatizes the ways in which gender roles become internalized:

Images of our anger
Images of our shouts
Why you don't fight back
Hush chile
Sometimes you have to play dead
To see what funeral you go get
So accustomed to the game
That even after the funeral over
We still playin dead
         (*Watchers and Seekers*, p. 25)

Here, the wry, melancholy note is one which subtly pervades the more recent collection, *Rotten Pomerack*. There *are* poems, such as 'Crick Crack', from which the title of the collection is drawn in which, in live performances, the poet actively involves the audience in voicing, 'Crick!/Crack!/Monkey break he back on a rotten pomerack' (p. 60). 'Crick Crack' effectively uses a 'traditional oral' form to make sharply satirical points:

> in South Africa de Klerk
> without a krick
> without a krack
> walking tall tall tall
> through the streets
> and they say he
> freeing the blacks
>
> I say for true?
> Where the blood?
> Where the sweat?
> Where the tears?
> sound like monkey well
> break he back
> on some rotten pomerack
>   (*Rotten Pomerack*, p. 62)

In other poems, though, there is a weariness mixed with the satire when the politics of location in Britain is dealt with. 'What Ting is Dat?' asks:

> You don't mean is a person?
> Is a being like me?
>
> That could walk? That could talk?
> Make up me own image an ting?
> Then is how come I become a
> Ethnic minority?
>   (*Rotten Pomerack*, p. 58)

While in 'Visiting Yorkshire Again', the speaker, no longer a tourist but resident in England, reads and understands the body language – 'the glances, the stares/the averted gaze/the quickened step' – of those who read *her* as a stranger:

> After the Brontës,
> I decided not to visit with Keats
> And Wordsworth
> Discovered that art
> In England
> Comes in Black and white
> In rich and poor

That an art called Black
Exists
For England
In some region called the Fringe
            (*Rotten Pomerack*, p. 18)

These poems offer a sobering commentary on the defiance of tone in 'No Dialects Please', suggesting that asserting the right to write in 'dialect' may not override the sense of loss which geographical distance from a live, familiar audience may represent. Indeed, many poems in *Rotten Pomerack* circle back and forth around notions of silences and chants. In 'Seduction', the ambiguous attractions of staying away from 'home' are foregrounded:

The longer you linger
in this seductive dying
the more silent, you'll see
You'll become
            (*Rotten Pomerack*, p. 14)

Meanwhile, in 'Schizophrenia', the poet speaks of

learning to speak in whispers
learning to shout in silence
[. . .]
listening for voices beneath the voices
for the words that weren't spoken
            (*Rotten Pomerack*, pp. 66–7)

And, in another poem, 'Where the Scattering Began', which focuses, like 'Schizo-phrenia', on the traumatic dislocations of the black 'disaporic' subject, the speaker concludes:

They come with hands that speak
In ways the tongue has forgotten
[. . .]
Here
hands and eyes and ears
begin to shape answers
to questions
tongue can find no words
for asking
            (*Rotten Pomerack*, p. 68)

The poem's point of departure is an unspecified African slave-trading port, and the lines suggest that it is (again) in body language that the traces of 'African ancestry' lie for diasporic blacks, that it is written deep within the black body. In 'Chant Me A Tune' (pp. 33–4), the poem's title acts as a soothing refrain as the poem outlines the painful legacy of the 'weeping atlantic', 'When you see me weak and wondering/as you sometimes will/chant me a tune'. Here, migration does not signify the possibilities and plenitude popularly associated with diaspora, but trauma and *silence*. Particularly when placed alongside the opening stanza from 'Because the Dawn Breaks!' (below), a sense of the *implosion* of poetic voice is striking:

> We speak
> Because
> When the rain falls
> In the mountains
> The river slowly swells
>
> Comes rushing down
> Over boulders
> > (*Because the Dawn*
> > *Breaks!*, p. 88)

By way of conclusion, I will briefly discuss the poem whose title, 'She Sits on the Train and Sings Inside' (*Rotten Pomerack*, pp. 25–9), conveys the shift in Collins's work outlined above. Using a third-person narrator, the poem focuses on a woman travelling on a grimy underground train to work in London. She 'Sits and sings snippets of remembered songs/To keep her feelings company' and thinks of her daughter back home. The daughter, meanwhile, fantasizes about her mother who works in London, with its exotic place names, like 'Piccadilly Circus'. Collins's skill here is in interweaving the snatches of song with the woman's thoughts and dreams, as well as those of the daughter, without the poem becoming incoherent. The mother, despite the evidence all around her on the tube of harsher realities, still succumbs to the magic of the city's names in much the same way that her daughter does – 'Covent Garden makes her sit straight/hold her head high/and yawn/delicately' – while the daughter boasts excitedly to her friends, 'Me mother in England/she working in Piccadilly Circus, now,/and she send ten pounds for me.' The constant shuttling between voices in the poem, between internal/external, over here/over there, reality/dream, suggests a poem which has been profoundly shaped – in terms of thematics *and* aesthetics – by the experience of migration. Collins productively exploits what might be described as the liminal, or limbo, space of the migrant to construct a poetic voice which hauntingly encapsulates the multiple dislocations attendant upon the process of 'relocation':

> Oy o yoy! Lord! Look at me crosses!
> She wonders if the women sleeping
> Have children too
> In St Kitts

St Lucia
Jamaica
Grenada

She sits on the train and sings
Inside
The songs that keep her thoughts company

Sad to say I'm on my way
                    (*Rotten Pomerack*, p. 26)

The poem, with its unfinished bits of song, resonates powerfully for those readers who are able to 'fill in' the gaps in the woman's snatches of song. So, for example, the lines which follow on from the fragment of an old calypso quoted above, 'sad to say I'm on my way', are:

Won't be back for many a day
My heart is down
My head is turning around
I had to leave a little girl
in Kingston town

Here, the familiar narrative of a man leaving behind a loved woman, when re-placed in Collins's poem, tells another story – familiar, though not often memor-ialized in calypso – of mother leaving beloved daughter. The haunting melody of the calypso (and other songs) is absent on the page, *completely* absent for the reader who is unfamiliar with the calypso/songs, and this, when compared to a live performance of the poem, or its performance on tape, may be deemed an unsatis-factory absence. As I argued in relation to Breeze's 'Riddym Ravings', however, I would suggest that the poem works sufficiently well on the page with the fragmen-tation of voices clearly indicated, syntactically and with regard to layout, for the reader to furnish for themselves the tenor and tone of the voicing of the poem. Indeed, the fact that much of the poem dramatizes an *internal* dialogue and there is only *imagined* communication between the woman and her fellow tube-travellers may even suggest that there is some poetic logic in reading the poem 'silently'. Read in relation to Collins's comments above about the genesis of her writing career – 'Before that [the end of the Bishop government], writing meant having a vocal and participatory audience, having people respond verbally to the work. So it was really with the loss of that audience that I began to think of publication'[91] – it is tempting to suggest that, disconnected from the intimacy and familiarity of her Grenadian constituency, the poet figure in 'She Sits on the Train and Sings Inside' emblematizes the importance of a 'real' community for the performance poet. 'Virtual' audiences 'met' via the page are no substitute.

It is important to stress here that it is not my intention to suggest that the trajec-tory I describe, from public performance poet to the lonely figure of the (name-less) woman journeying to work, accounts for the experiences of Merle Collins herself; rather, I am arguing that the construction of poetic identities in Collins's poetry dramatizes the importance of location to the construction of those identities. Further, the shift in identity outlined above has implications for the use of the body and voice for, as the poetic voice becomes less assured of public consensus (as in, say, 'Callaloo') and relinquishes the demotic for a more fragmented and private voice, the poet at times appears to be aspiring to – *escaping into* – 'pure sound'. The closing lines of 'She Sits on the Train' read:

> so now every night is a
> sitting on the sofa
> sitting on the sofa
> sitting on the sofa
> every night is a
> sitting on the sofa
> tra-la-la-la-la-la

But, while the trailing tra-la-la-las here may signal the embrace of a kind of madness, another poem, 'When It's All Over', uses the chant to signify a kind of release. In this poem, the end of a relationship allows for some positive thinking:

> and isn't it frightening
> and releasing
> this daily discovering
> that so much of loving
> is more a consequence of
> fear of loneliness
> Than sudden discovery of love?
> [. . .]
> . . . end up deciding
> Cho!
> Tra-la-la-la-la?
>   (*Rotten Pomerack*, p. 36)

This development in Collins's work makes an interesting point of connection with the work of Amryl Johnson, the last of the poets to be discussed in this chapter.

Amryl Johnson: coming out of limbo

Amryl Johnson is perhaps the least likely of the poets discussed so far to be closely associated with Creole or performative poetry. Certainly most of the poems in her first collections of poetry are fiercely private, employing dense layers of metaphor and a poetic language more readily associated with the page than the stage. So, for example, the title poem of *Long Road to Nowhere* opens:[92]

Distances between
a marginal error
I don't want to be
inside my head
sharing space with
this stranger who
is not
who is
the visible presence
of all things
unseen but felt
in the dark wells
of your mind

Many of Johnson's early poems have as their subject aspects of black history, particularly the legacy of slavery and her own relationship to this history. So, in 'The New Cargo Ship', the poet imagines a group of contemporary Trinidadians on a boat trip to Tobago in their 'historical' roles:

They came out of the belly of their suffering
into
the new cargo ship
joyful
singing songs
drinking rum
[. . .]
Still travelling
   in transit
always in transit
[. . .]
The one whose stomach heaves
with every wave
was the one who threw
himself overboard when
he could take no more
A people on the waves
   of the waves
And where was I in all this?
Where was I?

(*Long Road*, p. 39)

Or, in a poem about the New Cross fire in 1981, 'Circle of Thorns', the reverberations of slavery inflect her testimony to the young black man and woman who were killed. The poem concludes 'So/when they ask/For whom the bell tolls?/Tell them/Male black aged nineteen/Female black aged seventeen/Two faces/in/

a storm' (*Tread Carefully in Paradise*, p. 59). Johnson describes a comment made by one of her publishers in response to her early work: '"I would like to publish your work but how do I market it? It is like a scream of rage. How do I publish a scream of rage?"'[93] Where Habekost describes anger as the energy which propels dub poetry and gives his archetypal, dreadlocked dub poet his poetic identity (and market-ability?), anger, for the black woman poet, appears to be a more unwieldy identity.

There is a sense, too, in many of these poems, of an embattled poetic persona; an embattlement which is articulated more straightforwardly in the following, where Johnson elaborates on her mistrust of critical commentary on her work:

> It comes as quite a shock to read an article sounding off about the inappropriate title of the collection [*Long Road to Nowhere*]. The person then goes on to give the reason. He hasn't interviewed you. He has never met you in his life yet has the audacity to act as if he can get inside your head. He *knows* what you are thinking.[94]

I am suggesting, then, that Johnson is not keen, in her early work, to present herself as a public poet or to stage engagements with 'the people' in the accessibly performative mode characteristic of some of the work of the poets discussed above. There is, perhaps, too much introspection and questioning of her own role as poet for such a poetic identity to be articulated. Nonetheless, Johnson's attitude to, and use of, Creole offers interesting and complex insights into her own development as a poet and to the shift in poetic identities constructed in her more recent work. In *Long Road*, there are several poems which are written using various registers of Trinidadian Creole, but these poems have as their focus specifically Caribbean themes, such as carnival, or the 'sweet talk' of the peanut vendor, or the 'cussing-power' of 'Granny', or fragments of speech from 'the crowd'. The poems which are more conventionally poetic and introspective are written in Standard English and sit separate from the 'Creole poems'.

Amryl Johnson came to England from Trinidad with her parents when she was 11 and, apart from two holiday trips when she was 12 and 16, did not return to the Caribbean for an extensive visit until 1982. Johnson reflects on her relationship to Creole in an essay, 'Coming out of Limbo', in which she discusses her writing:

> I think racial prejudice was the first knife which starts to gouge. With this recognition came the urge to reclaim language. I did not feel confident, sure enough to attempt Creole in my writing. They were desperate times. I felt as if I was in a state of limbo. I had been away from the Caribbean too long. It was no longer mine by rights. As a joke sometimes, I would put on a Trinidadian accent. It always sounded false. Most certainly, not in the least authentic. When I eventually plucked up the courage to try writing in Creole, that also sounded false. The frustration I felt was coupled with a strange sense of guilt and shame. *Neither on paper nor verbally did I sound like a woman from the Caribbean.* Where did I belong? Who was I?[95] [My emphasis]

I am particularly struck by the suggestion here that Creole, far from being something 'natural' – a *noise in the blood* – is something which has to be, but *can be*, learned. Questions of *authenticity*, in this scenario, cannot be settled simply by the 'facts' of biology or the geography of birth; these questions become matters of aesthetic practice and judgement. The boundary between those inside the culture and those outside becomes much more difficult to define and maintain. This sense of being both in *and* outside of Creole culture is sometimes self-consciously fore-grounded in Johnson's poems as in, 'King of the Band', where the speaker acknowledges, 'You're swaying to the music/they're doing something else/ They're jamming' (*Long Road*, p. 17). Or, by implication, in 'Panorama from the North Stand', when the speaker comments on the capacity for involvement and enjoyment ('of true Bacchanalian proportions', p. 14) of the Trinidadians at the steelband competition:

> I am amazed at their capacity for enjoyment
> I am humbled by their generosity
> I am dwarfed by their spontaneity
> I am –
> Am I the only person looking at the band?
> Everyone else has his back to the stage
> Hailing his friends
>   Cedric, Merrill, Look meh!
>   (*Long Road*, p. 15)

Although, in the last three lines above, the poet mocks her own self-consciously poetic gaze on the cultural proceedings, the poem concludes with an unashamedly poetic declamation of admiration, consolidating her in the role of commentator, rather than participant:

> My people are like the leaves of an evergreen
> planted in the finest dawn
> Nurtured on their own audacious extravagance
> they are fresh and total
>   (*Long Road*, p. 16)

In other poems, such as 'Peanut Vendor' and 'Granny in de Market Place', the poet attempts to speak *as* a West Indian, using Creole throughout the text. Both poems are structured as a dialogue, and the point of both poems is, largely, to celebrate the expressive excesses of Creole speech itself:

> Girl, ah tell yuh dese nuts hot from de fire
> Ah does roas' dem meself wit' love an' desire
> Is de trut' Yuh tink ah is some kinda liar?
>   ('Peanut Vendor', *Long Road*, p. 47)

In 'Granny in de Market Place', the old woman's feisty responses to the market vendors dramatizes her refusal to fall for the 'sweet talk' associated with male traders, such as the peanut-sellers:

> De orange sweet?
>
> Ma, it eh hah orange in dis market as sweet as ah does sell
> It like de sun, it taste like sugar an' it juicy as well
>
> Yuh know, boy, what yuh sayin' have a sorta ring
> De las' time ah buy yuh tell meh exactly de same ting
> When ah suck ah fin' all ah dem sour as hell
> De dentures drop out an' meh two gums start tuh swell
>
> (*Long Road*, p. 31)

These two examples are reminiscent of, say, 'Cuss-Cuss' by Louise Bennett, in which the sheer exuberance of the people and their language becomes the point of the poem.[96] These poems, too, unlike some of the more introspective of Johnson's poems mentioned above, seem more obviously to be in the performative mode. In a cassette recording of her poems, *Blood and Wine*,[97] Johnson includes a reading of 'Granny in de Market Place', and I have also been in several audiences in which she has performed it.

I would argue that the poem on the page offers a convincing rendering of Trinidadian Creole, particularly so, of course, for the 'native' reader with an ear for the distinctive intonation and rhythm of this speech. For example, 'me' is spelt 'meh' and this is suggestive of the softer Trinidadian pronunciation than, say, the Jamaican, 'mi'. The orthography used does not make demands of the reader which that of other writers, such as Breeze, sometimes requires. Johnson usually indicates, with the use of apostrophes where a letter is 'missing' in the Creole representation of an English word on the page, as in, for example, 'Dulcine know wha' she talkin' 'bout!' (*Gorgons*, p. 57); this choice keeps the estrangement of those accustomed to Standard English text to a minimum. However, when Johnson reads or performs the poem herself, the English accent and intonation of her 'usual' speaking voice do not comfortably 'fit' the Trinidadian speech on the page. One could argue that her 'voiceprint', to use the evocative phrase of Rohlehr and colleagues,[98] 'betrays' her, or that Johnson's reading foregrounds the hybridity of her own location as a Trinidadian-British poet, based in the UK.

A parallel might also be drawn with David Dabydeen, who speaks in a strikingly English accent when he introduces his poetry but, when he performs from, say, *Coolie Odyssey*, is able to perform fluently the Guyanese dialect as he has 'scripted' it on the page. When performing a poem in Creole, both Johnson and Dabydeen (and there are other examples) have self-consciously to assume a different speaking voice from that of their 'normal' speaking voice and sometimes the 'fit' between voicing and language on the page is not a perfect match. All poets, to some extent, assume a performative persona when reading their poems to an audience – even the really 'cool' ones[99] – but the difference that I have in mind between the 'natural' and 'performance' vocal registers in relation to Johnson and Dabydeen is more fundamental than this.

Further, given the emphasis in many of the discussions outlined at the start of this chapter on orality as something 'innate' and 'natural', then the poet's 'live' presence should operate as an authenticating factor. If we return to the moment, cited in Chapter 2, when Una Marson's performance in an elocution contest earned the following comment from an English critic, Esther Chapman:

> Her principal fault is the pronunciation of certain words, especially the vowel sound in words like 'there' and 'stairs' which she pronounces as 'theere' and 'steers'. This in my opinion, should have disqualified her for second prize.[100]

Alternatively, briefly revisit Kamau Brathwaite's 'History of the Voice', where he discusses a recording of Claude McKay reading his (McKay's) 'St Isaac's Church, Petrograd':

> The only trouble is that McKay had 'trouble' with his syllables, his Clarendon syllables are very 'evident', and he didn't always say 'the', but sometimes said 'de' which is a form in nation language. And these elisions, the sound of them, subtly erode, somewhat, the classical pentametric of his sonnet.[101]

Chapman and Brathwaite are making a similar point, though the ideological motivation is different, about the way Marson's and McKay's voices respectively *betray* their control of a particular discursive form. Rather than attempting to 'police' the perceived 'mismatch' between the poet's voicing of a poem and the poem itself, I would rather read more permissively and recognize the diverse voices of, and *voicings by* Caribbean poets as examples of a productive commitment to hybridity and ventriloquy. What the discussion above also foregrounds is that, for some Caribbean poets, the representation of Creole on the page may read more 'naturally' than when they perform that Creole on the stage. Given the ever-widening diasporic reach of Caribbean culture and writing, hanging on to any notion of an 'authentic' Caribbean Creole voice is becoming a – welcome – impossibility. The kind of cultural and political agenda which may have motivated Johnson's desire to retrieve or relearn Creole will, it is to be hoped, be less of a requirement in the newer Caribbean disaporas.

There is another 'take' on this issue of pronunciation when, in the poem 'For a Sister', Johnson plays with the Creole enunciation of words, a wordplay which is only activated if the reader/listener has access to the page as well as to the sound. The poem, whose central metaphor is that of 'paddling one's own canoe', asks questions about the degree to which the embattlement associated with such defiant self-reliance is necessary or imagined:

> Is that what it is?
> > you
> > me
> de boat ah we

paddling that same
damn canoe
bailing for all we worth
            (*Long Road*, p. 6)

The phrase 'de boat ah we' refers to 'you me', but on the page the 'boat' resonance is also there. The poem concludes with lines which play on this phrasing further:

You
me
de boat
ah we
still
fighting
the monsters
which are
no longer
there
     (*Long Road*,
          p. 7)

Here, 'de boat ah we' resonates again with 'the both ah we' but, because of the arrangement of the lines, the words 'ah we' become an exclamation, 'ah oui', French patois for 'ah, yes'. Once again, the book and the spoken word are in intimate dialogue, 'infecting' and informing each other's discursive spheres.

In Johnson's more recent collection of poems, *Gorgons*, much greater use is made of Creole as a strategy for empowering her poetic voice. The metaphor of the Gorgon/Medusa figure which structures the collection is utilized as a device for speaking in diverse 'tongues', both in terms of the different personae in the collection (there are seven female speakers and one male speaker) and in terms of the use of a range of registers, including Standard English and Creole. The anxiety about location and voice which marked the earlier collection is largely eclipsed by a rhetorical *claiming* of voices and, indeed, the collection ends with the word, 'Shout!' Silence is represented as repressive and disempowering and, at the levels of theme and formal experimentation, finding and articulating voice is the recurring imperative. The Gorgon figure, its head a mass of writhing snakes, resonates with associations of 'dreadness'; the connection here with Rasta dread-ness is not accidental, especially when considered alongside the many references to 'Dan gorgons' (as hyper-macho men) in ragga music. Johnson's Gorgon figure appears to be in playfully formidable dialogue with these more customary male articulations of power. Clearly too, the classical myth of Medusa is also being reworked, so that the collection works to project the mythical Medusa figure into a positively creolized future.

In addition to the associations of power, dreadness and confrontational energy, the attraction of the Medusa figure for Johnson lies also in the possibilities for the more polyphonic poetic identity which it enables. Space does not allow for a discussion of the distinct personae in the collection, but many of the personae speak, 'shout' or 'sing' in voices which, on the page and in Johnson's perform-ances, are declamatory and suggest a much more *public* appeal to an audience than the poet's earlier work indicated. So, for example, 'Dulcine', 'the prophetess', often concludes her announcements with 'Dulcine know wha' she talkin' 'bout!' (*Gorgons*, p. 46).[102] But it is 'Inez' whose *coming to voice* is tracked most clearly in the collection. In 'Lookin' fuh a Voice', the process begins, stutteringly, with the basics of the alphabet:

Abc, def, ghij, klmnop
qrs, tuv
wxyz

Ah makin' babies since ah sixteen
nevah askin' fuh tings dat ah need
[. . .]
But ah strange ting happen today
meh tongue feel like it have somethin' to say
lips start movin' tuh sounds comin' down
an' now ah cahn stop singin' dis song

It goin'
Abc, def, ghij, klmnop
qrs, tuv
wxyz
[repeated again]

(*Gorgons*, p. 15)

After anxieties about the appropriate form and rhythm in which to articulate voice –

De tings ah sayin' wohn be dung on paper
ah usin' meh voice as if tellin' ah story
wen ah get it clear clear in meh min'
Ah hope den ah go mek meh poem rhyme
(' 'Fraid tuh Make Meh Poem Rhyme',
Gorgons, p. 30)

– Inez finds the form in which she *can* make her poems rhyme, the calypso:

An' is so ah come tuh start singin' meh song
Words and trut' tuh voice what is wrong
Usin' de power ah calypso as meh force
So me sistuhs can fin' de dignity dat dey los'
('Calypsonian', *Gorgons*, p. 41)

Eventually, Inez becomes so famous as a calypsonian that 'Now ah hah de prime minister kissin' meh hand/sayin' Miss Inez you is the most important person in the land' (p. 62). The attention paid, in both the layout of the lines, the rhyme scheme, and the rendering of the Creole, assists in a *reading* of it as calypso; Johnson's sung performance, however, offers a fuller rendition of the poem. But, in 'Lookin' fuh a Voice' (cited above), the reader may well be nonplussed about how to read the repeated 'Abc', which, in performance, Johnson sings to the jaunty melody used when children are being encouraged to memorize the alphabet.

Another poem, which in 'live' performance becomes a song, is 'Far and High', and here again the reader may feel a sense of being short-changed of the melody:

> Far and high
> Far and high
>
> We are climbing up the mountain side
> To where the air is sweet and the eagles fly
> A-n-d we ain't coming down
> We're going
> Far and high
>
> (*Gorgons*, p. 77)

Where, on the page, this poem appears rather contrived and too self-consciously poetic, in Johnson's performance of it, the haunting blues melody she sings it to almost *performs* it into poetry.

These questions surrounding the transition/translation from page to stage can be usefully foregrounded in a discussion of 'Wayward Ballerina'. In this poem, the poet dramatizes her perceived inability to control her poetic creations:

> Ballerina was fashioned for elegance
>
> but I flavoured my thoughts with wine before
> I sent her spinning
>
> She came back a stranger
>
> A stranger
> stepped out of her shoes
> sleek
> dangerous
> ravenous
> having tasted the spotlight would not leave
> would not bend to my will
> fought me for control of the page
>
> (*Gorgons*, p. 18)

In my reading of her work, the struggle between the well-behaved, poised ballerina and that of the rebellious dancer who moves 'in or out of the rhythm/never alongside it' (p. 18) is symptomatic of the struggle for, and between, poetic identities in Johnson's oeuvre. The poem concludes:

> but this dancer tensed every sinew
> scrutinized my composition
> defied its validity
>
> creating her own rhythm
> she spat off the page
> to what she assured me
> was her true destiny
> (Gorgons, p. 19)

In the essay cited earlier, Johnson explains her reasons for experimenting with Creole: 'Neither on paper nor verbally did I sound like a woman from the Caribbean.'[103] In *Gorgons*, in her sustained use of Creole, she *does* demonstrate a commitment and facility to write and perform 'as a Caribbean woman', that is, if one accepts Creole as the definitive marker of Caribbean authenticity. It is part of my larger argument in this book to explore some of the limitations and contradictions attendant on this definition of Caribbean-ness. That Johnson restlessly shifts away from Creole-use in the collection which follows on from *Gorgons* nuances this argument further.

The desire for belonging, location and community still haunts the poems in Johnson's most recent collection and remains in tension with a fierce commitment to privacy, control and introspection in her work. In *Gorgons*, this is addressed explicitly in the poem 'Learnin'', which I read as a comment on the poet/ commentator whose questions about 'roots' is answered sharply by the (unidentified) speaker of the poem:

> An' you askin' too much question
> Is like you ehn learn nuttin'
> fuh all de years yuh spen' in Englan'
> you would hah know much more 'bout life
> if yuh had kept yuh tail at home!
> (Gorgons, p. 11)

In another poem, 'Run de Bitch an' Dem', the query about roots gets an even sharper response:

> Li'l piss an' tail gul
> talkin' like she some damn white 'oman
> 'fraid?
> Ah shouldda cuff she 'cross she head!
> [. . .]
> Wen dey come in yuh yard

talkin' dey shew and dey shew
Dey tongue twis' up in dey mout'
wit' too much English
is tuh run dem
run dem
run de bitch an' dem!

Dem so?!
Dem is de wors' kind ah obeah 'woman!
                    (*Gorgons*, pp. 25–6)

    The interrogation of poetic identities and voices continues in Johnson's work; the reclamation of Creole and the performative identity associated with it do not appear to have exhausted the anxieties and self-questioning attendant upon the poet. In her most recent collection, *Calling*, there is a marked absence of Creole-use in the poems. Instead, some of the most powerful poems in the collection appeal to – or escape into – *sound*, unhampered by moorings in a specific language or by culturally specific rhythms. The collection's title, *Calling*, dramatizes the focus on an appeal to sound and is organized around the metaphor of the thorn bird, which sings only at the moment that it impales itself on the thorn bush. By way of conclusion, brief quotes from three poems will have to suffice to indicate the trajectory taken in Johnson's latest collection, 'Tree of Thorns', opens:

dah-d-d
da–da–da
d–d–d–d

Me–I–I–I
What I - ?
What is - ?
I am–is - ?
        (*Calling*,
            p. 17)

'The Earth – His Drum', opens:

Can you hear me?
Can you hear me?
Dumde-dah–dah–dedumdum
Dumdum–de–de–dahdumdum
                (*Calling*, p. 48)

and the opening stanza of 'Rhapsody' (p. 56), 'reads':

~~~Dah~~~~~~~~~deedeedah~~~~~~~~~~~~~~~~~
~~~~~~~~~~~dahdee~~~~~~~~~dah~~~~~~~~~~~~

Here the difficulties for the reading and/or performing of the poem are more profound and of a different nature than those associated with a specifically Creole performativity; perhaps one can argue that it is this very dilemma which the extract above dramatizes. That the difficulties, traumas and pleasures of *trying to find* a voice are staged here in ways which pose equal difficulties for page *and* stage suggests that, while Creole may have facilitated Johnson's 'coming out of limbo', it has also propelled her towards another dilemma.

While it is clear that the four poets discussed in this chapter have, in different ways, been influenced directly by Louise Bennett's work or, indirectly, by the debates about Creole-use generated by her work, the manifestation of this influence is varied and has taken these poets along diverse poetic paths. What these varied trajectories suggest is that Louise Bennett's pioneering work in documenting 'folk culture' has provided a valuable platform from which more hybrid possibilities for Creole-use have been generated. The work of Breeze, Collins and Johnson, in particular, has suggested that diasporic locations as well as the gendered implications of *performing* 'nation language' have had a complex impact upon the use of Creole and have resulted in a much more ambivalently inflected range of meanings to proliferate under the sign 'Creole'. Their work both questions the limitations of the protest tradition associated with their male counterparts, and inflects the more 'domestic' associations of Bennett's use of Creole with a more overtly feminist poetics.

In this chapter I have drawn attention to some of the ways in which Creole-use implies a particular kind of embodied presence for the woman poet, and in the next chapter I focus again on the body, though this time read through a parallel drawn between the sexual and the textual. Once again I focus on four contemporary women poets, allowing the evident differences of each both to support, and problematize, my argument.

Notes

1 Carolyn Cooper, *Noises in the Blood: Orality, Gender and the 'Vulgar' Body of Jamaican Popular Culture*, London, Macmillan, 1993, p. 4.
2 Walter J. Ong, *Orality and Literacy: The Technologizing of the Word*, London, Routledge, 1982, p. 168.
3 Judith Butler, *Gender Trouble: Feminism and the Subversion of Identity*, London, Routledge, 1990, pp. 140–1.
4 Bill Ashcroft, Gareth Griffiths and Helen Tiffin, *The Postcolonial Studies Reader*, London, Routledge, 1995, p. 321.
5 Rex Nettleford (ed.) *Jamaica Labrish: Jamaica Dialect Poems by Louise Bennett*, Kingston, Sangster's, 1966, p. 9.
6 George Lamming, 'The Peasant Roots of the West Indian Novel', in E. Baugh (ed.), *Critics on Caribbean Literature*, George Allen & Unwin, 1979, p. 25.
7 Nettleford, *Jamaica Labrish*, pp. 9–10.

8 Mervyn Morris, introduction to Louise Bennett, *Selected Poems*, Kingston, Sangster's, 1982, p. xi.

9 Edward Kamau Brathwaite, *The Arrivants: A New World Trilogy*, Oxford, Oxford University Press, 1978 [1967].

10 Edward Kamau Brathwaite, 'Francina', in *The Arrivants*, pp. 214–15.

11 Edward Kamau Brathwaite, 'History of the Voice: The Development of Nation Language in Anglophone Caribbean Poetry', in *Roots*, Ann Arbor, University of Michigan Press, 1993, p. 260.

12 Ibid., p. 266.

13 Ibid., p. 271.

14 Antony Easthope, *Poetry as Discourse*, London, Methuen, 1983, pp. 65–9.

15 Brathwaite, 'History of the Voice', p. 283.

16 Ibid., p. 298.

17 Derek Walcott, *What the Twilight Says: Essays*, London, Faber, 1998 [first published as the preface to Derek Walcott, *Dream on Monkey Mountain*, New York, The Noonday Press, 1970].

18 Ibid., p. 7.

19 Ibid., p. 25.

20 Antonio Benitez-Rojo, *The Repeating Island: The Caribbean and the Postmodern Perspective*, Durham, NC, Duke University Press, 1992, p. 10.

21 Patrick Chamoiseau, *Childhood*, London, Granta, 1999, pp. 56–7.

22 Lucien Taylor, 'Creolite Bites: A Conversation with Patrick Chamoiseau, Raphael Confiant and Jean Bernabé in *Transition* 74, 7, 2, pp. 154–5.

23 Walcott, 'A Letter to Chamoiseau', in *What the Twilight Says*, pp. 213–32.

24 Ibid., p. 18.

25 Christian Habekost, *Dub Poetry: 19 Poets from England and Jamaica*, Neustadt, Michael Swinn, 1986.

26 Ibid., p. 15.

27 Cooper, *Noises in the Blood*, p. 72.

28 Ibid., p. 71.

29 Stewart Brown, Mervyn Morris and Gordon Rohlehr (eds), *Voiceprint: An Anthology of Oral and Related Poetry from the Caribbean*, London, Longman, 1989, p. 17.

30 Ibid., p. 14.

31 Roger D. Abrahams, *The Man-of-Words in the West Indies: Performance and the Emergence of Creole Culture*, Baltimore, MD, Johns Hopkins University Press, 1983.

32 Cooper, *Noises in the Blood*, p. 141.

33 To be fair, Cooper does acknowledge this issue of essentialism, *Noises in the Blood*, p. 4:

> The emotive trope of blood and bone connotes what may be constructed as 'racist' assumptions about biologically-determined culture, if the label is applied by the alienating Other. Assumed by the in-group, this figure of speech denotes a genealogy of ideas, a blood-line of beliefs and practices that are transmitted in the body, in oral discourse.

However, invoking notions of an 'in-group' which revolves around a 'blood-line' does *not* avoid the dangers of essentialism. A strategic (to use Spivak's formulation) essentialism seems to me to be valid but in Cooper's paradigm the boundaries of the in-group appear fixed in relation to a black, nationalist Jamaican identification; a paradigm which is limited in both sociopolitical and aesthetic terms, given the diverse ethnicities encompassed in the region.

34 Erna Brodber, *Myal*, London, New Beacon, 1988, p. 109.

35 This is the term, along with 'spirit thievery', which Brodber uses in *Myal* to explore the variety of ways in which Caribbean people can become alienated from their 'true selves'.

36 Karin Barber, 'African-language Literature and Postcolonial Criticism', *Research in African Literature*, 26, 4, Winter, pp. 3–30.

37 Anthony Easthope, *Poetry as Discourse*, p. 15.

38 Mervyn Morris, 'Printing the Performance', in M. Morris, *Is English We Speaking and Other Essays*, Kingston, Ian Randle Publishers, 1999, p. 51.

39 Barber, 'African-language Literature', p. 5.

40 Linton Kwesi Johnson, Introduction, in Valerie Bloom, *Touch Mi; Tell Mi!* London, Bogle-L'Ouverture Publications Ltd., 1983.

41 Jamaica Kincaid, *A Small Place*, London, Virago, 1988, p. 25.

42 As performance often takes place at special events such as those listed by Cooper, *Noises in the Blood*, pp. 70–1, 'for example, African Liberation Day, International Women's Day; or festivals – Reggae Sunsplash in Jamaica, the International Bookfair of Radical Black and Third World Books in London', the sense of 'community' is often 'built-in' to the event.

43 One of Bloom's poems, 'Interview', was also included in Sylvia Paskin, Jay Ramsay and Jeremy Silver (eds), *Angels of Fire: An Anthology of Radical Poetry in the '80s*, London, Chatto & Windus, 1986, p. 95.

44 James Berry, *News for Babylon: The Chatto Book of Westindian-British Poetry*, London, Chatto & Windus, 1984, p. xxii.

45 Jimi Rand in Berry (ed.) *News for Babylon*, p. 113.

46 Valerie Bloom in Lauretta Ngcobo (ed.), *Let It Be Told: Black Women Writers in Britain*, London, Virago, 1988, p. 86.

47 Jean Buffong in Joan Anim-Addo (ed.) *Framing the Word: Gender and Genre in Caribbean Women's Writing*, London, Whiting & Birch, 1996, pp. 93–5.

48 See discussion in Ong, *Orality and Literacy*, of 'secondary orality', pp. 135–8.

49 Valerie Bloom in Ngcobo, *Let It Be Told*, p. 85.

50 Ibid., p. 86.

51 Morris, 'Printing the Performance', p. 5.

52 Valerie Bloom, *Yuh Hear Bout: Selected Spoken Works*, London, 57 Productions, 1997. Bloom is joined by Jean 'Binta' Breeze on two of the tracks recorded on this cassette.

53 But see the 'translations' of some of the poems in David Dabydeen, *Turner: New and Selected Poems*, London, Cape Poetry, 1994.

54 Stewart Brown, Mervyn Morris and Gordon Rohlehr (eds), *Voiceprint: An Anthology of Oral and Related Poetry from the Caribbean*, London, Longman, 1989. Rohlehr's introduction to this anthology suggests that the term 'voiceprint' signals both the emphasis on the voice and the distinctiveness of particular poetic voices in Caribbean poetry.

55 Jean 'Binta' Breeze, *Riddym Ravings*, London, Race Today Collective, 1988; *Spring Cleaning*, London, Virago, 1992; *On the Edge of an Island*, Newcastle upon Tyne, Bloodaxe, 1997; *Tracks*, London, LKJ Records, 1991; *Riddym Ravings*, Kingston, Jamaica, Ayeola Records, 1985; *Riding on de Riddym: Selected Spoken Works*, London, 57 Productions, 1997.

56 Jean 'Binta' Breeze, 'Can a Dub Poet Be a Woman?', *Woman: A Cultural Review*, 1, 90, 1990, pp. 47–9.

57 Mervyn Morris, quoted in Cooper, *Noises in the Blood*, p. 73.

58 Cooper, *Noises in the Blood*, p. 68.

59 Christian Habekost, *Verbal Riddim: The Politics and Aesthetics of African-Caribbean Dub Poetry*, Amsterdam-Atlanta, Editions Rodopi, 1993, p. 45.

60 Workshop held as part of the conference, 'Kicking Daffodils' at Oxford Brookes University, April 1989.

61 Breeze, 'Can a Dub Poet Be a Woman?', p. 48.

62 Morris describes Mutabaruka as having an 'impressive face, black with leonine locks, a grey patch just above the forehead', 'Mutabaruka' in Morris, *Is English We Speaking*, pp. 53–8. This essay offers a fine, detailed discussion of the ways in which Mutabaruka performs his poetry.

63 Breeze, 'Going Home' on audio cassette, *Riding de Riddym: Selected Spoken Works*.

64 Morris, 'Dub Poetry?' *Is English We Speaking*, p. 41.

65 'The Message Is the Most Important: An Interview with Lillian Allen', by Christian Habekost in Marlies Glaser and Marion Pausch, *Caribbean Writers: Between Orality and Writing, Matatu* No. 12, Amsterdam, Editions Rodopi, 1994, p. 49. Lillian Allen is based in Canada.

66 Oku Onuora, quoted in Morris, 'Dub Poetry?' in *Is English We Speaking*, p. 38.

67 Michael Smith, *It a Come*, Morris (ed.) London, Race Today Publications, 1986, p. 13.

68 Breeze, *On the Edge of an Island*, p. 22.

69 Breeze, *Riddym Ravings*, p. 58.

70 Breeze, *On the Edge of an Island*, p. 58.

71 Morris, 'Printing the Performance', p. 49.

72 Ibid.

73 Breeze, *Riding on de Riddym*; transcript of the lyrics is mine.

74 Oku Onuora quoted in Morris, 'Dub Poetry?', p. 38.

75 Breeze, 'Can a Dub Poet Be a Woman?', p. 49.

76 Breeze, *On the Edge of an Island* Breeze, *On the Edge of an Island*, p. 78.

77 Various other Caribbean writers and intellectuals became involved in Grenada; see Dionne Brand's, *In Another Place, Not Here*, London, The Women's Press, 1997, for a fictional account of her own involvement.

78 Merle Collins has published two volumes of poetry, *Because the Dawn Breaks!*, London, Karia Press, 1985, and *Rotten Pomerack*, London, Virago, 1992.

79 Merle Collins, 'Themes and Trends in Caribbean Writing Today' in Helen Carr (ed.), *From My Guy to Sci-Fi: Genre and Women's Writing in the Postmodern World*, London, Pandora, 1989, pp. 179–90.

80 There is an echo (via *The Tempest*) here of the last two lines of Martin Carter's 'Looking at Your Hands', You must know/I do not sleep to dream, but dream to change/the world. In *Martin Carter: Selected Poems*, Guyana, Red Thread Women's Press, 1997, p. 39.

81 'Up the Hill' refers to the location of Grenada's prison; while the specific addressee is not identified in the poem, it seems reasonable to assume that it is Bernard Coard, whose challenge to Maurice Bishop triggered the collapse of the Grenadian revolution.

82 Merle Collins, 'Themes and Trends in Caribbean Writing Today', p. 188.

83 The layout and spelling used when this poem is reprinted in *Rotten Pomerack* is interestingly different; the lines quoted above are 'tidied up' and rendered in less fragmented lines and in a slightly more 'standard' English, 'the' instead of 'de', for example: 'Is not no nancy-story, non/is a serious joke/I used to laugh at Grannie/repeat after her/till one day/I check the map/and find/the spelling/little different to how I did think/but the geography straight/like a arrow/tip focusing on the arctic ocean' (p. 55).

84 Merle Collins, *Butterfly: Selected Spoken Works*, 57 Productions, 1996.

85 Two recent performances stand out: one at the Caribbean Women Writers Conference in Grenada in 1998 and one at the Cave Hill Campus of the University of the West Indies for the 'Frank Collymore Conference' in July 1999.

86 Merle Collins, 'Themes and Trends in Caribbean Writing Today', p. 188. My emphasis.

87 In the version of this poem which Collins reads on the 57 Productions recording, *Butterfly: Selected Spoken Works*, there are substantial changes.

88 *Watchers and Seekers: Creative Writing by Black Women in Britain*, Rhonda Cobham and Merle Collins (eds), London, The Women's Press, 1987, p. 118.

89 Bennett, *Selected Poems*, pp. 4–5.

90 Collins, 'Themes and Perspectives in Caribbean Writing Today', p. 181.

91 Ibid., p. 188.

92 Amryl Johnson has published several collections of poetry: *Long Road to Nowhere*, London, Virago, 1985; *Tread Carefully in Paradise* (which combines poems from *Shackles* and *Long Road to Nowhere*) Coventry, Cofa Press, 1991; *Gorgons*, Coventry, Cofa Press, 1992; *Calling*, Oxford, Sable Productions, 1999.

93 Amryl Johnson, in Lauretta Ngcobo, *Let It Be Told*, p. 36.
94 Ibid., p. 44.
95 Amryl Johnson, 'Coming out of Limbo', in Susan Sellers (ed.) *Delighting the Heart: A Notebook by Women Writers*, London, The Women's Press, 1989, p. 204. [My emphasis]
96 Louise Bennett, 'Cuss-Cuss', in *Jamaica Labrish*, p. 188:

> Gwan gal yuh fava teggereg,
> Ah wey yuh gwine do?
> Yuh an yuh boogooyagga fren
> Dem tink me fraid o' yuh?

97 Amryl Johnson, *Blood and Wine*, Coventry, Cofa Press, 1992.
98 Brown, Morris and Rohlehr, *Voiceprint*.
99 I am thinking of a poet like Mervyn Morris, whose performance of his work often seems like a laconic extension of his 'regular', understated conversational style.
100 Delia Jarrett-Macauley, *The Life of Una Marson: 1905–1965*, Manchester, Manchester University Press, 1998, p. 28.
101 Brathwaite, 'History of the Voice', p. 277.
102 Despite this more 'public' voice, Johnson's own introductions to both *Gorgons* and *Calling*, in explaining the structure and artistic intention 'behind' the collections, appear to direct the reception of the poems in what is perceived as a hostile context of reception.
103 Johnson, 'Coming out of Limbo', p. 204. [My emphasis]

4 More body talk: righting or writing the body?

The work of Lorna Goodison, Mahadai Das, Grace Nichols and Marlene Nourbese Philip

When the African came to the New World she brought with her nothing but her body and all the memory and history which body could contain.[1]

Whenever the power of the nation is evoked [. . .] we are more likely than not to find it couched as a *love of country*: an eroticized nationalism. [. . .] Indeed, certain sexual identities and practices are less represented and representable in nationalism.[2]

We need languages that regenerate us, warm us, give birth to us. [. . .] In order to reconnect the book with the body and with pleasure, we must disintellectualize writing.[3]

In this sort of house lived people whose skin glistened with exhaustion and whose faces were sad even when they had a reason to be happy, people for whom history had been a big, dark room, which made them hate silence.[4]

The epigraphs above indicate some of the critical contexts relevant to my discussion of representations of women's bodies in the work of four Caribbean women poets. The previous chapter focused on women poets whose use of Creole involved a diverse range of choices with regard to the embodiment of poetic identity. This choice of Creole signalled a preference for working within the performative and oral modes, though I argued that these modes were being refashioned, in response to limitations which relate both to gender and to the poets' shifting geo-cultural locations. Although the poets discussed in this chapter make use of Creole in their work, they do so much less extensively and in ways which do not necessarily foreground the performative and oral modes. If, as I have argued above, the body image for women involved in performative Creole poetry requires a 'pruning' of their explicitly 'sexual selves' and that diasporic relocations often result in more internalized performative voices, then in this chapter I want to explore the ways in which the woman's body and sexuality are handled – or avoided – on the page, as opposed to the stage. Does the printed word afford a greater range of possibilities for writing about women's bodies? Indeed, is there any evidence of *writing the body*, French feminist style? Is the woman's body *righted*, *written* or *written out* of the text?

The body has always been central to feminism, and many have argued that, for woman, 'biology is destiny', and that it is woman's reproductive functions which have resulted in her being trapped in the 'private sphere' and limited her potential for active involvement in the 'public sphere'. Woman's body in this sociopolitical context is often associated with pain and anxiety, and the home as the context within which the repressive drama surrounding the woman's body is enacted. The resultant focus on marriage, the family and housework as oppressive was quickly challenged by black women, who argued that this emphasis did not take into account the specific ways in which 'race' impacts upon black women's experiences of themselves as 'embodied', complicating their interpretation of public/private spaces. Black feminist scholarship since the 1970s has been steadily filling in the 'blanks' in white feminist accounts. Barbara Omolade, for example, in 'Hearts of Darkness', argues:

> The very traditional experiences of motherhood and sex within marriage were not necessarily viewed as oppressive to black women, for they were the literal and symbolic weapons she could utilize to assure the biological and social reproduction of black people. Marriage and motherhood were humanizing experiences that gave her life meaning, purpose, and choice. These experiences were denied within the racist milieu where her humanity was questioned and her human rights and privileges to love and be loved were denied.[5]

Within the context of the Caribbean, 'the body' has always been of central importance, and the first of my epigraphs succinctly conveys the historical precedents which generated such a concern. Michael Dash argues that this concern with the body is crucial to an understanding of the region's writing: 'The ever shifting, unstable relationship between body and non-body, between dismembering and re-membering, is a continuous aesthetic and thematic concern.'[6]

Frantz Fanon had also emphasized this dynamic, arguing, in *Black Skin, White Masks*, that, in the white imagination, the black man is 'the biological-sensual-genital-nigger'[7] existing solely *as a body*. By contrast, Fanon's reluctance to analyse or speculate on 'the woman of color' is striking. In 'The Negro and Psychopathology', for instance, he says: 'Those who grant our conclusions on the psychosexuality of the white woman may ask what we have to say about the woman of color. *I know nothing of her.*'[8] While the invisibility of the black woman is worrying here, it is clearly also a recognition of the way in which it is the black *man* who is constructed as so menacing a presence in colonial representations of its 'other'. The potency and danger associated with the black male body in colonial discourse, and the relentless pathologizing of this body, perhaps also explain the robustness of the challenges generated in response to such distortions and the tendency for the black woman's embodied subjectivity to be consistently elided.

Nobody go f . . . with my poetry again

It is perhaps not surprising that the 'body at the centre of Caribbean literature' has, until very recently, continued to be that of the black *male* subject. The persona in 'Folkways', in Brathwaite's *The Arrivants*, for example, speaks out at the reader as the very 'biological-sensual-genital-nigger' described by Fanon:

> I am a fuck-
> in' negro,
> man, hole
> in my head,
> brains in
> my belly;
> black skin
> red eyes
> broad back
> big you know
> what: not very quick
> to take offence
> but once
> offended, watch
> that house
> you livin' in
> an' watch that lit-
> le sister.[9]

Brathwaite exploits a range of moods and voices in the remainder of the poem to convey the traumas of history which make such an articulation necessary. More recently, David Dabydeen, in *Coolie Odyssey* and *Slave Song*, frequently deploys what he describes as 'the erotic energies of the colonial experience'.[10] Dabydeen configures this as a fraught encounter between the black man (in Dabydeen's poetry, 'black' encompasses both 'Indian' and 'African') and a Miranda figure who functions as the 'forbidden fruit' or prized possession of the white man. So, in 'Slave Song', the speaker fantasizes, or boasts:

> Is so when yu dun dream she pink tit,
> Totempole she puss,
> Leff yu teetmark like a tattoo in she troat![11]

The violence of this image strikes an uneasy chord, however much one rationalizes the violence as being integral to the poetics of the persona being used. Clearly, Dabydeen is deliberately overdoing the 'savage' stereotype in a manoeuvre which seeks to deconstruct it, but there is, perhaps, too much sheer delight and rhetorical swagger in lines such as 'Bu yu caan stap me cack dippin in de honeypot/Drippin at de tip an happy as a hottentot!'[12] for this reader to be convinced that it is offered 'in good faith'. In a different vein, Derek Walcott's 'Shabine' figure in 'The Schooner Flight' is constructed as robustly male as he leaves his island behind, watching 'the sky burn/above Laventille pink as the gown/in which the woman I left was sleeping'. Later, on the journey, 'Vincie' makes fun of Shabine's poetic ambitions:

> Had an exercise book,
> this same one here, that I using to write
> my poetry, so one day this man snatch it
> from my hand, and start throwing it left and right
> to the rest of the crew, bawling out, 'Catch it,'
> and start mincing me like I was some hen
> because of the poems.

Shabine throws a knife and settles the matter:

> There wasn't much pain,
> Just plenty blood, and Vincie and me best friend,
> But none of them go fuck with my poetry again.[13]

Clearly, this is not the only kind of poetic persona which Derek Walcott constructs in his work, nor are the examples taken from Brathwaite and Dabydeen above. I have selected these texts as symptomatic examples of the kind of robustly male poetics and vigorous poetic identities which have been articulated in response to the violence of the colonial encounter, and to signal the way in which sexuality is crucially implicated in constructions of the nation. The diverse and nuanced range of poetic personae exploited in the postcolonial Caribbean by male West Indian poets, including Walcott, Brathwaite and Dabydeen, indicates more interrogative and subtle representations of the nation than constraints of space allow me to discuss here.

Forbidden fruit, fruit of the land

Woman, by contrast, has often been represented *as* the land; either by the colonizers in their depictions of the New World as virginal territory to be penetrated and conquered, or by nationalists for whom the woman/land conflation functions as the obvious symbol of what is being fought *for*. If the white woman, in this scenario, is often depicted as 'forbidden fruit', brown and black women are represented as 'the fruit of the land'. G.R. Coulthard, in an early exploration of the impact of race on literature, *Race and Colour in Caribbean Literature*, commented on the propensity in the pre-independence literary context for the rejection of white European cultural values to be projected onto and encapsulated in the figure of the white woman: 'Another aspect of the rehabilitation of the Negro woman in Caribbean literature is a criticism of the white woman as being over-civilized, over-sophisticated. In contrast, the Negro woman appears more elemental, more

of a woman.'[14] He quotes an extract from a poem by the Martiniquan poet Lionel
Attuly, where the white woman (who 'talked and talked and talked') is presented as
encased in the trappings of femininity (girdles, corsets, garters, brassieres) which
are symbolic of the deceitful trappings of 'civilization' itself. The 'rehabilitation'
of the black woman as the symbol of everything which the white woman is *not*
clearly has its limitations. In the extract below, from a poem by the Puerto Rican
poet Luis Pales Matos, the 'native' woman, conflated with the fruits of the land,
results in a poetic 'fruit salad' which verges on the farcical:

> Here is the sapodilla in its green suit
> with its fine soft muslin pants, here is the star-apple with its childish milk; here
>   the pineapple
> with its soprano crown. All the fruits, oh mulatto girl, you offer me all the
>   fruits
> in the clear bay of your body,
> burnished by the suns of the tropics.[15]

More explicitly in the poem, 'The Maroon Girl', published in 1950 by the
Jamaican poet W. Adolphe Roberts, the brown woman is again conflated with
the vegetation of the land:

> *She is Jamaica poised against attack.*
> Her woods are hung with orchids; the still flame
> Of red hibiscus lights her path, and starred
> With orange and coffee blossoms is her yard.
> Fabulous, pitted mountains close the frame.[16]

Here, the figure of the elemental brown (or 'mulatto') woman, embodying *all*
ethnicities, is conflated with Nature and with the land being fought for – by her
fathers – so that she *is* Jamaica. That both Matos and Roberts use the mulatto, or
'brown' woman, as symbol of the new nation, rather than a *black* woman, is also
interesting, reflecting both a desire to represent the racial diversity of their
respective new nations but perhaps also indicating the limits of their aesthetic
'rehabilitation' of the *black* woman. A more complete embrace of the black
woman came later with the negritude movement and the conflation of the black
woman with 'mother Africa'. In Kamau Brathwaite's *Mother Poem*, the clustering
of woman under the sign of 'the land' is extended so that motherland and mother
are invoked frequently enough to be interchangeable, 'But/muh/muh/muh/me
mudda/mud/black fat/soft fat man-/ure'.[17]

It is perhaps not surprising, given the overdetermined context outlined above,
that Caribbean women have only recently 'come out' in their writing as embodied
and sexualized subjects. Although there are numerous representations of the
maternal body in Caribbean women's texts, there are far fewer examples of the
explicitly sexual female body. Dionne Brand, for example, argues, 'And then again
it's self-preservation. In a world where Black women's bodies are so sexualized,

avoiding the body as sexual is a strategy.'[18] When representations of the 'non-maternal' woman's body *are* presented, it invariably signals anxiety and fear. Jamaica Kincaid's protagonist in her novel *Annie John* is alarmed by the changes in her body on reaching puberty: 'I thought of begging my mother to ask my father if he could build me a set of clamps into which I could screw myself at night before I went to sleep and which would surely cut back on my growing.'[19]

Erna Brodber, in her first novel, suggests that the black woman seek the protection of a kumbla (calabash) to avoid being trapped by her biology: 'What a life! What an abominable scrap heap thing is this thing womb.'[20]

Sexing the text: writing (about) the body

Western feminist discourses on sexuality have a well-documented history. Virginia Woolf, in 'Professions for Women', describes the taboo on writing about the body:

> To speak without figure she had thought of something, something about the body, about the passions which it was unfitting for her as a woman to say. Men, her reason told her would be shocked. [. . .] She could write no more.[21]

In response to this taboo, a range of positions have been articulated. One strand of feminism has interrogated, and exposed, the gendered assumptions of the received canon of English Literature and asked questions about if/where women writers might fit into conventional notions of literary traditions. Where, for example, Harold Bloom's argument about 'the anxiety of influence' suggests that male writers engage in an Oedipal battle with the patriarchs of literary tradition, many feminists have argued that women writers seek to embrace fellow women writers in an inclusive, rather than contestatory, notion of tradition.

Sandra Gilbert and Susan Gubar, in *No Man's Land*, quote several 'patriarchal bards' who explicitly metaphorize writing as male, including Auden's view, that 'The poet is the father who begets the poem which the language bears' and Emerson's call for 'spermatic, man-making words'.[22] Derek Walcott's use, in some of his earlier work, of a New World Adam figure, obviously invokes a particularly male sense of linguistic power – that of Adam naming the newly created universe. Alicia Ostriker, in her account of women's poetry, *Stealing the Language: Women and Poetic Identity*, argues that many women poets, by contrast to the 'white goddesses' and other gentle muses of their male counterparts, represent poetic inspiration as a violent invasion of their bodies.[23]

Several other feminist commentators have argued that the anxiety experienced by many women about their *right to write* often results in a preponderance of poems which focus on this theme. According to Cora Kaplan:

> A very high proportion of women's poems are about the right to speak and write. [. . .] To be a woman and a poet presents many women poets with such a profound split between their social, sexual identity (their 'human' identity) and their artistic practice that the split becomes the insistent

subject, sometimes overt, often hidden or displaced, of much women's poetry.[24]

Many of the Caribbean women poets I discuss reveal the kind of anxiety Kaplan describes, and this is evidenced in the many poems in which these poets agonize about their poetic roles, their choice of poetic identities, and the implications with regard to 'body image' associated with that choice of poetic identity.

Another approach to the link between the body and the text is one which focuses less on the thematics and more on the aesthetics of representing the body; this difference could perhaps be summed up as the difference between writing *about* the body and *writing* the body. In this latter approach, French feminists, associated with *écriture féminine*, have argued that woman's body needs to be *re-read* and *rewritten* as a site of multiple pleasures and possibilities, rather than as the site of limitation and repression: 'Why so few texts? Because so few women have as yet won back their body. Women must write through their bodies, they must invent the impregnable language that will wreck partitions, classes and rhetorics.'[25]

The kind of writing practice associated with *écriture féminine* is varied, and draws on the work of a range of French theorists, chiefly Julia Kristeva, Hélène Cixous and Luce Irigaray. Each of these writers has a particular focus, but all share a perception of patriarchal discourses as rigidly linear, clinical, abstracted and tightly structured around a hierarchized series of binary oppositions. *Écriture féminine* seeks not so much to unlock the code of patriarchal discourses as to undermine the linguistic structures which make meanings possible. A 'feminine writing', which Cixous and Kristeva suggest can be practised also by male writers, would see writing as the site of multiple possibilities, would seek to deconstruct or undo these binary oppositions, would celebrate a much freer play of signifiers, would challenge the dictates of 'proper' grammatical structures and make full use of polyphony and difference in textual practice. A recurring emphasis in *écriture féminine* is the importance of the body as a focus of signification. Chantal Chawaf, in the fourth of my epigraphs, urges a release of the body into the written text; 'If a music of femininity is arising out of its own oppression, it materializes through the rediscovered body.'[26]

Clearly, this focus on 'writing the body' does not imply the possibility of some unmediated transfer of body into text but suggests a *remetaphorization* of woman's body; a metaphoricity structured around a notion of difference between the female and male libidinal economies. In this account, the former is seen as diffuse, fluid and multiple, the latter as unified, solid and singular in focus. Further, Kristeva argues for a recognition of the multiple possibilities associated with the 'semiotic', the (ungendered) rhythmic pulsions and sensations experienced by the child in the pre-verbal stage when its identity is undifferentiated from any Other. Articulation of this non-verbal communication, if released into the writing, can undermine the Law of the Father and the status of the phallus as the transcendental signifier. Cixous also stresses the centrality of the mother as a source for textual empowerment; as Susan Sellers argues: 'Cixous believes the non-repression and inclusion of the maternal body in writing presents a link with the pre-symbolic plenitude between self and m/other, and hence a way round the loss, exile and perpetual alienation of the masculine schema.'[27] In this scenario, the maternal – and the womb – are re-installed as signifiers of plentitude and possibility; not the 'scrap-heap thing' of Erna Brodber's gritty construction above.

Retrieving the lost continent and the lost maternal body

In this scenario, the mother's body and voice/'milk' represent a space which is uncontaminated by the Law of the Father and the dictates and constrictions of patriarchal rules. It is the submerged or repressed voice of the mother which the woman writer is urged to reclaim. There are suggestive parallels between the nostalgic yearning for a return to the mother expressed by Cixous and the invocation of the mother in Brathwaite's work. In a short commentary, titled 'Submerged Mothers', he suggests that:

> Woman – especially the black woman – has always occupied a special place in books because she has always been a submerged/invisible presence and force. [. . .] In a world shaped by the acquisitive ego, the 'unconscious' female had an important part to play in the 'conscience' of the system; and in missile societies (that is, in expansionist, technological/industrial societies) where the male was war-head and explorer, the woman often acquiesced in, even insisted on, this role.[28]

Brathwaite implicitly *feminizes* black oppression as a group experience, with *woman* symbolizing the extreme boundary of this oppression. Black women, perceived as a submerged, archetypally oppressed group, are symbolically associated with 'the circle' of home, Creole culture, motherland and mother tongue by contrast to 'the missile' of aggressively imperialist and patriarchal European culture. Hélène Cixous, in a reverse critical move, claims the language of 'black power' to generalize *women's* oppression:

> We the precocious, we the repressed of culture, our lovely mouths gagged with pollen, our wind knocked out of us, we the labyrinths, the ladders, the trampled spaces, the bevies, – *we are black and we are beautiful.* [My emphasis][29]

Both Brathwaite and Cixous use metaphors here which result in somewhat problematic appropriative rhetorical gestures. The emphasis on *textual* empowerment, with which *écriture féminine* has been associated, has also been criticized for being apolitical and for overplaying the role of linguistic/semiotic resistance while underplaying that of sociopolitical activism. It is beyond the scope of this chapter to engage fully with the debate between the 'constructionists' and the 'essentialists' (to use Diana Fuss's shorthand).[30] However, while recognizing the limitations *and* excesses of *écriture féminine*, the playful textual strategies associated with it are useful correctives to the tendency, in Caribbean discourses, towards the privileging of realist modes.

Lorna Goodison: delivering the word

In an interview with *The Guardian* newspaper, cited in *I Am Becoming My Mother* (inside, back cover), Goodison says:

> I'm a poet, but I didn't choose poetry – it chose me [. . .] it's a dominating, intrusive tyrant. It's something I have to do – a wicked force.

Many of the poems in Goodison's first volume of poetry, *Tamarind Season*,[31] present an image of the poet as embattled, and poetry is configured as a physically abusive force, such as in 'For the Poet at Fort Augusta', which begins, 'Knowing how the muse has imperialist tendencies/How she colonizes your being and roomspace' (p. 60). Or in, 'I'm in Here Hiding', where the poet is besieged by words:

> I'm in here hiding from words
> they cloud my vision like wide-winged birds.
> Some darker ones harsh and crowlike
> picking issues to barebone.
> (*Tamarind Season*, p. 40)

This association of poetry with physical pain is also linked to the pain of giving birth, and there are several references to the *delivery* of poems. In 'For R & R in the Rain', the speaker rails against the intruder who interrupts 'what might have been the painless delivery of a poem' (*Tamarind Season*, p. 42). In 'My Last Poem', the writing of poetry is imaged throughout in terms of the woman's body, so that difficulties in the life and in the writing of that life find their most concentrated expression when mapped onto the body:

> you are too tightly bound, too whole
> he said
> I loosened my hair and I bled
> now you send conflicting messages they said
> divided I turned both ways and fled.
> (*I Am Becoming My Mother*, pp. 7–8)

But the connection between pain and poetry is perhaps most dramatically made in 'My Last Poem (Again)', in *Heartease*, where the speaker suggests that the tangled connections between the painful experiences of life and the impetus to record those moments results in an existence of intolerably heightened awareness. Goodison echoes Sylvia Plath in the vivid physicality of imagery in this poem, 'Goodbye poems, you bled me shiny bottles of red feelings./Poems, you were blood leeches attaching yourself to me' (*Heartease*, p. 14). And later in the same poem:

> When the King of Swords gutted me

and left me for dead, in my insides were found
clots of poems, proving that poets are made of poems
(Heartease, p. 14)

The 'King of Swords', referred to above, is pursued more sustainedly in the poem 'Ceremony for the Banishment of the King of Swords' (*Heartease*, pp. 51–5), where he represents a powerful but itinerant lover. Here, the 'king's' love is configured graphically as an invasion of the woman's body: 'He unsheathes the sword aligned with his backbone and sinks it into your chest.'

Love for her island, Jamaica, is sometimes also represented as the source of pain, as in 'Jamaica 1980', where the poet's role, following the violence of the 1980 elections when 800 people were killed, is a tragic one:

And mine the task of writing it down
as I ride in shame round this blood-stained town.
And when the poem refuses to believe
and slimes to aloes in my hands
mine is the task of burying the dead
I the late madonna of barren lands.
(I Am Becoming, p. 10)

These lines suggest a poet whose role as social conscience and commentator is taken on wearily, as an almost inescapable burden. Walcott's poem 'Mass Man' concludes in a similar vein:

Upon your penitential morning
Some skull must rub its memory with ashes,
Some mind must squat down howling,
Some hand must crawl and recollect your rubbish,
Someone must write your poems.[32]

Goodison's two most recent collections of poetry indicate a shift in poetic identity and poetic role which has interesting implications for the focus on the body which is the concern of this chapter. Taking the title poem of each of her five collections as emblematic (though clearly not exhaustive), I will trace this trajectory, arguing that Goodison moves towards the public role articulated in the extract from 'Jamaica 1980' above, and extended in the 'Heartease' poems and then shifts direction in the two most recent collections, *To Us, All Flowers Are Roses* and *Turn Thanks*, to a more individuated poetic role. This trajectory also suggests a return to the body.

In 'Tamarind Season', the fruits on the tamarind tree are used as a metaphor for the spinster woman (though in Jamaican culture 'tamarind season' is also a more generalized reference to hard times). The regularly indented shape of the long, hard, brown tamarind pod is exploited for its similarities to the shapely contours of the non-pregnant woman, and the uneven line lengths reiterate this visually on the page:

The skin atrophies
to a case of spinster brown.

the soft welcome within
needs protecting
so she grows wasp-waisted
again
wasp-waisted
(*Tamarind Season*, p. 73)

Goodison draws a parallel between the fruit and female sexuality, using the hard
case of the tamarind to represent the spinster's protective abstinence. In the third
stanza, the poet uses the image of the wizened fruit rattling in its now too-big case
to evoke the barrenness of the spinster in linguistic – as well as sexual – terms:

The welcome turns sour
she finds a woman's tongue
and clacks curses at the wind
for taking advantage
(*Tamarind Season*, p. 73)

Unfulfilled sexually, the spinster becomes that other female stereotype, the shrew,
whose tongue is her only weapon. The ambiguity of this stanza – is the wind
being cursed by the frustrated spinster who wants to be taken or because it *is*
taking advantage of her immobility by buffeting her as it likes? – leaves the reader
with a sense that the moment of 'delivery of the word', paralleling the spinster's
impotence, is also deferred and we are left with the image/sound of the
impotently clacking spinster – to 'wait'.

Instead of the hard, self-enclosed image of woman in 'Tamarind Season', in
the title poem of the collection, *I Am Becoming My Mother*, we are presented with a
sensuously fluid image of maternal fecundity – everything the spinster is not:

Yellow/brown woman
fingers smelling always of onions
My mother raise rare blooms
and waters them with tea
her birth waters sang like rivers
my mother is now me
[. . .]
I am becoming my mother
brown/yellow woman
fingers smelling always of onions.
(*I Am Becoming My Mother*, p. 38)

The poem celebrates creative processes in a series of deft, painterly strokes, in which the identity of mother and daughter overlap sensuously. The poem appeals to the senses: the smell and taste of onions; the 'sound' of birth waters singing; the texture of lace and linen (in the stanza omitted). The focus on hands 'smelling always of onions' draws attention to the idea of woman as creator/maker – of babies, homes, gardens, meals and, because the poem itself is a *creation*, of poems. The cyclical movement of the poem, beginning and ending as it does with the same two lines (except for the subtle shift in order of the yellow/brown combination), emphasizes the sensual merging of the two lives. This fluidity in movement is echoed, thematically, in references to the birth waters singing and, more generally, to the focus on *process* and *becoming* which the poem celebrates.

The woman-centredness and the powerful presence of the mother in this poem, as well as the fluidity of its movement and imagery, invite associations with the textual strategies associated with *écriture féminine*, as outlined above. While such a reading is productive, the affirmation of maternal plenitude offered in Goodison's poem is given a kind of materiality which connotes a difference in emphasis from that of the often exclusively psychoanalytical in *écriture féminine*. This poem perhaps finds a more accommodating context when read alongside other black women's texts, where the mother functions as a figure through whom painful histories can be confronted and reconciled. As in the title essay of Alice Walker's collection, *In Search of Our Mother's Gardens*,[33] Goodison suggests a blurring of the boundaries between 'Art' and the more everyday manifestations of artistry embodied in her mother.

'I Am Becoming My Mother' might also be read as a commentary on the view, expressed by many (particularly Anglo-American) feminists, that the relationship with the mother is fraught and difficult precisely because of the *sameness* which Goodison celebrates – because it is the mother who socializes the daughter into her gendered role. There is a substantial body of writing by women which explores the love–hate, mother–daughter relationship, what Adrienne Rich describes as, 'Matrophobia [. . .] the fear not of one's mother or of motherhood but of *becoming one's mother*';[34] it is this very process which Goodison celebrates. In balancing a reading of the poem between feminisms – 'French', 'Black' and 'Anglo-American' – the reader is afforded an opportunity to revisit and revise feminisms' various 'takes' on the mother. Further, the intimate identification of the poetic 'I' with the mother who is the subject of the poem, avoids the reification of the mother as a static, *monumental* figure, which characterized some early male representations.

'I Am Becoming My Mother' has a parallel in another poem, 'On Becoming a Mermaid', where the emphasis is also on identity *as process*, but where the water imagery of the former symbolizes fluidity and multiple possibilities, in the former, water signals freedom *and* limitation. The speaker muses on the attractions of an 'easy death' by drowning, imagining how:

the current pulls your bathing-plaits loose
your hair floats out straightened by the water
your legs close together fuse all the length down

your feet now one broad foot
the toes spread into
a fish-tail, fan-like
your sex locked under
mother-of-pearl scales
you're a nixie now, a mermaid
a green tinged fish/fleshed woman/thing
                    (*I Am Becoming*, p. 30)

Rather than signalling the *jouissance* and plenitude of water, or of 'birth waters', here water is presented more ambivalently, resulting in denial and the 'sealing off' of female sexuality; a denial which is also configured as a kind of release, suggesting the fraught dangers attendant upon female sexuality.

Where the very short title poems of Goodison's first two volumes focus quite specifically on questions of identity in relation to womanhood, in *Heartease* the title poems are a suite of three which increase in length as the poet catalogues the hardships faced by the poor of her own society and of powerless people everywhere. The poems take on an increasingly apocalyptic tone and spread out to speak of and for biblical crowds:

In this year of cataclysm pre-predicted
being plagued with dreams
of barefoot men marching
and tall civilizations crumbling
forward to where the gathering, gathering.
Crowdapeople, Crowdapeople weep and mourn,
crowdapeople I have seen
                    (*Heartease*, p. 36)

Goodison then clearly articulates her own role as poet within this materially deprived situation, providing healing images and evoking possibilities to keep the spirit and imagination alive: 'I speak no judgement/this voice is to heal/to speak of possibility.' This is reiterated later:

No judgement I speak
that function is not mine
I come only to apply words
to a sore and confused time
          (*Heartease*, pp. 37–8)

Goodison draws on a range of discourses in these poems, collapsing boundaries between them but privileging none consistently, to create a fluid, polyphonic voice. She *speaks in tongues*, as it were, and it is in this sense of *delivering* the word that she might easily be categorized as a 'performance poet'. Goodison exploits a style of delivery when she performs her poems which powerfully consolidates her role as poet-priestess, for she self-consciously signals a spiritual ambience, sometimes by first reading the prayer-like, 'I Shall Light a Candle to Understanding in Thine Heart which Shall Not Be Put Out' (*Heartease*, p. 7) and by reading many of her poems in a subdued, rhythmic, incantatory manner. In the *Heartease* poems, the speaker draws on the discourses of the Bible, of Jamaican Creole, and of the Rasta as well as using more obviously lyric/poetic language. She uses 'I' when making her observations or 'testifying' but uses 'we' when mapping healing possibilities, including herself in this process.

Goodison's voice in these poems is very much a public, *speaking* voice (indeed, a public-speaking voice), and the sense of a live audience is inscribed within the poems at several points. An example is 'If you did not see it I will tell you what/it said' or, 'you want to know how far this thing gone?' and there is a general appeal to an idea of this being a *collectively* difficult set of circumstances. The result is that at the level of content – and, more fundamentally, of form – Goodison's poetic identity is one which is so strongly allied to 'the people' that the individuated poetic voice merges with the collective, so that she *becomes the body politic*. The poet's carefully constructed poetic role of healer draws not only on the kind of *divining* traditionally associated with women but also on the linguistic power of the more conventionally *divine* in the biblical Word and other patriarchal discourses. That Goodison's distinctive 'performance of the nation' is generally not included alongside the other more obviously performative poets, such as Mutabaruka or 'Binta' Breeze, is an index of the degree to which 'the performative', within Caribbean poetry, has tended to encompass a very limited (Creole) speaking voice – and poetic identity.

Interestingly, in another poem in *Heartease*, 'My Father Always Promised Me', the poet explicitly links her artistry as healer/poet to her father, describing him as the axis of her world:

> Almost too late I learnt the flying steps
> father, look see me rising, lighter
> in the name of my father, dreamer
> who said I should be
> Of all worlds and a healer
>
> (*Heartease*, p. 9)

Here the father's association with the power of the symbolic order is made explicit, and it is, obviously, the order within which Goodison as woman poet must negotiate a space and empower her own voice. As argued above, Goodison does this by attempting to speak with the authority of her fathers – 'the' biblical Father as well as her own, 'biological' father – but she also derives power by attempting to speak with the authority of the voices of the people too.

This speaking of the body politic within the body of her own texts is achieved at some cost. In 'Heartease New England 1987', a bird marooned away from the flock and unable to negotiate its exit from the overpass inspires the poet to explore doubts and vulnerabilities in relation to her own role as poet: 'I too can never quite get the measure of this world's structure/somewhere I belong to community'. Bob Marley's music, wafting through the air, however, reconnects her to community and affirms her role as 'the sojourner poet carolling for peace' (p. 41). Bigger 'doubts' about a public poetic identity might be read in the suppression of a superabundant female sexuality which her role as poet/priestess/ healer seems to imply. The poem 'Wild Woman (I)' begins:

> I seemed to have put distance
> between me and the wild woman
> she being certified bad company.
> Always inviting me to drink
> bloody wine from clay cups
> and succumb to false promise
> in the yes of slim dark men.
> (*Heartease*, p. 49)

'Wild Woman II' begins, 'Sometime in this first half/the wild woman left' (p. 50). The two 'Wild Woman' poems point to a tension in Goodison's work between the private and the public; between the 'private' world of female sexuality and her 'public' role as healer/poet. Where many of the poems in Goodison's two earlier volumes might be described as womanist/feminist, focusing on explorations of woman's identity and the anxiety involved in writing *as woman*, there are fewer of these poems in *Heartease*. The poet, in opting for a poetic identity and voice which speaks to, for, and *as* 'the people', implies that her embodied woman's self has to be jettisoned. The association with *spiritual* delivery of the word, however, appears to be one which frees her from the kind of wounding associated with the more *female/reproductive* use of the word delivery.

The emphasis on spirituality harnessed to a public poetic role, which characterizes *Heartease*, is not evoked in so sustained a manner in the two later collections, though Goodison's concerns remain focused on Jamaicans and the hardships, pleasures – and courtesies – of their daily lives. In the title poem of *To Us, All Flowers Are Roses*, the poet meditates on the names of towns and villages in Jamaica, teasing out the historical associations of these names, sometimes playfully, always lovingly:

> I love so the names of this place
> how they spring brilliant like 'roses'
> (to us all flowers are roses), engage you
> in flirtation. What is their meaning? Pronunciation?
> A strong young breeze that just takes
> these names like blossoms and waltz
> them around, turn and wheel them on the tongue.
> (*To Us*, p. 69)

The varied provenance of these names – Spain, the Alps, Ghana, Egypt,

Stonehenge – 'There is everywhere here' (p. 69) – is celebrated, as evidenced in
the way these names have been claimed by the tongue: 'Chateau Vert slipped on
the Twi of our tongue/And fell to rise up again as "Shotover"' (p. 70). The history
of slavery, too, profoundly informs this catalogue of names:

> But there is blood, red blood in the fields
> Of our lives, blood the bright banner flowing
> Over the order of cane and our history.
> (*To Us*, p. 71)

The poem's conclusion resonates back to the *Heartease* poems: 'I recite these
names in a rosary, speak them/when I pray, for Heartease, my Mecca, aye
Jamaica' (p. 71). The emphasis on names and naming is also taken up in 'In City
Gardens Grow No Roses as We Know Them', where the impetus for the poem,
like that of the title poem, is to document and testify to the creativity of Jamaican
people:

> Necessary medicinal herbs, flowers easy to grow
> no delicate blooms could survive here.
> In city gardens grow no roses as we know them.
> So the people took the name and bestowed it
> generic, on all flowers, called them roses.
> So here we speak a litany of the roses that grow
> in the paint-pot chamber-pot gardens of Kingston.
> (*To Us*, p. 15)

The speaker's use of 'we' in both the title of the poem and in line 3 appears to
address a constituency of readers outside Jamaica: 'In city gardens grow no roses
as we know them' (my emphasis); that is, those for whom roses are a distinct, rather
than generic, entity. The poem, 'To Us, All Flowers Are Roses', which provides
the title for the collection, on the other hand, affirms identification unequivocally
between poet and the people for whom 'roses' are a generic term for *all* flowers.
This is a small distinction but one which indicates a shift in direction which *Turn
Thanks* exemplifies more fully – that is, that the identification between 'poet' and
'people' is negotiated in ways which signal the mediating consciousness of the
poet more explicitly, and suggests an appeal to audiences 'over here' *and* 'over
there'. In other words, where, in *Heartease*, the poet speaks *as* the people and
(sub)merges her own poetic identity in theirs, in more recent collections she
speaks *about* and *on behalf of* the people, using a clearly individuated poetic voice.

Many of the other poems in the collection *To Us All Flowers Are Roses*, in offering
individual poetic portraits of a variety of Jamaican people – 'Rassy', who re-fills
the mattresses (pp. 6–8); the 'elephant' man, harassed by the city's children (p. 9);
'Bun Down Cross Roads, ex-esquire, former gentleman', convicted of arson
(p. 11) – also contribute to this sense of a more individuated poetics.

This point can also be demonstrated in *Turn Thanks*, where the 'turn thanks' (returning thanks) of the title is taken up specifically in two poems, 'Turn Thanks to Miss Mirry' and 'Turn Thanks to Grandmother Hannah', in which the poet offers thanks and praises to two women in her life. One is Miss Mirry, the domestic helper, whose use of language is evoked below:

> She could not read or write a word in English
> but took every vowel and consonant of it
>
> and rung it around, like the articulated neck
> of our Sunday dinner sacrificial fowl.
> (*Turn Thanks*, p. 12)

The other is Grandmother Hannah, who 'aspired to sanctity/through the domestic vocation of laundering/the used, soiled vestments of the clergy' (p. 14) and whose philosphical understanding of her humble vocation appears to shape the poet's own recording of the 'extraordinariness' of the ordinary lives of Jamaicans:

> To be perfect in whatsoever you are called to do
> is counted in heaven as sincere prayer.
> My father's mother prayed through
> laundering the garments used in temple service.
> (*Turn Thanks*, p. 14)

More generally, many other poems in the collection record and testify to the layers of courtesy, wisdom and affection which characterize Goodison's Jamaicans. So, in 'Signals from the Simple Life':

> A poor man
> wears new gloves
> on his wedding day
> to say
> his hands
> are clean.
> This is
> his new beginning.
> (*Turn Thanks*, p. 23)

Or, in 'The Domestic Science of Sunday Dinner', the elaborate details of preparing the Sunday meal are described, as a ritual and then requiem for the father and mother with whom the speaker habitually shared this meal. There are also poems dedicated to the poet's mother and father as well as to aunts, uncles and a great-grandfather.

Alongside this more 'domestic' trajectory in thematic focus, the images of poetry – and of the poetic 'calling' – are more often presented in confidently sensual terms, than as a painful wounding. In 'Some Things You Do Not Know about Me', the poet-speaker presents herself as 'bohemian' – she eats with her hands, never wears shoes and drinks from a saucer – and the delivery of a poem as a 'wild whirling' dance. Reflecting on the way the tiny white dots stippled around the surface of her favourite coffee cup have worn away, the speaker concludes:

> I think I may have swallowed them, because some nights
> I feel like a trillion small punctuation
> periods are swarming inside me,
> waiting to attach themselves
> to the ends of my unwritten lines and sentences.
>   (*To Us*, p. 57)

This wonderfully indulgent image presents poetry and the poet in a whimsically visceral relationship; suspended between the body and the page, the delivery of a poem becomes the climax to an all-encompassing dance:

> If the poem is really coming now, straight and sure
> No holding back as it heads for its union with the page,
> Then I simply throw my hands up over my head
> Thereby releasing the poem.
>   (*To Us*, p. 57)

The poem concludes with the poet enjoying the equivalent of a post-coital cigarette: lighting a stick of incense while listening to Bob Dylan. This confident indulgence is again evident in 'The Mango of Poetry', in *Turn Thanks*, where, reading a book in which 'The writer defines it [poetry] as silence', the speaker offers the eating of a mango as a more convincing definition of poetry. The staging of the eating of the mango is elaborately theatrical and the poem concludes with the poet, dressed perfectly for the occasion, affirming both the mango – *and* herself, by implication – *as* poetry:

> I'd do all this while wearing
> a bombay-colored blouse
> so that the stain of the juice
> could fall freely on me.
>
> And I say that this too would be
> powerful and overflowing
> and a fitting definition
> of what is poetry.
>   (*Turn Thanks*, p. 44)

Unlike the static conflation of woman *as* the fruit of the land in the work of early male poets, the poet here offers the mango-eating woman as a symbol of

plenitude and agency. The poem also cheerfully both domesticates and sexual-
izes one of Wordsworth's famous definitions of poetry as 'the powerful overflow
of feeling'. Goodison, in an interview with Wolfgang Binder, comments on the
notion of poetry which prevailed while she was at school in Jamaica:

> I don't like 'The Daffodils' because in my whole life as a child I always
> recited 'a host of golden daffodils', and I had never seen one. It is a typical
> example of colonialism, where a bit of another culture is pushed on you,
> and you really have nothing to do with it. So we learned all of that, the
> Wordsworth, the Keats and Shelley. *And we were never encouraged to think that
> they and us were on the same level.* [My emphasis][35]

In 'To Mr William Wordsworth, Distributor of Stamps for Westmoreland', the
influence of the Romantics is simultaneously challenged and acknowledged in the
ironic recognition of their inspiration for other kinds of 'epiphanies':

> The host of golden flowers at my feet
> were common buttercups not daffodils,
> they danced and swayed so in the breeze
> though overseer thorns were planted among them.
>
> Still, it was a remarkable show of sorts
> which opened my eye, the inward one,
> which once opened enabled me to see
> the overflowing bounty of my peoples' poverty.
>
> (*Turn Thanks*, p. 45)

The poem, in drawing parallels between the speaker's great-grandmother and
Keats – 'Only Keats's nightingale/could compete with her guinea griot style.'
(p. 46) – insists that *both* poets occupy the same cultural level. Another poem,
'Country Sligoville' which opens, 'I arise and go with William Butler Yeats/to
country Sligoville/in the shamrock green hills of St Catherine' (*Turn Thanks*, p. 47),
continues the intimate cultural and poetic paralleling introduced in the close intertextual reference to Yeats's 'The Lake Isle of Innisfree', by coupling the myths of
Ireland and Jamaica (maroon warriors become 'bush comrades' of Cuchulain).
The confident intimacy of these intertextual relationships asserts the degree to
which Goodison refuses 'uncritical devotion' to the canonical texts disseminated
via colonial education, refusing a scenario 'where a bit of another culture is pushed
on you, and you really have nothing to do with it' (see the interview cited above).
Instead, she defines the terms on which she *does* have something to do with it.

The more frequent cross-cultural emphases in *To Us* and *Turn Thanks* might be
partly accounted for by the fact that, in recent times, Goodison has spent
extended periods of time away from Jamaica. This experience is the thematic
focus in several poems but, most interestingly, in 'I Have Spent These Snowbound
Days Away from Myself' (*Turn Thanks*, p. 79), which provides the platform for a

retrospective view of her own work as poet. The 'frozen foreign landscape' causes her heart to migrate:

> I wake up to find my heart has left a red note, saying,
> Gone in search of my identity, don't wait for me.

The quest for identity which the poem dramatizes –

> 'Who am I ?' I asked the woman that I was dressed in
> and she, not knowing either, shrank back from her skin.

– is 'resolved' in the final lines of the poem when the speaker refuses to equate her own 'self' with that of the many poetic selves featured in her own oeuvre: the wild woman, Amber, the Tightrope Walker, Penelope or the Mulatta. The insistence on a 'self' that cannot 'simply' be read via the various poetic identities constructed in her work suggests a revision of the painfully close identification between poet-woman and poetic personae articulated in some of the earlier poems. The self *beyond* poetic identities might be read here as a strategic necessity to challenge the submersion of self which the polyphony of the *Heartease* poems appeared to require. This view is supported by two other poems in *Turn Thanks* – 'Bringing the Wild Woman Indoors' (pp. 89–90), and 'The Revival Song of the Wild Woman' (pp. 91–2), in which the 'wild woman' whose disruptive plenitude did not fit with the poetic identity of 'Healer', is now generously embraced. Instead of being banished 'to live/under the house-bottom', the wild woman affords the poet a reconnection with the body via song and dance; a sensuality symbolized below in the red dress:

> This morning she caught your attention early, told you to dress
> in fiery red, and you who have been keeping your life colors
> in the range between muted and pastel are now garbed
> in brimstone red
>
> *(Turn Thanks,* p. 91)

In the interview with Wolfgang Binder, Goodison discusses another of her 'poetic selves', the mulatta figure. She argues for the embrace, on her own terms, of her multiple ethnic roots and her diverse poetic identities:

> It all belongs to me. I had a poem which I have never published that said something like 'All of it belongs to Me', because my great grandfather was a man called Aberdeen, who obviously came from Scotland. And my great grandmother came from Guinea, and because they had a mating and produced my grandmother, who looked like an American Indian – I have relatives who look like Egyptians and my son is an African prince – all of it belongs to me. If somebody tells you, take some and leave some, that is his or her problem. I am not going to do that. All of it belongs to me![36]

Later in the same interview, she mentions someone writing a paper about her work and reading 'these deep, serious connotations' about her seeing herself as a mulatta figure. Her dismissal is brisk: 'That's garbage! All it is is a persona' (p. 57). Given the emphasis on 'race' in Caribbean literature, Goodison's insistence that it is her prerogative as poet to make use of the mulatta in her work, regardless of political imperatives to identify *as black*, is important. As she says in the interview quoted from above, 'I am not a minority. I was not accustomed to think in terms of being a minority because I am not a minority where I come from' (p. 51). This fact, of living in a predominantly black/brown context, allows Goodison to reclaim colour as a *descriptive* category – the mother, in 'I Am Becoming My Mother', is presented as a 'yellow/brown woman' – and to harness the romantic associations of the mulatta to her own poetic ends. In poems in which she addresses injustices in black America or South Africa, Goodison mobilizes suitably political articulations of 'raced' terms. The confidence of her assertion of the right to write – and of poetic licence – along with the embrace of multiple selves (both 'poetic' and 'real') recalls Derek Walcott's Shabine, in 'The Schooner Flight':

> I'm just a red nigger who love the sea,
> I had a sound colonial education,
> I have Dutch, nigger, and English in me,
> and either I'm nobody, or I'm a nation.[37]

Turn Thanks ends with a love song, addressed to an unidentified 'you', in which the poet-speaker acquiesces, temporarily but willingly, to silence:

> I want to walk across this green island
>
> singing like the Guinea woman
> showers, showers of blessing
> until you cover my lips
> and I go silent and still
> and I will see your face
> and want then for nothing.
>
> (*Turn Thanks*, p. 95)

The image here of the poet striding confidently into her future(s) suggests a tentative reconciliation of many of the anxieties dramatized in the earlier work.

Mahadai Das: embracing the monster

Mahadai Das is an Indo-Guyanese who spent time in the 1980s in North America but now lives in Guyana. She has published three volumes of poetry, *I Want To Be a Poetess of My People* (1977), *My Finer Steel Will Grow* (1982) and *Bones* (1988).[38] With regard to the representation of the body in her work, the trajectory I trace, rather different from that outlined above in relation to Goodison, suggests a shift away from the robust, land-rooted female identity of her first collection to a presentation of the female body as vulnerable, battered and, finally, monstrous. At the same time, in a parallel shift, there is increasingly a move away from a nationalist to a feminist focus in her output.

That Das is the first Indian-Caribbean woman poet to be discussed so far in this book requires some consideration at the outset. The under-representation of 'Indians' in the literary output of the region has often been explained with reference to their 'late' arrival in the Caribbean (1838) and to their relatively small numbers except in Trinidad and Guyana; factors which, combined with the perceived reluctance of Indians to integrate fully into Creole culture, has resulted in the Afrocentric focus of Caribbean culture. This is clearly a provocative explanation and one which is being challenged as more detailed research is undertaken and as more Indian-Caribbean writers have their work published.

Most recent accounts emphasize the structural ways in which divisive economic and political policies have, in colonial *and* post-independence regimes, fostered suspicion and hostility between Indian- and African-Caribbeans.[39] Indians have, historically, been associated with the rural economy and stereotyped as simple peasants, while the African is stereotyped as a city hustler and spendthrift. Indian women arrived in very small numbers (one woman to three men) as indentured labourers, when they worked alongside men in the rice and cane fields (though paid two-thirds of the man's wage). With the shift away from plantation logies (barracks) to residences in villages in the interests of a more settled workforce, some Indian women were withdrawn from paid labour to bolster the prestige of the family. This, alongside the privileging of boys with regard to food, education and so on, gave many Indian women the dubious 'protection' of a traditional, domestic role. With regard to ethnic relations between Indian and African women, Linda Peake and Alissa Trotz, in a study that is, admittedly, limited to the Demerara county of Guyana, offer the following summary:

> Notions that each group was intrinsically different and culturally predisposed to certain types of activities were helped by relative residential and occupational segregation and low rates of intermarriage. The planters, for whom the benefits of a divided workforce were obvious, actively cultivated mutual suspicion and distrust along racialized boundaries. The inversion of the image of Indo-Guyanese women in the post-indentureship period to emphasize their 'traditional' domesticity, chastity and virtue now contrasted sharply with the representation of Afro-Guyanese women, who remained tainted with the image of sexual promiscuity and disorderliness.[40]

Jeremy Poynting, whose pioneering Peepal Tree Press has been active in publishing many Indian-Caribbean writers, offers a useful survey of Indian-Caribbean women's 'experience and voice'. He begins his discussion of their literary output as follows:

> The domestic, educational, occupational and social disadvantages suffered by
> Indo-Caribbean women are reason enough not to be surprised at the small
> quantity of imaginative writing they have produced. [. . .] Much of the writ-
> ing is undistinguished; many of the journal contributions are by adolescents
> who have subsequently gone silent.[41]

It is not my intention to repeat or extend Poynting's survey, though I have found
his work very helpful.[42] Since his article was published in 1987, there have been
substantial contributions from Indian-Caribbean women[43] but there is still, to
date, insufficient published poetry by Indian-Caribbean women for a substantive
exploration of their work as a discrete category. In any case, my interest, pursued
more fully in Chapter 5, lies less in constructing distinct categories along ethnic
lines than in mobilizing an awareness of the ways in which various kinds of
difference (ethnicity, sexuality, class and so on) may unsettle any easy homogeneous
or celebratory groupings. This book, in reading Caribbean women's poetry
alongside some of the main cultural debates in the literature of the region, has,
inevitably, resulted in an Afrocentric focus. Nonetheless, I am wary of attempting
to redress this by discussing Mahadai Das as a *representative* Indian female poet
because it risks trivializing the complexities which define Indian-Caribbean culture *and* Das's poetic oeuvre. Further, Das frequently challenges what it means to
be 'Indian' or 'Guyanese', and her work, in many ways, charts the failure of early
attempts in Guyana to refuse the limitations of identities forged along ethnic lines.

Mahadai Das's first collection, *I Want to Be a Poetess of My People*, was published
by the Guyana National Service Publishing Centre and includes a mini-bio which
proudly asserts:

> University student, teacher, beauty queen, Mahadai, up to October 1975,
> was a member of Guyana's leading para-military force – The Guyana
> National Service. She served as a pioneer in the Service's hinterland
> development and is intensely interested in music, drama and dance.
>
> (p. 28)

Das's active participation in the pro-nationalist initiatives of Forbes Burnham's
predominantly African Guyanese People's National Congress Party was strategically important to a party which, at least in the early part of its rule, was anxious
not to be accused of exclusively representing the interests of *African* Guyanese.
Burnham's increasingly socialist programme of reform and nationalization initially appealed to many Guyanese eager to implement the 1966 independence
motto: 'One people, one nation, one destiny'.[44] Many were also mistrustful of
Burnham's motives, however, and, by the time National Service was introduced
in 1973, a climate of fear prevailed:

> When GNS was made compulsory for both men and women wishing to enter
> higher education, it was seen by many Indians as an attempt to force racial
> integration, or rather the sexual integration of Indian girls. The fact that

when the lists for compulsory induction were published at the University of Guyana they contained 53 Indo-Guyanese of the 63 persons listed, and that of the 25 women listed 90% were Indian, meant only one thing to the majority of Indians.[45]

Das's enthusiastic involvement with the radicalism of the Burnham regime is charted in her first collection of poetry and, however naive it may appear with hindsight, her public endorsement of the PNC would have been read as progressive. Certainly it would have alienated many Indian Guyanese, signalling both a rejection of traditional definitions of Indian womanhood and a willingness to embrace an African Guyanese cultural identity. *I Want to Be a Poetess of My People* is propelled by a militant nationalism which Das uses to appeal energetically to Guyanese generally, and to women in particular. In 'Cast Aside Reminiscent Foreheads of Desolation' (pp. 8–10) (Das has a penchant for melodramatic and unwieldy titles in this collection), the speaker urges Indian women to refuse to see the future as predetermined by the traumatic past of indentureship and labour and to see the possibilities for 'newer patterns of meaning'. The land is depicted as 'husband' and the women urged to:

> Cast aside your apologetic philosophy of uprooted destiny!
> No bride regrets her entry
> Into the arms of her husband.
> Yet, she never ceases to love her father.

The sense in the formulation above of the young bride caught between husband and father resonates – inadvertently, here – with ironies. Later on in the poem, other strains appear in the marriage metaphor – 'This land has bequeathed you new meaning./*She is your husband./*No wife regrets her married state! '[my emphasis] – suggesting an uneasy tension between the speaker's concern to address both women's and nationalist concerns. The poem evokes powerful and daring (for the time) images of female sexuality –

> Today your Khukru-Beras tingle
> And glitter in the midday sun
> And your mali lies contentedly
> Until the dusk, when love's fingers
> Will unravel the dawn.
> Your breasts, like jars of jamoon wine
> Will yield their succinct flavours.

– before retreating into safer images of Indian womanhood:

> Sing your lullabies!
> Cradle the gifts of your womanhood serenely!
> Tomorrow,
> No more ships will come across the seas!

In 'Look in the Vision for Smiles of the Harvest' (pp. 11–12), the speaker, working in the cotton fields (one of the GNS projects involved planting cotton in the interior at Kimbia) alongside 'Hundreds of reapers/Green backs bent' (an allusion to the green GNS uniforms), surveys the land and asserts the owner-ship which distinguishes this labour as qualitatively different from that of the indentured labourers:

> Here I stand
> The palm of my brown hand shading two gleaming eyes from the
>   richness
> Of sunlight overhead.
> Here I stand and survey, all around born fruit of frustration and pain
> And hope.
> *Here I stand on my own soil*
>
>   (*I Want to Be*, pp. 11–12; my emphasis)

In 'Looking over the Broad Breast of the Land I Saw a Dream' (pp. 17–18), the 'broad breast of the land' signals fertility and 'A rooted dream. A green dream'; and the jungle is 'a symbolic womb, cradling and nurturing the generations/of yesterday's visions.' But another poem, 'Your Bleeding Hands Grasp the Roots of Rice', addressed to two old rice-farmers, suggests a much more ambivalent articu-lation of the 'new patterns of meaning' suggested by labour on the land: 'Don't you sense evolvement, misty-slow, painful, like new death' (p. 15).

If images of the land are of a 'Vibrantly green, verdantly green' (p. 17) land-scape and images of women are robustly active, the kind of poetic identity which Das asserts explicitly in this collection is declaimed equally energetically. 'Does Anyone Hear the Song of the River Wending Its Way through the Jungle?' (pp. 19–20) opens:

> Make me a poetess of my people.
> Let me too drink the sun that shines in early morning
> Knee-deep paddy-fields
> Drinking droplets dewing on endless acres of cane.

Here, Das invokes 'Nature' in the familiar mode of the Romantics but the poem quickly progresses to politicize this Romantic view and unsettle it; an unsettling perhaps already triggered in the unfamiliar invocation of 'paddy-field' and 'cane' as contexts which might inspire poetry. When compared to one of Una Marson's rhetorical appeals for poetic success, such as 'To Be a Poet' –

> If I were a poet with gifts divine
> And all the blessings of earth were mine
> I'd sit all day 'neath a shady tree
> And keep the Daisies company;
>   (*The Moth and the Star*, p. 9)

– the robustness of Das's construction of poetic identity is usefully fore-grounded. The poem then characterizes 'the people' – those of the 'logies' *and* the 'nigga-yards' – using the river as metaphor to convey their lack of represen-tation and voice: 'These same quiet veins of water that flow through the land/ Like blood vessels in the flesh of my mother' – and to conflate mother and motherland (as opposed to 'mother country'). The speaker is presented as a spokesperson for the people *and* the land. In 'Militant', the speaker, again invok-ing familiar tropes of blood in the service of nationalism, declaims her desire to represent the people:

> Militant I am
> Militantly I strive
> I want to march in my revolution.
> I want to march with my brother and sisters
> Revolution firing my song of freedom.
> *I want my blood to churn*
> Change! Change! Change!
>   (*I Want to Be*, p. 23; my emphasis)

The imagery of blood recurs later in the poem, 'In our veins run atoms of gall', and the country is described as being in the 'Throes of a bloody birth!/A scream of life!' and, again, an organic wholeness is evoked between the nurturing mother and the nurturing land: 'Seeds that I planted/For my child to nurture/Will shoot forth through my soil.' The speaker stresses her own 'militant' role as artist: 'I want my words scorching pages/Burning tongues/Paging my people's servility', and continues:

> I want to dance through patterns of pain
> Beaded to rooted, furrowed brows
> Of our sons of the land.
> *I want to be a son of my land.*
> [. . .]
> In history's sad march
> *Was I ever a son of my land?*
>   (*I Want to Be*, p. 23; my emphasis)

Here, the tension between the speaker's identity as a woman and that of a stri-dently male nationalist discourse is most apparent. The maleness of the poem's militancy is endorsed on the page by the inclusion of a charcoal drawing of a hand holding a rifle aloft. The question posed in the poem – 'Was I ever a son of the land?' – clearly refers to the colonized subject's historical lack of agency and 'ownership' of the land but has the added poignancy of foregrounding the dif-ficulties faced by the woman poet who seeks to speak in the name of an always, already *male* nation.

The collection concludes with 'He Leads the People', which I take to be a praise poem for Linden Forbes Burnham. The poem opens with an image of the poet/ speaker which is, deliberately, reminiscent of Soviet representations of the robust peasant-worker:

> In the era of the people
> I stand astride the excitement of reconstruction.
> Eagerness is a sparkling ray in my eye
>   The blood races through my veins.
>   (*I Want to Be*, p. 26)

The leader is presented as an idealized, Romantic figure:

> Tall, his vision communing with the light on the horizon.
> Beautiful hands, that caress so gently
> So firmly, those hands reconstruct.
> Clothed in jungle-green, like the forest
> And as silent
> He leads the people.
>   (*I Want to Be*, p. 26)

In Das's second volume, this image of Burnham as idealized leader is dramatically altered so that he is a gleeful 'tyrant' and a 'bullfrog who croaks'.

Before turning to Das's second collection, the poem 'They Came in Ships', with which *I Want to Be* opens, is worth noting. The poem, arranged on the page to mimic the shape of a pair of sails, offers a narrative of the arrival of the indentured labourers to Guyana, conveying historical information: the names of the ships – 'Whitby', 'Hesperus', 'Fatel Rozack' – wooden missions of young imperialist design; the conditions of the first 'arrivants' who were 'limpid, like cattle' and who, 'On the platter of the plantocracy', were offered 'disease and death'; as well as the early resistance on estates such as Enmore. But it also includes a sharply focused critique of colonial practices:

> The Commissioners came
> Capital spectacles with British frames
> Consulting managers
> About the cost of immigration
> They forgot their purpose in coming.
> The Commissioners left
> Fifty-dollar bounty remained.
> Dreams of a cow and endless calves
> and endless reality in chains.
>   (*I Want to Be*, p. 6)

Das, in placing this poem at the start of her collection, asserts the foundational importance of this history; while most of the other poems point to the future, 'They Came in Ships' attests to the shaping impact of such a history on the future.

My Finer Steel Will Grow, Das's second collection, signals its very different political provenance at the outset. The name of the publishers, Samisdat, indicates its
dissident affiliations, and the preface describes Das's response to their suggestion
that she use a pseudonym, 'I would prefer my own name . . . I will probably be
safe for a few years, as the Guyanese government is busy gunning down dissidents
at home.' Published in 1982, two years after Walter Rodney's assassination (one of
the poems in the collection is titled, 'For Walter Rodney & Other Victims'),
Guyana was, politically and economically, in turmoil and its government characterized as tyrannical.[16] Where expansive green landscapes and 'full-blooded'
imagery had characterized *I Want to Be,* the collection *My Finer Steel* is characterized by introversion, fear and an emphasis on psychic, rather than geographic,
landscapes. The effect of this 'wretched exile silencing me' (untitled, p. 13) is that
there is little attempt at the illusion of naturalism; instead, the poems make use of
dense layers of metaphor. Few of the poems are titled, removing another
'incriminating' clue to the poem's meaning. The untitled poem with which the
collection begins invokes a context of fear and suspicion at the outset – 'there are
eyes that watch behind/the shroud of darkness. The cancerous/prey is frantic'
(p. 3) – while, in the poem from which this collection takes it title, the speaker's
body is that of a flea-ridden dog:

> It is a dog's life. Today there are no bones.
> Yesterday there were too many.
> The common fleas irritate my hairy map.
> My legs are poles the world
> Cannot keep upright
> (*My Finer Steel*, p. 4)

Blood no longer 'races through the veins' for, here, the heart has 'gone dark/like
night and rotted blood' and the poem ends with an image of relentless assault,
'hammering/rains the bullets/on my back', which, in the slide from 'rain' to
'bullets' construes nature more malevolently – and politically – than in the earlier
volume. In another untitled poem, the speaker shivers in her 'inadequate skin',
and concludes:

> . . . This heart
> is a handful of tissue I must coat
> in warmth before the guerilla air.
> (*My Finer Steel*, p. 6)

In another poem, also untitled, in the same collection there is a piling up of
images of vulnerability which have their most intense expression in bodily
imagery. The poem, addressed to a lover, parallels throughout the disappointments and difficulties of both personal and political affiliations:

> the limbs of my whispers climb warily

the steep sides of your sternness.
[...]
My words are new leaves that constantly
bear fruit, little red flowers facing
the open high sun of love.
But your wall is a bitter garden
where my roots are not fed; your back
a keel of stone bruising the red lake
of my womb.

(*My Finer Steel*, p. 11)

In this collection, the body is repeatedly presented as the embattled site of multiple assaults: 'This body will bear the final calamity' (p. 8). Das's studies in America were disrupted by serious illness, and the images of pain which recur here and in *Bones* may well derive from this experience, as well as from the political disappointments indicated earlier. Images of the barren woman, in an untitled poem (p. 14), are also evident in the collection, with infertility being equated with voicelessness: 'Place your torch upon this cave/that cries/bringing down the roof of my emptiness/to a flat, silent shore where waves/visit' (p. 14).

By contrast to this embattled body, those who have abused power, the 'tyrant' and his 'murderers', 'those with paunches and their contented belches' (p. 7), are presented as corpulent and obscene in their over-consumption. Interestingly, the image of the *resisting* body is presented as naked, appealing to the universality of Shakespeare's 'unaccommodated man', but, more importantly, constructing Guyana's Amerindian peoples as symbolic of an uncontaminated power:

In this forest of green and great dreams,
in the unvanquished footsteps
of our first pride, we tread;
with our string of beads and our naked
spears we come with our shield of courage
to repossess our native waterfall.

(*My Finer Steel*, p. 5)

The reference to Amerindian culture is unusual in this collection for invoking a recognizable sociocultural world with some degree of naturalism, and optimism. It has a parallel in the penultimate poem, in which the speaker recreates a nostalgically utopian scenario in which Indian women, their wrists 'bangled' by the sun's rays, carry out their early morning domestic chores:

Our lords will wake
to hot curries and fresh-baked
wheat.
And while it is yet dark, they
Will make their way to the fields.

(*My Finer Steel*, p. 15)

Read against the grim disillusionment of many of the other poems in the collection, this poem appears to offer nostalgia for a golden past as a brief respite from
the disappointments with the 'revolutionary politics' which had shaped so many
of the earlier poems.

Das's third collection of poems, *Bones*, as the title suggests, continues to place
the body centre stage, but it is a body pared down to the essentials of its skeletal
frame and the tune played is dissonant and ethereal. The cover of the book, with
its 'floating' images of bones decorated with Amerindian-style designs, invites
connections to be made with the bone-flute of Amerindian mythology. Wilson
Harris has made extensive use of this mythology, tracing references, in early
anthropological writing on Guiana (as it then was), to a 'ritual cannibalism' practised by the Caribs who (and here Harris refers to Michael Swan's use of Richard
Schomburgh) 'usually brought back to the settlement an arm or leg of the slaugh-
tered enemy as a trophy, which would then be cooked so as to get the flesh more
easily off the bone; a flute was then made of this.' Harris argues that designating
the Caribs as 'cannibal' was essential in the Spanish conquistadors' relentless
extermination of the Amerindians.[47] But Harris is also attracted by the profound
and intimate cross-cultural exchange involved in this ritual cannibalism. He argues, 'The bone flute was a confessional organ involved in, yet subtly repudiating,
the evil bias of conquest that afflicted humanity.'[48]

'Flute', a short elegiac poem in Das's third collection, opens with an image of
the body as flute:

> my body's a hallowed
> stick of bone, a flute
> through which you pipe
> your melody.
> (*Bones*, p. 46)

Use of the word 'hallowed' suggests here both the hollowness of a flute and
the idea of something revered. The speaker, whose body is being 'played', is
presented/presents herself as dissociated from her embodied self; the only act of
agency being to ask to be played gently. While no specific contextual information
is provided to locate events in time or place, it is clearly the Amerindian bone-flute
myth which is being alluded to. In this myth, Das appears to find a suggestive
metaphor for the emphasis in the collection on the vulnerability of the human
body alongside a recognition of its power, against the odds, to produce sound. In
its refusal of specificity of time or place, it appeals to the sense of cosmic space
and time, which allows, in Harris's argument, for cross-cultural connections in the
vast 'womb of space'.

Interestingly, too, in 'Oars' – which opens with the line, 'I am an Indian woman'
(p. 44) – the detail and imagery which follow all suggest that Das is alluding to an
Amerindian rather than an '*East*' Indian woman. The 'Indian' woman speaker of
the poem has long hair and and a band of beads across her forehead and is
paddling a canoe with slender oars through the 'slow-dark river'. In the third

stanza the speaker says, 'My words, slender oars,/bear my boat forward' (p. 44), suggesting further poetic resonances to be drawn from Amerindian culture. By contrast, in 'If I Came to India', the speaker's quest for identity via a return to her 'roots' ends much more ambivalently: 'If I come/Will I find myself?' (p. 47). What this suggests is that for Das, Amerindian culture – perhaps because of its further distance from her personally but perhaps also because of its symbolic distancing in the political arena of Guyana where Amerindians have been routinely disregarded as 'bucks' – is a more productive site of poetic possibility.[19]

In the title poem of the collection, a similar 'other-worldliness' is suggested as the poem concludes with the bones ('white flutes') floating, 'forever', beyond the limits of geography and chronological time:

> So when these white flutes
> send a note out – a golden apple
> from the Mexican border – it takes to air,
>
> full shape climbing,
>   rising
>
> helium balloon   forever.
>   (*Bones*, p. 9)

Earlier in the poem, the bones, 'grotesque jewels', are described jangling dissonantly in the closet beside the conventional paraphernalia of femininity – prom dresses, red pumps, veils and petticoats:

> Long ago, they were supply fleshed.
> But then, all meat fell away
> from the bone. Some teeth
> and hair remained.
> Someone should examine their story.
>   (*Bones*, p. 8)

Here, the popular phrase 'skeleton in the cupboard' is wittily mobilized and their location in a feminine space suggests a feminist angle. This is taken further in the reference to the attic – doomed places in both Charlotte Brontë's and Jean Rhys's texts: 'They have no wish to stay in the attic/They want to be part of the world' (p. 8). The juxtaposition of images from different mythologies – and times – suggests a hybridity of approach and a rejection of more naturalistic techniques for constructing meaning, apparent in her first volume. The 'body' of the poems, too, in their more disjointed and fragmented format, often parallel the uncertainties involved in attempts to construct meaning.

Many of the poems collected here allude to the body-in-pain. 'Resurrection' charts the speaker's surprise recovery from illness, 'Triumphant, from dark days of starvation,/I rise from the grave,/blood thin, body weak' (p. 13). In its graphic imagery –

Maggots crawled through my hair,
between my teeth and eyes,
ate at places, which, in life's profane vanity,
I guarded with passion and suffering.

(*Bones*, p. 14)

– it recalls something of Sylvia Plath's 'Lady Lazarus', as does the threatening
tone of 'When I rise from this tomb/as if I were Jesus come again'. The poem
concludes with the hubris of the speaker-as-God:

I draw the sun out of his milky horizon
with invisible strings, as if I were a puppeteer,
and with my skill, I engineer the morning.

(*Bones*, p. 15)

Plath's 'Lady Lazarus' concludes:

Out of the ash
I rise with my red hair
And I eat men like air.[50]

Another poem, 'Deceived or Deceiving', in dramatizing the failure of patriarchal gods to help the speaker to make sense of the world, echoes another Plath
poem, 'The Colossus'. Plath's poem represents the woman poet confronting
patriarchy in the graphic image of a woman scaling the huge statue in Rhodes
trying to scrub the structure clean with her 'pails of Lysol'.[51] Das's poem also
focuses on the woman's impotence, and on the failure of the gods to speak to her:

I constantly sing my songs for you,
but you cannot hear them.

I write on this page
but the ink is invisible.

I take my confessions to every shrine
I know. Gods do not listen.
They watch my anxious face
with stony eyes.
[. . .]
Yet they are dumb.
Their lips may be broken with a hammer.

(*Bones*, pp. 19–20)

The poem concludes, bleakly, that there is no position from which to 'make sense'
of the world, and even repositioning oneself 'like a spider' would not provide
protection from 'this universal disorder of things'.

In the long poem 'For Maria de Borges', Das returns to the emphasis on the labouring body which was the focus of her first collection, demonstrating that political concerns still inform her take on the world. The poem, divided into nine parts and with the strongest narrative line of any of the poems in the collection, charts the process by which an immigrant woman in the metropolis is exploited relentlessly until, stripped of all sustaining dreams, she is reduced to her 'working parts', 'I am a pair of hands/A pair of feet' (p. 22). The speaker is presented here, exiled from the 'pastures' of home, as a ghost-like figure:

> Phantomlike,
> I move in long narrow streets.
> Down Broadway.
> A single head of cattle exiled
> from gentle grazings of our pasture.
> (*Bones*, pp. 21–2)

The poem is a passionate indictment of an international division of labour which treats the immigrant woman 'like a packcamel', diminishing her relentlessly:

> He grabs my tiara, my bangles
> Of silver. He gives me tokens
> To send me to his factory,
> Send me to his store,
> Cage me in his offices,
> Keep me in his kitchens.
>
> At gunpoint, he steals rubies in my cheeks,
> My full curve of hip.
> (*Bones*, p. 23)

The poem concludes with a powerful image of the distortion of self-hood which results from such treatment:

> into the real world I come
> with my muscles pumped
> so you may drain me
>
> with my hands polished, shining,
> my feet ready.
> (*Bones*, p. 30)

Again, to invoke Plath's work (Plath arguably being the poet who most dramatically placed the corporeal female body centre page), the parallels between Das's image of the commodified woman and that of Plath's in 'The Applicant' (below), are striking:

But in twenty-five years she'll be silver
In fifty, gold.
A living doll, everywhere you look.
It can sew, it can cook,
It can talk, talk, talk.[52]

Many of the poems in *Bones* construct the figure of the woman as the very antithesis of the robust female figure 'astride' a green landscape which characterized Das's first collection; instead, the images presented here are of a fragmented and traumatized body. Where in her first collection Das aspires to be a 'poetess' (with all its 'little' associations), in *Bones* it is precisely the deviation from this ideal which signals her new poetic power. So, in 'The Growing Tip', the final poem in *Bones*, the speaker refuses to deliver the decorous poetry expected by publishers:

They assumed a garden: English roses,
Palms of victory high-raised
On a history of thorns, thick
Hedges, neatly-trimmed.
                              (*Bones*, p. 51)

Instead, the poet delights in challenging their cosy expectations of 'a jolly post-man, a friendly milkman,/an ever-so-often handyman', by sending poems which are monstrous rather than sedate, and which reflect more gritty and troubled realities and a 'history of thorns':

What she sent reminded no one of a garden:
Pieces of skin, a handful of hair, broken
Teeth, bits of glass – an iron chest, rusty, grim . . .
She told of jungles, of suppers of snakes
And monkeys; of bills evaded by a change-of-address.
                              (*Bones*, pp. 51–2)

The cry of 'Aiee! [. . .] "What a monster!" ' with which the manuscript is greeted does not act as the cue for a poetic shift to conformity. Instead, the poem ends on an affirmative note, suggesting that the poet has embraced this 'monstrous' poetic identity as a platform for a powerful and distinctive voice:

As they watched,
In high shock,
From every tip,
It continued to grow.
                              (*Bones*, p. 52)

Grace Nichols: 'as a woman and a poet/I've decided to wear my ovaries on my sleeve'[53]

Like Das, Grace Nichols is Guyanese. She is an African-Guyanese and has lived in England since 1977. Nichols has published four collections of poetry and a novel as well as several books for children; her work is extremely well known in the UK and has been included in the GCSE and 'A' level curricula.[54] She is perhaps best known for her poetic representations of 'big-up' black women–women who are full of themselves, who delight in their sexuality and who use an irreverent humour to challenge and mock the power of patriarchy. Her poetry, then, is magnetically attractive to any feminist critic with an eye on the female body.

i is a long memoried woman, Nichols' first collection of poetry, won the Commonwealth Poetry Prize in 1983. It charts the experience of the slave woman in the New World, and, as such, the collection might be seen as an attempt to fill in the gaps evident in many texts concerning the specificity of women's experience of slavery. Indeed, at a talk given at the Commonwealth Institute as part of their 'Woman Writers' seminars in 1988, Nichols described how her first attempts at getting the volume published were greeted with the response that Brathwaite had already 'done it'. Since then, *i is a long memoried woman* has become well established in its own right and its epilogue has been used in many an article as a succinct symbol of the black woman's agency and of the process of 'coming to voice':

> I have crossed an ocean
> I have lost my tongue
> from the root of the old
> one
> a new one has sprung
> (*i is*, p. 80)

The collection opens with the following epigraph:

> From dih pout
> of mih mouth
> from dih
> treacherous
> calm of mih
> smile
> you can tell
>
> **i is a long memoried woman**
> (*i is*, p. 4)

The poems in this collection dramatize the experiences and processes which make it possible for the 'long memoried' black woman to move from the unspeaking – though clearly resisting – silence of the epigraph to the promise of speech with which the text ends. The black woman represented here *embodies* the memories and histories of all slave women, a kind of New World Everywoman, and, in the emphasis on *body language* as well as on the corporeality of language, Nichols signals her interest in the body as a site of densely coded meanings and inscriptions.

The first poem, 'One Continent/To Another', consolidates this corporeal focus with an image of the Middle Passage as womb:

> Child of the Middle Passage womb
> push
> daughter of a vengeful Chi
> she came
>   into the new world
> birth aching her pain
> from one continent/to another
>   (*i is*, p. 6)

The slave woman, 'delivered' painfully on the shores of the New World, lies in her own shit and blood, 'bleeding memories in the darkness' (p. 6), before going forth 'with others of her kind/to scythe the earth' (p. 7). The birthing imagery is obviously associated with pain here but the poem concludes on a note of tentative possibility, 'now she stoops/in green canefields/piecing the life she would lead' (p. 8). That this ability to salvage something from nothing is associated with women is indicated at the outset:

> But being born a woman
> she moved again
> knew it was the Black Beginning
> though everything said it was
> the end
>   (*i is*, p. 7)

Later on in the sequence, the 'contradictory' coupling of creativity and violence which characterizes Nichols' Caribbean is evident in

> these blue mountain islands
> these fire flying islands
> these Carib   bean
> Arawak   an
> islands
> *fertile*
>   *with brutality*
> (*i is*, p. 31; My emphasis)

Read alongside Naipaul's infamous statement below, Nichols' approach insists on the possibility of creation *despite* and *because of* the brutal history associated with the Middle Passage:

> The history of the islands can never satisfactorily be told. Brutality is not the only difficulty. History is built around achievement and creation; and nothing was created in the West Indies.[55]

Many of the poems catalogue the particular ways in which the slave woman was exploited under plantation slavery: as labour in the fields, as the reproducer of labour for the plantation, and as sexual object for the 'master' of the plantation. Part of Nichols' project is to *name* the brutal realities faced by the slave woman. So, in 'Ala', the speaker describes the punishment meted out to a slave woman who has killed her newborn rather than deliver the child into bondage:

> Face up
> they hold her naked body
> to the ground
> arms and legs spread-eagle
> each tie with rope to stake
>
> then they coat her in sweet
> molasses and call us out
> to see . . . the rebel woman
>
> (*i is*, p. 23)

The poem forces a revaluation of 'the maternal' in a context where such 'universal' human values as 'maternal love' have been traumatically disrupted. The poem also, in presenting the dignified way in which the women 'sing and weep' as they work – and pray for the repose of the rebel woman's soul – understatedly exposes the barbarity at the heart of the 'civilizing' colonial mission. 'Love Act' describes the way in which the slave woman is used by the entire family in the 'Great House':

> *Soon she is the fuel*
> *that keep them all going*
>
> He/his mistresswife/and his
> children who take to her breasts
> like leeches
>
> (*i is*, p. 49; my emphasis)

The poem effectively foregrounds the distorted meanings of the 'love act' in the context of slavery, where the mistress is presented as being relieved to be 'rid of the love act' and the master fantasizes that the 'act of love' he 'shares' with the slave woman means she can be trusted. 'Love Act' also hints at the ways in which any easy sisterly solidarity between women cannot simply be assumed; the white woman here at least has the privilege of passing the (sexual) buck. The poem ends with a reference to poison, one of the ways in which domestic slaves most frequently expressed their resistance to slavery: 'She hide her triumph/and slowly stir the hate/of poison in' (p. 49). 'Love Act' appears in Part Three, 'The Sorcery', in which other poems describe the slave woman's formidable powers to both haunt and heal.

Elsewhere in the sequence, other kinds of resistance are presented. In 'Water-pot', despite 'the overseer sneering/them along' (p. 14), the slave woman struggles to carry her waterpot with dignity, while in 'Skin-teeth', the 'smile' which the slave woman presents to 'Massa' speaks volumes:

> Know that I smile
> know that I bend
> only the better
> to rise and strike again
> > (*i is*, p. 50)

As with the epigraph and epilogue, Nichols suggests that both body language and silence can generate complex meanings. Here, parallels might be drawn with Brathwaite's recuperation of the smiling consent of the stereotypical 'Uncle Tom'; in this extract from 'All God's Chillun', Tom patiently outlines the harsh realities which make the articulation of overt resistance impossible:

> Boss man makes rules:
> Who works, who jerks
> The rope, who rips
> The patient dirt.
> [. . .]
> Boss man rates gain:
> I am his living vein
> Of sustenance:
> His corn, his meal, his grain.[56]

Recalling Nichols' lines – 'Soon she is the fuel/that keep them all going' (p. 49) – both poets offer reminders of the circumstances which make such dissembling necessary.

In other poems, slavery is presented as *unspeakably* brutal, rendering the poet tongue-tied or silent. The 'visionary' eye/I of the poet in 'Without Song', concludes reluctantly that the children who have 'fallen/into silence/uttering no cry/laying no blame' (p. 25) may represent the only sane response: 'Maybe the thing is to forget/to forget and be blind/on this little sugar island' (p. 26). In 'Eulogy', the speaker/poet, haunted by the 'ruptured tones' of the many slaves who died on the Middle Passage, repeatedly asks, 'How can I eulogise/their names?/What dance of mourning/can I make?' (p. 17). The stuttering repetition of the question punctuates the poem and echoes the literal silencing of those who died:

Kobidja, Nwasobi, Okolie
swallowing your own tongues
cold and stiff on your chains

How can I eulogise your names
What dance of mourning can I make?

(*i is*, p. 18)

In *i is a long memoried woman*, Nichols also affirms a belief in the capacity to resist by including poems in which the sensual/sexual are expressed *despite* harsh circumstances. 'Like a Flame' opens:

Raising up
from my weeding
of ripening cane

my eyes
make four
with this man

there ain't
no reason
to laugh

but
I laughing
in confusion

(*i is*, p. 37)

To swig my breasts in the face of history

It is this insistence that there doesn't have to be a *a reason*, that the body asserts its own 'rationale' which Nichols explores further in her second and third collections of poetry. In *The Fat Black Woman's Poems*, Nichols projects the battered black woman's body out of the nightmare of history and into the present with a persona who frequently speaks confidently *at* the reader, loves her body and challenges men with her sexuality. In making the fat black woman the speaking subject of many of these poems, Nichols signals her refusal to occupy the subject(ed) position designated for the black woman by history and to insist on more complex subject-ivities. The collection opens with 'Beauty', a poem in which descriptions of the black woman operate as *defining* beauty:

Beauty
is a fat black woman
walking the fields
pressing a breezed
hibiscus

to her cheek
while the sun lights up
her feet
>   (*The Fat Black
>   Woman's Poems*, p. 7)

In 'The Fat Black Woman Remembers', the speaker refuses the continued commodification of the black woman as 'mammie' figure. Having been used as the 'breeder' of labour and wet nurse on the plantations, the fat black woman refuses her continued commodification in the marketing of 'Aunt Jemima's Pancakes' (an American brand name) and asserts her autonomy: 'But this fat black woman ain't no Jemima/Sure thing Honey/Yeah' (p. 9). Nichols uses humour to deconstruct the supposedly benign and accommodating amplitude associated with the mammie figure by presenting her 'mammie' as 'tossing pancakes/to heaven/in smokes of happy hearty/murderous blue laughter' (p. 9). Making textual alliances with another 'large lady', the fat black woman recycles Hollywood's Mae West's famous invitation, 'Come up and see me sometime', inflecting it mischievously with her own black history:

there's a mole that gets a ride
each time I shift the heritage
of my behind

Come up and see me sometime
>   (*The Fat Black Woman's Poems*,
>   p. 13)

That Nichols is aware of the 'heritage' associated with the black woman's 'behind' is made even more explicitly in the indulgently titled 'Thoughts drifting through the fat black woman's head while having a full bubble bath'. Here, the repeated use of the word 'steatopygous' signals the long history of the fetishizing of the black woman's buttocks in anthropological discourse. Sander L. Gilman discusses the way Saartjie (or 'Sarah') Bartmann, the so-called 'Hottentot Venus', was exhibited in Europe:

> It is important to note that Sarah Bartmann was exhibited not to show her genitalia but rather to present another anomaly which the European audience found riveting. This was the steatopygia, or protruding buttocks, the other physical characteristic of the Hottentot female which captured the eye of early European travellers. Thus the figure of Sarah Bartmann was reduced to her sexual parts. The audience which had paid to see her buttocks and had fantasized about the uniqueness of her genitalia while she was alive could, after her death and dissection, examine both, for Cuvier presented to 'the Academy the genital organs of this woman prepared in a way so as to allow one to see the nature of the labia'.

Sarah Bartmann's sexual parts, her genitalia and her buttocks, serve as the central image for the black female throughout the nineteenth century.[57]

The speaker in Nichols' poem asserts her rejection of this demonizing of the black woman's body overtly:

> O how I long to place my foot
> On the head of anthropology
>
> To swig my breasts
> In the face of history
> (*The Fat Black Woman's Poems*,
> p. 15)

In the repetition of the word 'steatopygous', and its juxtaposition with words associated with the elements ('sky', 'sea', 'waves', 'me'), the speaker dramatizes her attempt to make the word itself resonate with new, uncontaminated meanings.

Nichols also deploys the fat black woman as a powerful challenge to the tyranny of Western notions of female beauty; instead of the tight contortions of the 'Barbie' figure, Nichols presents us, in 'Afterword', with the amplitude of the fat black woman who comes

> out of the forest
> brushing vegetations
> from the shorn of her hair
>
> flaunting waterpearls
> in the bush of her thighs
> blushing wet in the morning
>   sunlight
> (*The Fat Black Woman's Poems*,
> p. 24)

Just as in 'Taint' in *i is a long memoried woman* Nichols indicts black 'patriarchs' ('But I was traded by men/the colour of my own skin', p. 19) so too 'The Assertion' (p. 8) in this collection is equally aware of the exercise of male power in 'trad-itional' African culture. In this poem, the fat black woman sits on the golden stool, symbol of the Asante Chief's power, and refuses to budge.

Nichols continues this irreverent challenge to patriarchy in her third volume, *Lazy Thoughts of a Lazy Woman*, pitting the sexually fecund black woman's body against the sterility of patriarchal discourses. In 'My Black Triangle' the poet proclaims her power to transcend the dehumanizing violence of the history catalogued in *i is a long memoried woman*:

> And though
> it spares a thought for history

> my black triangle
> spread beyond his story
> beyond the dry fears of parch-ri-archy
>   (*Lazy Thoughts*, p. 25)

Here, black female sexuality is presented as 'spreading and growing/trusting and flowing' (p. 25) beyond the sterile world of His Word. In 'Configurations', the speaker lists the 'trade-off' between a representative black woman and white man: 'He gives her uranium, platinum, aluminium/and concorde./She gives him her 'Bantu buttocks' (p. 31). The poem concludes by invoking the familiar image of the adventuring Columbus 'discovering the Indies', but here it is reconfigured so that the New World woman menacingly uses her sexuality to take control:

> He does a Columbus –
> falling on the shores of her tangled nappy orchard.
>
> She delivers up the whole Indies again
> But this time her wide legs close in
>   slowly
>   Making a golden stool of the empire
>   of his head.
>   (*Lazy Thoughts*, p. 31)

The image conjured up here is both menacing and comical; that the white man's head is conflated with the Asante stool indicts patriarchal empires of *any* provenance. In other poems, the challenge to patriarchy has a more literary focus and intertextual relationships are given a sexual frisson. 'The Body Reclining' (p. 4), with its irreverent subtitle – '(with a thought for Walt)' – is a response to Walt Whitman's 'Song of Myself', which opens:

> I celebrate myself, and sing myself,
> And what I assume you shall assume,
> For every atom belonging to me as good belongs to you.
>
> I loaf and invite my soul,
> I lean and loaf at my ease observing a spear of summergrass.[58]

Nichols' version, much less grandly universal in scope than Whitman's, 'domesticates' his vision and celebrates the reclining woman's body (the 'lazy woman' alluded to in the title of the collection) as sweet release from the repetitive drudgery of dusting and scrubbing. There is a similarly whimsical approach in 'With Apologies to Hamlet', in which Shakespeare's famous 'To be or not to be' soliloquy is used as a kind of poetic template for the woman speaker trying to decide whether to 'break poetic thought for loo/As a course of matter/And by apee-sing end it' (p. 6). That Hamlet is riven by thoughts of suicide at the moment at which Nichols chooses to mimic his delivery effects a challenge to the anxious self-examination he is engaged in as well as insisting that the act of writing is always an *embodied* performance. In 'Wherever I Hang' the speaker, newly arrived in England from the West Indies, explores some of the circumstances of her current displacement; the use of the peculiarly English word 'knickers' in this context suggesting that the process of acculturation is well established. The poem concludes:

> To tell you de truth
> I don't really know where I belaang
>
>> Yes, divided to de ocean
>> Divided to de bone
>
> Wherever I hang me knickers – that's my home.
>> (*Lazy Thoughts*, p. 10)

Not only is Nichols inscribing a female speaker into a role more usually associated with men, that of the roving male lover who refuses to be anchored to one woman (as captured in the refrain of the popular song 'Wherever I Lay My Hat that's My Home'), but there is also an irreverent echo of Walcott's 'A Far Cry from Africa', which ends:

> I am who am poisoned with the blood of both,
> Where shall I turn, divided to the vein?
> I who have cursed
> The drunken officer of British rule, how choose
> Between this Africa and the English tongue I love?
> Betray them both, or give back what they give?[59]

Nichols is not dismissing the anguish of the 'divided self' which haunts so many Caribbean-authored texts; rather, as with the mischievous play on Shakespeare's soliloquy, she is positing the possibility of dealing with this existential angst in a more whimsical, if not 'slack', manner. In deploying an irreverent humour to undermine the seriousness with which patriarchal bards take themselves, Nichols offers a critique of the powerful, all-knowing poetic 'I' which is a feature of many male canons – 'little' and 'large'. Rather than the weight of a written tradition, Nichols suggests that it is the erotic energy of the sexual which propels her poetry into being. The poem 'On Poems and Crotches', dedicated to Ntozake Shange, consolidates this focus and is cheerfully dismissive of the more conventional ways of interpreting poetry, suggesting that the production of poetry is an altogether more messy and sensual affair:

> For poems are born
> in the bubbling soul of the crotch.
> Poems rise to marry good old Consciousness.
> Poems hug Visionary-Third-Eye.

Kiss intellect.
Before hurrying on down
to burst their way through the crotch.
(Lazy Thoughts, p. 16)

In indulging in the body for and of itself, Nichols is clearly refusing the historical legacy of distorted and demeaning colonial constructions of the black woman. In offering sensuously reclining black women, Nichols also refuses the continuing limitations and prescriptions of the black woman as victim. 'Of Course When They Ask for Poems about the "Realities" of Black Women' makes this agenda clear:

Maybe this poem is to say,
that I like to see
we black women
full-of-we-selves walking

Crushing out
with each dancing step
the twisted self-negating
history
we've inherited
(Lazy Thoughts, p. 54)

While the black woman's body is the specific focus of many of Nichols' poems, her work, in presenting the female body as a cause for celebration rather than commiseration, also appeals to a wide constituency of women readers. Many of the poems in both *The Fat Black Woman's Poems* and *Lazy Thoughts of a Lazy Woman*, foreground the ways in which so-called 'beauty regimes' operate tyrannically to tame the female body into its 'proper' feminine mould and to limit women's sexual selves. In 'Who Was It?' the speaker appeals to any woman who has struggled with razors in delicate places:

Also, let the hairline of the bikini
Be fringed with indecency
Let 'unwanted body hair' straggle free

O Mary Cant
O Estee Laud
O Helena Frankinstein
(Lazy Thoughts, p. 6)

'Ode to My Bleed', in celebrating the regular rhythms of the menstrual cycle, represents 'the curse' as 'a blessing' (though whether *all* women would share this enthusiasm equally is debatable):

Red warm
or livery
Shocking pink
or autumny

I will not part
with my cyclic bleed
my soft seed

Month after month
it tells me who I am
    reclaiming me
(*Lazy Thoughts*, p. 24)

Never enough to keep us rooted

In *Sunris*, Nichols shifts away from so dedicated a focus on the woman's body. While the collection is still clearly 'woman-centred', in that the speakers are generally female and the relationships explored are largely between women, the *embodied* presence of the woman is much less palpable than in other volumes. Instead, there is a much wider range of thematic concerns and a more dispersed range of voices. The poem 'First Generation Monologue' suggests an 'explanation' for this shift in focus for while the sensual appeal of 'back home' is noted –

Breezing out with Bo
in the shade of the backsteps,
Dress lapped between legs like a river.
Loud ice in lemonade.
Bird-picked mangoes hiding in foliage.
(*Sunris*, p. 33)

– the poem concludes, wistfully, that all of this is 'never enough to keep us rooted' (p. 33), suggesting an embrace of a diasporic sensibility as the preferred response to geocultural dislocations.

The title poem of the collection charts the progress of a Mas woman through a carnival procession in which she encounters and challenges an eclectic, culturally diverse range of historical, mythical and religious figures, including Montezuma, Isis, Iris, Kanaima, Papa Bois, 'Virgin Mary gyal', Christ, Kali and Mother Africa. These figures are interrogated and/or celebrated and the poem builds up to an emphatic conclusion:

O symbol of the emancipated woman, I come
I don't believe I see one frown
From dih depths of dih unconscious, I come
I come out to play Mas-Woman.
[. . .]

With the Gods as my judge
And dih people my witness,
Heritage just reach out
And give me one kiss.
From dih depths of dih unconscius
I hear dih snake hiss,
I just done christen myself, SUNRIS
(*Sunris*, p. 74)

In taking the male gods to account, the familiar challenge to patriarchal order(s) is delivered but, rather than suggesting that the erotic energy which propels poetry is located in the embodied female form, Nichols here uses the erotic energy of carnival as it is embodied in the cross-culturally representative mythical female figure 'Sunris'. The shift away from the grounded, embodied female form also has another expression in the poem 'Wings', in which the sometimes contradictory appeals of a 'return to roots' and 'flights elsewhere' are explored. This tension between 'roots' and 'wings' can perhaps be traced in the frequent shifting between perspectives throughout Nichols' four collections; between an insistence on a groundedness in the past, in history, and the desire to transcend that past. 'Wings' charts the many 'small' ways in which Caribbean people have 'risen above' the difficulties generated by their dislocated histories. It opens with a mournful recognition of the trauma associated with these dislocations:

Consigned to earth
we thought it fitting
to worship only
the sustenance of our roots,
so that when uprootment came
in its many guises
we moved around like
bereaving trees, *constantly touching*
our sawn-off places.
(*Sunris*, p. 77; my emphasis)

The image suggested here recalls that of 'the phantom limb': 'In such cases, which occur with near universality in the surgical removal of mobile limbs, the absence of a limb is as psychically invested as its presence. *The phantom can indeed be regarded as a kind of libidinal memorial to the lost limb.*'[60] The intensely physical image of the bereft trees 'constantly touching/their sawn-off places' foregrounds the continuing suggestions in her work that the disrupted histories of the Caribbean are intimately and profoundly experienced by 'embodied selves', and that this past is 're-membered' in/by the body.

Though this last collection shifts away from a specific focus on the black woman's body, there is ample evidence in Nichols' oeuvre of the body being placed 'centre page' as the site of most trauma but also as the site of multiple possibilities. To what extent might this focus be read as *writing the body*? Certainly, the *thematic* focus on the body in Nichols' work parallels many French feminist concerns: the frequent emphasis on woman's body as signifying plenitude and possibility, rather than limitation and despair; the celebration, rather than shame, attendant upon menstruation, childbirth and other 'messy' female bodily functions and fluids; the characterization of patriarchy as rigidly rational and uncreative; the irreverent tone and playful mockery of canonical, patriarchal texts and the deployment of the erotic as a counter-discourse; and suggestions of autoeroticism in the image of the fecund black woman enjoying her sensuality for and of itself.

Gabrielle Griffin discusses *i is a long memoried woman* as 'in many respects, the perfect example of an *écriture féminine*, of the notion of writing the body'.[61] This point is made in a discussion of Nichols' work alongside that of Joan Riley and Ntozake Shange in the context of a larger argument about issues of pedagogy and 'the blank that was the [white] students' knowledge of Black woman's writing' (p. 19). Griffin argues that *écriture féminine* provides a useful tool for reading these writers because they make the body such a central focus in their writing; but there is also the suggestion that these black women's texts are *especially* corporeal:

> what Kristeva offers us with her notions of *semiotic* and *symbolic* dispositions is celebration and cerebration of the female body. Both elevate – go to the head. They invite a formalist stance: animal existence and certain kind [*sic*] of physical reality are left behind in favour of metalinguistic explorations which deal in futures, possibilities of 'finding a woman's voice'.
>
> Meanwhile, back in the here and now, another kind of reality asserts itself, an unfamiliar reality for the white readers of white women's writing, much of which is still so *nice*, so polite, so middle-class and educated, so anxious and out of touch with her body except in the most subliminal way.[62]

The contrast made here between the celebration of the woman's body in Kristeva's work and the anxiety associated with the body in the work of the three black women writers she discusses is persuasive. However, the basis on which the distinction is made is questionable. The emphasis on 'formalist' concerns in Kristeva's 'celebration and cerebration' of the female body begs the question: surely all 'physical realities' are apprehended and represented within some kind of – if not 'the' – symbolic order? Kristeva's project inevitably involves 'cerebration' in that the re-metaphorizing of the woman's body with which she is concerned cannot be articulated *outside* of discourse. The implication that black women's experiences of their embodied realities are somehow free from 'nice, polite, middle-class, educated' constraints and that they are, therefore, more 'in touch' with their bodies is also questionable, suggesting that their representations are, somehow, *beyond? before?* 'cerebration'. The idea that black women are somehow more in touch with their bodies and more 'natural' may well be motivated by a radical feminist agenda – it has certainly had some mileage in black nationalist discourse – but it is an essentializing and limiting perspective. It may also lead to assumptions about *automatic* connections between the black woman writer and orality:

The body of the text is only very sparingly marked by the signs that come from a written tradition of language usage such as commas, question marks, dots. In fact, nothing comes to an end with a full-stop: there is no stopping the revolution. . . . It is not over.[63]

The awkwardly over-literal parallels being drawn between the text and the realities out of which the text is constructed are perhaps the result of a reading agenda which almost *wills* radical agency onto black women's texts. Nichols does make only sparing use of punctuation but her poems invariably utilize frequent and varied line lengths as an alternative way of signalling pauses on the page. Griffin also suggests that 'the presence of Creole, Standard English and a mixture of the two' (p. 32) in Nichols' *i is a long memoried woman*, points to a heterogeneity often associated with *écriture féminine* and an orality which resonates with Cixous's description of a woman speaking in public:

She doesn't 'speak' she throws her trembling body forward; she lets go of herself, she flies; all of her passes into her voice, and it's with her body that she vitally supports the 'logic' of her speech. Her flesh speaks true.[64]

It may be useful to pause here to consider the resonances between the 'oral' invoked in French feminist approaches and the 'oral' invoked by many Caribbean writers and critics. Both Brathwaite and Cooper, for example, though with slightly different emphases, argue that Caribbean writing and culture cannot be adequately contained or interpreted using European models based on written texts and page-bound rhythms. Instead, the Caribbean writer must tap into, or *mine for*, that oral culture associated with Africa, which was abruptly truncated by the slave trade. This cultural knowledge is carried in the body, 'a noise in the blood', which the responsive writer can release onto the page. French feminists, similarly, argue for *écriture féminine* as a writing which refuses the linearity associated with the page and which allows the pulsations, rhythms and sounds of the pre-verbal dyadic world of mother and baby to erupt onto the page to disrupt the Law of the Father. Both approaches yearn nostalgically for an 'uncontaminated' space and time *before* entry into the Symbolic Order in which their designated 'Otherness' is consolidated. And both read woman's body as the most likely repository for a rhythm and physical presence that can challenge patriarchal order. However, clearly both approaches also rely on articulating this challenge *discursively*, with the result that 'naturalness' must, inevitably, be read as a discursively achieved illusion.

To return to Nichols, then, I would argue that the fact that she uses a Creole register very economically in her work signals a reluctance to be read as somehow – *naturally* – the embodiment of Creole culture in the style of, say Louise Bennett. With regard to *écriture féminine*, Nichols' emphasis on presenting positive images of black women signals a belief in the power to shift the resonances of words and images without a radical challenge to the symbolic system which generates such images and words. As such, it is perhaps more appropriate to suggest that Nichols writes *about*, rather than *writes* the body. The discussion which follows on the challenge to the symbolic system represented in the work of Marlene Nourbese Philip may help consolidate this distinction.

Marlene Nourbese Philip: English is a foreign anguish

Marlene Nourbese Philip was born in Tobago and took her first degree, in Economics, at the University of the West Indies. She moved to Canada in 1970 to study Law and has remained resident there. Nourbese Philip's poetry has become increasingly centred on the body in ways which indicate a self-conscious and sustained interest in current arguments about the role of the body in the production of written texts. Where Nichols provides 'recognizable', or 'realistic', images of the black woman, Nourbese Philip seldom does, interrogating instead the language and symbolic systems which make this representation fraught, if not impossible. Nourbese Philip has published three collections of poetry: *Thorns* (1980), *Salmon Courage* (1983) and *She Tries Her Tongue: Her Silence Softly Breaks* (1989). Although *Looking for Livingstone: An Odyssey of Silence*[65] is not designated as 'poetry' but described as a postmodernist narrative,[66] I am taking the liberty of including a brief discussion of it here because it makes substantial use of poetry.

Nourbese Philip's first two collections of poetry are slim volumes in which the emphasis on the body is latent, rather than explicitly focused on, as it is in her later work. In *Thorns* the focus is often on the distortions of selfhood resulting from colonial regimes in the Caribbean as well as from the racism encountered in Canadian cities. Many of these poems invoke, and challenge, a variety of 'cants' – religious, political, liberal – through which subjectivities, particularly black subjectivities, are violated and constrained. The 'back home' of the Caribbean is also viewed with sharply ironic insight, as in *Oliver Twist*, in which a children's game acts as a metaphor for destructive colonial regimes. In this game, usually called 'O'Grady Says' (the English version is 'Simon Says'), one child, the 'O'Grady' figure, directs the other children to make particular movements; if these instructions are obeyed when *not* prefaced by 'O'Grady says to' that child is eliminated from the game. The arbitrariness and whimsy of such rules is exploited to suggest the impossible contradictions faced by the black child being 'educated into' English culture:

> mother oh grady says to cry
> mother oh lady says be white
> mother oh grady says be black,
> brown black
> yellow black
> black black
> black pickney stamped English
> (*Thorns*, p. 5)

The poem concludes with reminders of the ways in which the world of books works to eclipse and muffle lived realities and the more distant traditions of Africa:

> jus' like all dem school girls
> roun' de empire
> learning about odes to nightingales
> forget hummingbirds,
> [. . .]
> about princes shut in towers
> not smelly holds of stinking ships
> (*Thorns*, p. 6)

In a more abstract vein, the poinsettia flower, popular in many parts of the Caribbean, is referred to in 'E. Pulcherimma' (the Latin name for the poinsettia) as emblematic of a bloody history – and *her*story:

> e. pulcherrima came awake
> in a pool of blood
> birth blood
> trickling down
> thickening thighs
> sticky
> with her hot milky sap
> spilling from broken limbs
> milked white
> (*Thorns*, p. 48)

Two short poems, 'Nostalgia '64' and 'Poisson', arranged on adjacent pages, succinctly convey Nourbese Philip's sense of the Caribbean as a profoundly gendered culture. The former celebrates 'the boys' liming on the street corner but the celebration is sharply undercut by the repetition of 'liming by de street corner/ *dressed to kill*' (p. 2; my emphasis); the fish-selling women in 'Poisson', on the other hand, are celebrated without irony as having a physical amplitude which encapsulates a linguistic power:

> Bubaloops women
>
> behinds rolling madly
> dice thrown with abandon
> laughter lolling loudly
> [. . .]
> Come! Get your fresh poisson,
> vocal residue redolent
> of cultures long since forgotten
> (*Thorns*, p. 3)

The title poem of Nourbese Philip's second collection, *Salmon Courage*, suggests the rather more personal focus of this collection, though many of the poems included share a similar political agenda to those in *Thorns*. In this poem the speaker, born in Moriah and trained as a lawyer (paralleling Nourbese Philip's own circumstances), returns home. The visit becomes the occasion for the speaker to remember her mother ('This salmon woman of Woodlands, Moriah/took the sharp hook of death/in her mouth' (p. 14)) and to challenge her 'salmon father' whose pride in her qualification as a lawyer blinds him to the other 'salmon' possibilities his daughter might pursue:

> She a millstoned lawyer, his milestone
> To where he hadn't been.
> He pulls her out, a blood rusted weapon,
> To wield against his friends
> 'This, my daughter, the lawyer!'
> 　　　　　　　　　(*Salmon Courage*, p. 15)

The use of the salmon as a symbol of resistance, of 'swimming against the tide', is interesting in that it suggests a source of cultural authority and sustenance outside the Caribbean, implying a forging of connections in the 'adopted homeland', Canada. 'Sprung Rhythm' – a poem which opens with the confident assertion that 'It was there that I learnt to walk/in sprung rhythm,/talk in syncopated bursts of music' – ends on a much more ambivalent note, questioning the sources of cultural belonging:

> Was it there that I found the place
> to know from,
> to laugh and be from,
> to return and weep from?
> Was it there, or was it here?
> 　　　　　　　　　(*Salmon Courage*, p. 11)

Where the speaker in 'Sprung Rhythm' asks questions about a broader sense of cultural belonging, the speaker in 'Salmon Courage', in (firmly, lovingly) refusing the father's prescriptions, questions the cost of 'belonging' within the immediate family. If the daughter-speaker in 'Salmon Courage' must summon her own 'salmon courage' to resist the father, then the all-powerful mother-figure in 'She' is presented as more terrifying. Here, the daughter-speaker claims that the mother 'Taught me a language that couldn't be parsed' and 'Spelt my name in blood on her tongue/Showed me the only way to spill blood'. This woman's knowledge, however, includes a terrifying prohibition against loving other women sexually for 'She'

> Split the atom of silence,
> Threw her voice to the woman in the silent child

And warned,
'Women who do those things
Together are tarred and feathered.'
                    (*Salmon Courage*, p. 5)

Other poems associate the woman's body with pain in the familiar arena of childbirth. 'You Can't Push Now' dramatizes the tussle for control over the woman's body in the 'theatre' of the delivery room:

But the boys in white were there,
the boys in white are always
there with the words
    'You can't push now
    Your doctor's not here
    you can't bleed now
    Your doctor's not here
    You can't be now
    Your doctor's not here'
                    (*Salmon Courage*, pp. 34–5)

The controlling pronouncements of the doctors are echoed in references to other forms of patriarchal discourse – in particular, that of the Bible and the communion service – which also punctuate the proceedings: '*And in sorrow thou shalt bring forth children*' and '*This is my body/This is my blood*' (pp. 32 and 34). Famous male politicians are also listed (Lenin, Mao, Fidel, Mugabe), as representative of the limitations of a politics which underestimates the personal. And there is an irreverent reference to Christ in the lines, 'Sweet Jesus! even you/Can't push now/Wait for a second coming' (p. 35). Against these representatives of patriarchy are the competing voices of the goddesses Isis and Ta-urt, who laugh, belch and urge the speaker to push, offering a carnivalesque and anarchic challenge to 'the boys in white'. Ta-urt having 'belched her approval', the poem concludes:

'For the Goddess' sake push
Now
Give us all birth.'
                    (*Salmon Courage*, p. 35)

'Broken Spaces', in *Thorns*, p. 10, had described the womb, after a miscarriage, as 'softly plundered' and as 'a broken blood torn pact/an emptied wailing womb'. In 'Planned Obsolescence', in *Salmon Courage*, preventing conception by tying the fallopian tubes is presented as a mutilation (albeit embarked upon willingly):

Words of violence –
cut, crush, sear and burn.

Inner mutilation for outward freedom –
that bodily balance of terror.

The horned womb will weep always
blood.

(*Salmon Courage*, p. 36)

The womb, in these poems, is implicitly presented as the defining feature of woman's embodied self and is invariably associated with pain: 'The horned womb will weep always/blood.'

Thorns and *Salmon Courage* might be described as pinpointing and describing the sociocultural and political structures which oppress black subjects, particularly black female subjects. The implicit role of the poet in these two collections appears to be to record and testify to these experiences, both as an insider who must speak on behalf of the black community in Canada and as an individual with a particular experience of the realities of migrancy. In *She Tries Her Tongue: Her Silence Softly Breaks* and *Looking for Livingstone*, Nourbese Philip shifts away from representing these detailed sociocultural realities towards an interrogation of the structures through which such representations are enacted, dramatizing the difficulties attendant upon representation itself in a postcolonial context. This shift in focus is evident in the most cursory reading of *She Tries Her Tongue*: the poems comprise widely varied line lengths, different typefaces, quotes from other texts punctuate many of the poems and fragments of poetry are dispersed across the face of the page in unpredictable ways. Intertextual relationships are signalled in the many quotes from other texts which either preface the poems or are included as part of the poem. The texts referred to in *She Tries Her Tongue* include Ovid's *Metamorphoses*, Browning's *The Ring and the Book*, Klein's *Comprehensive Etymological Dictionary of the English Language*, Naom Chomsky's *Language and Responsibility*, Jeremy Campbell's *Grammatical Man* and Cecily Berry's *Voice and the Actor*, as well as invented 'quotes' from gardening, cookery and children's books and fragments of the Eucharist prayers.

Linguistic squatters, possessing adversely what is ours

Nourbese Philip prefaces the collection *She Tries Her Tongue* with an essay, 'The Absence of Writing or How I Became a Spy', which articulates clearly the aesthetic and thematic concerns which have inspired her poetic project. The essay begins with a short description, using a stylized Creole, of the way in which she started to write 'as a way of living my life' (p. 10) despite the pressure to pursue a more visibly upwardly mobile profession:

Books for so! Rows and rows of them at the library as greedy-belly I read my way through Dostoevsky, Moravia, Shakespeare, Dickens. Books for so! Other people were writing them. I was reading them.

(*She Tries Her Tongue*, p. 11)

The remainder of the essay also emphasizes the 'double-bind' generated by the knowledge contained in books in which 'the native', seeing herself represented as 'other' or not at all, is simultaneously silenced and empowered to speak:

> The paradox at the heart of the acquisition of this language is that the African learned both to speak and to be dumb at the same time, to give voice to the experience and I-mage, yet remain silent.
>
> (*She Tries Her Tongue*, p. 16)

In many ways the essay covers very familiar ground; indeed the argument that 'It is *in the continuum of expression* from standard to Caribbean English that the veracity of the experience lies' (p. 18, emphasis in original) is one which has been routinely made by Caribbean-based critics throughout the 1980s. This perhaps alerts us to the time-lag involved in many Caribbean diasporic contexts where old battles have to be fought again on each new journey. However, the suggestion that silence and speech are mutually constitutive categories for the New World subject and the emphasis on gender, *does* shift familiar arguments in a different direction. Nourbese Philip associates Caribbean popular cultural forms with a dynamic bodily and linguistic excess:

> A language also nurtured and cherished on the streets of Port-of-Spain, San Fernando, Boissiere Village and Sangre Grande in the look she dey and leh we go, in the mouths of the calypsonians, Jean and Dinah, Rosita and Clemintina, Mama look a boo boo, the cuss buds, the limers, the hos [whores], the jackabats, and the market women. These are the custodians and lovers of this strange wonderful you tink it easy jive ass kickass massa day done. [. . .] The excitement for me as a writer comes in the confrontation between the formal and the demotic within the text itself.
>
> (*She Tries Her Tongue*, p. 18; my emphasis)

In specifically foregrounding and celebrating women associated with street culture ('hos' and 'jackabats'), whose reputations are, in conventional terms, 'suspect', Nourbese Philip refuses the security of the more 'homely' model of Creole-use offered by Louise Bennett. In both the essay and the poems which follow, Nourbese Philip makes occasional and strategic, rather than naturalistic, use of Creole: Creole is often presented as being *in confrontation* with more formal discursive registers. This strategically limited use of Creole is part of a poetics which seeks both to expose the distortions rendered through colonial language and to transform this language in the process: '*I want to write about kinky hair and flat noses – maybe I should be writing about the language that* kinked *the hair and* flattened *noses,* made *jaws prognathous*' (p. 20). The poems in this volume seek to enact a poetics which might transform linguistic structures, particularly those associated with the written text. Nourbese Philip concludes her essay by asserting that 'There was a profound eruption of the body into the text of *She Tries Her Tongue*' (p. 24), and suggests that it is by inscribing the woman's body (in a variety of ways, as we shall see) into the written text that the formal structures of the written word can be disrupted.

The title poem of the collection, *She Tries Her Tongue; Her Silence Softly Breaks*, orchestrates fragments of a variety of texts in a mournful and tentative staging of 'coming to voice'. The poem opens with an epigraph taken from Ovid's *Metamorphoses* – '*All Things are alter'd, nothing is destroyed*' – suggesting both a willingness to enter into dialogue with a 'master discourse' while *also* embracing the mutability which the quote from Ovid proclaims.

Arranged over sixteen pages, the more familiarly lyric poet's voice appears on the left-hand side of the page, while quotes and short extracts from 'real' and invented texts (representative of a variety of discursive registers) are arranged on the right-hand side of the page. Nourbese Philip presents the poetic voice as stuttering and repetitive with many phrases suspended or unfinished: 'the me and mine of parents/the we and us of brother and sister/the tribe of belongings small and separate,/when gone'. The texts presented on the right-hand side of the page, by contrast, deliver a variety of 'truths': how to transplant plants without damaging their roots; how the limbic system operates human memory; the story of 'the three little pigs' becomes an instruction for 'How to Build Your House Safe and Right'; an extract from the Acts of the Apostles when they are visited by the Holy Ghost and speak in tongues; a description of a mother rejecting her child after it has been touched by a stranger; a fragment of prayer; definitions of 'history' and 'memory' taken from *Klein's Dictionary*, and, finally, a description of 'The oldest woman of the tribe' returning to the river the skeleton of the first salmon to be eaten as a way of ensuring future bounty.

Some of these texts are made ironic by their unfamiliar placing, while others take on new, more poetic, meanings. Cumulatively, they foreground the centrality of words in the worlding of the human subject. By contrast, the snatches of poetry suggest that narrative forms of discourse are inadequate to express the trauma and loss with which the poem is concerned. Instead, the unfamiliar arrangements of words on the left-hand side of the page seek to nudge the reader into less securely fixed associations:

> without the begin of word
> grist in a grind and pound of together
> in the absence of a past mortared with
> apart
> the harsh husk of a future-present begins
> (*She Tries Her Tongue*, p. 88)

In another section of the poem, the poet intersperses her own words between those of the prayer, 'Oh Lord I am not worthy', so that the processes of self-abnegation and dejection, acquired through force and then maintained through ritualized linguistic formulations (here, religion is taken as emblematic of powerful colonial discourses) are paralleled in the layout of the body of the text:

I am not worthy so much as to gather up the crumbs under thy table
forgive me this dumbness
but thou art the same Lord, whose property
this lack of tongue forgive
is always to have mercy
          upon

                  this

          thisthisand   this

                    disfigurement this

                          dis

        memberment

                this

                    verbal crippling
            (*She Tries Her Tongue*, p. 94)[67]

    The poem with which the collection opens, 'And Over Every Land and Sea', takes its title from Ovid's *Metamorphoses* and uses the drama of Ceres searching for her abducted daughter, Prosperine, as the literary platform from which the poet launches her own exploration of belonging. Nourbese Philip's version, reversing Ovid's structure, begins with the daughter looking for her mother, 'She whom they call mother, I seek' (p. 29). The first poem, 'Questions! Questions!' opens:

    Where she, where she, where she
    be, where she gone?
    Where high and low meet I search,
    find can't, way down the islands' way
    I gone – south:
    [. . .]
    Before the questions too late,
    before I forget how they stay,
    crazy or no crazy I must find she.
           (*She Tries Her Tongue*, p. 28)

    In addition to the quest for the lost daughter/mother, it is the epic scale and operatic mode of Ovid's narrative that appear to be attractive to Nourbese Philip; the figure of Ceres, powerful in her grief and fury, provides an evocative 'literary mouthpiece' to express larger historical griefs. In appropriating this figure, Nourbese Philip also, to some extent, succeeds in creolizing 'the original', and *performs* the very metamorphosis at the heart of Ovid's stories. A short extract from 'The Search' demonstrates this:

    all day long she dreaming about wide black nights,
    how lose stay, what find look like.
    A four-day night of walk bring me
    to where never see she:

is 'come child, come' and 'welcome' I looking –
the how in lost between She
and I, call and response in tongue and
word that buck up in strange;

(*She Tries Her Tongue*, p. 31)

Clearly, Nourbese Philip's poems do not offer narratives whose meanings can be readily summarized. Rather, she eschews the illusion of 'wholeness' in the body of her texts, dispersing authorial authority in the numerous references to, and inclusion of, other texts within the body of her own text. The meanings generated in the poems must be actively constructed by the reader through the exploration of the relationships *between* fragments of texts and between different uses of familiar words; sometimes, too, the poet's wordplay, in its emphasis on *sound*, signals the importance of the sensual, embodied self in the construction of meanings. Clearly, *all* texts require active interpretation, but Nourbese Philip explicitly foregrounds this requirement, implicating the acts of writing and of interpretation in the thematic concerns of many of the poems. The poem 'Discourse on the Logic of Language' is perhaps the clearest example of the poetics/thematics I have just described.

English is a foreign anguish

The poem is spread over four pages and makes use of different typefaces and linguistic registers. Placed vertically along the edge of the left-hand side of the first and third pages, in capital letters, is a matter-of-fact description of a mother licking her newborn baby girl clean and then blowing words into the child's mouth. Alongside this, arranged horizontally in the middle of these pages, is a more obviously lyrical poetic voice in which the yearning for a 'true' mother tongue is dramatized:

English

is my mother tongue.
A mother tongue is not
not a foreign lan lan lang
language
l/anguish
  anguish
– a foreign anguish.

(*She Tries Her Tongue*,
p. 56)

Alongside this, on the right-hand side of the first and third pages, in italics, are '*Edicts I and II*', which, in a legalistic register, briskly map out the prohibition against slaves speaking to each other in their 'native' tongues on the plantations, and the punishment attendant upon disobedience:

Where necessary,
removal of the tongue is
recommended. The offending
organ, when removed,
should be hung
on high in a central place,
so that all may see and
tremble.
> (*She Tries Her Tongue,*
>   p. 58)

The facing pages, 2 and 4, are devoted to replicating 'scientific' discourse used in support of racist agendas:

> Dr Broca believed the size of the brain determined intelligence; he devoted much of his time to 'proving' that white males of the Caucasian race had larger brains than, and were therefore superior to, women, Blacks and other peoples of colour.

The use of a smaller typeface and the quotation marks around 'proving' signal the parodic intention motivating this re-presentation of 'scientific racism'. This is followed by a 'straight' description of the workings of the left temporal lobe and the motor cortex which make speech possible, but, coming as it does after Dr Broca's racist pronouncements, its 'facticity' – and that of scientific discourse more generally – is undermined. On page 4 are posed a series of multiple-choice questions about the tongue and the related muscles necessary for speech:

> Air is is forced out of the lungs and up the throat to the larynx where it causes the vocal chords to vibrate and create sound. The metamorphosis from sound to intelligible word requires
>
> (a)   the lip, tongue and jaw all working together.
> (b)   a mother tongue.
> (c)   the overseer's whip.
> (d)   all of the above or none.
>
> (*She Tries Her Tongue*, p. 59)

The parodic tone of these 'choices' works to undermine the very discourse which the poet is mimicking – *undoing* the discourse by *overdoing* it – and to refuse the possibility of the categorizing impulse which motivates such discourses. The poet's strategic use of patriarchal discourses works both to convey the linguistic context in which the hegemony of English was enforced and to suggest possibilities for the dismantling of that hegemony.

In addition to the strategic use of mimicry and parody, the suggestive juxtaposition of different discourses is also employed. The most dramatic of these juxtapositions foregrounds the sterile 'rationality' and monologism of patriarchal discourse by placing it alongside the embodied sensuality of the female word, arranged on the right- and left-hand sides of the page respectively. The capitalized text on the far left of the page, which describes a mother licking her newly born infant clean, is evocative of Kristeva's 'semiotic' in which mother and daughter communicate fluidly and sensually in the language of the body. In the second of the capitalized sections, the poet offers a rewriting of the story of how the female, colonial subject enters the symbolic order, challenging the primacy of the phallus in Lacanian accounts of language acquisition and transferring that power to the mother:

THE MOTHER THEN PUT HER FINGERS INTO HER CHILD'S MOUTH – GENTLY FORCING IT OPEN;/SHE TOUCHED HER TONGUE TO THE CHILD'S TONGUE, AND HOLDING THE TINY MOUTH OPEN,/SHE BLOWS INTO IT – HARD. SHE WAS BLOWING WORDS – HER WORDS, HER MOTHER'S WORDS,/THOSE OF HER MOTHER'S MOTHER, AND ALL THEIR MOTHERS BEFORE – INTO HER DAUGHTER'S/MOUTH.

(She Tries Her Tongue, p. 58)

The corporeal and sensuous image of the mother blowing words into her baby's mouth – with its resonances of 'mouth-to-mouth resuscitation' – is operatic in scale; the mother is presented here as all-powerful, rather like the gigantic goddesses of Ovidian myth. In her insistence on asserting a new myth of language acquisition, Nourbese Philip offers metaphoric possibilities with which to challenge the relentless determinism and pessimism of the Law of the Father. Importantly, too, the inclusion of the edicts in the poem remind the reader of a violent history which disallows an *exclusively* gendered reading. The sensuousness of the image of the mother breathing language into the daughter is placed alongside the slender stanzas in a more lyrical voice in which the speaker stutters and stumbles in her yearning towards speech – and towards a mother tongue untainted by colonial histories.

If the capitalized text represents the mother as a monumental figure, the frequent repetitions of different words for 'mother' – 'mammy/mummy/moder/ mater/macer/moder' – represent a different strategy for challenging the Law of the Father. Here, the speaker wishes for the security of a mother tongue, unproblematically acquired, and explores the impossible contradictions of her 'real' situation: 'I have no mother/tongue/no mother to tongue/no tongue to mother/to mother/tongue/me' (p. 56). The logical conclusion of this is that 'I must therefore be tongue/dumb/dumb-tongued/dub-tongued/damn dumb/ tongue' (p. 56). Paradoxically, however, the very process of the delivery of the poem itself contradicts such a conclusion. When the poem is enunciated aloud, the use of repetition also forces an awareness of speech as a physiological phenomenon as the linguistic estrangement caused by the 'unnatural' breaks in stanza lines and the play on similar-sounding words produce a 'tongue-twisting' effect.

Read in dialogue with the pseudo-scientific 'rationalizing' about the physiology of speech, represented on the right-hand side of the page, the tongue-tied lyricism on the left of the page acts as a reminder of the embodiedness of speech. The fact that, when first faced with the poem, the reader must decide how and where to begin reading the poem, holding the book sideways and so on, also functions as a reminder of the embodiedness of reading.

Nourbese Philip, in this poem, appears to suggest that the historical contamination of the 'mother tongue' in the Caribbean can be challenged by deploying a poetics which recognizes – and releases – the sensual potential of words. There are obvious parallels to be drawn with the work of Kamau Brathwaite here, for, like Nourbese Philip, he too suggests the possibility of pushing against the boundedness of words by exploiting similarities in sounds to forge new words, or new resonances from old words. Both poets suggest that the colonially inherited language – English – can be mined to release the traces of the repressed or submerged pre-colonial language and culture: of the mother, of Africa, of 'Mother Africa'. Nourbese Philip does not share quite the same emphasis on rhythm as does Brathwaite, who represents 'talking drums', calypso, reggae and pan beat in his poems. In *Mother Poem*, Brathwaite dramatizes the process of *mining* for the suppressed mother's voice by giving the illusion of playing with similar sounding words until he 'stumbles' on some telling similarity: 'But/muh/muh/muh/me mudda/mud/black fat/soft fat man-/ure'.[68] Or, in 'Negus':

> It is not
>
> it is not
> it is not enough
> to be pause, to be hole
> to be void, to be silent
> to be semicolon, to be semicolony,
> (*The Arrivants*, p. 224)

Nourbese Philip, in the play on 'mother' and 'language/l/anguish' in 'Discourse on the Logic of Language', uses a similar kind of wordplay. In 'Meditations on the Declension of Beauty by the Girl with the Flying Cheek-bones', there is an even more striking parallel with Brathwaite's 'Negus':

> If not in yours
>
>   In whose
> In whose language
>   Am I
>   Am I not
>   Am I   I am yours
>   Am I not   I am yours
>   Am I   I am

If not in yours
                    In whose
In whose
In whose language
                    Am I
If not in yours
                    Beautiful
                    (*She Tries Her Tongue*,
                              p. 53)

Both Brathwaite and Nourbese Philip suggest that the reader acquaint themselves intimately and sensuously with the process of constructing meanings by *performing* the words, rather than relying on silent, intellectual *recognition* of meaning. Clearly, this 'recognition' of the slippages in meanings in the examples given above involve *both* 'sight' and 'sound', so that the play in meanings of the word results from a play-off between page and performance.

If Brathwaite's poetic project suggests that, for the West Indian, the suppressed 'mother tongue' has its cultural moorings in the lost 'mother land' of Africa, then *Looking for Livingstone: An Odyssey of Silence*, attempts to read and re-present the familiar representation of Africa and of the black woman ('worded over' by David Livingstone's grand narrative of discovery and conquest), through the 'travelogue' of a solitary black woman. She exploits metaphors for writing (mentioned earlier in this chapter) in which patriarchal word power, particularly that associated with the written word, is predicated upon woman's invisibility and silence, exploring the 'logic' of this metaphor fully and using exaggeration to undermine *his* power and empower *her* silence:

> HE – LIVINGSTONE – AND I COPULATE LIKE TWO BEASTS – HE RIDES ME – HIS WORD SLIPPING IN AND OUT OF THE WET MOIST SPACES OF MY SILENCE – I TAKE HIS WORD – STRONG AND THRUSTING – THAT WILL NOT REST, WILL NOT BE DENIED IN ITS SEARCH TO FILL EVERY CREVICE OF MY SILENCE – I TAKE IT INTO THE SILENCE OF MY MOUTH – AND IN A CLEARING IN A FOREST HE SITS AND WEEPS AS STANLEY COMFORTS HIM –
> 'I SAY, OLD CHAP, WHAT'S THE MATTER?'
> 'MY WORD, MY WORD IS IMPOTENT –'
> 'FUCK THE WORD, LIVINGSTONE.'
> 'THAT'S WHAT I'M TRYING TO TELL YOU, OLD CHAP –'

                                        (*Looking for Livingstone*, p. 25)

Nourbese Philip attempts to map the silence, reading the silences and gaps in the discursive terrain previously mapped by colonial 'adventurers' who, supposedly, name the continent into existence. Where Livingstone travels with all the latest technology – compass, sexton, gun – and the Bible, Nourbese Philip's woman is armed only with her *body*, a mirror and a crude map.

The illusion of 'order' suggested by chronological, linear time is eschewed as the speaker travels in vast loops of time, encountering along the way several communities of women – the names of which are all anagrams for the word 'silence'. The concept of silence is explored in a range of ways, stressing the sensuality of body language or contrasting the spareness of silence with the excessive proliferation of the word, in what the poet characterizes as a patriarchal 'market place' of words. In one scene, for example, the traveller is forced to spend time in a sweat lodge to 'sweat away' and cleanse herself of the 'taint' of patriarchal language; as in *Salmon Courage*, Nourbese Philip draws on native Canadian culture for inspiration. In another encounter, with the 'NEECLIS', the woman traveller has a passionate affair with one of the women of this 'land of needle-women and weavers'. Eventually abandoned by her lover, Arwhal, in a room 'ablaze with coloured fabric and yarn', the traveller is told to 'piece together the words of [her] silence'. Memories of her lover sustain her:

> watching the noon-day sun play hide-and-go-seek with water-damp bodies –
> first a flank then a nipple, challenging finger or tongue to follow – now a
> buttock, next the soft surround of navel, soon the long, swift curve of back . . .
> tufted, secret triangles of crinkly pleasure.
>
> (*Looking for Livingstone*, p. 53)

The traveller returns with the quilt of silence she has woven to spend fifty years sleeping under it with her lover, before moving on again in search of Livingstone. In 'The Museum of Silence', the traveller, appalled at 'the many and varied silences of different peoples' (p. 57) collected there, contemplates peeing on the structure but, instead, spits on the ground and leaves. By the end of this 'odyssey of silence', the reader is given a set of indulgently imaginative images and vocabularies with which to imagine silence.

The many and various meanings suggested in the exploration of silence also work to undermine and mock the monologic authority of Livingstone's account. The contrast between the woman's version of 'the quest', her openness to suggestions, to difference and to sharing, and that of the single-minded determination of Livingstone and Stanley's attitudes, works to unravel and diminish the latter. When the woman traveller finally meets Livingstone, for instance, she greets him with, 'You're new here aren't you?' (p. 61), having earlier wondered, 'Would I be cool enough to give him a first rate black hand shake and say, "Yo there, Livi baby, my man, my main man!"?' (p. 60). Philip here undermines the composed 'civility' of Stanley's fabled greeting, 'Dr Livingstone, I presume?' Elsewhere in the text, the traveller imagines Stanley and Livingstone squabbling like two schoolboys, and Livingstone says, 'Now see here, Stanley – this is *my* expedition – you just can't horn in on it like that, you know' (p. 24). Here, Nourbese Philip's use of 'horn in' also playfully *creolizes* Livingstone's speech ('horn in' is a Trinidadian expression which refers to the sexual appropriation by one man of another man's 'woman'). The dialogue between the two famous discoverers becomes increasingly farcical when Stanley cautions Livingstone: 'Gimmie, gimmie never gets – come on, let's be men about this Livingstone.'

It is important to stress that Nourbese Philip does not simply reverse hierarchies, replacing patriarchal discourse (as exemplified by Livingstone's narrative) with some innately superior women's discourse. Rather, she dramatizes the kinds of power relationships involved in any interaction between cultures, languages and epistemes, and suggests ways in which writing might be mobilized to expose the distortions, excesses and gaps in male discourses and so destabilize them. That *Looking for Livingstone* concludes with the black woman claiming both her silence *and* Livingstone's hand signals a belief in the power of textual forays which *can* transgress the impasse of Patriarchal Law; it asserts, too, a belief in the possibility of reclaiming something, however fractured, from the black woman's silence.

Though I have differentiated the way the body figures in the work of Goodison, Das, Nichols and Nourbese Philip from how it is used by the four poets discussed in Chapter 3, I would insist that I am not valorizing one group over another in some kind of feminist league table, whereby some women writers are perceived as more radical than others. I would prefer to stress the variety of ways in which the body is explored in these women's texts and the interesting possibilities for interpretation which this poses. 'Interpretation' of individual women's work through individual poems has been the thrust of my approach so far. In the following, and final, chapter of this book I shall seek to interpret larger textual entities: anthologies of writing by, and critical discussions of, Caribbean women poets, with a view to exposing the various mechanisms whereby the object of this study itself has been constituted.

Notes

1 Marlene Nourbese Philip, 'Managing the Unmanageable', in S. Cudjoe (ed.) *Caribbean Women Writers*, Wellesley, MA, Calaloux Publications, 1990, p. 298.
2 A. Parker, M. Russo, D. Sommer and P. Yaeger (eds), *Nationalisms and Sexualities*, London, Routledge, 1992, p. 1.
3 Chantal Chawaf, 'Linguistic Flesh', in S. Marks and I. de Courtivron (eds), *The New French Feminisms*, Brighton, Harvester, 1981, pp. 177–8.
4 Jamaica Kincaid, *The Autobiography of My Mother*, London, Virago, 1996, pp. 61–2.
5 Barbara Omolade, 'Hearts of Darkness', in A. Snitow, C. Stansell and S. Thompson (eds), *Desire: The Politics of Sexuality*, London: Virago, 1984, p. 371.
6 Michael Dash, 'In Search of the Lost Body: Redefining the Subject in Caribbean Literature', *Kunapipi*, 11, 1, 1989, p. 20.
7 Frantz Fanon, *Black Skin, White Masks*, London, Pluto, 1986.
8 Ibid., pp. 179–80.
9 Edward Kamau Brathwaite, *The Arrivants: A New World Trilogy*, London: Oxford University Press, 1978 [1967], p. 30.
10 David Dabydeen, 'Slave Song', *Turner: New and Selected Poems*, London, Cape Poetry, 1994 [originally published in *Slave Song*, 1984], p. 46.
11 Paula Burnett, *The Penguin Book of Caribbean Verse in English*, London, Penguin, 1986, p. 363.
12 Ibid.

13 Derek Walcott, 'The Schooner Flight', in *Collected Poems 1948–1984*, New York, The Noonday Press, Farrar, Straus & Giroux, 1986; pp. 345–61.

14 G.R. Coulthard, *Race and Colour in Caribbean Literature*, London, Oxford University Press, 1962, p. 91.

15 Ibid., p. 90.

16 W. Adolphe Roberts, 'Maroon Girl', in Burnett, *Penguin Caribbean Verse*, p. 141.

17 Edward Kamau Brathwaite, 'Nametracks', in *Mother Poem*, London, Oxford University Press, 1977, p. 56.

18 Dionne Brand, *Bread out of Stone: Recollections, Sex, Recognitions, Race, Dreaming, Politics*, Toronto, Coach House, 1994, p. 27.

19 Jamaica Kincaid, *Annie John*, London, Picador, 1985, p. 27.

20 Erna Brodber, *Jane and Louisa Will Soon Come Home*, London, New Beacon Books, 1980, p. 143.

21 Virginia Woolf, 'Professions for Women', in *Collected Essays*, vol. 2, London, Hogarth, 1966, pp. 287–8.

22 Sandra Gilbert and Susan Gubar, *No Man's Land*, New Haven, Yale University Press, 1990, p. 254.

23 Alicia Ostriker, *Stealing the Language: Women and Poetic Identity*, London, The Women's Press, 1987, pp. 91–121.

24 Cora Kaplan, *Sea Changes: Essays on Culture and Feminism*, London: Verso, 1986, p. 71.

25 Cixous, Hélène, 'The Laugh of the Medusa', in Marks and de Courtivron (eds), *New French Feminisms*, p. 256.

26 Chawaf, 'Linguistic Flesh', p. 177.

27 Susan Sellers, *Language and Sexual Difference*, London, Macmillan, 1991, p. 140.

28 Edward Kamau Brathwaite, 'Submerged Mothers', *Jamaica Journal*, 9, 2 and 3, p. 48.

29 Cixous, 'The Laugh of the Medusa', p. 248. My emphasis.

30 Diana Fuss, *Essentially Speaking*, New York, Routledge, 1989.

31 Lorna Goodison's publications include: *Tamarind Season*, Kingston, The Institute of Jamaica, 1980; *I Am Becoming My Mother*, London, New Beacon, 1986; *Heartease*, London, New Beacon, 1988; *To Us, All Flowers Are Roses*, Urbana and Chicago, University of Illinois Press, 1995; *Turn Thanks*, Urbana and Chicago, University of Illinois Press, 1999.

32 Walcott, 'Mass Man', in *Collected Poems*, p. 99.

33 Alice Walker, *In Search of Our Mothers' Gardens*, London, The Women's Press, 1984, pp. 231–43.

34 Adrienne Rich, *Of Woman Born: Motherhood as Experience and Institution*, London, Virago, 1977, p. 235.

35 'An Interview with Lorna Goodison', Wolfgang Binder, *Commonwealth Essays and Studies*, 13, 2, Spring 1991, pp. 49–59.

36 Ibid., p. 57.

37 Walcott, *Collected Poems*, p. 346.

38 Mahadai Das, *I Want to Be a Poetess of My People*, Georgetown, Guyana National Service Publishing Centre, 1976; *My Finer Steel Will Grow*, Richford, Vermont, Samisdat, 1982; *Bones*, Leeds, Peepal Tree Press, 1988.

39 See, for example, Ralph Premdas, 'Race and Ethnic Relations in Burnhamite Guyana', in D. Dabydeen and B. Samaroo (eds), *Across the Dark Waters: Ethnicity and Indian Identity in the Caribbean*, London, Macmillan, 1996 pp. 39–64.

40 L. Peake and D.A. Trotz, *Gender, Ethnicity and Place: Women and Identities in Guyana*, London, Routledge, 1999, p. 51.

41 Jeremy Poynting, 'East Indian Women in the Caribbean: Experience and Voice' in D. Dabydeen and B. Samaroo (eds) *India in the Caribbean*, London, Hansib, 1987, p. 243.

42 I am also indebted to Jeremy Poynting for his generosity in sending me photocopies of Das's earlier work and that of Shana Yardan and Rajkumari Singh.

43 See writers such as Ramabai Espinet, Shani Mootoo, Lelawattee Manoo-Rahming and Oonya Kempadoo, among others.
44 Burnham came to power in 1964; Guyana gained independence in 1966 and became a 'co-operative republic' in 1970.
45 Poynting, 'East Indian Women in the Caribbean', p. 243.
46 Walter Rodney was the leader of the multi-racial Working People's Alliance which formed in the mid-1970s to challenge Burnham's increasingly totalitarian government.
47 See Peter Hulme and Neil Whitehead (eds), *Wild Majesty: Encounters with Caribs from Columbus to the Present Day*, Oxford, Clarendon Press, 1992.
48 Wilson Harris, 'The Schizophrenic Sea', in A. Bundy (ed.), *Selected Essays of Wilson Harris: The Unfinished Genesis of the Imagination*, London, Routledge, 1999, p. 106.
49 See Pauline Melville, *The Ventriloquist's Tale*, London, Bloomsbury, 1997, for a sustained exploration of 'Amerindian' life in Guyana (Melville focuses in particular on the Macusi and Wapisiana peoples).
50 Sylvia Plath, 'Lady Lazarus', *Collected Poems*, Ted Hughes (ed.), London, Faber, 1981, p. 247.
51 Ibid., pp. 129–30.
52 Ibid., pp. 221–2.
53 Ntozake Shange, 'wow . . . yr just like a man!' *Nappy Edges*, London, Methuen, 1987, p. 16.
54 Grace Nichols' publications include: *i is a long memoried woman*, London, Karnak House, 1983; *The Fat Black Woman's Poems*, London, Virago, 1984; *Lazy Thoughts of a Lazy Woman*, London, Virago, 1989; *Sunris*, London, Virago, 1996.
55 V.S. Naipaul, *The Middle Passage*, Harmondsworth, Penguin, 1969 [1962], p. 29.
56 Brathwaite, *The Arrivants*, pp. 18–19.
57 Sander L. Gilman, 'Black Bodies, White Bodies: Toward an Iconography of Female Sexuality in Late Nineteenth-century Art, Medicine, and Literature', in Henry Louis Gates, Jr. (ed.), *'Race', Writing, and Difference*, Chicago, University of Chicago Press, 1985, pp. 232–5.
58 Walt Whitman, from 'Song of Myself', in *The Norton Anthology of Poetry*, 3rd edn, A.W. Allison *et al.* (eds), New York, W.W. Norton & Co., 1983, p. 760.
59 Walcott, *Collected Poems*, pp. 17–18.
60 Elizabeth Grosz, *Volatile Bodies: Toward a Corporeal Feminism*, Bloomington and Indianapolis, Indiana University Press, 1994, p. 41; my emphasis.
61 Gabrielle Griffin, '"Writing the Body": Reading Joan Riley, Grace Nichols and Ntozake Shange', in Gina Wisker (ed.), *Black Women's Writing*, London, Macmillan, 1993, p. 33.
62 Ibid., p. 21.
63 Ibid., p. 26.
64 Cixous, 'The Laugh of the Medusa', p. 251.
65 Marlene Nourbese Philip's collections of poetry include: *Thorns*, Toronto, Williams-Wallace, 1980; *Salmon Courage*, Toronto, Williams-Wallace, 1983; *She Tries Her Tongue, Her Silence Softly Breaks*, Charlottetown, Ragweed Press, 1989; *Looking for Livingstone*, Stratford, Ontario, Mercury Press, 1991.
66 Carol Morrell (ed.), *Grammar of Dissent: Poetry and Prose by Claire Harris, M. Nourbese Philip and Dionne Brand*, Fredericton, New Brunswick, Goose Lane, 1994, p. 98.
67 The poems included in the section 'Cyclamen Girl' pursue further the specific oppressions engendered by religion, and its consequences for the black girl-child.
68 Edward Kamau Brathwaite, 'Nametracks', in *Mother Poem*, p. 56.

5 Playing the field

Anthologizing, canonizing and problematizing Caribbean women's writing

God, what a trade to ply
distilling cris de coeur
with one sly eye
on metropolitan markets conditions.[1]

Now in a space she claims
that feels sometimes
like home
a woman poet of the new tongue
at evening time
sings alone.[2]

O Adam
make me a poet please
and not no wo-man poet
let me be free
and gender
less dear Ad . . .

At this point I stopped Eaves-dropping[3]

In the previous chapters I discussed the work of individual Caribbean women poets in relation to a variety of issues, including the quest for literary models, and literary mothers, gendered debates about the aesthetics and politics of Creole poetry, and the connections between textuality and sexuality. This final chapter has a much broader remit in that it shifts away from a focus on the individual poet to interrogate the category 'Caribbean women's writing' itself. Using a range of anthologies of Caribbean women's prose and poetry, as well as collections of critical essays about this writing, I want to explore how 'the' Caribbean woman writer has come to be defined and read. What characterizes the archetypal Caribbean woman writer? Who qualifies? What gets left out? Beginning with a comparison of two anthologies of Caribbean women's poetry – *Jamaica Woman*, published in 1980, and *Creation Fire*, published in 1990 – the discussion which follows is more concerned with what these anthologies represent as publications which have signposted Caribbean women's poetry as a distinct field of writing than with detailed discussion of the poems included in these anthologies.

Jamaica Woman, edited by Pamela Mordecai and Mervyn Morris,[4] was the first anthology of Caribbean poetry to appear which selected texts by women only. The title of the collection, *Jamaica Woman*, signals its focus clearly, suggesting in its use of the singular that the constituency of poets included is to be taken as representative of the broader constituency of Jamaican women. The title also recalls Louise Bennett's poem 'Jamaica Oman', which opens:

> Jamaica oman cunny, sah!
> Is how dem jinnal so?
> Look how long dem liberated
> An de man dem never know![5]

The poem goes on to praise the clever ('jinnal') way in which Jamaican women exercise their strength and power without arousing suspicion in their men. The limitations of this *covert* exercise of women's power might be demonstrated in the preface to *Jamaica Woman* in the somewhat ambiguous stance taken in relation to feminism by the editors in their short preface:

> Because these poets are all women, one may be tempted to raise the issue of whether they are 'poets who happen to be women', or something called 'woman poet'. But that is not the point. The poems are various. [. . .] there is nothing limp in the responses of the poets here, nor is there any aggressive feminism in their work.
>
> (*Jamaica Women*, p. xi)

The preface simultaneously acknowledges and denies the relevance of gender to poetic output and attempts to avoid knotty gender politics by asserting that 'These are some poems we like'. This caginess about feminism perhaps suggests a suspicion about 'feminism' as an 'imported' ideology and a reluctance to risk alienating a readership for whom a nationalist, rather than feminist, agenda is paramount. The preface then, perhaps inadvertently, highlights the tensions between 'Jamaica' and 'woman'. There is a similarly defensive tone in the reassurances that the poems are not 'limp' but neither are they 'aggressive' and that the poets 'often demonstrate a striking "distance" from their content'. In other words, although these poets 'happen' to be women, the poems are strong but balanced, truthful but not embarrassingly confessional. Interestingly, the editors suggest that the poets included *do* share a distinctive use of language: 'What these poets most noticeably share is a language, flexible in its range; they revel in the long continuum of Jamaican English; they push "nation language" in all kinds of directions' (p. xii). While this point is made too fleetingly for sustained discussion, it does resonate with the arguments presented in earlier chapters of the present work about the gendered use of Creole.

If the title and preface of *Jamaica Woman* generate interesting ambivalences, examination of the cover of the book is also instructive. The image used, an untitled work by Ras Daniel Hartmann,[6] is a close-up of a black woman's face. She gazes wearily from beneath her head-tie with lips sealed, conveying a sense of long-suffering patience and strength. Clearly, the choice of this image to 'front' the collection reflects a commitment to identifying with the struggles of the most poor in Jamaica. But, in the implication that it is the black working-class woman who is the representative Jamaican woman in the text, it might also be seen as signalling an anxiety about being 'misread' as more indulgently feminist. In other words, the image functions to signal the text's worthiness. However, while many of the poems *do* reflect a concern with 'the folk', the collection also includes the treatment of a diverse range of themes and concerns which do *not* speak directly to the stoicism of the image of woman on the cover.

In Cyrene Tomlinson's 'Foam, Foment, Ferment', the persona is clearly identifiable with the image of the oppressed woman on the cover of the text, charting the way in which the poor black Jamaican woman is the most vulnerable to the vacuous promises of politicians and 'big men':

> An all di official dem a do
> Is siddung wid 'a nuh mi, a yu'
> So dem call fi di whole heapa ism
> All mi can see is pure 'pass-di-buck-ism'
> Big man dis an big man dat
> all mi a hear a so-so chat
> > (*Jamaica Woman*, p. 87)

Pamela Mordecai also speaks on behalf of the poor Jamaican woman, but her speech is framed by a range of politically 'radical' patriarchal discourses which dramatize their implication in her marginalization:

> On the corner, again and again, see
> me sit with my needle and spoon, see me
> puffin' my spliff, see me splittin' my mind,
> see me teenager dead from the blows of
> your words that baptize me according to
> Lenin and Marx – 'You are no one, no one.'
> > (*Jamaica Woman*, p. 101)

Christine Craig's 'Poem' offers another perspective on the image of the 'loud silence' conveyed in the resolutely sealed lips of the woman on the cover of *Jamaica Woman*:

> And you must know this now.
> I, me, I am a free black woman.
> My grandmothers and their mothers

knew this and kept their silence
to compost up their strength,
kept it hidden
and played the game of deference
and agreement and pliant will.
                    (*Jamaica Woman*, pp. 8–9)

While these three poems reflect the mood of survivalism suggested in the image
on the cover of this collection, others reflect more diverse experiences. Many
question the degree to which the 'sexual revolution' liberated women – or
disappointed them. Bridget Jones, for example, in 'Thermo-static', captures that
1970s imperative to be 'cool' after a night of 'free love':

Today
We pass
By Barclays bank
Your left lid flickers
I crook a digit

Cool cool.
        (*Jamaica Woman*,
                    p. 47)

Dorothea Edmondson, in 'The Roots-man', exposes the ways in which 'the
brother's' radical black politics is dramatically compromised in the bedroom:

He calls her his Union Jack
she calls him her black.
but when he's wracked
with rebel rage
she purrs, tiger in my cage,
when he nightly prays
to fix just that one imperialist
when he struggles with that there flag,
she goads, fakir-nigger
                    (*Jamaica Woman*, p. 23)

Edmondson depicts the 'red-haired woman' with 'Her mistress-of-the manor
style' as ruling the roost, and she juxtaposes this to the black brother's insistence
that 'you, black woman woman,/stand behind your man,/build your black man'
(p. 23) to foreground the way in which 'race politics' are compromised by 'sex
politics'. Like the poems by Mordecai and Tomlinson, Edmondson's 'The
Roots-man' poses its challenge to 'the brothers' assertively, indicting nationalist
patriarchs for ignoring black women's realities. Edmondson complicates this
indictment further by drawing attention to the white woman's complicity in this
process.

Another aspect of *Jamaica Woman* which is pertinent to this discussion concerns the identity of the contributors. The preface suggests that the function of the anthology is to provide a platform for women to be published: 'Each author is a woman who has not yet had a separate volume of her poems published' (p. xi). Beyond this, however, the notes on contributors are largely devoted to identifying their areas of work: the majority of the women included work either in the field of education or in various arts/media arenas. The nationality and/or 'race' of the contributors is not addressed as an issue, although the anthology includes Jamaican-born women, of diverse ethnicities, as well as those from outside the region who resided in Jamaica. Such casual permissiveness makes an interesting contrast to some later publications where an uneasiness about 'origins' can lead to rather anxious identifications, as in the following:

> I'm not a *real* Jamaican. Let me explain. I was born in the island's capital. [. . .] But, I've got a strong Lancashire accent which *real* Jamaicans find funny [. . .] still I suppose I'll always be a displaced person – an African-Jamaican-English-Boltonian a long way from home. [My emphasis][7]

That *Jamaica Woman* is less self-conscious about pinpointing the racial, cultural or national identities of its various contributors is partly accounted for by the fact that it predates this 'identity politics'. But it might also be explained as deriving from the characteristically hybrid nature of Jamaican ethnicities, while the category 'black woman' appears to be a more 'obvious' category. And the contributors to *Jamaica Woman* do embody a very diverse range of ethnic and cultural identities. That such plurality is elided in the choice of image for the cover of the text, however, suggests the pervasiveness of an Afrocentric identity as the normatively nationalist one, despite the simultaneous recognition and embrace of multiple ethnicities in the choice of contributors.

Where the editors of *Jamaica Woman* frame the collection on a carefully placatory note, Ramabai Espinet, the editor of *Creation Fire*,[8] adopts a much more assertive tone. *Creation Fire* was published, in Toronto, ten years after *Jamaica Woman* and, where the latter had included eighty-two poems by fifteen poets, the former is a much more substantial collection and includes over 250 poems by 121 women. This anthology has its genesis in an explicitly stated feminist context, that of the Caribbean Association for Feminist Research and Action (CAFRA): 'The idea of such an anthology was born at the launching of CAFRA as an association in 1985. The formation of an organization dedicated to feminist research was an exciting and thrilling one' (pp. xiii–xv). Espinet describes the collection as one of CAFRA's first projects, initiated by the desire to create a context in which women of the region would feel more confident in their ability to write – and to make that writing public. So, where the editors of *Jamaica Woman* suggest that 'whether they are "poets who happen to be women" or something called "woman poet" [. . .] is not the point', *Creation Fire* wears its ideological commitment to feminism boldly on its sleeve; being a woman and a writer is precisely the point here. This clearly stated ideological agenda is both the strength and weakness of the anthology. On the one hand, the unequivocal alignment with feminism insists on its relevance to Caribbean women and on the commitment of Caribbean feminists to redefining the term to suit their needs. As Rhoda Reddock and Rawwida Baksh-Soodeen argue in the preface:

> The incorporation of the word 'feminist' in our name claimed for Caribbean and other Third World women the right to focus on all the strategic issues facing women in our societies; issues which span the range of the social, economic, cultural, political and social.
>
> (*Creation Fire*, p. ii)

What is less clear is how literary production can be harnessed to such overtly political ends. If, in the image of the long-suffering woman on the cover of *Jamaica Woman*, a degree of affinity with 'grassroots women' is being claimed by the editors, then this identification with women as oppressed subjects is more pronounced in *Creation Fire*. The editors of the anthology were clear that 'We sought originally to reach the so-called "grassroots constituency" (p. xx). However, when the original call for poems elicited only fifty poems, Espinet wrote an essay in which she spelt out the difficulties facing the would-be woman poet, and this essay, along with information about CAFRA and about the purpose of the anthology, "formed the basis of a kit which we distributed throughout the Region" (p. xv):

> Recent research throughout the Caribbean region reveals that there are many more struggling literary females than the printed output would lead us to believe. [. . .] It is in the interest of redressing this perceived deficiency in the publication of women's poetry in the Caribbean that CAFRA has initiated the task of compiling an anthology of contemporary poetry. The problem of writing and publishing is compounded by our history of slavery and indentureship, colonialism and its attendant disabling mechanisms.
>
> (*Creation Fire*, p. xiv)

The response resulting from the circulation of this 'kit' was, in Espinet's words, 'a torrential array of poetry. Over 500 poems were received.' The editor suggests that the preoccupation with resistance in many of the poems 'arose organically out of the mass of the poetry lying in front of us'. Given the method in which poems were solicited, it is clearly no surprise that many women delivered 'feminist' poems. However, rather than acknowledging the role of the anthology *in constructing* this feminist agenda, the editors coyly elide responsibility and suggest instead that a literary sisterhood was, somehow, already there simply awaiting the encouragement to go public:

> Somewhere in Suriname, late at night or very early in the morning, a woman is sitting in a room alone, writing. Somewhere in Guyana another woman sits doing exactly the same thing. [. . .] She writes because she must. She is writing for her life. And in other parts of the Caribbean too – Trinidad,

Curacao, St Lucia, Jamaica, Barbados, – throughout the archipelago all the way to Belize, and further down into South America, women are writing themselves into being.

(*Creation Fire*, p. xiii)

This organicist view of women's writing is consolidated further on in the introduction: 'one of the literary rewards of editing this anthology was the sense of *discovering the voice of the Caribbean woman*' (p. xix; my emphasis).

Another strategy used to consolidate this notion of a collective/representative Caribbean woman's voice is the adoption of as *all-inclusive* an editorial strategy as possible; ideally, *all* the poems submitted would have been included, 'none of us wanted to lose any of this poetry although it was clear that it could not all be published. It was an important historical record' (p. xvi). This archival approach perhaps also explains the lack of stringent aesthetic criteria; contributions included 'the voices of schoolgirls who show as yet undeveloped potential, and some are older women with dreams of writing channelled, out of necessity, into other familial enterprises, but resurrected for this anthology' (p. xxi). Earlier in the introduction Espinet suggested that not only were there more women writing than publication statistics would suggest but that 'invariably, the product is poetry. It is not difficult to understand why. It is easier, after all, to write a poem if one has a few minutes between cooking, looking after children and coping with house-work than a novel or a play' (p. xiv). To some extent, this interpretation of the connection between gender and genre sounds convincing; and it probably *is* the case that shorter forms (short stories and poetry) are being published in greater numbers than novels by Caribbean women. However, the quote above implies that poems – *because* they are short – can be 'knocked off' in between household chores. This approach appears also to conflate *testimony* unproblematically with poetry. Perhaps, too, it points to the contradictory nature of poetry as a genre. In 'Poetic License', Helen Carr argues that:

> Poetry is regarded in our culture in very contradictory ways, and those contradictions seem intimately bound up with gender. It is seen both as a prestigious, elite and esoteric form, and as a private, intimate, intensely subjective one. And whilst considered in the former way women may feel intimidated, in the latter they, and less privileged men, can regard poetry as a place in which they are enfranchised.[9]

I agree with Carr that poetry, despite being a genre which is tightly governed by conventions and artifice with regard to language-use, is invariably the literary genre most closely associated with 'feelings', expressions of self and spontaneity. Indeed, Espinet implies this connection when she says, 'To mark the birth of CAFRA many women spontaneously wrote poetry' (p. xiii). Here, poetry is presented as a genre that is 'naturally' suitable for expressing emotions; when one adds to this the familiar assumption that women are 'naturally' better than men at expressing emotions, the 'naturalness' of the link between women and poetry –

particularly 'confessional poetry' – is consolidated. The reference in the introduction of *Creation Fire* to the 'torrential array of poetry' (p. xv) and the elemental resonances of the title of the collection itself further solidifies the sense of there being a *natural* fit between women and poetry.

But the notion of poetry as 'spontaneous outpouring' is at odds with the materialist focus which engendered the anthology itself, for it suggests that writing poetry does not involve *labour*. Instead the introduction at several points implies that *real* work involves physical exertion – the photograph which precedes the section entitled 'The Worker' most obviously underscores this implication: it features a woman, who appears to be a field worker, displaying a pair of overworked, weather-beaten hands. The ideological imperative to valorize the hard-working women of the Caribbean, particularly agricultural labourers, is laudable, but perhaps other types of work might also have been recognized as valid in the struggle against oppressive patriarchal structures. Indeed, the biographical blurbs on each of the women included in *Creation Fire* indicate that many of these women are active politically in a range of women's groups and in the fields of education and culture, where the vast majority of them are employed. The selective use of images and the political claims made for the anthology inflate the political role of the woman poet while simultaneously offering a reductive account of the production of poetry.

Finally, the cover of this anthology also begs commentary: it is a batik painting (by the Jamaican, Sharon Chacko) depicting a naked black woman suckling a baby in a lush tropical setting, with water, mountains, various flora and fauna, and an erupting volcano in the background. The woman is lean and muscular and both she and the baby wear their hair in short dread locks, signalling their black identity unequivocally. Chacko's tableau reconfigures the familiar madonna and child icon of Christianity, inflecting it with a powerful black female presence. This strong image frames the text and signals a particular kind of identity to the prospective reader: the fact that the woman is naked, is suckling a baby *and* is embedded in nature works to emphasize her elemental strength; she is one with nature. That the blackness of the woman is also clearly signalled consolidates the black woman as mother earth. The image, however inadvertently, occludes the diversity and differences of/between the women represented in the anthology. It is apparent that the editorial committee exerted considerable effort to include a representative range of women; the photographs and mini-bios provided in the text demonstrate the diverse ethnicities of the contributors and indicate an almost exhaustive spread of Caribbean locations as well as including contributions from some women born in the UK and USA who have spent time in the region. The anthology is also inclusive linguistically, seeking to challenge colonially defined divisions within the region by including poems in French, Spanish and Dutch/ Papiamento, with English translations. Clearly, no one image can contain such diversity, but it is interesting that it is the black woman who is, again, used as a 'default' representative of Caribbean woman, even as diversity and difference are again embraced, consolidating further the defining parameters outlined in the discussion of *Jamaica Woman* above. Nonetheless, despite these quibbles, both anthologies represent a commitment to Caribbean feminism in the collating of these women's voices and, as such, provide the crucial platform which makes possible discussion and contestation about the constituency 'Caribbean woman writer' in the first place.

This sensitivity to linguistic diversity in the region is a feature of another anthology, *The Literary Review: Women Poets of the Caribbean*, guest edited by Pam Mordecai and Betty Wilson in summer 1992.[10] As in *Creation Fire*, the editors link the transgression of linguistic boundaries with a broadly transgressive women's poetics and are similarly anxious to establish the anthology's radical pedigree. The editors of this collection, however, privilege those Caribbean women poets actually based within the region, arguing that 'owing to space constraints we would use this issue for the work of those who live here, who have limited access to publication, and whose work would be unlikely to reach a US audience save for an opportunity like this' (*The Literary Review*, p. 445).

This editorial choice, indicative of a commitment to challenging the privileged access to publication of those poets based in various metropolitan centres, is shared by Margaret Watts, who edited another anthology of poetry, published in 1990: *Washer Woman Hangs Her Poems in the Sun: Poems by Women of Trinidad and Tobago*.[11] Watts's criteria for inclusion – 'the writers must be born, bred and resident in Trinidad or Tobago or citizens who live here' (p. x) – are also contextualized, interestingly, with regard to the prolific output of *Jamaican* women poets. Both collections, inevitably, result in the problematic omission of poets based 'abroad' and point to an area of tension between locatedness within the region and broader, diasporic poetic identities.

Both of these anthologies also draw attention, as did *Jamaica Woman* and *Creation Fire*, to the question of literary value. Mordecai and Wilson acknowledge, for instance, that some of the poems are 'strong and powerful, others simple, naive, almost childish. Some are less "evolved" and are still imitatively linked to traditional forms' (p. 447). Watts argues that 'form is perhaps the weakest element in the collection' and 'Many of the rhymed poems submitted suffered from inferior word choices and sentence structures, made in order to accommodate the rhyme (and rhythm).' She goes on to suggest that 'There is a profound need for critics. Poetry will improve and flourish when it can respond to some serious criticism' (pp. xiii–xiv). This attitude to the aesthetic qualities and merit in the establishment of a women's tradition of poetry, while markedly more permissive than that taken in response to the originary texts in a national(ist) canon of West Indian poetry (as discussed in Chapter 1), is not without its own problems. In particular, it is difficult to know how to read those (many) poems included in these anthologies which suffer from poor crafting of various kinds.

The editors of both these anthologies also share an emphasis on an explicitly archival approach and a self-consciousness about their place in relation to their literary antecedents:

> This publication joins *Jamaica Woman* and the ground-breaking CAFRA anthology [. . .] *Creation Fire*, as well as an increasing number of collections by

individual poets; together these books BEGIN the work of documenting the writing of Caribbean women in this most ancient of literary genres.

(*The Literary Review*, p. 446)

In *Washer Woman*, the appeal to a broader-based, grassroots constituency of women is consolidated in the choice of title for the collection:

> The symbol of Washerwoman is an old one, and not in some ways, an appealing one. The communal exercise of washing and gossiping and laughing has nearly disappeared. Many modern women want to drown the washerwoman part of their lives, for washing seems a drudgerous domestic duty which has kept them from realizing their more attractive and lasting potential.
>
> (*Washer Woman*, p. xiv)

A photograph of Minshall's Washerwoman (carnival Queen of the 'River' band, 1984) is used for the cover of the anthology. The parallel drawn by the editor between washerwomen and poets and between the public 'airing' of washing and of poems perhaps strains to make the connection; though the fact that it is a *carnival* version of this reality which is privileged helps to emphasize that it is the symbolism of this connection which is paramount. The image on the cover of *The Literary Review* similarly draws attention to its status as 'art' rather than inviting a 'realistic' reading; the image, painted by Seya Parboosingh, is of two women's faces suspended in a brightly coloured surround of flowers, foliage and sea in which bold brush strokes and geometric lines declare its abstractness.

Caribbean women have also featured prominently in anthologies of black British women's writing and I shall discuss a selection of these briefly to highlight the shifting definitions of both 'Caribbean' and 'black'. I draw attention to the British context because it is here, more than in other metropolitan locations, that Caribbean women have signalled a distinct literary identity. Clearly, there are historical reasons for the high profile of Caribbean writers in the UK. The USA, with a very different pattern and history of migration, has a strong African American tradition which has tended to *include* – or subsume – Caribbean/black writing under its rubric. Canada, with a more recent history of Caribbean migration in comparison to Britain, appears to be repeating Britain's divisive discriminations despite its rhetoric of multiculturalism. In the Canadian context, publishing houses such as Sister Vision, which published *Creation Fire*, have recently been instrumental in providing Caribbean women writers with a platform alongside other women of colour.

Watchers and Seekers: Creative Writing by Black Women in Britain, published in 1987 by The Women's Press, was edited by Rhonda Cobham and Merle Collins (the former a Trinidadian, the latter Grenadian).[12] It could be argued that this is the foundational text for black British women's writing, being one of the first to anthologize black women's texts as a discrete category. James Berry had edited *News for Babylon* three years earlier, in 1984, but this had included only four women out of a total of forty poets and this fact, along with the robustly challenging, 'in-your-face' attitude implied in the title, perhaps suggests an agenda in which the challenge to British culture eclipses a focus on gendered issues.[13] *Watchers and Seekers* is an anthology of poems and short stories (illustrations and an autobiographical essay are also featured), which includes work by twenty-six women whose 'origins' are extremely diverse. The 'Notes on Contributors' indicates that the majority of the women are West Indian (of varied ethnicities), or of West Indian origins, though there are also contributors from India and Nigeria. Not all of the contributors declare their national or cultural origins, endorsing the sense that it is their shared identification as 'black' which shapes the anthology.

Interestingly, Rhonda Cobham's introductory essay begins, 'In the search for foremothers to the writers presented in this anthology, the figure and work of the poet, Una Marson, cannot be overlooked' (p. 3). She cites Una Marson as an appropriate literary foremother for *all* the women included in this text, suggesting that Marson's anxious quest to find 'an authentic literary style', her restless journeyings, and the lack of recognition accorded her during her lifetime, all resonate with the concerns of the women included in *Watchers and Seekers*:

> The writers whose works have been brought together in this anthology share with Marson an awareness of themselves, as Black people and as women, that informs their relationship to their art and their societies. Like her, many of them have lived between societies.
>
> (*Watchers and Seekers*, p. 5)

In Cobham's construction, Marson is a symbolic mother-figure for all the women included in the anthology, regardless of their 'origins', because of her literal – and literary – mobility; she functions as a black Everywoman. Further, Cobham argues that Marson's 'significance [. . .] goes further than the coincidence of race, gender and social situation' because of her recognition of the need for a style that could 'reflect and utilise *the heritage of those half-forgotten voices, skills and gestures*' (p. 7; my emphasis). The emphasis here on the *embodiment* of culture is consolidated in the concluding paragraph of the introduction, where she harnesses all the women's voices together in an image of the anthology itself as 'back home':

> Perhaps then you will understand why, each time I read through the collection, I have the illusion of being 'back home' for that family reunion of sisters and cousins we've been promising ourselves for years: where we'll cook home food, laugh raucously at the most inane jokes, share political obsessions and spiritual insights, rap about relationships and generally heal each other of all the scars of all those years of achieving and surviving like the strong Black women we cannot always be.
>
> (*Watchers and Seekers*, p. 11)

This notion of a sisterhood of black women has been articulated in various ways and is often designated as an example of Alice Walker's term 'womanism';

so, perhaps one can read Cobham's deliberate location of this anthology's 'home' in the Caribbean as a way of relocating black feminism away from its more familiar African American location to the UK. Cobham does not address the issue of the misfit between her use of the label 'black' – which applies to those Indian and Chinese women included in the anthology – and its use within the Caribbean, where it generally refers exclusively to those of African origin. Unlike the anthologies discussed above, whose definition included the 'white' West Indian (as well as, in some cases, the European and North American) woman, this anthology is organized as a specific platform for *black* women writers in Britain. This was clearly an expedient political necessity in Britain in the 1980s when black women rightly challenged the complacently white, middle-class associations of the category 'women writer', or indeed 'feminist'. Nonetheless, in this deployment of the category, 'Caribbean black' again operates as the dominant ethnicity, raising questions about the coupling of 'black' and 'Caribbean' as a suitably diverse category of analysis.

One of the poems included in this anthology and in *Creation Fire*, by the Chinese Guyanese writer Meiling Jin, speaks to this issue of invisible racial difference:

> My grand-father sailed on the ship
> Red-riding Hood:
> part of a straggly band
> of yellow humanity.
> They severed the string
> that tied them to the dragon,
> and we grew up never knowing
> we belonged
> to a quarter of the world's people.
> [. . .]
> One day I learnt
> a secret art,
> Invisible-Ness, it was called.
> I think it worked
> as even now, you look
> but never see me.[14]

It is also worth noting that the image on the cover of this anthology shares many features with those of the anthologies discussed above and might be seen as contributing to the process of 'invisibilizing' in the poem above. The image is of a lone black woman whose expression of gritty determination serves to consolidate the representation of the black woman as long-suffering, patient and strong. This image is also one which many of the pieces in the book are at pains to question; Maureen Ismay's poem, for example, 'Frailty Is Not My Name', opens:

> Frailty is not my name
> yet,

On the other hand,
I'm not a big strong, black woman
iron hard and carrying
all the sorrows of the world on my back.
                    (*Watchers and Seekers*, p. 15)

Another anthology, published a year after *Watchers and Seekers*, in 1988, is *Let It Be Told: Essays by Black Women in Britain*, a collection of essays by black women, focused on their roles as writers in a hostile 'host' country.[15] Of the eight writers featured in this anthology, four originate from the Caribbean and the remainder from Africa or Asia (interestingly, those from the Caribbean are all poets). Lauretta Ngcobo, the editor, argues:

> In the mainstream of life in Britain today, Blackwomen [*sic*] are caught between white prejudice, class prejudice, male power and the burden of history. [. . .] We want to materialize in the heart of this racist and sexist society where Blackwomen are invisible.
>
> > (*Let It Be Told*, p. 1)

As with the introduction to *Creation Fire*, Ngcobo's emphasis on the shared experiences and identities of 'Blackwomen' sometimes has the reverse effect of calling the collective identity of the category into question. This is most evident towards the end of the introduction, where Ngcobo states that there is now such a thing as 'the Blackwoman's viewpoint':

> From now on we exist. Where we had no collective considered viewpoint, now we have. In books such as this, we are carving for all Blackwomen a niche in British society.
>
> Needlesss to say, the critical opinions expressed in this introduction are my own. They are not necessarily shared by the women writers who have contributed to this volume.
>
> > (*Let It Be Told*, p. 34)

This disclaimer is indicative of a tension between the individual and the collective which inflects many of these anthologies. It foregrounds, too, some of the problems and anxietes generated by the category 'black woman writer' itself and the some of the limitations of mobilizing publications under such a heading.

Ngcobo's lengthy introduction outlines the contexts in which black women's texts are produced and read, and often there is a sense that the reader being addressed here is white and middle-class, if not male and hostile:

> We as Black writers at times displease our white readership. Our writing is seldom genteel since it springs from our experiences which in real life have none of the trimmings of gentility. If the truth be told, it cannot titillate the

aesthetic palate of many white people, for deep down it is a criticism of their values and their treatment of us throughout history.

(Let It Be Told, p. 4)

Here, experience is invoked as automatically authorizing. The suggestion that black women's texts are not 'genteel' – therefore 'raw'? – and unable to 'titillate' the white reader is, obviously, insultingly reductive of *both* constituencies of writers and readers. Further, Ngcobo's stance appears to want both to speak from the margins and to reject the very marginalization which that position signifies. This approach ignores the fact that experience must, necessarily, be mediated through a range of discursive conventions, and appeals to moral, rather than aesthetic, criteria for interpretation. Sara Suleri addresses these issues cogently in 'Woman Skin Deep: Feminism and the Postcolonial Condition', in which she argues: 'While lived experience can hardly be discounted as a critical resource for an apprehension of the gendering of race, neither should such data serve as the evacuating principle for both historical and theoretical contexts alike.'[16] I share Suleri's suspicion of the way in which 'theoretical interventions within this trajectory become minimalized into the naked category of lived experience' (p. 248), though this problematizing of 'experience' must, clearly, be accompanied by a commitment to exploring other, more nuanced ways in which marginalized realities *can* be articulated, and recognized.

With regard to poetry, Ngcobo argues, like Espinet, that it is the most spontaneous of literary genres. She suggests that 'Many Blackwomen writers prefer to communicate through poetry, a medium of expression which effectively enables them to deal *immediately* with the subjects that engage Black society' (*Let It Be Told,* p. 2; my emphasis). Experience is again presented as easily transferable to the page, and any critical gap between the 'life experiences' of the author and the text is elided.

Finally, while for the greater part of the introduction 'black' is the preferred term of reference, it is interesting to see that, although the involvement of Asian and black women in trade union action is noted, there is no discussion of the cultural implications of including Asian women within the category 'black', though one of the contributors is an Indian South African. Ngcobo notes that 'The majority of our community are people of Caribbean extraction' (p. 20) but there is no reference in the essay to those of other kinds of Caribbean extraction and the image on the cover of the book is of a young, black, dreadlocked woman.

When specific reference is made to Caribbean culture, interestingly, it is in relation to Caribbean women poets' use of Creole: 'the language which arouses more emotion than most, forged as it was in those centuries of darkness, out of scraps of human speech from everywhere. It is the language of triumph and achievement' (*Let It Be Told,* p. 2). And later: 'The various dialects of the Caribbean are not maimed English, but a creative reconstruction of language by people deprived of their own and thrown together in mute work teams. *This is our language,* and it should be accorded literary recognition' (p. 26; my emphasis). Here, Creole is valued for its subversive potential and is designated a paradigmatic 'black' language. Instead of invoking the more familiar associations of plurality and hybridity, however, Creole here consolidates the esssential *Blackwoman*'s identity. The refusal of more complex Creole identities is emphasized in the argument made with regard to 'mixed race' people:

> Instead of being drawn to identifying with either half of themselves, they are often pushed one way or another or else repelled both ways. The choice to be Black and accepted as such by other Black people has to be an emphatic one. *They have to live demonstrably Black lives and make a conscious decision to renounce their white heritage.*
>
> (*Let It Be Told*, p. 33; my emphasis)

The rigidity of the racial categories invoked here and the either/or choice suggested by Ngcobo are both radically out of step with the permissiveness and plurality usually associated with Creole. This calls into question the degree to which Caribbean women writers can be comfortably accommodated in the category 'Black British Woman Writer', at least as it is defined here. The St Lucian poet, Jane King, in her 'Yellow Girl Couplets', conveys the impossibility of Ngcobo's prescription above:

> Any more yellow girls out here
> fed up to their underwear
>
> of the double colour bar
> that haunts those with too little tar?[17]

Or, in 'Letter from Me', the speaker comments on her invisibility in a metropolitan landscape:

> I saw three black people walking
>   in Saratoga Springs but
> they didn't see me.
> I was so glad to see them but too pale
>   for them to notice
> not black enough to see.
> I've never anywhere in the world walked into
>   a room full of folk
> who look like me.[18]

Honor Ford-Smith conveys the complexity elided by Ngcobo, in a poem, 'Amputation: For Two Voices', in which the (brown) mother and ('mixed') daughter speak to/of the intimacies and contradictions of their difference:

> Mother:
> Cold, white
> invulnerable as alabaster,
> patronizing the impoverished

with visions of upliftment
handing down writs of judgement
on the colonized bourgeois – like me.

Daughter:
Wrong colour too.
But she would never say that out loud.
And she's the one who said she couldn't go
to the US with me when I was little.
Said they'd put me in the bus for whites
and her in the one for coloureds.[19]

The Guyanese writer Pauline Melville offers a more generous and lyrical portrait of her sister writer, Honor Ford-Smith (the daughter-figure in the poem above) in 'Honor Maria':

A dark mother, familiar with the names of plants
Birthed a daughter
Eyes green as Negril sea,
Hair blond as the golden sea-horse
That dances upside down in the waves.
Fair Jamaica.[20]

The following remarks, taken from another anthology of black women's writing, *Charting the Journey: Writings by Black and Third World Women*, might usefully be placed in dialogue with Ngcobo's introduction:

[T]here is the tendency towards the collective adornment of moral and political superiority which is supposed to derive from the mere fact of being a Black woman. [. . .] No longer do we succumb to spurious notions of unity when that 'unity' is based on conservative or even reactionary ideas.[21]

This anthology, which includes fiction, poetry, essays and interviews, is organized around the broader category, 'Black and Third World', and, perhaps inevitably given the diverse 'origins' of the forty-two contributors (all of whom now reside away from 'home'), it refuses to offer images of an imagined, collective homeland. Instead, the editors embrace the idea of migration as making possible profound remappings of the boundaries of home – and of self:

Migrations away from past social norms, from different realities, from petri-fied ideas, and from past selves. [. . .] This is what we are doing – preserving, extending and redefining ourselves in order to create a situation in which 'blackness' as commonly understood, has no social meaning. In effect we are consciously choosing to continue our migration into a better, more comfortable place where we are made in our own, ever-changing image.

(*Charting the Journey*, pp. 4–5)

Here, there is no nostalgic appeal to the homeland left behind but a commitment to, and engagement with, the place migrated *to*, with all its difficulties *and* possibilities. The abstract image on the cover of this anthology, of a multi-coloured splash of paint, perhaps also conveys the refusal of bounded identities and refuses some of the framing devices, discussed above, which have tended to render 'Indian', 'Chinese', 'mixed-race', or 'white' Caribbean women invisible.[22]

Increasing numbers of women have been included in more recent, 'male-stream' anthologies of Caribbean poetry and most of these include remarks on the 'phenomenon' of the increased visibility of women poets. Significantly, the other observation regularly made about current trends in Caribbean poetry is the increasing experimentation with oral forms, though connections are not made between these two trends (my argument in Chapters 2 and 3 suggests that attention to the gendering of Creole discourse foregrounds some interesting connections between these two developments). While this recognition of the increased output of women poets is not manifested in equal representation, numerically, in these anthologies, it complements the work of the specifically female-focused anthologies. So, for example, *The Penguin Book of Caribbean Verse in English*, edited by Paula Burnett (1986),[23] includes seventeen women and ninety-nine men. *Voiceprint: An Anthology of Oral and related Poetry from the Caribbean*, edited by Stewart Brown, Mervyn Morris and Gordon Rohlehr (1989), includes fourteen women and seventy-four men. *Hinterland Caribbean Poetry from the West Indies and Britain*, edited by E.A. Markham (1989), includes four women and ten men.[24] *The Heinemann Book of Caribbean Poetry*, edited by Ian McDonald and Stewart Brown (1992), features eighteen women and forty-three men.[25] While *Crossing Water: Contemporary Poetry of the English-speaking Caribbean*, edited by Anthony Kellman (1992),[26] includes twelve women and twenty-five men. The greater commitment to representing women poets evident in Kellman's collection is somewhat undermined by the tone of paternalism in the introduction, where he welcomes 'the unprecedented (and long overdue) visibility of female authors', but also issues a warning: 'However, just as the polemical bias tended to off balance the well-meaning nationalism of the 50s and early 60s, the politics of feminism, if they are not to be deepened and widened in aesthetic terms, can fall into this same monolithic trap' (p. xxv).

Trading on the margins[27] or playing the field?

The increasingly high profile of Caribbean women poets in the anthologies discussed above needs to be read alongside some of the other publications and processes which have contributed to the constitution of Caribbean women's writing as a discrete 'field' of study. I will now look briefly at a selection of conferences and collections of critical essays which have developed around the field of Caribbean women's writing to explore the degree to which these kinds of emphases are replicated in more self-consciously 'academic' discourse.

In April 1988, the Black Studies Department of Wellesley College hosted the First International Conference on Caribbean Women's Writing. First-hand reports confirm that, as Sue Greene describes, in a discussion of the second conference, 'everyone was aware that something momentous was happening'.[28] The proceedings of the conference were published in 1990 and include a lengthy introduction by the organizer of the conference, Selwyn Cudjoe, as well as some forty contributions by writers and critics.[29] General overviews of Caribbean women's writing in the English, Dutch, French and Spanish-speaking Caribbean were included; creative writers offered short fiction or reflections on being a writer, and critics offered a range of pieces on the sociocultural context as well as detailed readings of individual women's texts. There is a strong sense in this collection of the recognition and celebration of the Caribbean woman writer and less of an emphasis on the role of the critic, an emphasis which was reversed at the second conference. The celebratory mood of the conference perhaps explains why there is little attempt to interrogate the grounds upon which such a conference was organized: what Caribbean women writers have in common with each other is taken to be self-evident in the very *fact* of their Caribbean female identity.

What is also interesting is the self-conscious way in which the editor/conference organizer, Selwyn Cudjoe, presents the role of the conference, the publication – and, by implication, himself – in *creating* the category 'Caribbean woman writer'. In his acknowledgements Cudjoe says:

> I will always be grateful to A.J. Seymour [. . .] for triggering this idea in my mind. It was because of our conversation in January 1987 that I began to think of the possibility of having this conference. Certainly the publication of these essays represents a continuation of a project he started forty-five years ago and thus can be seen as a fitting tribute to his memory and his work.
>
> (*Caribbean Women Writers*, p. xii)

In this construction, Cudjoe aligns himself with one of the father-figures of the Caribbean literary tradition and, thus coupled, Seymour and Cudjoe appear as the founding fathers of Caribbean women's writing, as a branch of Caribbean Literature. In the opening paragraph of the introduction, Cudjoe consolidates this sense of paternity by implying that these women writers had had no other fora for meeting prior to the conference: 'For the first time since their ancestors came to the New World in the sixteenth century these women and men were able to come together to talk about their writing' (p. 5). He continues, 'This conference was the founding event of Caribbean women's writing.' There is no sense of irony in these declamations about the originary status of this conference/publication, a lack of irony made even more pointed given the juxtaposition on the left-hand side of the page of the image of the New World (an engraving by Jan van de Straet), configured as a naked woman reclining in a hammock surrounded by tropical flora and fauna being 'discovered' by a fully clothed male representative of Europe.[30] One is thus left with the unfortunate image of the editor as a modern-day, black Columbus-figure. Cudjoe does not place himself in relation to the material he is editing, nor does he ask questions about what it is about his location – as a *male* academic in an *American* university – which makes it possible for him to host such a conference, and for Caribbean women to have been inhibited from doing so. Given the dramatic claims being made by Cudjoe about the 'achievements of this conference' (listed under the heading, 'The Achievements of the Conference' at the end of the introduction) and the definitive way he maps out the terrain of Caribbean women's writing, some sense of his own location was necessary, beyond the claim of paternity.

A later publication, critical writings on a selection of Caribbean women prose writers, edited and introduced by Harold Bloom, provides an interesting parallel with Cudjoe's authoritative summarizing. Bloom prefaces his brief introduction to the collection with a few remarks on his own role as a Patriarchal Critic, and concludes:

> Sometimes I sadly think of myself as Bloom Brontosaurus, amiably left behind by the fire and the flood. But more often I go on reading the great women writers, searching for the aesthetic difference that yet may prove to be there, but which has not yet been found.[31]

It is puzzling, given these views, why Bloom was asked (and, indeed why he agreed), to edit such a collection (to promote 'rigorous' debate?). His short introduction briskly ranks the Caribbean women writers discussed in the book (Jamaica Kincaid's stance is 'rather less revolutionary than her highly ideological critical supporters stress it as being', and Paule Marshall's 'conventional style and sentimental characterizations [. . .] are likely to diminish the intrinsic importance of her achievement') before concluding with a sweeping and authoritative finale, 'the novel [*Wide Sargasso Sea*] remains the most successful prose fiction in English to emerge from the Caribbean matrix.' Caribbean women's writing might be described here as caught between a rock and a hard place, between the 'kind' and 'stern' paternalisms of Cudjoe and Bloom, respectively.

But to return to Cudjoe, his overall approach constructs Caribbean women's writing as a *branch* of Caribbean writing, rather than speculating on the ways in which women's texts may have a more complex and contestatory relationship to the male-dominated tradition of writing in the Caribbean.[32] Cudjoe's concluding paragraph merits quoting in full:

> The diversity and timeliness of these essays represent particular strengths of this volume and provide a basis upon which we can begin to understand the new configuration of Caribbean Literature. Probably one of the more imaginative volumes to come out on Caribbean Literature, *Caribbean Women Writers* may prove to be as important an intervention in the literature of the Americas as was Alain Locke's *The New Negro*, Addison Gayle's *The Black Aesthetic*, and Kenneth Ramchand's *The West Indian Novel and Its Background*. Just as important, it enlarges the boundaries of Caribbean literary discourse and thus outlines another of the many histories of America's literary imagination.
>
> (*Caribbean Women Writers*, p. 48)

Here, Caribbean women's writing is deftly nested in Caribbean Literature, which is nested in African American Literature, which is nested, in turn, in American Literature. Cudjoe does not make any connections between other *women's* literary traditions and practices, effectively muffling Caribbean women's writing as a gendered discourse.

Questions might also be asked about the processes involved in the selection and editing of the pieces included in *Caribbean Women Writers*. For example, Dionne Brand's contribution to the conference is not included and its absence not explained. In her essay, 'This Body for Itself', in *Bread out of Stone*, Brand describes her decision to abandon her proposed talk on 'poetry and politics' after listening to the other papers and deciding, 'what is missing: the sexual body'.[33] Instead, she read a short story, 'Miss Alaird's Breasts', which focused on the obsessive fascination of a class of 13-year-old girls with their French teacher's breasts. The response, in Brand's words, was:

> Outrage. I hear that some think I have ridiculed the woman in the story. I've been indecorous. No one tells me directly, but I sense that I've crossed the line. Only the feminists and lesbians talk to me after that. I'm late and I hear that the next session is charged with questions about lesbianism and homosexuality. It has taken the lunch hour for the story to sneak up on the audience. The lesbian *double entendre* has just dawned on some. [. . .] To write this body for itself feels like grappling for it, like trying to take it away from some force. Reaction to the story confirms this territorial pull and tug.[34]

Brand points to an area of tension centred on issues related to sexuality generally but to lesbianism in particular which has yet to be fully addressed in Caribbean women's writing. Later in the same essay, Brand suggests a recuperation of the figure of the 'Jamette' (Creole for a 'loose' or 'bad' woman) as a symbol of the possibilities for Caribbean women to define and control their own sexualities. Interestingly, in Brand's poetic oeuvre, the image of the old woman recurs as one which provides the possibility of escape from 'the prisoned gaze of men'[35] and from anxieties about sexual roles in women's relationships with each other:

> At least two poets
> one hundred other women I know, and I,
> can't wait to become old and haggard,
> then, we won't have to play coquette
> or butch –
> or sidle up to anything.[36]

Of course, this witty refusal of the sexual is not the final word in Brand's work; there are many poems which luxuriate in the pleasures of woman's sexual body. Space permits only a brief citation:

> this is you girl, this is the poem no woman
> ever write for a woman because she 'fraid to touch
> this river boiling like a woman in she sleep

that smell of fresh thighs and warm sweat
sheets of her like the mitan rolling into the atlantic[37]

Cudjoe's decision to exclude Brand's presentation (it is, of course, possible that she may have withdrawn it herself) forecloses on any discussion of differences between women, presenting a seamlessly 'decorous' and celebratory version of the conference.

As with many of the anthologies of Caribbean women's writing already mentioned in this chapter, the image on the cover of *Caribbean Women Writers*, of a sculpted African woman's head, again takes the African Caribbean woman as representative of Caribbean woman. All the other illustrations used in the text (apart from the Van de Straet engraving) are also of African women, and the collection is prefaced by a poem which consolidates this focus, 'The Sorrows of Yamba; Or, the Negro Woman's Lament'.[38]

The Second International Conference of Caribbean Women Writers was held in Trinidad in April 1990. At this conference it was almost immediately apparent that it could not simply be taken for granted that we were all gathered together with the same gendered agenda in mind. One of the most obvious areas of tension was the perceived emphasis on 'critics' rather than on 'creative writers'. Sue N. Greene, in her report on the conference, quotes the disgruntled comment of one writer: 'I'm never coming back to one of these things. It's all about ideology. There's no discussion about art.'[39] Similarly explosive grumbles led to a newspaper report on the conference under the headline, 'Women Writers Wrangle!' The very title of the conference, as with the first conference, with its focus on Caribbean women *writers*, rather than on Caribbean Women's *writing*, might be read as cultivating this emphasis. In any case, what this highlights is a resistance to theorizing Caribbean women's writing in favour of a more celebratory, 'sisterly' approach, in which 'experience' becomes the authorizing discourse. As Evelyn O'Callaghan argues, the very decision to group Caribbean women's texts together is itself an ideological decision.[40] Greene, however, appears to endorse this resistance to theory in her concluding remarks:

> It may be that, for now, literary critics can best serve the study of Caribbean women's literature by expanding their concept of literature and by looking more deeply at the world from which it has arisen than by applying critical theories of any kind.
>
> (Greene 1990, p. 538)

Clearly, contextual information *is* necessary, but this should not preclude critical approaches. In her discussion of 'orality', Greene also seems to collude with romantic generalizations made throughout the conference, but particularly on the panel, 'Oral Traditions and the Woman Writer in the Caribbean'. She says: 'most of the conferees perceived orality as primarily the province of women and perhaps the most significant aspect of Caribbean women's reality' (p. 533). This romantic privileging of the oral led to some presenters abandoning their prepared papers and making passionate statements about 'breaking the silence' by reciting from their literary works or by prefacing their presentations with evidence of their own ability to 'talk that talk'; namely, to speak Creole. Greene reports two telling examples:

> When Elaine Savory Fido remarked that Caribbean women were so 'richly oral' that she felt 'voiceless' – so much so that she had gotten laryngitis twice when she was to speak on Caribbean women's writing, one under- stood her predicament. [. . .] When Afua Cooper began her presentation, she said, 'I am not going to talk *about*, I am going to *talk* oral traditions.' Saying she had come to the conference 'to hear women's voices,' she switched back and forth between 'English English English' and Jamaican Creole and between recitation and singing, emphasizing the power of sound.
>
> (Greene 1990, pp. 533–7)

Where, despite speaking for the most part with a fairly strong American accent, Afua Cooper's ability, as a Jamaican-*born* woman, to *deliver* Creole speech estab- lishes her 'insider' status, Elaine Savory Fido, not a 'native' of the Caribbean, presents herself as 'voiceless' because of her inability to talk Creole. The emphasis on the oral was invoked by many at the conference as something which dis- tinguished Caribbean women from men. But it became apparent that Creole also functions as an authorizing and excluding discourse.

Two books, launched at the Second International Conference of Caribbean Women Writers, were also instrumental in establishing Caribbean women's writ- ing as a discrete category of writing. *Out of the Kumbla*,[41] edited by Carole Boyce Davies and Elaine Savory Fido, is a collection of critical essays, while *Her True- True Name*,[42] edited by Pamela Mordecai and Betty Wilson, is a collection of short stories and extracts from novels by thirty-one women.[43] *Out of the Kumbla* was the first sustained collection of critical essays on Caribbean women's writing to be published, and the excitement attendant upon this publication is signalled in the celebratory title of the collection and invoked in the stylized image of the defiantly upbeat African women on the cover (with calabash, sun and tropical trees in the background). What is interesting about this collection for the purpose of my argument here, beyond the way in which the image on the cover repeats the emphasis on the African Caribbean woman, and the scant attention paid to poetry, is the way in which the text is framed by a preface and an 'afterword' which foreground some of the tensions and difficulties involved in the category 'Caribbean woman', itself. In their preface, 'Talking It Over: Womanism, Writing and Feminism' (pp. ix–xx), Savory Fido and Boyce Davies discuss the relative merits of the terms 'feminism' and 'womanism'; the former favours womanism, with its emphasis on 'women's talk, customs, lore', as a 'softer, more flexible option than feminism' (pp. xii–xv) while the latter leans towards feminism as a term with more political bite, though she concludes: 'In the end, though I find myself using "womanist" in a few contexts and "feminist" in most. A lot of us talk, though, of an "international feminism" [. . .][which] instead addresses women's struggles globally' (p. xiii).

This preface, which opens with the statement, 'Sometimes it is important to be personal' (p. ix), is careful to locate both editors in terms of their own personal connections to 'women's issues' and to the Caribbean (Boyce Davies was born and grew up in Trinidad while Savory Fido was born in England and came to the Caribbean in her twenties). It concludes with Savory Fido's words:

> Giving voice to women's concerns means fighting back against the pressures which obstruct women from finishing things, from engaging fully on professional projects over and above those of the working day. So this collection is for me a matter for celebration.
>
> (*Out of the Kumbla*, p. xix)

In the jointly authored introduction, the editors argue that

> *the most urgent and central concern we must have in the sphere of women's writing is to encourage writing.* The first essential is to find all the lost writers – those many, many women all over the region who have poems in drawers and inside books, pieces of fiction unpublished and confined to obscurity.
>
> (*Out of the Kumbla*, p. 17; my emphasis)

As with some of the anthologies discussed earlier, the imperative here is to encourage, collate and document women's writing. The editors' unequivocal commitment to the analysis of Caribbean women's realities and writing, despite quibbles about definitions of feminism or womanism, is thoroughly problematized by Sylvia Wynter's 'Afterword'. That the editors included it as 'the final word' of the collection suggests an admirably open-minded willingness to 'talk it over'. In 'Beyond Miranda's Meanings: Un/silencing the "Demonic Ground" of Caliban's "Woman" ',[44] Wynter argues for a 'demonic model of cognition' outside of the discourses of *both* patriarchy *and* feminism. Taking Shakespeare's *The Tempest* as a powerful example of one of Western Europe's 'foundational endowing texts' (p. 358), Wynter argues that there was, at this juncture in history, a 'mutational shift from the primacy of the *anatomical* model of sexual difference as the referential model of *mimetic* ordering, to that of the *physiognomic* model of racial/*cultural* difference':

> In other words, with the shift to the secular, the primary code of difference now became that between 'men' and 'natives,' with the traditional 'male' and 'female' distinctions now coming to play a secondary – if none the less powerful – reinforcing role within the system of symbolic representations.
>
> (*Out of the Kumbla*, p. 358)

Although Wynter's argument usefully functions to unsettle the tendency of Boyce Davies and Savory Fido to lapse into a too cosily consensual literary sisterhood, it does perhaps disregard the degree to which the contributors to *Out of the Kumbla* do demonstrate an acute awareness of the centrality of 'race' in constructions of 'the' Caribbean woman. Further, Wynter's repeated invocation of Caliban's female counterpart (only alluded to in *The Tempest*) as 'Caliban's woman' inadvertently emphasizes the very necessity for a distinctly feminist perspective in the Caribbean. As Kathleen Baluntansky argues, in a review of *Out of the Kumbla*, the Caribbean woman, in Wynter's model, is still the property of Caliban:

> [I]t is extremely troubling to find this relationship, even in Wynter's configuration, mediated by the possessive: Caliban's woman is *his* woman, the object of *his* desire – in essence, she thus emerges triply marginalized by her race, her gender, and her status as the dispossessed 'native savage.'[45]

More recently, Natasha Barnes, in an article entitled, 'Reluctant Matriarch: Sylvia Wynter and the Problematics of Caribbean Feminism',[46] goes further in her response to Wynter's argument:

> But let us return to Wynter's provocative statement: that a Caribbean feminism is impossible because gender difference was not part of the constitutive makeup of European colonialism and white supremacy. [. . .] Not only does it reiterate a version of the classic defence that many Third World nationalisms offer as an explanation for putting the question of feminism on the political back burner, but it rehearses a troubling problematic that sees racial oppression as the primary determining social force of Caribbean identity and, in effect, admonishes regional feminists for the false conscious act of 'choosing' gender over race. [. . .] I stand by Third World feminists around the world who have said that no nationalist liberation movement anywhere has given women equal access to political, economic and social power under these terms.
>
> (Barnes 1999, pp. 41–2)[47]

Barnes's article, published some ten years after Wynter's 'Afterword', testifies to the continuing challenge posed by Wynter's argument – *and* to the continuing commitment to, and contestation over, feminism in Caribbean discourses.

The other book launched at the Second International Conference of Caribbean Women Writers, *Her True-True Name: An Anthology of Women's Writing from the Caribbean*, edited by Pamela Mordecai and Betty Wilson, includes an introduction which, though brief, raises similarly contentious issues about how 'the' Caribbean woman writer – and by implication Caribbean women's realities more generally – might best be characterized. The editors argue that, where male-authored writing of the region had been 'a literature of middle-class values and bourgeois preoccupations [. . .] The focus of most of the women's writing – especially recent writing – has been on grass roots concerns and ordinary people' (p. xiii). That 'ordinary', 'grass roots', people here implies 'black people' is not stated, but this implication resonates in the rather brisk way in which Michelle Cliff's work is singled out. Cliff, the 'only one of the recently published Caribbean writers who does not affirm at least aspects of being in the Caribbean place' is linked to Jean Rhys, and both writers' personal identities are invoked as explanations for the alienation evident in their texts:

> Personal history perhaps provides important clues: like Rhys, who also felt isolated, Cliff is 'white' – or as light-skinned as makes, to the larger world, little difference. Also like Rhys, she went to the kind of school [. . .] which promoted the values of the metropole. Like Rhys, she left her island early and never really came home. One of the prices she has paid is a compromised authenticity in some aspects of her rendering of the creole.
>
> (*Her True-True Name*, p. xvii)

Several objections come to mind: while it may be the case (albeit debatable) that 'the larger world' does not racially stigmatize the light-skinned 'foreigner,' it *is* the case that within the Caribbean, where Cliff grew up, very clear distinctions are made between persons who are 'properly' white – namely, 'European white' – and those who are not (that is, 'mixed-race' or creolized 'not-quite-whites'). That the discrimination which may result from such a racial hierarchy will certainly be less extreme the 'lighter' one's skin, does not negate the fact of difference. On the second point, surely most schools within the Caribbean would have, until very recently, 'promoted the values of the metropole'? And with regard to the issue of leaving the Caribbean and never 'really' coming home, geographical rootedness here seems to be required of Cliff to compensate for the 'distance' from the 'grass-roots' realities equated with 'home' which her 'light-skinned' identity suggests. The geographic mobility of many of the other writers included in the collection is not questioned in this way. Once again, too, 'authentic' use of Creole is invoked as the arbiter of insider status. Kathleen M. Balutansky, reviewing *Her True-True Name* alongside *Out of the Kumbla*, summarizes succinctly some of my reservations with Mordecai and Wilson's introduction, and with some of the anthologies discussed earlier:

> Like the Caribbean itself, Cliff's protagonist is a mixture of cultures and races; and though she is the offspring of a privileged class, she did not choose her legacy. It is of greater importance that, in matters in which she has a choice, she gives her allegiance to the dispossessed. [. . .] Although the editors' inclusion of writers who include middle-class women's experiences demonstrates that they recognize the diversity of Caribbean life, their critical comments nevertheless imply that the Caribbean woman who is not immersed in her African past is somehow not 'authentic' and cannot know her 'true-true' name. This is a prescriptive stand that seems to undermine the stated purpose of the anthology.[48]

Michelle Cliff herself offers a much more nuanced sense of her own troubled location(s) within *and* outside the region than Mordecai and Wilson allow for, in her poem, 'Love in the Third World':

> I know the price of cooking oil and rice.
> I know the price of Blue Mountain coffee and Canadian saltfish.
> I have a sense of the depth of our self-hatred.
> I speak from a remove of time and space – I have tried to hold
> your shape and history within me. I keep track of you through
> advertisements and photographs. Through *The Harder They*
> *Come* and 'Natty Dread.' By entering the patty shops in Bedford-
>   Stuyvesant.
> By watching a group of applepickers stroll
> through a Massachusetts hilltown. Through shots of graffiti
> on the walls of Tivoli Gardens. My homeland. My people.[49]

Writing from Canada rather than the USA, Ramabai Espinet similarly conveys the sense of ambivalent belonging(s) of the migrant (Indian) woman in her poem 'Hosay Night' –

> This land is home to me
> now homeless, a true refugee
> of the soul's last corner
> Saddhu days and babu days
> and Mai in ohrni days
> lost to me – like elephants
> and silks, the dhows of Naipaul's
> yearning, not mine.[50]

– while Lelawattee Manoo-Rahming, in a poem entitled 'Ode to My Unknown Great-Great Grandmother', echoes something of Espinet's mournful lament:

> I heard you were the first
> to belong nowhere.
> Born on the wide Kali pani
> between Calcutta and Port-of-Spain
> on a ship unknown.[51]

Dionne Brand, in one of the poems in the 'Land to Light On' cycle, is more emphatic about the rejection of 'solid ground' as a source of belonging:

> I'm giving up on land to light on, slowly it isn't land,
> it is the same as fog and mist and figures and lines
> [. . .]
> . . . Look. What I know is this. I'm giving up.
> No offence. I was never committed. Not ever, to offices

or islands, continents, graphs, whole cloth, these sequences
or even footsteps[52]

Two more recent collections of essays take pains to stress the importance of resisting imperatives towards fixity and homogeneity in the critical discourses which respond to this writing. The first of these, Evelyn O'Callaghan's *Woman Version: Theoretical Approaches to West Indian Fiction by Women*,[53] published in 1993, makes explicit in its title the commitment to theorizing Caribbean women's texts, rather than celebrating an assumed collective identity. A brief comparison of the approaches taken by O'Callaghan and Boyce Davies indicates some interesting shifts in the field of Caribbean women's writing and perhaps signals their greater willingness to play the field in the foregrounding of diversity and difference which is evident in their texts. O'Callaghan suggests in her introduction that there are many diverse thematic and aesthetic connections linking Caribbean women's writing, some of which parallel the concerns and formal innovation associated with male writers of the region and some of which are a distinct feature of texts by women. She argues for an eclectic combination of theoretical approaches which, in its multiplicity and hybridity, would be responsive to the full range of literary concerns and forms of Caribbean women's writing:

> What *kind* of approach would it be, to be able to account for 'unity in diver-
> sity'? Obviously, a theory in the best Creole tradition, as syncretic and inclu-
> sive as the women's literary voices it seeks to elucidate [. . .] [W]hat I suggest
> is that we approach this writing, in the light of the above, as a kind of remix
> or dub version, which utilizes elements from the 'master tape' of Caribbean
> literary discourse (combining, stretching, modifying them in new ways);
> announces a gendered perspective; adds individual styles of 'talkover';
> enhances or omits tracks depending on desired effect; and generally alters by
> recontextualization to create a *unique* literary entity.[54]

O'Callaghan focuses exclusively on Caribbean women's fiction, deploying post-colonial and feminist approaches to explore a range of thematic and aesthetic concerns. A significant new departure in this book is the sustained attention given, in the first chapter, to the work of early 'white' West Indian women, convention-ally excluded as 'outsiders' from discussions of West Indian (women's) writing. O'Callaghan argues, here, for the inclusion of '*all* voices (however problematic in terms of historical/racial/political context' (p. 34).

The introduction concludes with an unequivocal statement of the book's intentions:

> For in the end, my intention – and that of *all* studies of West Indian women's
> writing – is to bring to public awareness and appreciation a body of litera-
> ture that articulates, with spirit and feeling and wit, what it means to be a
> woman in this wonderful region.
>
> (*Women Version*, p. 16)

Apart from such declamations, O'Callaghan's commitment to, and location within, the region is evident throughout the text in the many detailed ways in which West Indian culture and writing are referenced. This commitment to a West Indian-centred approach, however, coupled with the critical use of both feminist and postcolonial discourses, avoids a narrowly regionalist emphasis.

In *Black Women, Writing and Identity: Migrations of the Subject*, published a year after *Woman Version*, Carole Boyce Davies, like O'Callaghan, stresses the need for a critical practice which is eclectic in its borrowings from 'Theory'.[55] But where O'Callaghan places her discussion of Caribbean women's texts very firmly in the geographical and cultural context of the Caribbean, Boyce Davies works within a black diasporic model, which obviously, deliberately, limits her discussion of Caribbean women writers to those of African descent and those living outside the Caribbean. Both Boyce Davies and O'Callaghan note the under-representation of Indian women in their respective texts, though neither focuses on such writing. Within Boyce Davies's framework, then, 'Caribbean' is subsumed under 'black' and, although the work of African writers such as Ama Ata Aidoo is discussed, there is a strong African American feminist/womanist focus in the text.

The 'migratory subjectivities' indicated in Boyce Davies's title refer to the literal displacement of black women around the world but also to the way in which many black women's texts exploit multiple subject positions as a textual strategy for challenging the marginal position allocated them in dominant discourses. The book is organized around the premise that this fluid subject position has been generated by the lived realities which have made such multiple 'migrations' necessary :

> I believe that questions of Black female subjectivity bring a more complex and heightened awareness to all theoretics and feminist concerns rather than an escape from them. In other words, if we take any feminist issue and run it up the scale to its most radical possibility, its most clarifying solution will be the experience of Black women.[56]

African Caribbean women writers in the British context are discussed separately in the chapter 'From "Post-coloniality" to Uprising Textualities', in which Boyce Davies discusses the work of a selection of black British writers (including Beryl Gilroy, Merle Collins, Joan Riley and Grace Nichols). What is most interesting about this discussion is the way these Caribbean/black British women are positioned, in relation to her overall argument within the book, as representative of a 'natural' (or at least, untheoretical) rebellion or oppositionality. In the introduction, Boyce Davies argues, 'The passion behind much of the work of Black British women writers is creative rather than "high academic". In fact, this in my view is a strength' (p. 33). Michael Eldridge, commenting on the symbolic value currently associated with black British writing in the USA, despite its falling from fashion in the UK, suggests: 'the experiences that these black-and-Asian poets perform is also making waves on the other side of the Atlantic, especially in the academy, where "black British" has become a full-blown flavor-of-the-month'. His suggestion that these writers (mostly male) represent a certain chic black style, read in tandem with Boyce Davies's construction of black British women as 'more passionate', raises provocative questions about the traffic in black representations and nuances the ongoing discussion of America's post-coloniality.[57]

Boyce Davies extends her argument about the role of black British women in chapter 4, 'From "Post-coloniality" to Uprising Textualities', where she argues:

> Black British women writers then become crucial in this articulation [of the dynamics of 'post-colonialism'], for, positioned as they are, they are able to launch an internal/external critique which challenges simultaneously the meanings of Empire, the project of post-coloniality as well as the various nationalistic identifications of home.
>
> (*Black Women, Writing and Identity*, p. 96)

For Boyce Davies, Caribbean/black British women appear to have a particular purchase on the 'postcolonial' which their African American and African counterparts do not have. Further, because of their location 'in the former colonial heartland, they create different spaces for women's work' (p. 112). She concludes:

> Creative activity therefore takes place within and outside contexts of publishing and sometimes more as an affirmation of creativity and existence as Black women in Britain. Thus, much of what exists may never see the published forum nor have any desire to be thus exposed. Black women writers in England are therefore articulating assertive presences, rather than belatedness – voicing creative uprisings.
>
> (*Black Women, Writing and Identity*, p. 112)

While Boyce Davies's argument has the effect of presenting Caribbean British women's writing as rather naively 'from the heart' – 'passionate'and 'creative', rather than 'high academic' – her point here is also to suggest a strategic use of the literary text to challenge the hegemony of 'Theory'. O'Callaghan and Boyce Davies both include extended discussions of 'Theory' in their texts, anxiously outlining and defending the particular eclecticisms of their choices and scrupulously citing a dense network of theoretical positions. This sustained engagement with theoretical interventions is clearly indicative of a broader shift within academic institutions. Within feminist discourses, this shift has undermined the celebratory sisterliness characteristic of earlier versions of feminism.[58] Both O'Callaghan and Boyce Davies, then, offer substantial accounts of the critical terrain in which they locate their discussion of West Indian and black women's texts – the former in relation to feminist and postcolonial perspectives; the latter in relation to nationalist, black, feminist, womanist and postcolonial discourses. This careful citation of theorists and critics, despite, on occasion, cramping O'Callaghan's and Boyce Davies *own* voices and styles of writing, marks a welcome commitment to interrogating the constituency of the fields of Caribbean and black women's writing.

Alongside the commitment to a serious engagement with 'Theory', both texts include an explicit inscription of 'the personal'. O'Callaghan, a ('white') Jamaican, who teaches at the Cave Hill Campus of the University of the West Indies, places herself in relation to her engagement with West Indian women's literature as a student in the 1970s and then as a lecturer at the University of the West Indies. She signals her unease about being any more 'personal' than this by using the playfully self-deprecating heading, 'The obligatory "personal state-ment"' (p. 1) and by limiting the discussion of 'the personal' to her professional engagement with West Indian women's writing. Carole Boyce Davies, a ('black') Trinidadian, who lectures at the State University of New York at Binghamton, makes a more directly personal connection between herself and the book by describing her own 'migratory critical position' in relation to the (literal) migra-tions of her mother and by punctuating the critical discourse of her introduction with a series of emotive 'migration horror stories'. The forthrightness with which the personal is introduced in Boyce Davies's text might be explained, using her own model, in terms of her own experience, as a black woman, of marginality, but it might also be read, paradoxically, in relation to the 'centrality' of her current location in a North American academic institution which affords her the cultural confidence to construct a constituency which overrides the specifics of geo-cultural locatedness in its global reach. For O'Callaghan the detailed intim-acies of location are paramount and provide the ground for her own authority to speak about Caribbean women's writing. But perhaps O'Callaghan's relative reluctance to personalize her critical discourse also reflects a recognition that her personal identity, as a 'white' West Indian woman, precludes such disclosure?

Another collection of essays, edited by Susheila Nasta, *Motherlands: Black Women's Writing from Africa, the Caribbean and South Asia*,[59] though it pre-dates the two texts discussed above, is relevant to this discussion. This collection of essays, as the title clearly indicates, focuses on the writing of 'black women' and is prefaced by an extract from Marlene Nourbese Philip's poem, 'Discourse on the Logic of Language', in which the impact of race and gender on the 'mother tongue', English, in the historical context of plantation slavery in the West Indies, is dramatized. But Nasta's introduction also privileges the work of another West Indian woman writer in the framing of this collection, that of Jean Rhys. Discussing the short story, 'Let Them Call It Jazz', Nasta argues:

> The story of Selina who nearly loses her song and then encounters it trans-lated into another version which she almost doesn't recognize is a familiar one and is perhaps in danger of being re-enacted in some Western critical discourses which appropriate texts by women writers of the 'Third World' in order to elucidate their theories.
>
> (*Motherlands*, pp. xiv–xv)

Here, Nasta suggests that Rhys's story can be read as a paradigm of the unequal exhange between Western critical discourses and 'Third World' women's texts, with the latter perceived as functioning as 'literary fodder' for the former. Beyond the caginess about 'Theory' which is again in evidence here, Rhys's anomalous inclusion, as a *white* woman writer, in a collection explicitly designated as focusing on *black* women's writing, is instructive. In addition to Nasta's discussion of Rhys's story in the introduction, at least four of the essays in *Motherlands* include a focus on Rhys's *Wide Sargasso Sea*. It appears that, both in challenging a canonical text's representation of the West Indian woman as racial 'other',[60] and in the exploration of a racially hybrid protagonist (Antoinette), Rhys offers a more nuanced inscription of racial difference than the 'discrete' categories of 'black' or 'white' imply. What this suggests is that Rhys's handling of marginality speaks across the boundary of 'race' and perhaps problematizes the usefulness of 'race' as an anthologizing category, at least in the Caribbean. Many Caribbean women poets have memorialized Jean Rhys in their poems, further endorsing her place in their literary history.[61] Olive Senior's poem 'Meditation on Red', for example, opens, 'You, voyager/in the dark/landlocked/at Land Boat Bungalows no. 6' and continues:

> Right now
> I'm as divided
> as you were
> by that sea.
>
> But I'll
> be able to
> find my way
> home again
>
> for that craft
> you launched
> is so seaworthy
> tighter
> than you'd ever been
> dark voyagers
> like me
> can feel free
> to sail.
>
> That fire
> you lit
> our beacon
> to safe harbour
> in the islands.[62]

One might argue further that the way in which Rhys 'passes' for black in a collection of essays devoted to black women's writing is indicative of a shift in emphasis in the critical contexts within which Caribbean women's texts are received. This shift in emphasis has been facilitated by postcolonial discourse with its destabilizing of fixed identities, of either the colonizer or colonized, and its privileging of ambivalence, liminality and hybridity. Rhys, whose racial credentials as an 'authentic' West Indian writer have, historically, been perceived as 'suspect',[63] now becomes central to the discussion of postcolonial women's identities. The fact that Nasta frames her discussion of 'Black women's writing from Africa, the Caribbean, and South Asia' with reference to two West Indian women writers of very different provenance clearly suggests the importance of Caribbean women writers in definitions of 'black' and 'postcolonial' literary constituencies, but it indicates that it is perhaps also *because* of such differences that Caribbean literary identities are so resonant. So, the explicit inscription of black, female Caribbean identity in Marlene Nourbese Philip's work, when placed in dialogue (however fraught) with the more racially ambivalent inscription of the Creole woman's identity in Rhys's work, might perhaps offer the 'truly Creole' interpretative approach suggested by Evelyn O'Callaghan.

Indeed, perhaps the 'in-betweenness' which Rhys's fiction so persistently rehearses might offer a suitable model for the reading of Caribbean women's writing. For, in foregrounding the indeterminacy of all kinds of identities, whether of geography, culture, race, class, sexuality or gender, her work speaks to the complexity and mutability of 'the' Caribbean woman's identities. If some of the publications discussed above have asserted a more bounded notion of the Caribbean woman, often using the figure of the black woman as a shorthand definition for the Caribbean woman in general, these texts have also, despite the many quibbles and concerns I have outlined, provided the necessary ground upon which further debate and contestation can be staged. Similarly, while I would argue that the poetry which I have discussed in this book cannot be productively engaged with if kept frozen on the margins, where marginality itself becomes the defining feature of this 'tradition', it has also been necessary, for the moment, to construct these poets as constituting a 'marginal' tradition, while seeking *simultaneously* to deconstruct this constituency. In reading Caribbean women's poetry in relation to the predominantly male poetics of the region, my aim has been to provide a critical platform from which to envisage a move beyond a binary poetics of *his* and *hers*, where 'man-talk' and 'woman-talk' might occupy less discretely bounded spaces than those articulated below.[64]

Man-Talk

His words
   strut
  swaggering
he steps his words
flaunts his sayings
   cocksured
slips them from

zip-opened lips
and they throb
    rising
[. . .]
his words mean[65]

A space in which *his* words might begin to mean differently and where *hers* might be recognized more widely. Dionne Brand's work often conveys powerfully the kind of amplitudinous possibilities associated with women's words:

> This
> grace, you see come as a surprise and nothing till
> now knock on my teeming skull, then, these warm
> watery syllables, a woman's tongue so like a culture,
> plunging toward stones not yet formed into flesh,
> language not yet made . . . I want to kiss you deeply,
> smell, taste, the warm water of your mouth as warm as
> your hands. I lucky is grace that gather me up and
> forgive my plainness.[66]

While this book has been concerned to expose the normatively male contours of poetic discourse in the Caribbean to date, and has traced some of the contours emerging from contemporary women's poetry, it is to be hoped that poetic trajectories in the future will suggest a much more promiscuous criss-crossing of such contours.

Notes

1 Pamela Mordecai, 'In Verse', *Journey Poem*, Kingston, Jamaica, Sandberry Press, 1989, p. 38.
2 Joan Anin-Ado, 'Creation Story', *Haunted by History*, London, Mango Publishing, 1998, p. 13.
3 Velma Pollard, 'Version', *Considering Woman*, London, The Woman's Press, 1989, no page reference.
4 Pamela Mordecai and Mervyn Morris (eds), *Jamaica Woman: An Anthology of Poems*, London, Heinemann, 1980.
5 Louise Bennett, *Selected Poems*, ed. Mervyn Morris, Kingston, Jamaica, Sangster's Bookstores Ltd, 1982, p. 23.
6 This image, by Ras Daniel Hartmann, is an example of a recognizable genre of portraiture in the postcolonial Caribbean which sought to make 'ordinary' black Jamaicans the proper focus of Caribbean art.
7 Lorraine Griffiths, *Talkers through Dream Doors: Poetry and Short Stories by Black Women*, Manchester, Crocus, 1989, p. 92. This collection was compiled by Cultureword and credits no individual editors.
8 Ramabai Espinet (ed.), *Creation Fire: A Cafra Anthology of Caribbean Women's Poetry*, Toronto, Sister Vision Press, 1990.
9 Helen Carr, *From My Guy to Sci-Fi: Genre and Women's Writing in the Postmodern World*, London, Pandora, 1989, p. 136.

10 Pam Mordecai and Betty Wilson (eds), *Women Poets of the Caribbean*, special issue of *The Literary Review*, 35, 4, Summer 1992.

11 Margaret Watts (ed.), *Washer Woman Hangs Her Poems in the Sun: Poems by Women of Trinidad and Tobago*, Tunapuna, Trinidad, Gloria V. Ferguson Ltd.,1990, p. xi.

12 Rhonda Cobham and Merle Collins (eds), *Watchers and Seekers: Creative Writing by Black Women in Britain*, London, The Women's Press, 1987.

13 James Berry (ed.), *News for Babylon*, London, Chatto & Windus, 1984.

14 Meiling Jin, 'Strangers in a Hostile Landscape', in *Creation Fire*, pp. 130–1.

15 Lauretta Ngcobo (ed.), *Let It Be Told: Black Women Writers in Britain*, London, Virago, 1988.

16 Sara Suleri, 'Woman Skin Deep: Feminism and the Postcolonial Condition', in P. Williams and L. Chrisman (eds), *Colonial Discourse and Postcolonial Theory: A Reader*, Hemel Hempstead, Harvester Wheatsheaf, 1993, p. 248.

17 Jane King, *Fellow Traveller*, Kingston, Sandberry Press, 1994, p. 20.

18 Ibid., p. 36.

19 Honor Ford-Smith, *My Mother's Last Dance*, Toronto, Sister Vision Press, 1996, p. 71. Ford-Smith established the working-class Jamaican women's theatre collective, Sistren.

20 Pauline Melville, 'Honor Maria', in *Creation Fire*, p. 55.

21 Shabnam Grewal *et al.* (eds), *Charting the Journey: Writings by Black and Third World Women*, London, Sheba, 1988, p. 3.

22 The publication of Karen McCarthy (ed.), *Bittersweet: Contemporary Black Women's Poetry*, London, The Women's Press, 1988, attests to the continued valency of the category 'black woman writer'.

23 Paula Burnett (ed.), *The Penguin Book of Caribbean Verse in English*, Harmondsworth, Penguin, 1986.

24 E.A. Markham (ed.), *Hinterland: Caribbean Poetry from the West Indies and Britain*, Newcastle, Bloodaxe, 1989, p. 21.

25 Ian McDonald and Stewart Brown (eds), *The Heinemann Book of Caribbean Poetry*, London, Heinemann, 1992, p. xv.

26 Anthony Kellman (ed.), *Crossing Water: Contemporary Poetry of the English-speaking Caribbean*, Greenfield, NY, The Greenfield Review Press, 1992, p. xxv.

27 See Henry Louise Gates, 'Trading on the Margins: Notes on the Culture of Criticism', *Loose Canons: Notes on the Culture Wars*, New York, Oxford University Press, 1992.

28 Sue Greene, 'Report on the Second International Conference of Caribbean Women Writers', *Callaloo*, 13, 3, 1990, pp. 532–8.

29 Selwyn R. Cudjoe (ed.), *Caribbean Women Writers: Essays from the First International Conference*, Wellesley, MA, Calaloux, 1990.

30 This image might also be suggestively compared with that on the cover of *Creation Fire*, both images conflating woman and land as harmoniously elemental.

31 H. Bloom (ed.), *Caribbean Women Writers*, Philadelphia, Chelsea House Publishers, 1997.

32 Sylvia Wynter's challenge to Louis James's construction of West Indian writing as a branch of 'English Literature' is pertinent here. Wynter questions James's elision of his own position as a white academic from 'the mother country' writing about West Indian literature and insists that he place himself in relation to the colonial structures he so carefully outlines in his introductory essay. See Louis James, *The Islands In Between*, London, Oxford University Press, 1968 and Sylvia Wynter, 'Reflections on West Indian Writing and Criticism: Part 1', *Jamaica Journal*, 11, December 1968, pp. 23–32.

33 Dionne Brand, *Bread out of Stone: Recollections, Sex, Recognitions, Race, Dreaming Politics*, Toronto, Coach House Press, 1994, pp. 9–49.

34 Ibid., pp. 29–31.

35 Dionne Brand, 'Hard against the Soul', *No Language Is Neutral*, Toronto, Coach House Press, 1990, p. 48.

36 Dionne Brand, *Winter Epigrams and Epigrams to Ernesto Cardenal in Defense of Claudia*, no. 31, Toronto, Williams-Wallace, 1983, p. 29.

37 Brand, *No Language Is Neutral*, p. 7.
38 *Caribbean Women Writers*, pp. xv–xvi; a poem by Grace Nichols also prefaces the collection.
39 Sue Greene, 'Report on the Second International Conference of Caribbean Women Writers', *Callaloo*, 13, 3, 1990, p. 536.
40 Evelyn O'Callaghan, *Woman Version: Theoretical Approaches to West Indian Fiction by Women*, London, Macmillan, 1993, pp. 97–8.
41 Carole Boyce Davies and Elaine Savory Fido (eds), *Out of the Kumbla: Caribbean Women and Literature*, New Jersey, Africa World Press, 1990.
42 Pamela Mordecai and Betty Wilson (eds), *Her True-True Name: An Anthology of Women's Writing from the Caribbean*, London, Heinemann, 1989.
43 Space does not permit me to discuss the many conferences with a specific focus on Caribbean women writers which were held after 1990, except to note that the Caribbean Women Writers Alliance, based in London at Goldsmith's College, has published the conference proceedings of one such conference in *Framing the Word: Gender and Genre in Caribbean Women's Writing*, Joan Anim-Ado (ed.), London, Whiting & Birch, 1996, and there is another forthcoming. See also *Caribbean Women Writers: Fiction in English*, Mary Conde and Thorun Lonsdale (eds), London, Macmillan, 1999; and *Caribbean Portraits: Essays on Gender Ideologies and Identities*, Christine Barrow (ed.), Kingston, Ian Randle in association with the Centre for Gender Studies, Mona, UWI, 1998.
44 Boyce Davies and Fido (eds), *Out of the Kumbla*, pp. 355–72.
45 Kathleen M. Baluntansky, 'Naming Caribbean Women Writers: A Review Essay', *Callaloo*, 13, 3, Summer 1990, p. 543.
46 Natasha Barnes, 'Reluctant Matriarch: Sylvia Wynter and the Problematics of Caribbean Feminism', *Small Axe*, 5, March 1999, pp. 34–47.
47 Barnes goes on to offer a persuasive reading of Sylvia Wynter's *The Hills of Hebron*, which demonstrates the way in which Wynter offers – 'whether she intends it or not' – a challenge to the foundational moment of nationalism in the 'forceful *feminist* critique' which the text embodies. Ibid., p. 47.
48 Baluntansky, 'Naming Caribbean Women Writers', p. 545.
49 Michelle Cliff, in Espinet (ed.), *Creation Fire*, p. 147.
50 Ramabai Espinet, *Nuclear Seasons*, Toronto, Sister Vision Press, 1991, p. 10.
51 Lelawattee Maoo-Rahming, *Curry Flavour*, Leeds, Peepal Tree Press, 2000, p. 12.
52 Dionne Brand, *Land to Light on*, Toronto, McClelland & Stewart, 1997, p. 47.
53 O'Callaghan, *Woman Version*.
54 Ibid., pp. 10–11.
55 Carole Boyce Davies, *Black Women, Writing and Identity: Migrations of the Subject*, London, Routledge, 1994.
56 Ibid., p. 29.
57 Michael Eldridge, 'The Rise and Fall of Black Britain', *Transition*, 7, 2, 74 1998, p. 33.
58 The anxiety concerning 'Theory' is perhaps best summarized in Barbara Christian's 'The Race for Theory', *Cultural Critique*, 6, Spring 1987, pp. 51–63.
59 Susheila Nasta, *Motherlands: Black Women's Writing from Africa, the Caribbean and South Asia*, London, The Women's Press, 1991.
60 Jean Rhys's *Wide Sargasso Sea*, London, Penguin, 1966, 'writes back to' Charlotte Brontë's *Jane Eyre*, challenging the representation of the 'mad' West Indian woman in the attic, Bertha.
61 Another recent anthology takes its title from a Jean Rhys story; see *The Whistling Bird: Women Writers of the Caribbean*, Elaine Campbell and Pierrette Frickey (eds), Boulder, London and Kingston, Three Continents Press, Lynne Rienner Publishers and Ian Randle Publishers, 1998.
62 Olive Senior, *Gardening in the Tropics*, Toronto, McClelland & Stewart, 1994, pp. 51–2.
63 A recent debate in *Wasafiri* between E.K. Brathwaite and Peter Hulme over Jean Rhys's

position with regard to postcolonial and West Indian writing highlights the continuing importance of Rhys as a contested cultural figure. See Peter Hulme, 'The Place of *Wide Sargasso Sea*', *Wasafiri*, 20, Autumn 1994, pp. 5–11; E.K. Brathwaite, 'A post-cationary tale of the Helen of our wars', *Wasafiri*, 21, Spring, 1995, pp. 69–78; see also Elaine Savory, Evelyn O'Callaghan and Denise deCaires Narain, 'The Jean Rhys Debate: A Forum', *Wasafiri*, 28, Autumn 1998, pp. 33–8.

64 See also Belinda Edmondson, *Making Men: Gender, Literary Authority and Women's Writing in Caribbean Narrative*, Durham, NC, Duke University Press, 1999, for an approach which reads Caribbean women's writing in subtle relationship to that of their male counterparts.

65 Jennifer Rahim, 'Meditations upon the Word', *The Literary Review*, 35, 4, Summer 1992, p. 564.

66 Brand, 'Hard against the Soul', *No Language Is Neutral*, p. 36.

Bibliography

Poetry and fiction

Agard, J., *Mangoes and Bullets*, London, Pluto, 1985.
Allfrey, P., *In Circles*, London, Raven, 1940.
—— *Palm and Oak I*, London, the author, 1950.
—— *Contrasts*, Bridgetown, Barbados, Advocate Press, 1955.
—— *Palm and Oak II*, Roseau, Dominica, Star Printery, 1973.
—— *The Orchid House*, London, Virago, 1982 [1953].
Anim-Ado, J., *Haunted by History*, London, Mango Publishing, 1998.
Antoni, R., *Blessed Is the Fruit*, London, Faber, 1998.
Bennett, L., *Jamaica Labrish: Jamaica Dialect Poems*, ed. Rex Nettleford, Kingston, Sangster's, 1966.
—— *Selected Poems*, ed. Mervyn Morris, Kingston, Sangster's, 1982.
Bloom, V., *Touch Mi; Tell Mi!*, London, Bogle-L'Ouverture, 1983.
Brand, D., *Winter Epigrams & Epigrams to Ernesto Cardinal in Defense of Claudia*, Toronto, Williams-Wallace, 1983.
—— *No Language Is Neutral*, Toronto, Coach House Press, 1990.
—— *Land to Light On*, Toronto, McClelland & Stewart, 1997.
—— *In Another Place, Not Here*, London, The Women's Press, 1997.
Brathwaite, E.K., *The Arrivants: A New World Trilogy*, Oxford, Oxford University Press, 1978 [1967].
—— *Mother Poem*, London, Oxford University Press, 1977.
Breeze, J.B., *Spring Cleaning*, London, Virago, 1982.
—— *Riddym Ravings*, London, Race Today, 1988.
Brodber, E., *Jane and Louisa Will Soon Come Home*, London, New Beacon, 1980.
—— *Myal*, London, New Beacon, 1988.
Bronowski, J. (ed.) *William Blake*, London, Penguin, 1982 [1958].
Brown, S., Morris, M. and Rohlehr, G. (eds), *Voiceprint: An Anthology of Oral and Related Poetry from the Caribbean*, Harlow, Longman, 1989.
Burford, B., Pearse, G., Nichols, G. and Kay, J., *A Dangerous Knowing: Four Black Women Poets*, London, Sheba, 1985.
Burnett, P. (ed.), *The Penguin Book of Caribbean Verse in English*, Harmondsworth, Penguin, 1986.
Cameron, N. (ed.) *Guianese Poetry 1831–1931*, Georgetown, Argosy, 1931.
Campbell, E. and Frickey, P. (eds) *The Whistling Bird: Women Writers of the Caribbean*, Boulder, London and Kingston, Three Continents, Lynne Rienner, Ian Randle Publishers, 1998.

Césaire, A., *Notebook of a Return to My Native Land*, London, Bloodaxe, 1995 [1971].

Cobham, R. and Collins, M. (eds), *Watchers and Seekers: Creative Writing by Black Women in Britain*, London, The Women's Press, 1987.

Collins, M., *Because the Dawn Breaks!*, London, Karia Press, 1985.

— *Angel*, London, The Women's Press, 1987.

— *Rotten Pomerack*, London, Virago, 1992.

Craig, C., *Quadrille for Tigers*, Sebastopol and Berkeley, CA, Mina Press, 1984.

Dabydeen, David, *Slave Song*, Mundellstrup, Denmark, Dangaroo, 1984.

— *Coolie Odyssey*, Coventry, Dangaroo, 1988.

— *Turner: New and Selected Poems*, London, Cape Poetry, 1994.

Das, M., *I Want to Be a Poetess of My People*, Georgetown, Guyana National Service Publishing Centre, 1977.

— *My Finer Steel Will Grow*, Richford, VT, Samisdat, 1982.

— *Bones*, Leeds, Peepal Tree, 1988.

Escoffery, G., *Loggerhead*, Kingston, Sandberry Press, 1988.

Espinet, Ramabai (ed.), *Creation Fire: A Cafra Anthology of Caribbean Women's Poetry*, Toronto, Sister Vision Press, 1990.

— *Nuclear Season*, Toronto, Sister Vision Press, 1991.

Ford-Smith, H., *My Mother's Last Dance*, Toronto, Sister Vision Press, 1996.

Goodison, L., *Tamarind Season*, Kingston, Hummingbird, 1980.

— *I Am Becoming My Mother*, London, New Beacon, 1986.

— *Heartease*, London, New Beacon, 1988.

— *To Us, All Flowers Are Roses*, Urbana and Chicago, University of Illinois Press, 1995.

— *Turn Thanks*, Urbana and Chicago, University of Illinois Press, 1999.

Hamilton, J., *Rain Carvers*, Kingston, Sandberry Press, 1992.

Harris, C., *Fables from the Women's Quarters*, Toronto, Williams-Wallace, 1984.

— *The Conception of Winter*, Toronto, Williams-Wallace, 1989.

Hodge, Merle, *Crick Crack Monkey*, London, Heinemann, 1981 [1970].

James, C.L.R., *Minty Alley*, London, Secker & Warburg, 1936.

Johnson, Amryl, *Long Road to Nowhere*, London, Virago, 1985.

— *Gorgons*, Coventry, Cofa, 1992.

— *Calling*, Abingdon, Oxon, Sable Publications, 1999.

Keens-Douglas, P., *Tim Tim*, Port of Spain, Keensdee Productions, 1976.

Kellman, A. (ed.), *Crossing Water: Contemporary Poetry of the English-speaking Caribbean*, Greenfield, NY, The Greenfield Review Press, 1992.

Kincaid, J., *Annie John*, London, Picador, 1985.

— *A Small Place*, London, Virago, 1988.

— *Lucy*, New York, Plume, 1991.

— *The Autobiography of My Mother*, London, Vintage, 1996.

King, J., *Fellow Traveller*, Kingston, Jamaica, Sandberry Press, 1994.

Lamming, G., *In the Castle of My Skin*, London, Longman, 1953.

McDonald, I. and Brown, S. (eds), *The Heinemann Book of Caribbean Poetry*, London, Heinemann, 1992.

Mais, Roger, *Brother Man*, London, Longman, 1956.

Markham, E.A. (ed.) *Hinterland: Caribbean Poetry from the West Indies and Britain*, Newcastle, Bloodaxe, 1989.

Marson, U. *Tropic Reveries*, Kingston, Jamaica, The Gleaner, 1930.

— *Heights and Depths*, Kingston, Jamaica, The Gleaner, 1931.

— *The Moth and the Star*, Kingston, Jamaica, The Gleaner, 1937.

—— *Towards the Stars*, Bickley, London University Press, 1945.

Mordecai, P. and Morris, M. (eds), *Jamaica Woman: An Anthology of Poems*, London, Heinemann, 1980.

Mordecai, P. and Wilson, B. (eds), *Her True-True Name: An Anthology of Women's Writing from the Caribbean*, London, Heinemann, 1989.

—— (eds), 'Women Poets of the Caribbean', special issue of *The Literary Review*, 35, 4, Summer 1992.

Naipaul, V.S., *The Mimic Men*, Harmondsworth, Penguin, 1969 [1967].

Nichols, G., *i is a long memoried woman*, London, Karnak House, 1983.

—— *The Fat Black Woman's Poems*, London, Virago, 1984.

—— *Lazy Thoughts of a Lazy Woman*, London, Virago, 1989.

—— *Sunris*, London, Virago, 1996.

Nourbese Philip, Marlene, *Thorns*, Toronto, Williams-Wallace, 1980.

—— *Salmon Courage*, Toronto, Williams-Wallace, 1983.

—— *She Tries Her Tongue; Her Silence Softly Breaks*, Charlottetown, Prince Edward Island, Ragweed, 1989.

—— *Looking for Livingstone*, Stratford, Ontario, Mercury, 1991.

Plath, S., *Collected Poems*, Hughes, T. (ed.), London, Faber, 1981.

Pollard, V., *Crown Point and Other Poems*, Leeds, Peepal Tree Press, 1988.

—— *Considering Woman*, London, The Women's Press, 1989.

—— *Shame Trees Don't Grow Here . . . But Poincianas Bloom*, Leeds, Peepal Tree Press, 1992.

Rhys, Jean, *Wide Sargasso Sea*, Harmondsworth, Penguin, 1968 [1966].

—— *Voyage in the Dark*, Harmondsworth, Penguin, 1988 [1934].

Riley, Joan, *The Unbelonging*, London, The Women's Press, 1988.

Savory, E., *Flame Tree Time*, Kingston, Sandberry Press, 1993.

Selvon, S., *The Lonely Londoners*, London, Longman, 1956.

Senior, O., *Talking of Trees*, Kingston, Jamaica, Calabash, 1985.

—— *Gardening in the Tropics*, Toronto, McClelland & Stewart, 1994.

Walcott, D., *Dream on Monkey Mountain*, New York, The Noonday Press, 1970.

—— *Collected Poems: 1948–1984*, New York, The Noonday Press, 1990 [1986].

Watts, M. (ed.), *Washer Woman Hangs Her Poems in the Sun: Poems by Women of Trinidad and Tobago*, Tunapuna, Gloria V. Ferguson, 1990.

Recordings

Bloom, V., *Yuh Hear Bout: Selected Spoken Works*, London, 57 Productions, 1997.

Breeze, J.B., *Riddym Ravings*, Kingston, Jamaica, Ayeola Records, 1985

—— *Tracks*, London, LKJ Records, 1991.

—— *Riding on de Riddym: Selected Spoken Works*, London, 57 Productions, 1997

Collins, M., *Butterfly: Selected Spoken Works*, London, 57 Productions, 1996.

Johnson, A., *Blood and Wine*, Coventry, Cofa Press, 1992.

Secondary sources

Abrahams, R.D., *The Man-of-Words in the West Indies: Performance and the Emergence of Creole Culture*, Baltimore, MD, Johns Hopkins University Press, 1983.

Allison, A.W. *et al.* (eds), *The Norton Anthology of Poetry*, New York, Norton & Co., 1983.

Allsopp, R., *Dictionary of Caribbean English Usage*, Oxford, Oxford University Press, 1996.

Anim-Ado, J., *Framing the Word: Gender and Genre in Caribbean Women's Writing*, London, Whiting & Birch, 1996.

Ashcroft, B., Griffiths, G. and Tiffin, H., *The Empire Writes Back*, London, Routledge, 1989.

—— *The Postcolonial Studies Reader*, London, Routledge, 1995.

Ashcroft, W.D., 'Intersecting Marginalities: Postcolonialism and Feminism', *Kunapipi*, 11, 2, 1989.

Baluntansky, K.M. 'Naming Caribbean Women Writers: A Review Essay', *Callaloo*, 13, 3, Summer 1990.

Barnes, N., 'Reluctant Matriarch: Sylvia Wynter and the Problematics of Caribbean Feminism', *Small Axe*, 5, 1999.

Baugh, E., *West Indian Poetry: A Study in Cultural Decolonization*, Kingston, Jamaica, Savacou, 1970.

—— (ed.) *Critics on Caribbean Literature*, London, George Allen & Unwin, 1978.

Benitez-Rojo, A., *The Repeating Island: The Caribbean and the Postmodern Perspective*, Durham, NC, Duke University Press, 1992.

Bennett, L., 'Bennett on Bennett', Louise Bennett interviewed by Dennis Scott, *Caribbean Quarterly*, 14, 1 and 2, March–June 1968.

—— Louise Bennett interviewed by Dennis Scott', in *Hinterland: Caribbean Poetry from the West Indies and Britain*, ed. E.A. Markham, Newcastle, Bloodaxe, 1989.

Besson, J., 'Reputation and Respectability Reconsidered: A New Perspective', in J.H. Momsen (ed.), *Women and Change in the Caribbean*, London, James Curry, 1992.

Bhabha, H., *The Location of Culture*, London, Routledge, 1994.

Black Womantalk (Choon, D., Wilson, O.C., Evaristo, B. and Pearse, G.) (eds), *Talkers through Dream Doors: Poetry and Short Stories by Black Women*, Manchester, Crocus, 1989.

Bloom, H., *Caribbean Women Writers*, Philadelphia, Chelsea House Publishers, 1997.

Bowlby, R., *Still Crazy after All These Years: Women, Writing and Psychoanalysis*, London, Routledge, 1992.

Boyce Davies, C., *Black Women, Writing and Identity: Migrations of the Subject*, London, Routledge, 1994.

Boyce Davies, C. and Savory Fido, E. (eds), *Out of the Kumbla: Caribbean Women and Literature*, Trenton, NJ, Africa World Press, 1990.

Brand, D., *Bread out of Stone: Recollections, Sex, Recognitions, Race, Dreaming Politics*, Toronto, Coach House, 1994.

Brathwaite, E.K., *Contradictory Omens*, Kingston, Savacou, 1974.

—— Introduction' to Hazel Campbell, *The Rag Doll and Other Stories*, Kingston, Savacou, 1978.

—— Submerged Mothers', *Jamaica Journal*, 9, 2 and 3, 1979.

—— History of the Voice: The Development of Nation Language in Anglophone Caribbean Poetry', in *Roots*, Ann Arbor, University of Michigan Press, 1993.

Breeze, J.B., 'Can a Dub Poet Be a Woman?' *Women: A Cultural Review*, 1, 90, 1990.

Breiner, L., 'How to Behave on Paper: The *Savacou* Debate', *Journal of West Indian Literature*, 6, 1, 1993.

Brown, Lloyd, *West Indian Poetry*, London, Heinemann, 1984.

Butler, J., *Gender Trouble: Feminism and the Subversion of Identity*, London, Routledge, 1982.

Carr, H., 'Poetic License', in Helen Carr (ed.), *From My Guy to Sci-Fi: Genre and Women's Writing in the Postmodern World*, London, Pandora, 1989.

Chamberlin, J.E., *Come Back to Me My Language: Poetry and the West Indies*, Toronto, McClelland, 1993.

Christian, Barbara, 'The Race for Theory', *Cultural Critique*, 6, Spring 1987.

Cixous, Hélène, 'The Laugh of the Medusa', in E. Marks and I. de Courtivron (eds), *New French Feminisms*, London, Harvester, 1980.

Clarke, E., *My Mother who Fathered Me*, London, Allen & Unwin, 1966.

Collins, Merle, 'Themes and Trends in Caribbean Writing Today', in H. Carr (ed.), *From My Guy to Sci-Fi: Genre and Women's Writing in the Postmodern World*, London, Pandora, 1989.

Cooper, C., 'Afro-Jamaican Folk Elements in Brodber's *Jane and Louisa Will Soon Come Home*', in C. Boyce Davies and E. Savory Fido (eds), *Out of the Kumbla*, Trenton, NJ, Africa World Press, 1990.

—— 'Something Ancestral Recaptured', in S. Nasta (ed.), *Motherlands: Black Women's Writing from Africa, the Caribbean and South Asia*, London, The Women's Press, 1991.

—— *Noises in the Blood: Orality, Gender and the 'Vulgar' Body of Jamaican Popular Culture*, London, Macmillan, 1993.

Coulthard, G.R., *Race and Colour in Caribbean Literature*, London, Oxford University Press, 1962.

Cudjoe, S.R. (ed.), *Caribbean Women Writers*, Wellesley, MA, Calaloux, 1990.

Dabydeen, D. and Samaroo, B. (eds), *Across the Dark Waters: Ethnicity and Indian Identity in the Caribbean*, London, Macmillan, 1996.

Dash, Michael, 'In Search of the Lost Body: Redefining the Subject in Caribbean Literature', *Kunapipi*, 11, 1, 1989.

deCaires Narain, D., 'Reading and Writing the Creole Woman in a Selection of Caribbean Women's Texts', in S. Nasta (ed.), *Reading the 'New' Literatures in a Postcolonial Era*, London, Bowdell & Brewer, 2000.

deCaires Narain, D. and O'Callaghan, E., 'Anglophone Caribbean Women Writers', in A. Rutherford, L. Jensen and C. Chew (eds), *Into the Nineties: Postcolonial Women's Writing*, Armidale, NSW, Dungaroo, 1994.

Donnell, A., 'Una Marson', *Kicking Daffodils: Twentieth Century Women Poets*, ed. V. Bertram, Edinburgh, Edinburgh University Press, 1997.

Easthope, Antony, *Poetry as Discourse*, London, Methuen, 1983.

Edmondson, B., *Making Men: Gender, Literary Authority and Women's Writing in Caribbean Narrative*, Durham, NC, Duke University Press, 1999.

Fanon, Frantz, *Black Skin, White Masks*, London, Pluto, 1986.

Fryer, Peter, *Staying Power: The History of Black People in Britain*, London, Pluto, 1984.

Fuss, Diana, *Essentially Speaking*, New York, Routledge, 1989.

Gates, H.L., Jnr, *'Race', Writing and Difference*, Chicago, University of Chicago Press, 1985.

—— *The Signifying Monkey: A Theory of Afro-American Literary Criticism*, New York, Oxford University Press, 1988.

—— 'Critical Fanonism', *Critical Inquiry*, 17, Spring 1991.

—— *Loose Canons: Notes on the Culture Wars*, New York, Oxford University Press, 1992.

Gilbert, S. and Gubar, S., 'The Blank Page and Female Creativity', in E. Showalter (ed.), *The New Feminist Criticism*, London, Virago, 1984.

—— *No Man's Land*, New Haven, CT, Yale University Press, 1990.

Gilman, S., 'Black Bodies, White Bodies', in H.L. Gates Jnr (ed.), *'Race', Writing and Difference*, Chicago, University of Chicago Press, 1985.

Greene, S., 'Report on the Second International Conference of Caribbean Women Writers', *Callaloo*, 13, 3, Summer 1990.

Grewal, S. *et al.* (eds), *Charting the Journey: Writings by Black and Third World Women*, London, Sheba, 1988.

Griffin, G., 'Writing the Body: Reading Joan Riley, Grace Nichols and Ntozake Shange', in G. Wisker (ed.), *Black Women's Writing*, London, Macmillan, 1993.

Grosz, E., *Volatile Bodies:Towards a Corporeal Feminism*, Bloomington and Indianapolis, Indiana University Press, 1994.

Habekost, Christian, *Dub Poetry: 19 Poets from England and Jamaica*, Neustadt, Michael Swinn, 1986.

—— *Verbal Riddim: The Politics and Aesthetics of African-Caribbean Dub Poets*, Amsterdam, Rodopi, 1993.

Harris, W., *Selected Essays: The Unfinished Genesis of the Imagination*, Bundy, A. (ed.), London, Routledge, 1999.

Homans, Margaret, *Women Writers and Poetic Identity*, Princeton, NJ, Princeton University Press, 1980.

Hulme, P., *Colonial Encounters: Europe and the Native Caribbean*, London, Routledge, 1992 [1986].

—— *Naked Majesty*, Oxford, Clarendon Press, 1992.

Hurston, Z.N. and Walker, A. (eds), *I Love Myself When I Am Laughing: A Zora Neale Hurston Reader*, New York, The Feminist Press, 1979.

James, L., *The Islands in Between*, London, Oxford University Press, 1968.

Jarrett-Macauley, D., *The Life of Una Marson 1905–1969*, Manchester, Manchester University Press, 1998.

Jekyll, W., *Jamaica Song and Story*, New York, Dover Publications, 1966 [1906].

Johnson, Amryl, 'Coming out of Limbo', in S. Sellars (ed.), *Delighting the Heart: A Notebook by Women Writers*, London, The Women's Press, 1989.

Jones, D. and Cameron, D. (eds) *The Feminist Critique of Language*, London, Routledge, 1990.

Kaplan, C., *Sea Changes: Essays on Culture and Feminism*, London, Verso, 1986.

Knight, F.W., *The Caribbean: The Genesis of a Fragmented Nationalism*, New York, Oxford University Press, 1978.

Kozain, R., 'Shakespeare's Silences in Search of the People: South African Literary Criticism and the Poetry of Mzwakhe Mbuli', *Wasafiri*, 19, Summer 1994.

Lamming, G., 'The Peasant Roots of the West Indian Novel', in E. Baugh (ed.), *Critics on Caribbean Literature*, London, George Allen & Unwin, 1978.

McFarlane, B., *A Literature in the Making*, Kingston, Pioneer Press, 1956.

Montefiore, J., *Feminism and Poetry: Language, Experience, Identity in Women's Writing*, London, Pandora, 1994 [1987].

Moore, G., 'The Language of West Indian Poetry', in E. Baugh (ed.), *Critics on Caribbean Literature*, London, George Allen & Unwin, 1978.

—'Use Men Language', *Bim* 57, 1974.

Morrell, C. (ed.) *Grammar of Dissent: Poetry and Prose by Claire Harris, M. Nourbese Philip, Dionne Brand*, Fredericton, NB, Goose Lane, 1994.

Morris, M., 'Printing the Performance', *Aspects of Commonwealth Literature*, 3, London, University of London/Institute of Commonwealth Studies, 1993.

—— *Is English We Speaking and Other Essays*, Kingston, Ian Randle, 1999.

Naipaul, V.S., *The Middle Passage*, Harmondsworth, Penguin, 1969.

Nasta, Susheila (ed.), *Motherlands: Black Women's Writing from Africa, the Caribbean and South Asia*, London, The Women's Press, 1991.

Ngcobo, L. (ed.), *Let It Be Told: Essays by Black Women in Britain*, London, Virago, 1988.

O'Callaghan, Evelyn, *Woman Version: Theoretical Approaches to West Indian Fiction by Women*, London, Macmillan, 1993.

Omolade, Barbara, 'Hearts of Darkness', in A. Snitow, C. Stansell and S. Thomson (eds), *Desire: The Politics of Sexuality*, London, Virago, 1984.

Ong, W.J., *Orality and Literacy: The Technologizing of the Word*, London, Routledge, 1989 [1982].

Paravisini-Gebert, L., *Phyllis Shand Allfrey: A Caribbean Life*, New Brunswick, NJ, Rutgers University Press, 1996.

Parker, A., Sommer, D. and Yaeger, P., *Nationalisms and Sexualities*, London, Routledge, 1992.

Paskin, A., Ramsay, J. and Silver, J. (eds), *Angels of Fire: An Anthology of Radical Poetry in the 80s*, London, Chatto & Windus, 1986.

Peake, L. and Trotz, A., *Gender, Ethnicity and Place: Women and Identities in Guyana*, London, Routledge, 1999.

Pearn, J., *Poetry in the Caribbean*, London, Hodder & Stoughton, 1985.

Ramchand, K., 'Terrified Consciousness', *Journal of Commonwealth Literature*, 7, July 1969, pp. 8–10.

—— *The West Indian Novel and Its Background*, London, Faber, 1970.

Rich, A., *Of Woman Born: Motherhood as Experience and Institution*, London, Virago, 1977.

Rohlehr, G., 'West Indian Poetry: Some Problems of Assessment', *Bim*, 54 and 55, 1971.

—— The Folk in Caribbean Literature', *Critics on Caribbean Literature*, E. Baugh (ed.) London, George Allen & Unwin, 1978.

—— Images of Men and Women in 1930s Calypsos', in *Gender in Caribbean Development*, P. Mohammed and C. Shepherd (eds), St Augustine, Trinidad, University of the West Indies Women and Development Project, 1988.

Sander, R., *From Trinidad*, London, Hodder & Stoughton, 1978.

Sellers, S., *Delighting the Heart: A Notebook by Women Writers*, London, The Women's Press, 1989.

—— *Language and Sexual Difference*, London, Macmillan, 1991.

Senior, O., 'Interview with Olive Senior by Anna Rutherford', *Kunapipi*, 8, 1986.

—— Interview with Janice Shinebourne', *Everywoman*, June 1991.

—— Interview with Miles Glaser', *Caribbean Writers: Between Orality and Writing*, Amsterdam-Atlanta, Editions Rodopi, 1994.

—— Interview with Charles Rowell', *Callaloo*, 36,11, Summer 1998.

Smilowitz, E., 'Una Marson: Woman before Her Time', *Jamaica Journal*, 16, 2, May 1983.

Snitow, A. and Stansell, C. (eds), *Desire: The Politics of Sexuality*, London, Virago, 1984.

Spivak, G.C., *In Other Worlds: Essays in Cultural Politics*, New York, Methuen, 1997.

Suleri, S., 'Woman Skin Deep: Feminism and the Postcolonial Condition', *Colonial Discourse and Postcolonial Theory: A Reader*, P. Williams and C. Chrisman (eds), Hemel Hempstead, Harvester Wheatsheaf, 1993.

Walcott, D., 'The Muse of History', *Critics on Caribbean Literature*, E. Baugh (ed.), London, George Allen & Unwin, 1978.

Walker, A., *In Search of Our Mothers' Gardens*, London, The Women's Press, 1984.

Williams, P., 'Difficult Subjects: Black British Women's Poetry', *Literary Theory and Poetry*, D. Murray (ed.), London, Batsford, 1989.

Wilson, P., *Crab Antics: The Social Anthropology of English-speaking Negro Societies in the Caribbean*, New Haven, CT, Yale University Press, 1973.

Wisker, G., *Black Women's Writing*, London, Macmillan, 1993.

Woolf, V., 'Professions for Women', *Collected Essays*, vol. 2, London, Hogarth, 1966.

Index